MCAT

CHEMISTRY AND PHYSICS

Strategy and Practice

Printed in the United States of America

Third Printing, 2017

ISBN 978-1-944935-04-7

Next Step Pre-Med, LLC
4256 N Ravenswood Ave
Suite 303
Chicago, IL 60613

www.nextstepmcat.com

ABOUT THE AUTHORS

Bryan Schnedeker is Next Step Test Prep's Vice President for MCAT Tutoring and Content. He manages all of our MCAT and LSAT instructors nationally and counsels hundreds of students when they begin our tutoring process. He has over a decade of MCAT and LSAT teaching and tutoring experience (starting at one of the big prep course companies before joining our team). He has attended medical school and law school himself and has scored a 44 on the old MCAT, a 525 on the new MCAT, and a 180 on the LSAT. Bryan has worked with thousands of MCAT students over the years and specializes in helping students looking to achieve elite scores.

Anthony Lafond is Next Step's MCAT Content Director and an Elite MCAT Tutor. He has been teaching and tutoring MCAT students for nearly 12 years. He earned his MD and PhD degrees from UMDNJ - New Jersey Medical School with a focus on rehabilitative medicine. Dr. Lafond believes that both rehabilitative medicine and MCAT education hinge on the same core principle: crafting an approach that puts the unique needs of the individual foremost.

To find out about MCAT tutoring directly with Anthony or Bryan visit our website:

http://nextsteptestprep.com/mcat

Updates may be found here: http://nextsteptestprep.com/mcat-materials-change-log/

If you have any feedback for us about this book, please contact us at mcat@nextsteptestprep.com

Version: 2017-01-01

FREE ONLINE MCAT DIAGNOSTIC and

FULL-LENGTH EXAM

Want to see how you would do on the MCAT and understand where you need to focus your prep?

TAKE OUR FREE MCAT DIAGNOSTIC EXAM

Timed simulations of all 4 sections of the MCAT

Comprehensive reporting on your performance

Continue your practice with a free Full Length Exam

These two exams are provided free of charge to students who purchased our book

To access your free exam, visit:

http://nextsteptestprep.com/mcat-diagnostic/

TABLE OF CONTENTS

Introduction

Hello and welcome to Next Step's Strategy and Practice book for the new Chemical and Physical Foundations of Biological Systems Section of the MCAT. Since that name is quite the mouthful, we're just going to keep it simple for this book and call it "the Chem/Phys section".

The book you're holding contains all of the information and practice that you need to start mastering this challenging new part of the MCAT. We'd like to start by giving you a brief overview of the Chem/Phys Section here in the Introduction.

The new Chem/Phys Section will consist of 59 questions which you'll have 95 minutes to answer. Those 59 questions will be presented in a mix of independent questions and questions associated with a reading passage (much like the old MCAT). The section includes 10 passages with a total of 44 questions and 15 stand-alone questions. We've followed these exact specifications for the practice sections in this book.

Each section of 59 questions will have roughly 40% of its questions drawn from physical principles underlying biological systems and 60% from the chemical principles that govern the dynamics of living systems. Within those broad categories, the AAMC estimates that the 59 questions will break down further as:

Introductory biochemistry, 25%
Introductory biology, 5%
General chemistry, 30%
Organic chemistry, 15%
Introductory physics, 25%

The key to mastering this section involves taking a step-by-step approach, starting with reinforcing foundational content, then putting that content into an overall context, and finally practice, practice, practice!

Everyone here at Next Step would like to wish you the best of luck with your studies!

Thank you,

Bryan Schnedeker
Co-founder
Next Step Pre-Med, LLC

How to Use This Book

This workbook has five different components:

Section I is an outline of all of the content areas that will be covered in the Chem/Phys Section, arranged by content area and topic. This outline is provided primarily as a reference tool. If you want to double-check if a particular topic will be on the Chem/Phys Section, come back to check this outline.

Appendix C is the self-study outline. Here, we have taken the first several points from the outline in Section I and expanded them. This is where you learn and summarize new content. This book is not a textbook. It is focused on practice and, if you want, content self-study. If you are looking for content review, consider picking up Next Step's Content Review books.

Instead, in Appendix C we model for you the way to develop your own notes on these topics. By building up your own self-study outline, you will learn the material far better than simply skimming through a pre-written outline. If you wish to develop your own self-study outline, simply create a Word document and expand the entire outline from Chapter 1, following the template we've demonstrated for a few pages in Appendix C.

To use the Self Study version of the outline, fill in the space labeled "CL" with your confidence level (1, 2, 3, 4) on that topic. We suggest a simple self-assessment such as:

4 = total confidence. I could take the MCAT today and questions on this topic would be fine.
3 = strong confidence. I'd like to just refresh quickly, but I'd feel good seeing this topic on my MCAT.
2 = weak confidence. I've heard of it but can't explain it and I'd be nervous on this topic on my MCAT.
1 = no confidence. Is this even English? I've never even heard of this before.

Once you've gone through and done a self-assessment, then use the large blank spaces under each topic to fill in your own definition or description of that topic for each topic you labeled 3 and 4. Once you've finished that, briefly investigate those topics using additional resources. If your descriptions were accurate, great. If you left things out or got things wrong, then highlight that topic. It's easy to learn new information, but harder to un-learn wrong information. So stuff you thought you knew (but didn't) will have to be a priority in your studies.

After you're done with your strengths, move to the topics you're not sure on. For those, simply go through your outside content (old textbooks, Next Step Content Review books, Khan Academy, Wikipedia, etc.) and fill in a short description of each topic and sub-topic. If it looks like there's too much info to sum up in a few sentences, create a separate study sheet for your notes.

Once that's all done, give yourself a big pat on the back – that's the first major step in the process. As we said, the act of building up your own notes will have led to much more learning than simply whizzing through a pre-written review book.

Appendix D is a glossary of every key term you will be expected to know for the Chem/Phys Section. With the same goal of turning this workbook into an active tool for learning (rather than something passive), we've arranged the glossary as a series of study sheets.

To use them, simply fold over the right-hand side of the page to cover the definitions. Then quiz yourself on the words on the right and check yourself.

It's important when learning these terms to avoid simply plowing through the terms in the same order over and over. You'll end up learning the terms in the context of the study sheet, rather than really learning each idea. We recommend that you use the following pattern:

1) Go through the words in order, twice.

2) Go through the odd-numbered pages, then the even-numbered pages, then repeat.

3) Quiz yourself on the first word on each page, then the second word on each page, and so on.

4) Finally, go through the whole glossary backwards, twice.

By breaking up the order in which you review the words, you help your brain focus on learning each individual term rather than subconsciously memorizing the pattern in which the words are printed on the page.

Section II presents several practice passages and independent questions and discusses some simple strategies for organizing the information they present. Work through this section **after completing the self-study outline** and **after learning the terms** in the glossary.

Section III consists of four full, 95 minute, timed sections. Complete each of these sections in order, under timed conditions. You do yourself no favors by "cheating" and not holding yourself to time. It takes a lot of practice to get used to the tight time constraints on the test, and these sections are your first chance to practice.

When going through the passages, we discuss the use of a highlighter pen (the new version of the MCAT will still retain the on-screen highlighting function). For these timed sections, a valuable way to review is to go back into the passages with a different color of highlight after you've reviewed your work. If there are any questions you got wrong because you didn't highlight something important in the passage, then highlight after the fact with the new color.

This lets you come back and review your work a couple of days later with a clear visual representation of how you should have been highlighting the first time through.

At the end of this book you will see an appendix listing key formulas to know for this section. It is by no means exhaustive, but it does contain some of the traditionally highest yield physical and chemical concepts tested by the MCAT.

If you ever find yourself stuck and would like to ask questions or offer feedback contact us at mcat@nextsteptestprep.com or visit www.NextStepTestPrep.com if you'd like to arrange for tutoring.

Outline of the Chem/Phys Section

The AAMC has organized the MCAT content around general concepts that cut across disciplinary boundaries. To make the material more manageable for you, we have sorted it based on the core sciences: chemistry, biochemistry, organic chemistry, and physics. You will see certain topics listed more than once. For example, the concept of Gibbs Free Energy shows up in both the biochemistry and chemistry sections. When a topic can be covered under multiple sciences, you may get questions that ask about that topic as it's normally taught in a biochemistry class, or as it's normally taught in a chemistry class.

PART I: PHYSICS

1. Translational Motion
   A. Units
   B. Vectors
   C. Vector addition
   D. Speed, velocity
   E. Acceleration

2. Force
   A. Newton's 1st Law
   B. Newton's 2nd Law
   C. Newton's 3rd Law
   D. Friction, static and kinetic

3. Equilibrium
   A. Free body diagrams
   B. Torques, levers

4. Work
   A. Work Energy theorem
   B. Mechanical work
   C. Conservative forces

5. Energy
   A. Kinetic
   B. Potential

6. Thermodynamics
   A. Energy Types

7. Periodic Motion
   A. Springs
   B. Pendulums
   C. Transverse and longitudinal waves

8. Fluids
   A. Density, specific gravity
   B. Buoyancy
      1. Archimedes' Principle
   C. Hydrostatic pressure
      1. Pascal's Law
      2. Hydrostatic pressure
   D. Viscosity: Poiseuille Flow
   E. Continuity equation
   F. Turbulent flow at high velocities
   G. Surface tension
   H. Bernoulli's equation
   I. Venturi effect

9. Electrostatics
   A. Coulomb's Law
   B. Electric Fields
   C. Electrostatic Energy

10. Circuits
    A. Current
    B. Electromotive force
       1. Voltage
    C. Resistance
       1. Ohm's law
       2. Resistors in series
       3. Resistors in parallel
       4. Resistivity

D. Capacitance
1. Parallel plate capacitor
2. Energy of charged capacitor
3. Capacitors in series
4. Capacitors in parallel
5. Dielectrics
E. Conductivity
1. Metallic
2. Electrolytic
F. Meters

11. Magnetism
A. Magnetic Field
B. Motion of charged particles in magnetic fields; Lorentz force

12. Properties of Sound
A. Relative speed of sound in solids, liquids, and gases
B. Intensity of sound
1. Decibel units, log scale
C. Doppler Effect
D. Pitch
E. Resonance
F. Ultrasound

13. Light, Electromagnetic Radiation
A. Interference
B. Diffraction grating
1. Single-slit diffraction
C. X-ray diffraction

14. Polarization of light
A. Properties of electromagnetic radiation
B. Visual spectrum, color

15. Geometrical Optics
A. Reflection from plane surface: angle of incidence equals angle of reflection
B. Refraction
1. Refractive index
2. Snell's law
C. Dispersion, change of index of refraction with wavelength
D. Conditions for total internal reflection
E. Spherical mirrors
F. Center of curvature
G. Focal length
H. Real and virtual images
I. Thin lenses
J. Converging and diverging lenses
K. Use of lensmaker's formula
L. Lens strength
M. Combination of lenses
N. Lens aberration
O. Optical Instruments, including the human eye

16. Atomic & Nuclear Physics
A. Atomic number, atomic weight
B. Neutrons, protons, isotopes
C. Nuclear forces, binding energy
D. Radioactive decay
1. Alpha decay
2. Beta decay
3. Gamma decay
E. Half-life, exponential decay, semi-log plots
F. Mass spectrometer

17. Properties of Solids
A. Thermal expansion

PART II: GENERAL CHEMISTRY

1. Electronic Structure
A. Orbital structure
B. Principal quantum number n, number of electrons per orbital
C. Ground state, excited states
D. Absorption and emission line spectra
E. Use of Pauli Exclusion Principle
F. Paramagnetism and diamagnetism
G. Conventional notation for electronic structure

H. Bohr atom
I. Heisenberg Principle

2. Gas Phase
A. Absolute temperature
i. Kelvin Scale
ii. Celsius Scale

B. Pressure
    i. Mercury barometer
C. Ideal gas Definition, Ideal Gas Law
D. Kinetic Molecular Theory of Gases

3. Thermochemistry, Thermodynamics
    A. Zeroth Law – concept of temperature
    B. First Law – conservation of energy in thermodynamic processes
    C. Endothermic/exothermic reactions
    D. Measurement of heat changes (calorimetry), heat capacity, specific heat
    E. Heat transfer – conduction, convection, radiation
        i. Endothermic reactions
        ii. Exothermic reactions
    F. Enthalpy, H, and standard heats of reaction and formation
    G. Hess's Law
    H. Bond dissociation energy as related to heats of formation
    I. Free energy
        i. Spontaneous reactions and the change in standard free energy
    J. Heat of fusion, heat of vaporization

4. Deviation from Ideal Gas Law

5. The Periodic Table
    A. Classification of Elements
    B. Chemical Properties

6. Stoichiometry
    A. Molecular weight
    B. Empirical and molecular formula
    C. Metric units commonly used in the context of chemistry
    D. Description of composition by percent mass
    E. Mole concept, Avogadro's number
    F. Oxidation number
    G. Oxidizing and reducing agents
    H. Disproportionation reactions
    I. Chemical equations
    J. Writing chemical equations

    K. Balancing equations
    L. Limiting reactants
    M. Theoretical yields

7. Electrochemistry
    A. Galvanic cells
    B. Voltaic cells

8. Solubility
    A. Units of concentration
    B. Titration

9. Free energy (G)
    A. Spontaneous reactions

10. Phase Changes and Phase Equilibria
    A. Phase diagram: pressure and temperature

11. Chemical Reaction Rate
    A. Kinetics and Equilibrium
    B. Rate-determining step
    C. Activation energy
    D. Catalysts

12. Equilibrium in chemical reactions
    A. Equilibrium Constant
    B. Le Châtelier's Principle

13. Covalent Bond
    A. Lewis Electron Dot formulas
    B. Resonance structures
    C. Dipole Moment
    D. Hybrid orbitals and geometries
    E. VSEPR theory and molecular shapes
    F. Stereochemistry of covalently bonded molecules

14. Liquid Phase - Intermolecular Forces
    A. Hydrogen bonding
    B. Dipole Interactions
    C. Van der Waals' Forces

PART III: ORGANIC CHEMISTRY

1. Molecular Structure and Absorption Spectra
   A. Infrared region
   B. Visible region Absorption (color)
   C. Ultraviolet region
   D. NMR spectroscopy

2. Isomers
   A. Structural isomers
   B. Stereoisomers
   C. Conformational isomers
   D. Absolute and relative configuration
      1. Conventions for R and S forms
      2. Conventions for E and Z forms

3. Separations and Purifications
   A. Extraction: distribution of solute between two immiscible solvents
   B. Distillation
   C. Chromatography

4. Separation and purification of peptides and proteins
   A. Electrophoresis
   B. Quantitative analysis

5. Carbohydrates
   A. Disaccharides
   B. Polysaccharides
   C. Aldehydes and Ketones
      1. Keto-enol tautomerism
      2. Aldol condensation
      3. Kinetic versus thermodynamic enolate

6. Alcohols

7. Carboxylic Acids
   A. Acid Derivatives
   B. Oxidation and reduction

8. Aromatic Compounds
   A. Biological aromatic compounds

PART IV: BIOCHEMISTRY

1. Acid/Base Equilibria
   A. Buffers, definition and concepts
   B. Influence on titration curves

2. Ions in Solutions
   A. Nucleotides and nucleic Acids
   B. Nucleotides and nucleosides: composition
   C. Sugar phosphate backbone
   D. Pyrimidine, purine residues
   E. Deoxyribonucleic acid: DNA; double helix
   F. Chemistry
   G. Other functions

3. Amino Acids, Peptides, Proteins
   A. Amino acids: description
   B. Absolute configuration at the α position
   C. Dipolar ions
   D. Classification
      1. Acidic or basic
      2. Hydrophilic or hydrophobic
   E. Synthesis of alpha amino acids
   F. Strecker Synthesis
   G. Gabriel Synthesis
   H. Peptides and proteins: reactions
      1. Sulfur linkage for cysteine and cystine

4. Peptide linkage: polypeptides and proteins
   A. Hydrolysis
   B. General Principles
      1. Primary structure of proteins
      2. Secondary structure of proteins
      3. Tertiary structure of proteins
   C. Isoelectric point

5. Three-Dimensional Protein Structure
   A. Conformational stability
   B. Hydrophobic interactions
   C. Solvation layer (entropy)
   D. Quaternary structure
   E. Denaturing and Folding

6. Non-Enzymatic Protein Function
   A. Binding
   B. Immune system
   C. Motor

7. Lipids
   A. Description, Types
   B. Storage
      1. Triacyl glycerols
      2. Free fatty acids
      3. Saponification
   C. Structure
      1. Phospholipids and phosphatids
      2. Sphingolipids
      3. Waxes
   D. Signals/cofactors
   E. Fat-soluble vitamins
   F. Steroids
   G. Prostaglandins

8. Enzymes
   A. Classification by reaction type
   B. Mechanism
   C. Substrates and enzyme specificity
      1. Active site model
      2. Induced-fit model
      3. Cofactors, coenzymes, and vitamins
   D. Kinetics
      1. General (catalysis)
      2. Michaelis–Menten
   E. Cooperativity
   F. Effects of local conditions on enzyme activity
   G. Inhibition
   H. Regulatory enzymes
   I. Allosteric effects
   J. Covalently modified enzymes

9. Principles of Bioenergetics
   A. Bioenergetics/thermodynamics
   B. Free energy
   C. Concentration
   D. Phosphorylation/ATP
      1. ATP hydrolysis
      2. ATP group transfers

10. Biological oxidation–reduction
      1. Half-reactions
      2. Soluble electron carriers

11. Flavoproteins

CHAPTER 2
Introduction to MCAT Strategies

The Chem/Phys section can be difficult for many students. These sciences are not as familiar to many pre-meds as the biological science ones. However, a focused strategy can help you turn this area into a place to score more points by allowing you to truly master the material, as opposed to recognition-level memorizing. This will enable you to recognize these classic science topics in the unique format the MCAT uses.

As we mentioned in the Introduction, each Chem/Phys Section will consist of 15 independent questions and 44 questions that are attached to a passage. Time is tight on the MCAT and you'll want to make sure you make the most of each minute.

To that end, you must make sure you stick strictly to a timing breakdown of ~8 minutes on each passage and ~1 minute on each discrete question. The discrete questions come in four chunks of 3-5 questions, and the section always ends with one of these sets. You don't want to miss out on these relatively easy points because you took too long on a passage.

1. By interrupting the network of intermolecular interactions between water molecules, surfactant helps lung function by:

    A. decreasing surface tension, allowing the alveoli to expand with less effort.
    B. increasing surface tension, contributing significantly to the passive rebound elasticity needed for exhalation.
    C. reducing the thickness of the aqueous layer coating the alveoli, increasing the rate at which respiratory gases may diffuse.
    D. reducing the structural integrity of the cell walls and plasma membranes of any bacteria entering the lungs.

This is an example of a relatively straightforward biology question. When reading through these independent questions, start by asking yourself, "***Exactly what is the question asking me for?***". A classic sort of trap answer will be something that's the "right answer to the wrong question" - that is, it will be related to the topic of the question but not ***exactly*** answer the question.

Here, the question is asking us what the purpose of surfactant is, though in a roundabout way. Once you've read the question and answer choices, and you know ***exactly*** what the question is asking for, ask yourself, "***What information is provided?***". You've got to be careful not to make any unwarranted assumptions. The MCAT is a picky test and will expect you to pay attention to the exact information provided. We're told that surfactant aids lung function by reducing interactions (bonding) between water molecules.

Next, ask yourself, "***What outside information do I need?***". The independent questions, especially, will draw heavily on outside knowledge. Here, you need to be familiar with the typical chemical and physical properties of lung function. The alveolar sacs that inflate during breathing can be compared to gas in water, as the alveoli are wet and surround a central air space. The surface tension acts at the air-water interface and tends to make the bubble smaller (by decreasing the surface area of the interface). Gas pressure is needed to keep equilibrium between the collapsing force of surface tension and the expanding force of gas in an alveolus. Thus, it is possible that by reducing interactions between water, this equilibrium is maintained, and the alveoli do not collapse during expiration.

Finally, *evaluate the choices, either by prediction or process of elimination*. In "prediction" you simply skim quickly through the choices looking for what you already know the answer will say. That's often the case when you have a good content background in an area. If you're not exactly sure what they're looking for, don't delay – start eliminating choices.

Remember, *answer every question, even if you're not sure!*

In this question, the answer is (A). The inside of the alveoli are lined with a thin aqueous layer. The surface tension in the water is constantly pulling on the alveolar walls. If left unimpeded, this surface tension could contribute to alveoli collapsing. Surfactant breaks up that surface tension, helping the alveoli to remain open. Thus choice A is correct.

B: This is a classic opposite wrong answer, as it starts off by saying surfactant INCREASES surface tension, which would throw off the force equilibrium and leads to alveolar collapse, thus hindering respiration.

C: This first part of the answer is tempting, because surface tension forces also draw fluid from capillaries into the alveolar spaces. Surfactant reduces fluid accumulation and keeps the airways dry by reducing these forces. Surfactant does not alter the aqueous layer thickness and the rate of gas diffusion would not be affected by the presence of surfactant.

D: This answer is another MCAT favorite, the one that comes out of left field, but may seem plausible if you're unsure of your content. Under typical breathing conditions, there should not be bacteria entering the cells, and surfactant cannot have any impact on microbial membranes though it does have a lesser known immune role in that it contains moieties that can bind to sugars on the surface of pathogens and thereby label them for uptake by phagocytes. However, this would not aid in respiration.

Now try another question:

2. An object with a density of $\rho = 0.75$ g/cm^3 floats on the surface in a fluid with a specific gravity of 0.81. The object has a mass of 2 kg and floats with only a portion of the volume above the surface of the water. The buoyant force, F_B = (assume g = 10 m/s^2)

    A. 15 kg
    B. 15 N
    C. 20 kg
    D. 20 N

Exactly what is the question asking me for?

You need to calculate the buoyant force acting upwards on the object from the fluid.

What information is provided?

The values of the object's density, mass, specific gravity are given. A description is also given that the object is not completely submerged and is floating.

What outside knowledge do I need?

The MCAT will expect you to be familiar with various formulas related to physics and general chemistry. We need to do some scratchwork (our prediction) to calculate the buoyant force and compare our result to the answer choices and be able to match our results to the correct answer. So, you might be tempted to jump into calculation buoyant force, which is calculated with the formula:

$$F_{buoyant} = \rho g V$$

Where ρ is the density of the fluid, g is the acceleration due to gravity (a must know for test day, 9.8 m/s^2) and V is the volume of the object submerged underwater. At first glance, this question looks like it will involve lots of calculation and involve information we do not have directly. In fact, it's much easier than it looks.

First, we can eliminate choices A and C. The question asks for force, so the answer must be in newtons.

Next, the object is floating and not accelerating anywhere. By Newton's 2nd law that means the sum of the forces must be 0. Here, the downward force of gravity, F_g is being offset by the upward buoyant force, F_B:

$$F_g = F_B$$
$$mg = F_B$$
$$(2)(10) = F_B$$
$$20 = F_B$$

Now it is clear, we need to match answer D, 20 N.

A: This is a result of miscalculation, and is not in newtons. Thus, it cannot be a force.
B: This is a result of miscalculation; you must practice your math skills as there is NO calculator allowed on the exam.
C: This is a result of accurate calculation but it is not in newtons. Thus, it cannot be a force. On the MCAT you must be careful to ensure you know what the question is asking for so that you do not grab wrong answers.

Now that we've carefully examined a couple of questions, complete these questions to practice this process. The explanations follow.

3. A student builds a small catapult that uses a spring to launch a small ball bearing straight up. The student pushes the spring down 20 cm and the ball bearing is launched 3 meters into the air. Approximately how far would the student have to push down the spring to launch the ball bearing 9 meters into the air?
   A. 20 cm
   B. 34 cm
   C. 60 cm
   D. 180 cm

4. An unknown compound with a molecular weight of 110 g/mol is determined to have an approximate mass percentage of carbon, hydrogen, and oxygen of 65.5%, 5.5%, and 29%, respectively. Which of the following gives the molecular formula and the empirical formula of the unknown compound?
   A. $C_6H_6O_2$ and C_3H_3O
   B. C_3H_3O and C_3H_3O
   C. C_3H_3O and $C_6H_6O_2$
   D. $C_6H_8O_2$ and C_3H_4O

5. Which of the following will result in the emission of a photon?
   I. The ejection of an electron
   II. An electron moving from a higher energy level to a lower energy level
   III. An electron moving from a lower energy level to a higher energy level

   A. I only
   B. II only
   C. I and II only
   D. I and III only

6. Which reagent should be used for the following reaction?

   A. $KMnO_4$
   B. $K_2Cr_2O_7$
   C. $LiAlH_4$
   D. PCC

Independent Question Explanations

3. A student builds a small catapult that uses a spring to launch a small ball bearing straight up. The student pushes the spring down 20 cm and the ball bearing is launched 3 meters into the air. Approximately how far would the student have to push down the spring to launch the ball bearing 9 meters into the air?
    A. 20 cm
    B. 34 cm
    C. 60 cm
    D. 180 cm

As with many physics problems, the most efficient way to approach this is using conservation of energy. The ball originally flew 3 meters into the air and the question asks us to launch the ball 9 meters into the air. To triple the height, we must triple the gravitational potential energy the ball has (PE = mgh). That means we will need to triple the energy stored in the spring at the start of the experiment. The energy stored in a spring is given by:

$$PE = ½\,kx^2$$

Since we're using the same spring, the spring constant k doesn't change. Thus we must increase x. To store triple the energy, we must increase x by a factor of $\sqrt{3}$ which is approximately 1.7. Rounding will be a great strategy to utilize on the exam.

20 cm x 1.7 is 34 cm, making **B** the right answer.

> A: This is a result of miscalculation.
> C: This is a result of miscalculation.
> D: This is a result of miscalculation.

4. An unknown compound with a molecular weight of 110 g/mol is determined to have an approximate mass percentage of carbon, hydrogen, and oxygen of 65.5%, 5.5%, and 29%, respectively. Which of the following gives the molecular formula and the empirical formula of the unknown compound?

    A. $C_6H_6O_2$ and C_3H_3O
    B. C_3H_3O and C_3H_3O
    C. C_3H_3O and $C_6H_6O_2$
    D. $C_6H_8O_2$ and C_3H_4O

This question tests your knowledge of molecular formula and empirical formula determination. To determine the molecular formula using mass percentage, assume that the total mass of the substance is 100 grams. Therefore, in 100 grams of the substance, 65.5 grams is carbon, 5.5 grams is hydrogen, and 29 grams is oxygen. To convert to moles, divide the mass of each element by its molecular weight.

Carbon: 65.5/12 = 5.5 moles
Hydrogen: 5.5/1 = 5.5 moles
Oxygen: 29/16 = 1.8 moles

Thus, the best approximation for the molecular formula is $C_{5.5}H_{5.5}O_{1.8}$. Based on the answer choices, $C_6H_6O_2$ is the correct answer. To determine the empirical formula, you divide each subscript by the largest common denominator, or 2 in this case, yielding C_3H_3O. A is the correct answer.

B: This answer shows the molecular and empirical formula as the same. The empirical formula must be the lowest whole number ratio of the atoms in the molecule but the molecular formula may be larger, as it is in this case.

C: This answer reverses the order of the answer to empirical formula, molecular formula. Close, but no cigar.

D: This answer is due to not using the % values given in the question stem properly.

5. Which of the following will result in the emission of a photon?
   I. The ejection of an electron
   II. **An electron moving from a higher energy level to a lower energy level**
   III. An electron moving from a lower energy level to a higher energy level

   A. I only
   B. **II only**
   C. I and II only
   D. I and III only

This question tests your understanding of Bohr's model of electron configurations. Electrons orbit around the nucleus of an atom at various energy levels; the further from the nucleus, the higher the energy level. Therefore, when an electron goes from a higher energy level to a lower energy level, energy is released. However, when an electron goes from a lower energy level to a higher energy level, the input of energy is required. Thus, an atom emits radiation when an electron moves from a higher energy level to a lower energy level making B the correct answer. I and III both involve an electron going to a higher energy level which requires the input of energy.

6. Which reagent should be used for the following reaction?

   A. $KMnO_4$
   B. $K_2Cr_2O_7$
   C. $LiAlH_4$
   D. **PCC**

This question shows a typical oxidizing reaction you will need to recognize for test day, that of a primary alcohol oxidized into an aldehyde. So, we need to use a relatively mild oxidizing agent like PCC. Thus, D is correct. Recognizing classic strong/weak oxidizing/reducing agents is a must for the MCAT.

A: This is a strong oxidizing agent, and as a result will oxidize the alcohol to the carboxylic acid.

B: This is a strong oxidizing agent, and as a result will oxidize the alcohol to the carboxylic acid.

C: This is a reducing agent and would not be able to oxidize the alcohol.

Science Passages

The science passages on the MCAT will be anywhere from 250 − 550 words, and will often come with one or more diagrams. The types of information they present can be broadly categorized as informational or experimental. There are a number of different approaches possible here, but in this book we will opt for a relatively simple one: use the on-screen highlighter.

Some folks may like to go slowly and use the scratch paper provided to take notes, and others prefer to skim very quickly through the passage to get to the questions as quickly as possible. For some students those strategies might work. But at least at first, we suggest you start with our "middle of the road" approach: don't skip right to the questions, don't bother taking notes on the scratch paper. Instead, read briskly − a little faster than you're normally comfortable with − and highlight important ideas as they come up.

When you come to experimental information, slow down and focus on one question: *what did they measure?* The MCAT loves to test your understanding of a passage by focusing on exactly what the experiment measured.

So what should you highlight?

There are four general categories of things worth highlighting: **Key terms, Opinions, Contrasts, Cause and Effect Relationships.**

Keep in mind, we're using these category names *very* loosely. What matters is that you've spotted a key idea, not what name you give it. Having said that, here's what to watch for:

Key terms:	These are things like proper nouns, technical terms, numbers, dates, etc. They're the words that you're going to want to be able to find again quickly if a question asks about them.
Opinions:	Most importantly, the author's. Opinions can be a view expressed by a particular scientist, or a view espoused by a school of thought. The main thing to watch for here are emphasis words like should, ought, must, better, worse, etc. These tend to be rare in science passages.
Contrast:	Just what it says. Watch for conflicting views, old vs. new, traditional vs. radical and so on. In science passages, contrasts tend to be contrast in function (e.g. osteoclasts vs. osteoblasts).
Cause and effect:	We're going to use the phrase "cause and effect" to refer to any logical connection, association, correlation, or literal cause-and-effect relationship presented in the passages. Any time the passages offers us a "because this, therefore that" relationship, we'll call it "cause and effect". To be clear, we don't mean these are always literal, scientific causes. Rather, we're using this phrase in a loose, rhetorical way.
Figures:	When you are presented with a figure on the MCAT, approach it as you do the text. Focus on identifying the main purpose of the figure. For example, what relationship, findings, results, or data does it present? What kind of information is it (numbers, graphs, a schematic). Once you have identified what type of information it presents and what implications it could have on the type of questions asked, move on. You do not need to decipher the entire graph now; if it's important the questions will ask about it and we can earn points.

While using this book, have a highlighter handy. Highlight in the book just like you would want to on the real exam. When you review the explanations afterwards, you'll see that we break down the material a couple of ways.

First, we use **bold and underline** text to show you the words and phrases you should have highlighted. Then, underneath each paragraph, we use bold text to describe why you should highlight those terms. The material is analyzed using the four categories above.

If you're the type of test-taker who likes to take notes on the scratch paper, then our **bold text** notes under the paragraph can serve as an example of the sorts of things you should have jotted down. Recall that on test day, time is a factor so when note taking, shorthand and abbreviations are an ideal way to convey full sentences worth of information without needing to write in complete sentences.

Another valuable strategy for the MCAT is to prioritize your quicker, easier points while saving tougher passages for later. Thus, it is in your best interest to practice all relevant topics on the exam. This will allow you to identify areas of strength and areas of weakness. Once identified, weaker areas can be attacked with diligent practice.

Passage Format

In addition to using content, you can also utilize the type of passage and the category of figures presented to prioritize passages. The images will also allow you to quickly identify the passage content.

Before jumping into a passage, take a few seconds to **scan the passage** for any figures, graphs, and equations. Next try to **identify the topic of the passage**. This will allow you to ask yourself several important questions before you begin reading.

1) *"How comfortable am I with the presented topic?"*
2) *"How well do I recognize the ideas presented in the figures?"*
3) *"Is the format of the passage one with which I am comfortable?"*

The MCAT will present science passages in three different formats. In the Chem/Phys section they are:

1. **Information-based passages**
   These passages will be dense on information about a topic, and may present equations or figures related to that topic. However, they will not be centered around a research principle or experimental procedure.
2. **Experiment-based passages**
   These passages will be built around a specific experimental procedure. The goal here will be to identify the goals, results and implications of the experiments. A solid understanding of what and why the experimenters carried out tasks is more important than the exact details of the procedure.
3. **Research-based passages**
   These passages are a bit of a hybrid of the other two passage formats. They will present a core concept of Chem/Phys (typically with a medical slant) but they will do so in the context of a research project. The research passages released so far are broader in their scientific focus than the experiment-based passages. This also allows the MCAT to introduce questions that specifically test you on the design and execution of medically-related research.

Once you have completed the passage reading, it is on to the **questions**, which is **where all the points are**! Just like the passages, each question the exam presents is looking to test your ability to complete a task. The four question types will be presented as follows:

Task 1: Recall, 35% of questions
Task 2: Problem Solving, 45% of questions
Task 3: Research Design, 10% of questions
Task 4: Data and Statistics, 10% of questions

Task 1: Recall of Scientific Concepts

A big part of your success both in medical school and on the MCAT is demonstrating a solid understanding of scientific concepts and principles. The exam will test your ability to recall key formulas and concepts and your ability to identify the relationship between closely-related concepts.

Task 1 Example Question

7.   Which of the following is NOT a polyprotic acid?
     A. Carbonic acid
     B. Acetic acid
     C. Sulfurous acid
     D. Phosphorous acid

This is a task 1 question because it simply requires you to recall the idea that a polyprotic acid has more than one ionizable hydrogen atom in the formula. The formula for acetic acid is $HC_2H_3O_2$. While there are four hydrogen atoms in the formula, only the one hydrogen atom bonded to the oxygen atom, is ionizable. Choice **B** is the correct answer.

A: The formula for carbonic acid is H_2CO_3, having two ionizable hydrogen atoms.
C: The formula for sulfurous acid is H_2SO_3, having two ionizable hydrogen atoms.
D: The formula for phosphorus acid is H_3PO_3, having three ionizable hydrogen atoms.

Task 2: Problem Solving within Scientific Concepts

The MCAT is not just about recall. The exam seeks to test a student's critical reasoning about scientific concepts, theories, and applications. Solving these questions will involve analyzing and assessing scientific explanations and predictions across chemistry and physics. You will see plenty of task 2 questions in this book, but take a look at the sample question below.

Task 2 Example Question

8.   The radius of the trachea is about 1 centimeter and air passes through it at a velocity of 20 centimeters per second. A typical bronchiole has a radius of about 4×10^{-4} cm with air passing through at a velocity of 5×10^{-2} centimeters per second. Using this data, what is the approximate number of bronchioles in a human body?

     A. 1×10^6
     B. 1.5×10^8
     C. 2.5×10^9
     D. 3.5×10^{12}

This is a task 2 question because it requires you to use a mathematical model to make predictions about physiological phenomena. To answer this question, you must recognize the concepts underlying flow characteristics of air in the human respiratory system and apply the appropriate mathematical model to an unfamiliar scenario.

$$\text{Total airflow in trachea} = \text{Total airflow in bronchioles}$$

From the continuity equation we can estimate flow in a system $=$ Area x Velocity

(Area of trachea) x (velocity trachea) $=$ (Area of bronchiole) x (velocity in bronchiole) x (# of bronchioles)

$$\pi \times 1^2 \text{ cm}^2 \times 20 \text{ cm/s} = \pi \times (4\times10^{-4})^2 \text{ cm}^2 \times (5\times10^{-2}\text{cm/s}) \times (\text{\# of bronchioles})$$

$$(\text{\# of bronchioles}) = [\pi \times 1^2 \text{ cm}^2 \times 20 \text{ cm/s}] \, / \, [\pi \times (4\times10^{-4})^2 \text{ cm}^2 \times (5\times10^{-2}\text{cm/s})]$$

$$(\text{\# of bronchioles}) = 2.5 \times 10^9$$

Answering this question correctly first requires recognition that the volume of air flowing through the trachea is the same volume of air flowing through the bronchioles. It is a task 2 question because you then need to use reasoning to find the difference in the volumes that the aorta and capillaries can each carry in order to calculate the total number of bronchioles. The correct answer is **C**.

A, B, D are all a result of miscalculation.

Task 3: Research Design and Execution

The new MCAT is looking to identify well-rounded future physicians. It will ask you to display a clear understanding of crucial components of scientific research. These questions will test your scientific inquiry skills by showing that you can actually design can carry out the "business" of science. You will be tested on your mastery of important components of scientific methodology.

To answer these questions correctly you will need to understand the methods that social, natural, and behavioral scientists execute research designed to test and expand the boundaries of science. These questions may seek to test your ability to recognize the ethical guidelines scientists must follow to ensure the rights of research subjects, the integrity of their work, and the interests of research sponsors.

Task 3 Example Question

9. A common screening for white blood cells in urine involves precipitation. False positive results are often reported due to precipitation of $MgSO_4$. Which of the following procedures would prevent precipitation of the salt?

    A. Add magnesium hydroxide
    B. Add of sodium sulfate
    C. Add a buffer to maintain neutral pH
    D. Add a buffer to maintain high pH

This is a task 3 question because it requires you to identify a modification to an experiment that would remove a frequently encountered problem. The problem mentioned is related to the test for white blood cells and involves precipitation. The test will give a false positive if $MgSO_4$ precipitates. In order to answer this question correctly, you must think about how changing experimental parameters will eliminate the problem.

Precipitation occurs when there are too many solutes in solution for the system to maintain equilibrium. If there are too many solutes dissolved in solution, the system will shift to relive this stress by precipitating out excess salts. The salt mentioned $MgSO_4$, will ionize in solution to produce a basic solution. If the pH of the test solution is too high, the system will seek to precipitate out excess basic salts. Of all the choices given, only C mentions using a buffer to keep the pH neutral. Thus, the correct answer is **C**.

A, B, D would all cause the precipitation of $MgSO_4$ by adding magnesium, sulfate ions to the solution or by raising the pH of the solution.

Task 4 Data-Based and Statistical Reasoning

The last task for the new MCAT is really not that new. Interpreting figures, tables, graphs and equations has long been a necessary skill in reading passages efficiently. With these questions, the test will make this task more formal. To succeed you must train yourself to be able to deduce patterns in data presented in graphs tables and figures. It will also ask you to draw conclusions based on the scientific data given in a passage or question.

Task 4 Example Question

10. Nitric oxide has been shown to be an important molecule that can affect blood pressure. Nitric oxide is known to react with elemental oxygen in the gas phase to form nitrogen dioxide. The following data was collected concerning the initial rate of this reaction.

Trial	[NO] (mol/L)	[O_2] (mol/L)	Initial Rate (mol/L•s)
1	1.3×10^{-2}	1.1×10^{-2}	3.2×10^{-3}
2	1.3×10^{-2}	2.2×10^{-2}	6.4×10^{-3}
3	2.6×10^{-2}	1.1×10^{-2}	1.3×10^{-2}

What is the rate law for this reaction?

A. rate = $k[O_2]^2$
B. rate = $k[NO]^{0.5}[O_2]$
C. rate = $k[NO]^{0.5}[O_2]^2$
D. rate = $k[NO]^2[O_2]$

This is a task 4 question because to answer it, you must consult the table of experimental data. To determine the proper rate law, you must identify how changing the concentration of a given reactant, [Reactant], affects the rate of reaction.

Comparing trial 1 to trial 2, the [NO] is held constant and the [O_2] is doubled, resulting in a doubling of the rate of the reaction. Thus, the reaction is first order with respect to oxygen. Choice A and C can now be eliminated.

Comparing trial 1 to trial 3, the [O_2] is held constant and the [NO] is doubled, resulting in the rate of reaction quadrupling. With this data, you can say the reaction is second order with respect to nitric oxide. Choice B can be eliminated, and choice **D** is the correct answer.

Use the four passages on the following pages as a way to practice your highlighting technique and to begin to get comfortable with the different questions types on the exam. For now, don't worry about time. Speed will come with practice.

Passage 1

The Doppler Effect, commonly used to describe frequency changes in sound waves, applies to all waves including electromagnetic radiation. One everyday application of these effects can be found in police radar guns, which use microwave signals in order to gauge the speed of drivers. In order to detect a target's speed, radar guns emit a microwave pulse in the direction of the target at a known frequency, and subsequently measure the frequency of the return microwave as it reflects off of the target vehicle. The frequency of this return wave – also known as the Doppler frequency – will be given by the Doppler equation. A graph displaying the observed frequency change of an electromagnetic wave versus target vehicle speed is shown below in Figure 1.

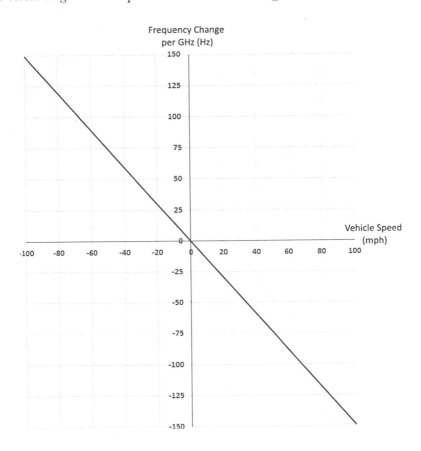

Figure 1 The frequency change per GHz (Hz) at a given target vehicle speed (mph). The frequency change is calculated as the difference between the Doppler frequency, f_D, and the emitted frequency, f. The results shown in the figure are for a 1 GHz microwave pulse.

In order to accurately measure a vehicle's speed using the Doppler Effect, however, there are multiple complicating factors that must be taken into account. Perhaps the most important of these obstacles is referred to as the 'Cosine Error', which accounts for the fact that the Doppler Effect is only observed for target motion in the same direction as the microwave pulse. The angle formed between the direction of the microwave pulse and the target vehicle's trajectory, therefore, will have a significant effect on the measured speed, with the observed speed given by $V_t \cos(\beta)$, where V_t is the actual target's speed and β is the angle formed (Figure 2).

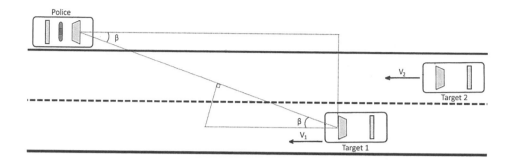

Figure 2 The angle formed between the direction of the target vehicles motion and the direction of the microwave pulse, β, affects the measured target speed.

Discrepancies due to the cosine error can be particularly significant when radar guns are set to 'moving radar', a mode used to measure the speed of a target vehicle from inside of a moving police car. In moving mode the radar calculates the speed of a target vehicle by calculating both the speed of the police car itself (often using a nearby object as a reflective surface) as well as the speed of the target vehicle relative to the police car. Both measurements are subject to inaccuracies due to the cosine effect, and therefore can contribute to inaccuracies in the measured speed of a target vehicle (Figure 3).

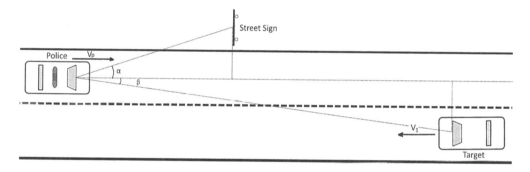

Figure 3 In moving radar mode, the measured speed of a target vehicle is dependent upon the angle α, which is based upon the direction of the police car's motion, as well as the angle β.

11. A stationary police officer directs his radar gun directly ahead at a target vehicle. The initial radar frequency is 0.5 GHz, and the observed frequency change is -60 Hz. Based on Figure 1, which of the following best approximates the speed of the target vehicle?
    A. 40 miles per hour toward the radar gun
    B. 80 miles per hour toward the radar gun
    C. 40 miles per hour away from the radar gun
    D. 80 miles per hour away from the radar gun

12. A radar gun within a police car travelling at 25 mph is pointed directly ahead at a target vehicle. The initial radar frequency is 1 GHz, and the observed frequency change is 75 Hz. Based on Figure 1, which of the following answers best approximates the speed and direction of the vehicle?
    A. 25 MPH toward the police officer
    B. 50 MPH toward the police officer
    C. 25 MPH away from the police officer
    D. 50 MPH away from the police officer

13. In the situation shown in Figure 2, how will the measured speed of target 1 compare to the measured speed of target 2, assuming both are moving at the same speed?
    A. Target 1's measured speed will be greater than Target 2's measured speed, and closer to the vehicle's actual speed.
    B. Target 1's measured speed will be greater than Target 2's measured speed, and further from the vehicle's actual speed.
    C. Target 1's measured speed will be smaller than Target 2's measured speed, and closer to the vehicle's actual speed.
    D. Target 1's measured speed will be smaller than Target 2's measured speed, and further from the vehicle's actual speed.

14. In the situation shown in Figure 3, how will the measured speed of the target vehicle compare to its actual speed? Assume that $\alpha > \beta$ as is consistent with the diagram.
    A. The measured speed on radar will be consistent with the vehicle's actual speed
    B. The measured speed on radar will be less than the vehicle's actual speed
    C. The measured speed on radar will be greater than the vehicles actual speed
    D. There is not enough information to answer this question.

15. A stationary police officer directs his radar gun at a vehicle travelling away from him at 80 mph. When the angle between the vehicle's direction of motion and the direction of the microwave pulse is at 60°, which of the following would be closest to the observed vehicles frequency change? Assume the microwave pulse has a frequency of 1 GHz.
    A. -120 Hz
    B. -60 Hz
    C. 60 Hz
    D. 120 Hz

16. Instead of microwave radiation, a new form of radar is designed to use infrared radiation. Which of the following is NOT an accurate description of the differences between the two systems?
    A. The frequency shift per GHz would remain consistent between the infrared and microwave radar systems
    B. The infrared system would require a more sensitive detection system for reflected waves
    C. It would require more energy to emit the infrared radiation
    D. Using infrared radiation would eliminate the effectiveness of radar jamming devices that emit microwaves to interfere with police radar guns.

17. A police officer situated on an overpass above a highway is using a radar gun to measure the speed of directly oncoming traffic. Which of the following statements are accurate?
    I. The measured speed of target vehicles will depend on the height of the overpass.
    II. The measured speed of target vehicles will depend on their horizontal location relative to the radar gun.
    III. The measured speed of target vehicles will become less accurate the closer they get to the radar gun.

    A. II only
    B. III only
    C. II and III only
    D. I, II, and III

Passage 1 Explanation

The **Doppler Effect**, commonly used to describe frequency changes in **sound waves**, applies to all waves including **electromagnetic radiation**. One everyday application of these effects can be found in police **radar guns**, which use **microwave signals** in order to gauge the speed of drivers. In order to detect a target's speed, radar guns emit a microwave pulse in the direction of the target at a known frequency, and subsequently measure the frequency of the **return microwave** as it **reflects** off of the target vehicle. The frequency of this return wave – also known as the **Doppler frequency** – will be given by the **Doppler equation**. A graph displaying the observed frequency change of an electromagnetic wave versus target vehicle speed is shown below in Figure 1.

Key terms: Doppler Effect, sound waves, electromagnetic radiation, radar guns, microwave signals, emit, return microwave, reflect, Doppler frequency, Doppler equation.

Cause-and-Effect: The reflected frequency of a wave is given by the Doppler equation. The Doppler Effect is used in police radar guns to measure a vehicle's speed.

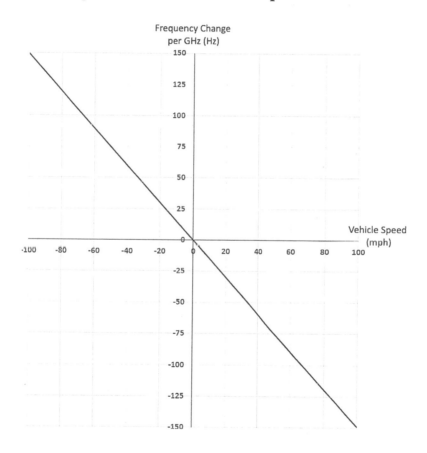

Figure 1 The frequency change per GHz (Hz) at a given target vehicle speed (mph). The frequency change is calculated as the difference between the Doppler frequency, f_D, and the emitted frequency, f. The results shown in the figure are for a 1 GHz microwave pulse.

Figure 1 The frequency change per GHz (Hz) at a given target vehicle speed (mph). The frequency change will be given by $f_d - f$, so a positive frequency change would imply that the return frequency is greater than the emitted frequency, and a negative frequency the opposite. This means that a negative speed in the diagram corresponds to a vehicle approaching the radar gun (and therefore created a greater reflected frequency) while a positive speed corresponds to a vehicle moving away from the radar gun. The results shown in the figure are also for a 1 GHz microwave pulse, so we'll have to be careful to adjust the observed changes for a microwave pulse at a different frequency.

In order to accurately measure a vehicle's speed, however, there are multiple complicating factors that must be taken into account. Perhaps the most important of these obstacles is referred to as the '**Cosine Error**', which accounts for the fact that the **Doppler Effect** is only observed for target motion in **the same direction** as the microwave pulse. The **angle formed** between the direction of the microwave pulse and the target vehicle's trajectory, therefore, will have a significant effect on the measured speed, with the observed speed given by $\mathbf{V_t \cos(\beta)}$, where V_t is the actual target's speed and β is the angle formed (Figure 2).

Key terms: 'Cosine Error', Doppler Effect, same direction, angle formed, $V_t \cos(\beta)$, V_t, β.

Cause-and-Effect: The angle formed between the target vehicle's motion and the direction of the microwave pulse affects the measured speed of the vehicle on radar.

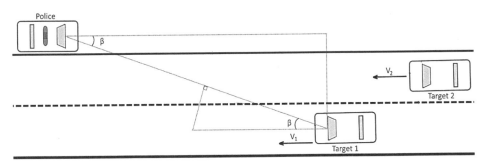

Figure 2 The angle formed between the direction of the target vehicles motion and the direction of the microwave pulse, β, affects the measured target speed.

Figure 2. The angle formed between the direction of the target vehicles motion and the direction of the microwave pulse, β, affects the measured speed of the target. The measured speed will be given by $V_t \cos(\beta)$, so in this circumstance it will always be smaller than the actual speed of the vehicle.

Discrepancies due to the cosine error can be particularly significant when radar guns are set to '**moving radar**', a mode used to measure the speed of a target vehicle from **inside of a moving police car**. In moving mode the radar calculates the speed of a target vehicle by calculating both **the speed of the police car** itself (often using a **nearby object as a reflective surface**) as well as the **speed of the target** vehicle **relative to the police car**. Both measurements are subject to inaccuracies due to the cosine effect, and therefore can contribute to inaccuracies in the measured speed of a target vehicle (Figure 3).

Key Terms: 'moving radar', inside of a moving police car, the speed of the police car, nearby object as a reflective surface, speed of the target, relative to the police car.

Cause-and-Effect: In moving radar mode the radar gun is used to estimate the speed of the police car as well as the target vehicle, therefore the angle formed with the reflective object used to measure the police's speed has to be considered as well.

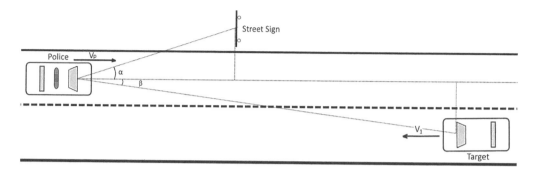

Figure 3 In moving radar mode, the measured speed of a target vehicle is dependent upon the angle α, which is based upon the direction of the police car's motion, as well as the angle β.

Figure 3. When radar gun is set to its moving mode, the angle between formed between the police car's direction of motion and the reflective surface upon which the police's speed is measured, α, also has an effect on the measured speed of the target vehicle.

11. A stationary police officer directs his radar gun directly ahead at a target vehicle. The initial radar frequency is 0.5 GHz, and the observed frequency change is -60 Hz. Based on Figure 1, which of the following best approximates the speed of the target vehicle?
    A. 40 miles per hour toward the radar gun
    B. 80 miles per hour toward the radar gun
    C. 40 miles per hour away from the radar gun
    D. **80 miles per hour away from the radar gun**

Choice **D** is correct. If the observed frequency change is -60 Hz for a 0.5 GHz pulse, the corresponding frequency change for a 1 GHz pulse would -120 Hz. Looking at Figure 1 we can see that a frequency change of -120 Hz corresponds to a target speed of 80 mph. A negative frequency change also means that the Doppler frequency is smaller than the emitted frequency, which means that the target vehicle must be moving away from the radar gun. Choice D is therefore the correct answer.

12. A radar gun within a police car travelling at 25 mph is pointed directly ahead at a target vehicle. The initial radar frequency is 1 GHz, and the observed frequency change is 75 Hz. Based on Figure 1, which of the following answers best approximates the speed and direction of the vehicle?
    A. **25 MPH toward the police officer**
    B. 50 MPH toward the police officer
    C. 25 MPH away from the police officer
    D. 50 MPH away from the police officer

Choice **A** is correct. Given that the initial radar frequency is 1 GHz, we can look directly at the results in Figure 1 to answer this question. Looking at Figure 1 we can see that a frequency change of 75 Hz corresponds to a target velocity of -50 mph, and furthermore a positive frequency means that the Doppler frequency is larger than the emitted frequency, which in turn implies that the target vehicle is moving towards the police car. The 50 mph, however, is relative to the speed of the police car, and therefore the speed of the police vehicle must be taken into account. We already know that the police car is travelling at a speed of 25 mph, however, and as a result the actual speed of the target vehicle must be closest to 50 - 25 = 25 mph. Choice A is therefore the correct answer.

13. In the situation shown in Figure 2, how will the measured speed of target 1 compare to the measured speed of target 2 assuming both are traveling at the same speed?
    A. Target 1's measured speed will be greater than Target 2's measured speed, and closer to the vehicle's actual speed
    B. Target 1's measured speed will be greater than Target 2's measured speed, and further from the vehicle's actual speed
    C. Target 1's measured speed will be smaller than Target 2's measured speed, and closer to the vehicle's actual speed
    D. **Target 1's measured speed will be smaller than Target 2's measured speed, and further from the vehicle's actual speed**

Choice **D** is correct. Looking at the figure the angle β for target vehicle 1 will be greater than the corresponding β for target vehicle 2. Since the measured speed is given by $V_t \cos(\beta)$, a larger value of β will correspond to a smaller measured speed, and a larger discrepancy between the measured speed and the actual speed of the target. Choice D is therefore the correct answer.

14. In the situation shown in Figure 3, how will the measured speed of the target vehicle compare to its actual speed? Assume that α > β as is consistent with the diagram.

    A. The measured speed on radar will be consistent with the vehicle's actual speed
    B. The measured speed on radar will be less than the vehicle's actual speed
    C. The measured speed on radar will be greater than the vehicles actual speed
    D. <u>**There is not enough information to answer this question.**</u>

Choice **D** is correct. In moving radar mode the inaccuracies in measuring both the speed of the police car and the relative speed of the target vehicle must be considered. A large α value will help contribute to a smaller measured police car speed, while a large β value would make the speed of the target vehicle relative to the police car appear smaller as well. Since the speed of the target vehicle is based upon the difference between the two, a large α would make the target appear to be going faster than it actually is (because more of the relative velocity would be attributed to the motion of the target vehicle), while a large β would make it appear to be going slower than it actually is. The numerical value of the discrepancy, however, is also dependent on the speed of the vehicles. Even if a police car has a large α value, if it isn't moving very fast that discrepancy won't have that large of an overall affect. (If a cop car is only travelling at 1 mph, the cosine effect could at most make the target vehicle appear to be travelling 1 mph faster). As a result, even though we know that α > β, we do not have enough information to solve this question because we also need to know the speeds of both vehicles. The answer, therefore, is choice D.

15. A stationary police officer directs his radar gun at a vehicle travelling away from him at 80 mph. When the angle between the vehicle's direction of motion and the direction of the microwave pulse is at 60°, which of the following would be closest to the observed vehicles frequency change? Assume the microwave pulse has a frequency of 1 GHz.
    A. -120 Hz
    B. <u>**-60 Hz**</u>
    C. 60 Hz
    D. 120 Hz

Choice **B** is correct. If β = 60°, cos(β) will be 0.5 and the measured speed of the target vehicle will be given by 80(0.5) = 40 mph. The vehicle is travelling away from the officer, therefore this will correspond to a positive speed and a negative frequency change when we look at Figure 1. Based on Figure 1 a speed of +40 mph corresponds to a frequency change of roughly -60 Hz, therefore choice B is the correct answer. (Note we were able to directly use the results of Figure 1 since we were told to assume the microwave pulse has a frequency of 1 GHz).

16. Instead of microwave radiation, a new form of radar is designed to use infrared radiation. Which of the following is NOT an accurate description of the differences between the two systems?

    A. The frequency shift per GHz would remain consistent between the infrared and microwave radar systems
    B. <u>**The infrared system would require a more sensitive detection system for reflected waves**</u>
    C. It would require more energy to emit the infrared radiation
    D. Using infrared radiation would eliminate the effectiveness of radar jamming devices that emit microwaves to interfere with police radar guns.

Choice **B** is correct. Infrared radiation has a higher frequency than microwave radiation, and both travel at the speed of light. Since both waves travel at the same speed, the percent (or per GHz) change in frequency due to the Doppler effect will be the same, and the higher frequency infrared waves will therefore have a larger overall frequency change. A larger frequency change could be detected by a less sensitive detection system, therefore choice B is an incorrect statement.

17. A police officer situated on an overpass above a highway is using a radar gun to measure the speed of directly oncoming traffic. Which of the following statements are accurate?

   I. The measured speed of target vehicles will depend on the height of the overpass.

   II. The measured speed of target vehicles will depend on their horizontal location relative to the radar gun.

   III. The measured speed of target vehicles will become less accurate the closer they get to the radar gun.

   A. II only
   B. III only
   C. II and III only
   D. <u>**I, II, and III**</u>

Choice **D** is correct. Statement I is accurate. The vertical displacement created by the height of the overpass creates an angle between the direction of the vehicle's motion and the direction of the microwave pulse. Just like in Figure 2 and Figure 3, this makes the measured speed smaller than the actual speed due to the cosine effect. Statement II is also accurate. This is the cosine error effect described specifically in Figure 2 and Figure 3. Lastly, statement III is accurate as well. The closer the vehicle gets to the radar gun, the angle corresponding to the horizontal displacement as well as the angle to the vertical displacement gets larger, making the cosine error more prominent. Answer D is therefore the correct answer.

THIS PAGE LEFT

INTENTIONALLY BLANK

Passage 2

Polycyclic aromatic hydrocarbons (PAHs) are hydrocarbons composed exclusively of aromatic rings. Polynuclear aromatic hydrocarbons (PNAs) are a subset of PAHs that contain two or more fused aromatic rings. PAHs are formed by the incomplete oxidation of organic materials, and many have been identified as carcinogenic.

One such PNA is benzo[*a*]pyrene. When ingested, it is metabolized by the human liver enzymes cytochromes P450 1A1 (CYP1A1) and P450 1B1 (CYP1B1) to a benzo[*a*]pyrene diol epoxide.

The Ames test indicates the mutagenic characteristics of a compound and is used as a test for suspected carcinogens. The test works by placing a mutant strain of the bacterium *Salmonella typhimurium* in a medium that lacks the amino acid histidine. The mutant strain lacks an intrinsic DNA repair mechanism and the ability to synthesize histidine. Wild type *Salmonella* grow well in the histidine-deficient medium, but the mutant *Salmonella* do not survive. In the Ames test, a potential carcinogen is added to growth medium. If the chemical is mutagenic, visible colonies of back-mutated *Salmonella* will form.

Figure 2 shows the results of the Ames test in four plates containing either *Salmonella* alone, *Salmonella* and a human liver preparation, *Salmonella* and benzo[*a*]pyrene, or *Salmonella*, a human liver preparation, and benzo[*a*]pyrene.

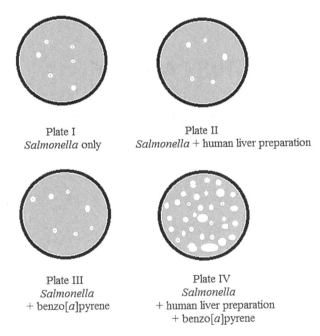

Plate I
Salmonella only

Plate II
Salmonella + human liver preparation

Plate III
Salmonella
+ benzo[*a*]pyrene

Plate IV
Salmonella
+ human liver preparation
+ benzo[*a*]pyrene

Figure 1 Illustration of the results of the Ames test for *Salmonella* with human liver preparation, benzo[*a*]pyrene, human liver preparation and benzo[*a*]pyrene.

18. Based upon the results shown in Figure 1, which of the following compounds is potentially mutagenic in the absence of further metabolism?

    I. benzo[*a*]pyrene
    II. CYP1A1
    III. CYP1B1
    IV. (+)-benzo[*a*]pyrene-7,8-dihydrodiol-9,10-epoxide

    A. I only
    B. IV only
    C. I and IV only
    D. I, II, III and IV

19. Why is the Ames test, which detects mutagens, an effective tool to screen potential carcinogens?
    A. Mutagens are metabolized by *Salmonella*, forming carcinogens.
    B. Oncogenes are transferred from *Salmonella* to the tested compounds.
    C. *Salmonella* is unable to grow in the presence of carcinogens.
    D. Mutagens are often also carcinogens.

20. Which of the following best explains why greater bacterial growth occurred in Plate IV than in Plate II?
    A. Cytochrome P450 enzymes present catalyzed the formation of mutagens.
    B. CYP1A1 and CYP1B1 enzymes inhibited bacterial digestion of mutagens in the sample.
    C. Enzymes present in the human liver can cause *Salmonella* backmutation.
    D. Histidine is a byproduct of the conversion of benzene[*a*]pyrene by cytochrome P450 enzymes.

21. Based upon passage information, back-mutated *Salmonella*:
    A. inhibit CYP1A1 and CYP1B1 enzymes.
    B. synthesize a carcinogenic compound.
    C. produce a visible pigment.
    D. synthesize histidine.

22. By binding to the aryl hydrocarbon receptor, a transcription factor, in the cytosol, benzo[*a*]pyrene increases the rate of its metabolism by inducing a change in cytochrome CYP1A1 expression. In order to mediate this action, the bound receptor must:
    A. increase expression of CYP1B1.
    B. bind to an enhancer region.
    C. translocate to the nucleus.
    D. recruit a histone acetyltransferase.

Passage 2 Explanation

Polycyclic aromatic hydrocarbons (PAHs) are hydrocarbons composed exclusively of aromatic rings. **Polynuclear aromatic hydrocarbons (PNAs)** are a subset of PAHs that contain two or more fused aromatic rings. PAHs are formed by the incomplete oxidation of organic materials, and many have been identified as **carcinogenic**.

Key terms: polycyclic aromatic hydrocarbons (PAH); polynuclear aromatic hydrocarbons (PNAs); carcinogenic

Cause-and-Effect: PAHs are hydrocarbons composed entirely of aromatic rings; PNAs are PAHs composed of two or more fused aromatic rings; PAHs are formed from the incomplete oxidation of organic materials; many PAHs are carcinogenic

One such PNA is **benzo[a]pyrene**. When ingested, it is metabolized by the human liver enzymes **cytochromes P450 1A1 (CYP1A1)** and **P450 1B1 (CYP1B1)** to a **benzo[a]pyrene diol** epoxide.

Key terms: benzo[a]pyrene, cytochrome P450 1A1 (CYP1A1), cytochrome P450 1B1 (CYP1B1), benzo[a]pyrene diol

Cause-and-Effect: benzo[a]pyrene is metabolized by the liver enzymes cytochrome P450 1A1 (CYP1A1) and cytochrome P450 1B1 (CYP1B1) to form a benzo[a]pyrene diol.

The **Ames test** indicates the **mutagenic** characteristics of a compound and is used as a test for suspected carcinogens. The test works by placing a mutant strain of the **bacterium Salmonella typhimurium** in a medium that lacks the amino acid **histidine**. The mutant strain lacks an intrinsic DNA repair mechanism and the ability to synthesize histidine. Wild type *Salmonella* grow well in the histidine-deficient medium, but the mutant *Salmonella* do not survive. In the Ames test, a potential carcinogen is added to growth medium. If the chemical is mutagenic, visible colonies of back-mutated *Salmonella* will form.

Key terms: Ames test, mutagen, *Salmonella typhimurium*, histidine

Cause-and-Effect: The Ames test is used as a test for suspected carcinogens to indicate mutagenic character; a nutritionally deficient strain of Salmonella that is both unable to synthesize histidine and which lack a DNA repair function; histidine is required for the growth of Salmonella; wild type Salmonella grow normally in the media, but the mutant strain does not; when a carcinogen is added in the Ames test, visible bacterial colonies will form if a mutagenic carcinogen is present.

Figure 1 shows the results of the Ames test in four plates containing either *Salmonella* alone, *Salmonella* and a human liver preparation, *Salmonella* and benzo[a]pyrene, or *Salmonella*, a human liver preparation, and benzo[a]pyrene.

Key terms: liver preparation

Cause-and-Effect: The Ames test was conducted in four plates containing either *Salmonella* alone, *Salmonella* and a human liver preparation, *Salmonella* and benzo[a]pyrene, or *Salmonella*, a human liver preparation, and benzo[a]pyrene.

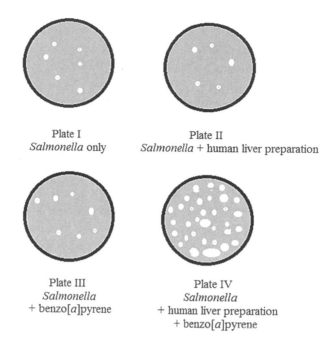

Plate I
Salmonella only

Plate II
Salmonella + human liver preparation

Plate III
Salmonella
+ benzo[*a*]pyrene

Plate IV
Salmonella
+ human liver preparation
+ benzo[*a*]pyrene

Figure 1. The Ames test for *Salmonella* shows minimal growth with in Plate I, or with human liver preparation in Plate II or with benzo[*a*]pyrene in Plate III, but considerable growth in Plate IV when human liver preparation and benzo[a]pyrene are both present.

18. Based upon the results shown in Figure 1, which of the following compounds is potentially mutagenic in the absence of further metabolism?

    I. benzo[*a*]pyrene

    II. CYP1A1

    III. CYP1B1

    IV. (+)-benzo[*a*]pyrene-7,8-dihydrodiol-9,10-epoxide

    A. I only

    B. **IV only**

    C. I and IV only

    D. I, II, III and IV

Choice **B** is correct. The absence of significant bacterial growth in Plate III, when compared to the controls in Plates I and II, demonstrate that benzo[*a*]pyrene (roman numeral I) is not, without additional metabolism, mutagenic. Thus choices A, B, D are all wrong because they indicate that it is.

By a similar logic, the contents of human liver preparation, including the enzymes CYP1A1 (roman numeral II) and CYP1B1 (roman numeral III), contained in Plate II, are not mutagenic. Only the three metabolites of benzo[*a*] pyrene shown in Figure 1, including, (+)-benzo[*a*]pyrene-7,8-dihydrodiol-9,10-epoxide (roman numeral IV) could be potential mutagens, as demonstrated by the significant growth in Plate IV when benzo[*a*]pyrene was present. Choice B correctly indicates that roman numeral IV only is potentially carcinogenic without undergoing further metabolism. Choices A, C and D incorrectly indicate at least one compound is carcinogenic without undergoing further metabolism.

19. Why is the Ames test, which detects mutagens, an effective tool to screen potential carcinogens?
    A. Mutagens are metabolized by *Salmonella*, forming carcinogens
    B. Oncogenes are transferred from *Salmonella* to the tested compounds.
    C. *Salmonella* is unable to grow in the presence of carcinogens.
    D. Mutagens are often also carcinogens.

Choice D is correct. If mutagens are also often carcinogenic because of their mutagenic quality, then a test for mutagens can also identify carcinogens (choice D). The passage gives no indication that the action of *Salmonella* is responsible for the conversion of mutagens to carcinogens. If this were true, then only mutagens exposed to *Salmonella* or some other compound with a similar action, would be carcinogenic, and the test would not be a good indicator of the general carcinogenic properties of compounds (choice A). For a reasons similar to that which applied to choice A, if *Salmonella* is required for the conversion of mutagens to carcinogens then the Ames test would not be a good indicator of the general (choice B). If carcinogens inhibited *Salmonella* growth, then a positive Ames test—the growth of *Salmonella* colonies—would not indicate the presence of carcinogens in the medium.

20. Which of the following best explains why greater bacterial growth occurred in Plate IV than in Plate II?
    A. Cytochrome P450 enzymes present catalyzed the formation of mutagens.
    B. CYP1A1 and CYP1B1 enzymes inhibited bacterial digestion of mutagens in the sample.
    C. Enzymes present in the human liver can cause *Salmonella* backmutation.
    D. Histidine is a byproduct of the conversion of benzene[*a*]pyrene by cytochrome P450 enzymes.

Choice **A** is correct. The absence of significant bacterial growth in Plate III, when compared to the growth in Plates I and II, demonstrate that benzo[*a*]pyrene is not, without additional metabolism, mutagenic. However, the significant growth in Plate IV when benzo[*a*]pyrene was present along with human liver preparation suggests that its metabolites, when acted upon by the cytochrome P450 enzymes contained in the sample, could have led to the formation of mutagenic products (choice A). If growth in Plate IV occurred because CYP1A1 and CYP1B1 enzymes inhibited bacterial digestion of mutagens in the sample (choice B), then mutagens must already have existed in the sample as benzo[*a*]pyrene, or in the human liver preparation. If this were true, then growth would also occur in either plate II or III. If enzyme present in the liver can, alone, cause back-mutation of *Salmonella*, then growth should have been found in Plate II (choice C). The reactions catalyzed by CYP1A1 and CYP1B1 during the metabolism of benzene[*a*]pyrene are shown in Figure 1. Neither of those reactions involve the production of the amino acid histidine (choice D).

21. Based upon passage information, back-mutated *Salmonella*:
    A. inhibit CYP1A1 and CYP1B1 enzymes.
    B. synthesize a carcinogenic compound.
    C. produce a visible pigment.
    D. synthesize histidine.

Choice **D** is correct. Back-mutated *Salmonella* must synthesize histidine in order to grow. As the rate of back-mutation increases due to the presence of a mutagen, so too does the rate of bacterial growth because of the increased number of now wild type *Salmonella* that are present in the media and capable of synthesizing histidine (choice D). If back-mutated *Salmonella* inhibited CYP1A1 and CYP1B1 enzymes, then growth due to their mutagenic metabolites would be affected. There is no indication based upon the information presented in the passage to suggest this occurs (choice A). Back-mutated *Salmonella* occur due to the presence of a carcinogenic compound. If *Salmonella* synthesized a carcinogenic compound upon back-mutation, then the rates of *Salmonella* growth in Plates I, II and III should be greater, as spontaneous back-mutation should cause further mutagen-derived back-mutation (choice B). There is nothing in the passage to indicate that *Salmonella* colonies are visible because of a pigment, or that they produce such a pigment (choice C).

22. By binding to the aryl hydrocarbon receptor, a transcription factor, in the cytosol, benzo[*a*]pyrene increases the rate of its metabolism by inducing a change in cytochrome CYP1A1 expression. In order to mediate this action, the bound receptor must:
    A. increase expression of CYP1B1.
    B. bind to an enhancer region.
    C. **translocate to the nucleus.**
    D. recruit a histone acetyltransferase.

Choice **C** is correct. Transcription factors contain DNA-sequence-specific binding domains that attach adjacent to the genes which they regulate. Thus they must move into the nucleus to affect transcription.

A, B, D: For the aryl hydrocarbon receptor to induce a change in CYP1A1 expression, it must translocate from the cytosol to the nucleus where it could bind the region of DNA to which it is specific (choice C). Once bound, it may perform its regulatory function alone, or as a complex, by either activating (promoting) or repressing (blocking) the recruitment of RNA polymerase and the transcription of a specific region of DNA. Increased expression of CYP1B1 is not necessarily required to accompany the up-regulation of CYP1A1 expression, as there is nothing to indicate that they are encoded by a common gene or that their expression is regulated by a shared mechanism (choice A). While a transcription factor such as the aryl hydrocarbon receptor that upregulates expression of a particular protein may do so by binding to a cis-regulatory enhancer region, it may also do so by binding a promoter region which initiates transcription of the genes necessary for production of that protein (choice B). One mechanism by which a transcription factor can up-regulate transcription of a gene is by recruitment of a histone acetyltransferase (HAT) enzyme. Such an enzyme weakens the association of histones with DNA, making the DNA more accessible to the cell's transcriptional machinery. However, a transcription factor may upregulate expression by a variety of molecular mechanisms, including by recruitment of a co-activator protein to the transcription factor-DNA complex, or by stabilizing the binding of RNA polymerase to DNA (choice D).

Passage 3

Aldehydes and ketones are functional groups found in a number of biologically important molecules. The structural formulas for a few examples are shown in Figure 1. The shapes of these molecules play an important role in their function and how they interact with different types of nerve receptors. For example, carvone has two optically active forms that have distinctly different flavor sensations, i.e. R-carvone is known as oil of spearmint, whereas S-carvone is the oil of caraway seeds.

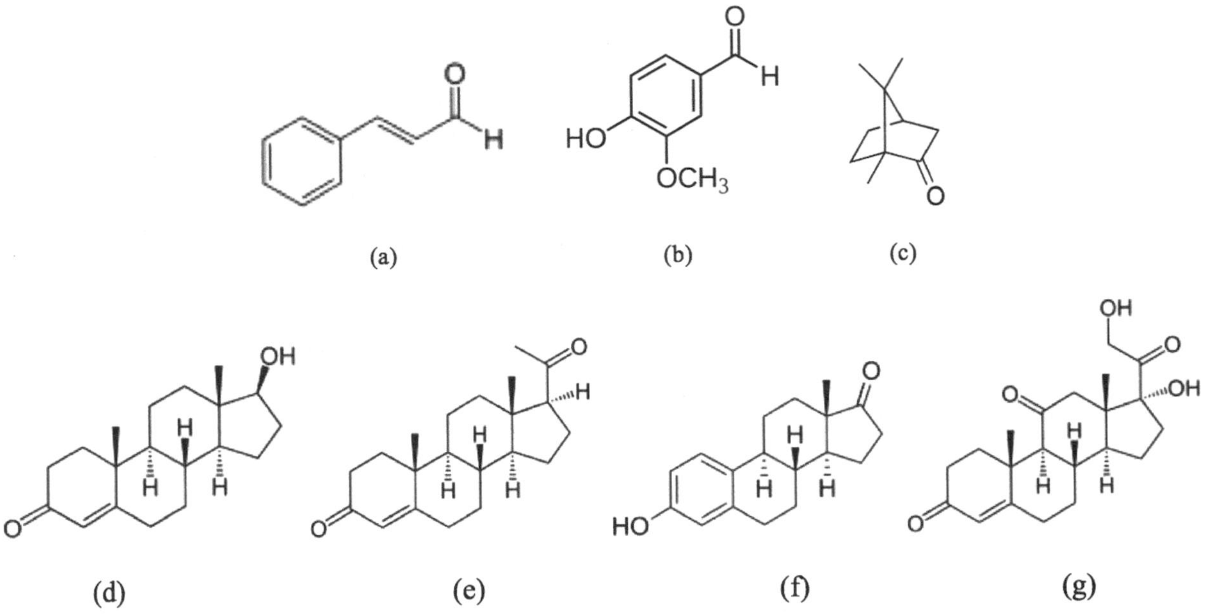

Figure 1 Structural formulas for examples of naturally occurring aldehydes and ketones: (a) cinnamon; (b) vanillin; (c) camphor; (d) testosterone; (e) progesterone; (f) esterone; and (g) cortisone.

Both Benedict's solution and Tollens' solutions are useful reagents to test for aldehydes. In the former, a positive test results when the basic royal blue cupric solution is reduced to form a precipitate of cuprous oxide. A positive test for the latter results when the ammoniacal solution of silver ion is reduced to silver metal.

23. Which of the following would NOT give a positive Benedict's test?
    I. Cinnamon
    II. Vanillin
    III. Camphor
    IV. Carvone
    A. I and II only
    B. I and III only
    C. II and IV only
    D. III and IV only

24. What are the oxidation numbers of the silver species in the Tollens' test before and after a positive test?
    A. 1+ and 0, respectively
    B. 2+ and 1+, respectively
    C. 3+ and 2+, respectively
    D. 2+ and 0, respectively

25. Which of the following best describes the isomer of 2-Methyl-5-(1-methylethenyl)-2-cyclohexenone shown below?

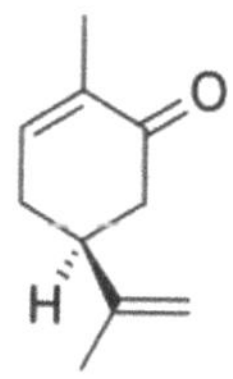

    A. This isomer is R-carvone, which is oil of spearmint.
    B. This isomer is R-carvone, which is oil of caraway.
    C. This isomer is S-carvone, which is oil of spearmint.
    D. This isomer is S-carvone, which is oil of caraway.

26. Which of the following would be most useful in distinguishing propanal from propanone?
    A. Proton NMR spectroscopy
    B. IR spectroscopy
    C. UV-Vis spectroscopy
    D. Rotation of plane-polarized light

27. Cholesterol, whose structure is shown below, is the precursor to which of the following hormones?

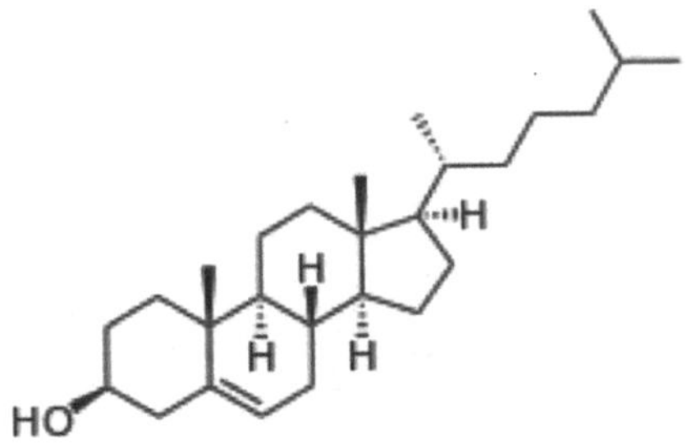

I. Testosterone
II. Progesterone
III. Estrogen
IV. Cortisone

   A. I only
   B. I and II only
   C. I, II, and III only
   D. I, II, III, and IV

Passage 3 Explanation

Aldehydes and **ketones** are functional groups found in a number of **biologically important molecules**. The structural formulas for a few examples are shown in Figure 1. The **shapes** of these molecules play an important role in their function and how they **interact with different types of nerve receptors**. For example, **carvone** has two optically active forms that have distinctly different flavor sensations, i.e. R-carvone is known as oil of **spearmint**, whereas S-carvone is the oil of **caraway** seeds.

Key terms: Aldehydes, ketones, carvone, spearmint, caraway
Cause-and-Effect: the shape of the molecule can change interactions with nerve receptors; the two stereoisomers of carvone have different tastes (indicating the react differently with nerve receptors in taste buds

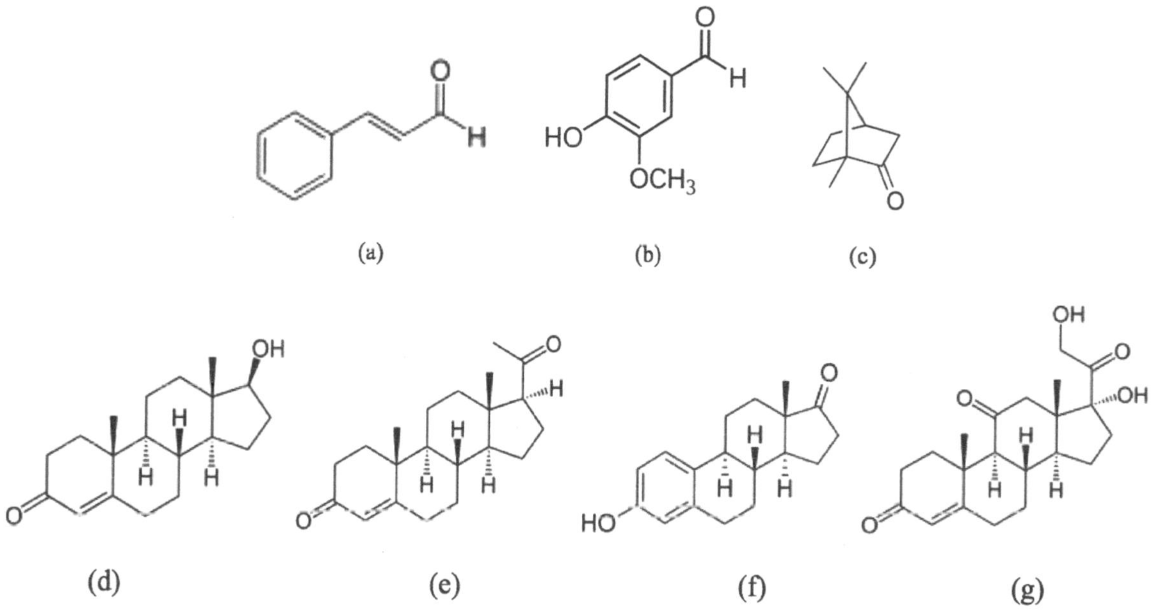

Figure 1 Structural formulas for examples of naturally occurring aldehydes and ketones: (a) cinnamon; (b) vanillin; (c) camphor; (d) testosterone; (e) progesterone; (f) esterone; and (g) cortisone.

Figure 1 shows us the structures of various molecules with a carbonyl carbon, including both aldehydes such as cinnamon and ketones such as testosterone.

Both **Benedict's** solution and **Tollens'** solutions are useful reagents to test for aldehydes. In the former, a positive test results when the basic **royal blue cupric solution is reduced to form a precipitate of cuprous oxide**. A positive test for the latter results when the **ammoniacal solution of silver ion is reduced to silver metal**.

Key terms: Benedict's, Tollens'
Contrast: Benedict's test involves reducing copper from cupric to cuprous solution vs. Tollens' test involves reducing a positive silver ion to silver metal

23. Which of the following would NOT give a positive Benedict's test?

I. Cinnamon
II. Vanillin
III. Camphor
IV. Carvone

   A. I and II only
   B. I and III only
   C. II and IV only
   D. <u>**III and IV only**</u>

Choice **D** is correct. As seen in the structure shown in Figure 1, the structures for cinnamon and vanillin have aldehyde functional groups, which would give a positive Benedict's test. Choices A and B can be eliminated. Also as seen in Figure 1, the structure of camphor has a ketone as a functional group. Ketones do not give a positive Benedict's test. Choice C can be eliminated and choice D is the best answer. While the structure of carvone is not shown in Figure 1, the suffix -one, indicates that it is a ketone.

24. What are the oxidation numbers of the silver species in the Tollens' test before and after a positive test?

   A. <u>**1+ and 0, respectively**</u>
   B. 2+ and 1+, respectively
   C. 3+ and 2+, respectively
   D. 2+ and 0, respectively

Choice **A** is correct. As stated in the passage, Tollens' test involves the reduction of silver ion, Ag^+, to silver metal, whose oxidation number is 0. Therefore the oxidation number changes from 1+ to 0 and choice A is the answer.

25. Which of the following best describes the isomer of 2-Methyl-5-(1-methylethenyl)-2-cyclohexenone shown below?

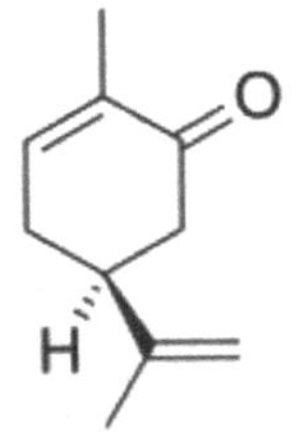

   A. This isomer is R-carvone, which is oil of spearmint.
   B. This isomer is R-carvone, which is oil of caraway.
   C. This isomer is S-carvone, which is oil of spearmint.
   D. <u>**This isomer is S-carvone, which is oil of caraway.**</u>

Choice **D** is correct. The chiral carbon of carvone in the structure shown is at the bottom of the six membered ring. We need to assign priority to the groups attached to this carbon. The hydrogen is easily assigned the lowest priority. Since the other three positions all are directly attached to a carbon atom, we then need to turn our attention to the atoms attached to those carbons. The highest priority is assigned to the carbon that is attached to two other carbon atoms, rather than part of the ring. We now need to consider the carbons that are part of the ring. The second highest priority is on the right side of the ring because of the ketone, followed by the carbon on the left side of the ring. When looking along the chiral C-H bond and following the direction of priority, this is the S-enantiomer.

Choices A and B can be eliminated. As stated in the passage, the S-enantiomer is "oil of caraway", making choice D the best answer.

26. Which of the following would be most useful in distinguishing propanal from propanone?

   A. <u>Proton NMR spectroscopy</u>
   B. IR spectroscopy
   C. UV-Vis spectroscopy
   D. Rotation of plane-polarized light

Choice **A** is correct. Propanal and propanone are both expected to have a carbonyl stretches in the 1700-1800 cm^{-1} region of the IR spectrum and would be difficult to distinguished based on IR spectroscopy. Choice B can be eliminated. Both molecules are colorless organic compounds and would only absorb ultraviolet radiation. It would be difficult to distinguish these compounds based on UV-Vis spectroscopy. Choice C can be eliminated. Neither propanol nor propanone have chiral carbon atoms and will not rotate plane-polarized light. Choice D can be eliminated.

Propanone, or acetone, has two methyl groups on either side of the carbonyl and would produce a singlet in the ^{1}H NMR spectrum between 1-2 ppm. Propanal has an ethyl group and aldehyde hydrogen on either side of the carbonyl. The ethyl group will produce a triplet in the 1-2 ppm methyl region and a quartet in the 2-3 ppm methylene region. In addition, the aldehyde hydrogen will produce a singlet somewhere significantly downfield, in the 8-13 ppm range. Choice A is the best answer.

27. Cholesterol, whose structure is shown below, is the precursor to which of the following hormones?

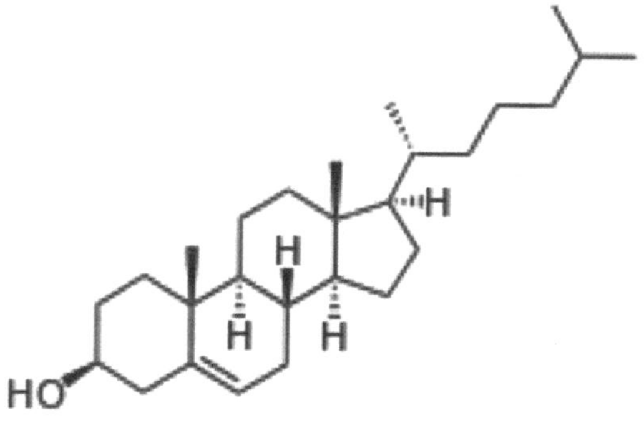

   I. Testosterone
   II. Progesterone
   III. Estrogen
   IV. Cortisone

   A. I only
   B. I and II only
   C. I, II, and III only
   D. <u>I, II, III, and IV</u>

Choice **D** is correct. The ring structure in cholesterol is similar to the ring structures in all of the steroid hormones and cholesterol is transformed by way of a series of enzymatic reactions into steroid-based sex hormones such testosterone, progesterone and estrogen. Choices A and B can be eliminated. Cortisone is a steroid-based hormone produced by the adrenal gland, which uses cholesterol as the precursor. Choice C can be eliminated and choice D is the best answer.

THIS PAGE LEFT

INTENTIONALLY BLANK

Passage 4

Newton was able to demonstrate that when a thin beam of sunlight was passed through a prism, Figure 1, the light was dispersed due to refraction into the familiar colors of the rainbow. He subsequently was able to reconstruct the white light by using a second prism. Newton apparently favored an explanation of this phenomena based on the corpuscular theory of light, which describes light in terms of discrete particles that pass through matter at different speeds due to collisions with atoms. He also recognized the utility of Huygens' wave theory, which was useful in describing other aspects of light, such as diffraction, and interference. The angle (q) of refraction is dependent upon the index of refraction (n) for a particular material, and Snell's Law (Equation 1), where n is a constant relating the ratio of the speed of light in a vacuum (c = 3.0 x 10^8 m/s) to the speed (v) of light in a material.

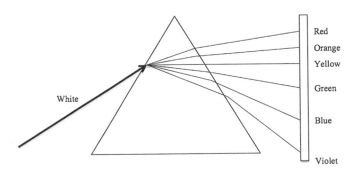

Figure 1 A schematic representation of a beam of white light passing through an equilateral triangular glass prism, resulting in the dispersion of the various color components of white light.

Equation 1 $$n_1 \sin \theta_1 = n_2 \sin \theta_2$$

The current understanding of why we see colors is based on a person's ability to perceive reflected, transmitted or emitted wavelengths of visible electromagnetic radiation, between 400 and 800 nm. There are two basic types of photosensitive cells, rods and cones on the retina, located on the back of the eye, where the lens focuses light based on the principles of refraction, producing an image. The rods are not significantly involved in the perception of color, but are important in the perception of colorless images under conditions of low illumination. The cones can be subdivided into three basic types, blue, green and red, based on the wavelengths of maximum sensitivity, however, each cone has sensitivity to a range of wavelengths. Monochromatic light is perceived by the brain due to the degree of optic nerve stimulation that is generated by the combination of each type of photosensitive cell. Materials that reflect multiple colors produce complex responses from the cones, explaining the multitude of perceptions of colors. The most common type of color dysfunction is known as red-green color blindness, in which the red or green cones are either missing or function with diminished efficiencies. This abnormality is often associated with a recessive X chromosome mutation. As a result males are much more likely to suffer from red-green color blindness than females.

28. A red-green colorblind man is married to a red-green colorblindness carrier woman. What are the probabilities that a male child and female child in this family will be red-green colorblind?
    A. The probability for green-red colorblindness will be 100% for the male children and 0% for the female children.
    B. The probability for green-red colorblindness will be 50% for the male children and 25% for the female children.
    C. The probability for green-red colorblindness will be 50% for the male children and 50% for the female children.
    D. The probability for green-red colorblindness will be 100% for the male children and 50% for the female children.

29. If a red laser pointer is focused on the surface of a rectangular piece of crown glass (n = 1.50) at an angle of 30° with respect to the normal, what would be the angle that the laser beam exits the other side of the glass? The index of refraction of air at 0°C is 1.000293, the sin of 20° is 0.342, the sin of 30° is 0.500, the sin of 45° is 0.707 and the sin of 60° is 0.866.
    A. 20°
    B. 30°
    C. 45°
    D. 60°

30. Which of the following monochromatic colors has the lowest velocity while passing through a glass prism?
    A. Red
    B. Yellow
    C. Green
    D. Blue

31. Which of the following best describes a corpuscle of light?
    A. A proton
    B. An electron
    C. A neutron
    D. A photon

32. If the human eye has a converging lens, which of the following best describes the image that is formed on the retina for an object that is more than one focal length away from the lens?
    A. The image is real and inverted.
    B. The image is real and erect.
    C. The image is virtual and inverted.
    D. The image is virtual and erect.

33. What is the speed of light in water if its index of refraction is 1.33?
    A. 1.2×10^8 m/s
    B. 2.3×10^8 m/s
    C. 3.0×10^8 m/s
    D. 4.0×10^8 m/s

34. Which of the following most likely represents the wavelengths of maximum sensitivity for the red, green and blue cones of the human eye?
    I. 435 nm
    II. 540 nm
    III. 575 nm

    A. I, II and III, respectively
    B. II, III and I, respectively
    C. III, I and II, respectively
    D. III, II and I, respectively

Passage 4 Answers and Explanations

Newton was able to demonstrate that when a thin beam of sunlight was passed through **a prism**, Figure 1, the light was **dispersed due to refraction into the familiar colors of the rainbow**. He subsequently was able to reconstruct the white light by using a second prism. Newton apparently favored an explanation of this phenomena based on the **corpuscular theory** of light, which describes light in terms of discrete particles that pass through matter at different speeds due to collisions with atoms. He also recognized the utility of Huygens' **wave theory**, which was useful in describing other aspects of light, such as **diffraction, and interference**. The angle (q) of refraction is dependent upon the **index of refraction** (n) for a particular material, and **Snell's Law** (Equation 1), where n is a constant relating the ratio of the speed of light in a vacuum (c = 3.0 x 108 m/s) to the speed (v) of light in a material.

Key terms: prism, refraction, corpuscular theory, wave theory, diffraction, interference, and index of refraction.

Cause-and-Effect: White light is composed of electromagnetic radiation with wavelengths encompassing the entire visible range of the spectrum. Passing white light through a prism causes refraction at the surface interfaces between the air and prism, in which the different wavelengths have increasing indices of refraction as wavelength decreases, resulting in dispersion and the separation of the various fundamental colors associated with the rainbow.

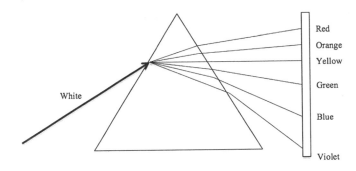

Figure 1 A schematic representation of a beam of white light passing through an equilateral triangular glass prism, resulting in the dispersion of the various color components of white light.

Figure 1 When light rays pass from a material with a low index of refraction (air) into a material with a higher index of refraction (glass) at some angle with respect to the normal for the surface, the angle of the light beam bends towards the normal. The extent of this bending depends upon the speed that the electromagnetic radiation travels through the materials, which determines the index of refraction. The longer wavelengths have larger speeds than shorter wavelengths, because the short wavelengths are more likely to interact with the atoms of the material. Upon exiting the prism on the other side, the light beam bends away from the normal, as a result of going from a material with a higher index of refraction to a lower index of refraction. Since the two surfaces of the prism are not parallel, the resulting refraction causes a separation of the wavelengths. When Newton used two prisms, he essentially created a piece of glass with two parallel surfaces, which causes the light to refract back to the same angle with respect to the normal as the beam initially entered.

Equation 1 $n_1 \sin q_1 = n_2 \sin q_2$

Equation 1   For a light ray passing from one material into another, Snell's law states that the ratio of the sine of the angles of a light ray with respect to the normal of the surface, will be proportional to the speed of the light in the two materials, which is then also proportional to the ratio of the indices of refraction.

$$(\sin \theta_1)/(\sin \theta_2) = v_1/v_2 = n_1/n_2$$

Rearrangement of this relationship provides Equation 1.

The current understanding of why we see colors is based on a person's ability to **perceive reflected**, **transmitted or emitted wavelengths of visible electromagnetic radiation**, between 400 and 800 nm.   There are two basic types of **photosensitive cells, rods and cones on the retina**, located on the back of the eye, where the lens focuses light based on the principles of refraction, producing an image. The rods are not significantly involved in the perception of color, but are important in the perception of colorless images under conditions of low illumination. **The cones can be subdivided into three basic types, blue, green and red, based on the wavelengths of maximum sensitivity**, however, each cone has sensitivity to a range of wavelengths. Monochromatic light is perceived by the brain due to the degree of **optic nerve** stimulation that is generated by the combination of each type of photosensitive cell. Materials that reflect multiple colors produce complex responses from the cones, explaining the multitude of perceptions of colors. The most common type of **color dysfunction is known as red-green color blindness,** in which the red or green cones are either missing or function with diminished efficiencies. This abnormality is often associated with a **recessive X chromosome mutation**. As a result human males are much more likely to suffer from red-green color blindness than females.

Key terms: electromagnetic radiation, photosensitive cells, rods, cones, retina, image, optic nerve, dysfunction, color blindness, recessive, X chromosome, and mutation.

Cause-and-Effect: Shining light on the photoreceptors can result in stimulation of the optic nerve.

Cause-and-Effect: Since there are three different types of color photoreceptors, or cones, in the retina of the eye, sensitive to different wavelengths of visible light, the degree of this simultaneous stimulation of all three types, results in the interpretation of this information by the brain as a particular color.

Cause-and-Effect: A sex-linked mutation on the X chromosome can lead to a dysfunction of one or more of the color receptors, or cones, associated with maximum sensitivity for either red or green light, resulting in a common form of color blindness.

28. A red-green colorblind man is married to a red-green carrier woman. What are the probabilities that a male child and female child in this family will be red-green colorblind?
    A. The probability for green-red colorblindness will be 100% for the male children and 0% for the female children.
    B. The probability for green-red colorblindness will be 50% for the male children and 25% for the female children.
    C. **The probability for green-red colorblindness will be 50% for the male children and 50% for the female children.**
    D. The probability for green-red colorblindness will be 100% for the male children and 50% for the female children.

Since the father is color blind, he carries the mutated gene (*) on his X chromosome (X*Y) and the mother is heterozygous for the mutation (X*X). The Punnett square is:

	X*	X
X*	X*X	X*X*
Y	X*Y	XY

Since the mutated gene is recessive, 50% of the female children will be colorblind and 50% of the male children will be color blind. Choice **C** is the correct answer.

29. If a red laser pointer is focused on the surface of a rectangular piece of crown glass (n = 1.50) at an angle of 30° with respect to the normal, what would be the angle that the laser bean exits the other side of the glass? The index of refraction of air at 0°C is 1.000293, the sin of 20° is 0.342, the sin of 30° is 0.500, the sin of 45° is 0.707 and the sin of 60° is 0.866.
    A. 20°
    B. **30°**
    C. 45°
    D. 60°

When the light beam goes from the air into the glass the angle will be bent towards the normal as predicted by Snell's law,

$$1.000293 \sin 30° = 1.50 \sin \theta \text{ glass}$$
$$(1.000293/1.5) \sin 30° = \sin \theta \text{ glass}$$
$$(1.000293/1.5)\, 0.5 = \sin \theta \text{ glass}$$

however, on the other side of the glass the beam will bend back away from the normal, therefore

$$1.5 \sin \theta \text{glass} = 1.000293 \sin \theta \text{ air}$$
$$(1.5/1.000293) \times (1.000293/1.5)\, 0.5 = \sin \theta \text{ air}$$
$$0.5 = \sin \theta \text{ air}$$
$$\sin^{-1} 0.5 = \theta \text{ air}$$
$$30° = \theta \text{ air}$$

The light beam that exits the glass on the other side is parallel to the incident light beam, with the angle with respect to the normal being 30°. Choice **B** is the correct answer.

30. Which of the following monochromatic colors has the lowest velocity while passing through a glass prism?
    A. Red
    B. Yellow
    C. Green
    D. <u>**Blue**</u>

Based on Figure 1, the blue light is refracted the most. In order for this to happen the index of refraction (n) for this color must be the highest. Since $n = c/v$, where c is the speed of light in a vacuum and v is the velocity in the prism. The velocity of the blue light will be the slowest and red light will be the fastest. Choice **D** is the correct answer.

31. Which of the following best describes a corpuscle of light?
    A. A proton
    B. An electron
    C. A neutron
    D. <u>**A photon**</u>

Choices A, B and C all correspond to components of atoms and have mass. Light does not have mass.

As stated in the first paragraph of the passage, "…corpuscular theory of light, which describes light in terms of discrete particles…" and photons are the modern term used to describe a particle of electromagnetic radiation (light). Choice **D** is the correct answer.

32. If the human eye has a converging lens, which of the following best describes the image that is formed on the retina for an object that is more than one focal length away from the lens?
    A. <u>**The image is real and inverted.**</u>
    B. The image is real and erect.
    C. The image is virtual and inverted.
    D. The image is virtual and erect.

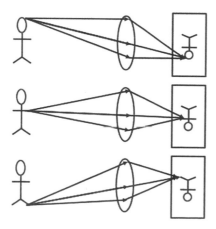

A converging lens produces a real and inverted image for objects located beyond the focal point of the lens, as shown in the ray diagrams for a convex lens shown below. Choice **A** is the correct answer.

33. What is the speed of light in water if its index of refraction is 1.33?
    - **A.** 1.2×10^8 m/s
    - **B.** $\underline{\textbf{2.3} \times \textbf{10}^8 \textbf{ m/s}}$
    - **C.** 3.0×10^8 m/s
    - **D.** 4.0×10^8 m/s

As stated in the passage, the index of refraction is the ratio of the velocity of light in a vacuum to the speed of the light in the water. Substituting into the equation gives

$$n = c/v$$
$$1.33 = (3.0 \times 10^8 \text{ m/s}) \, / \, v$$
$$v = (3.0/1.33) \times 10^8 \text{ m/s}$$
$$v = 2.3 \times 10^8 \text{ m/s}$$

Choice **B** is the answer, since it is slightly less than the speed of light in a vacuum. The speed of light in the presence of matter is always slower than in a vacuum, eliminating choice C. The speed of light can not be greater than 3.0×10^8 m/s, eliminating choice D.

34. Which of the following most likely represents the wavelengths of maximum sensitivity for the red, green and blue cones of the human eye?
    - I. 435 nm
    - II. 540 nm
    - III. 575 nm

    - **A.** I, II and III, respectively
    - **B.** II, III and I, respectively
    - **C.** III, I and II, respectively
    - **D.** $\underline{\textbf{III, II and I, respectively}}$

On the visible spectrum as you move across ROYGBIV, wavelength decreases from 700 to 400 nm and frequency increases. Red light would have the longest wavelength and would correspond to III, eliminating choices A and B. Blue light would have the shortest wavelength, eliminating C. Choice **D** is the correct answer.

TIMED
SECTION 1
59 Questions, 95 Minutes

(Use the tear-out answer sheet provided in Appendix E)

Passage 1 (Questions 1-5)

The structure of a polypeptide was determined beginning with the identification of its constituent amino acids. A purified sample of the polypeptide was denatured and then hydrolyzed by a strong acid at 110°C for 24 hours. The individual amino acids released by the treatment were then separated by cation-exchange chromatography. In this technique, amino acids bind to, with differing affinities, negatively charged groups attached to resins applied along the column.

Following treatment with a series of eluting solutions, the separated amino acids contained in the eluate from the column were heated with ninhydrin—a reagent that forms the blue-purple compound Ruhemann's Purple with most amino acids, amines and ammonia.

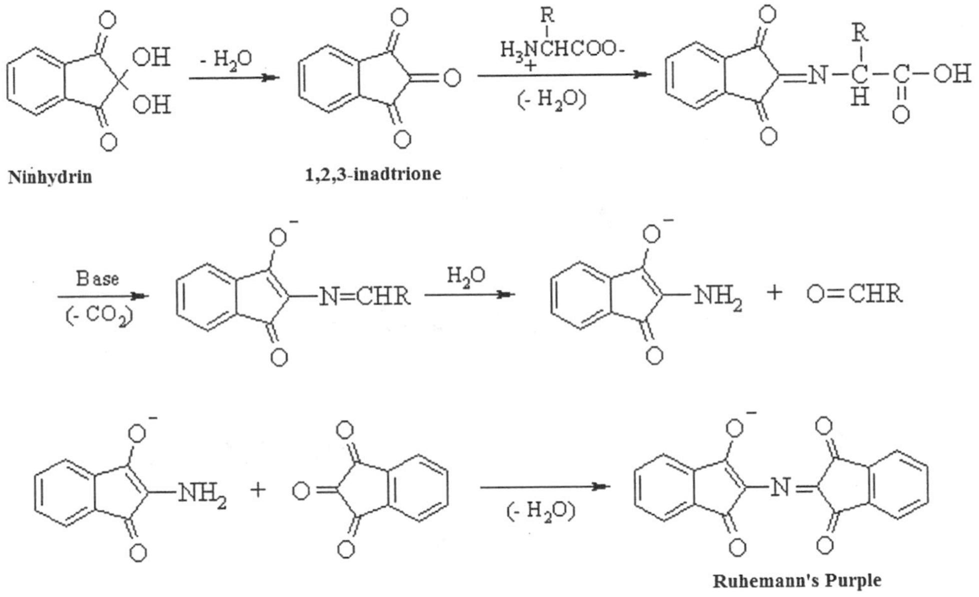

Figure 1 The ninhydrin reaction between ninhydrin and a free amino acid.

The amount of each amino acid present was then determined spectrophotometrically by measuring the amount of blue-purple light absorbed.

The specific position of each amino acid in the polypeptide chain was also found. Edman reagent (phenylisothiocyanate) was used to label a terminal residue under mildly alkaline conditions, resulting in the formation of a phenylthiocarbamoyl. Under acidic conditions, the terminal amino acid of the polypeptide was cleaved, releasing free polypeptide and phenylthiohydantoin (PTH), an amino acid derivative that can be identified. Edman reagent was applied repeatedly, shortening the peptide bond obtained following each cycle. The steps of the Edman degradation are shown in Figure 2.

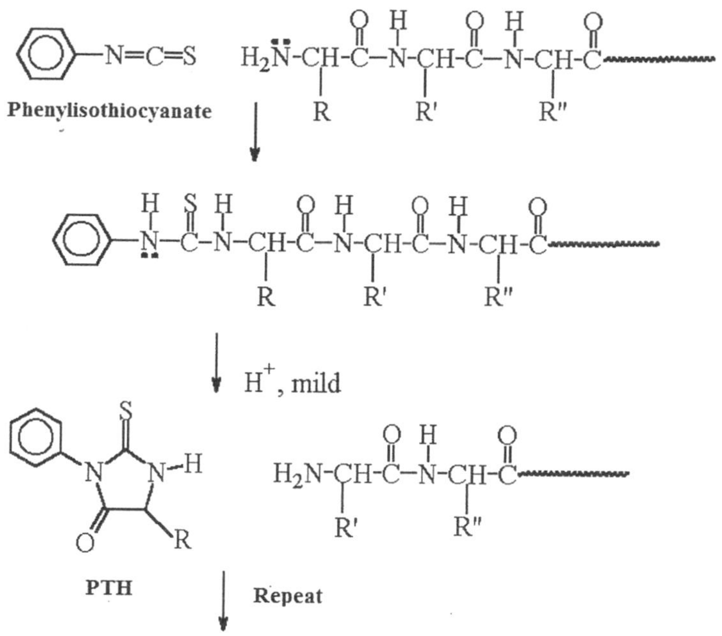

Figure 2 Edman degradation of a polypeptide

There are limits on the length of polypeptides that can be sequenced by this method. Over time, the yield of PTH-amino acid products decreases relative to the background level of PTH-amino acids. Repetitive yield is a measure of the percent of detectable material remaining after each turn of the cycle. Longer polypeptides can be sequenced from greater initial sample sizes and larger repetitive yields. They may also be cleaved by peptidase enzymes to create shorter polypeptides for sequencing.

1. The kinetics of the ninhydrin reaction were shown to be first order with respect to 1, 2, 3-indantrione and α-alpha amino acid, and second order overall. The reaction rate was shown to vary with solution pH. The initial reaction rate was greatest when the product of which two concentrations was maximized? (Note: $R=C_8H_4O_2$.)

    A. $[RC=O^+H][H_2NCHRCOO^-]$
    B. $[RC=O][H_3^+NCHRCOO^-]$
    C. $[RC=O^+H][H_3^+NCHRCOOH]$
    D. $[RC=O][H_2NCHRCOOH]$

2. Which of the following molecules is the product obtained at the end of the Edman degradation of the polypeptide H_2N-Ala-Gly-Arg-Met-COOH?

    A. PTH-Ala
    B. PTH-Gly
    C. PTH-Arg
    D. PTH-Met

3. What is most likely true of the eluant solutions used to recover free amino acids from the ion-exchange column employed?

    A. They are hydrophobic.
    B. They possess a characteristic salt concentration.
    C. They must be capable of denaturing disulfide linkages.
    D. They must contain digestive enzymes.

4. Unfolding of the polypeptide in the presence of the denaturant preceded unimolecularly with rate constant, k. What are the units for this rate constant?

    A. s^{-1}
    B. $M \cdot s$
    C. $M^{-1} \cdot s^{-1}$
    D. $M \cdot s^{-1}$

5. Which of the following reaction types best describes the formation of the bond between phenylisothiocyanate and a polypeptide during the first reaction in Figure 2?

    A. Addition
    B. Dehydration
    C. Neutralization
    D. Elimination

THIS PAGE LEFT

INTENTIONALLY BLANK

Passage 2 (Questions 6-9)

Carbon dioxide is a molecular compound with a linear structure and exists primarily in the gas phase under normal temperature and pressure conditions. The solid is often referred to as dry ice, in which the molecular units form a trigonal unit-cell crystal structure, in which the O-C-O angle is essentially 180° and the C=O bond lengths of 1.16 Å are shorter than the C=O bond lengths observed in organic carbonyl compounds (1.23 Å), and only slightly longer than that observed in carbon monoxide (1.13 Å).

As seen in the phase diagram shown in Figure 1, the liquid phase does not exist under standard conditions of temperature and pressure, and relatively high pressures are required to condense the gas to the liquid. Below the triple point pressure the gas will condense directly to the solid, or the solid will sublime directly to the gas. These properties are clearly the result of the weak intermolecular interactions, which stands in stark contrast to the properties of its silicon homolog, silica (SiO_2), which forms a network solid in which each silicon atom is bonded to four oxygen atoms. Supercritical carbon dioxide has received considerable interest as a solvent for the extraction of organic compounds from complex matrices, such as in the preparation of decaffeinated coffee (as opposed to using chlorocarbon solvents such as chloroform ($CHCl_3$) or methylene chloride (CH_2Cl_2)). The structure of caffeine is shown in Figure 2.

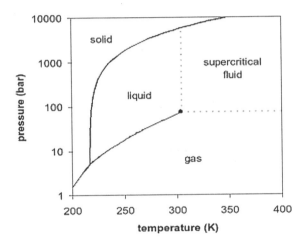

Figure 1 Phase diagram for carbon dioxide, (1.01 bar = 1 atm = 101 kPa)

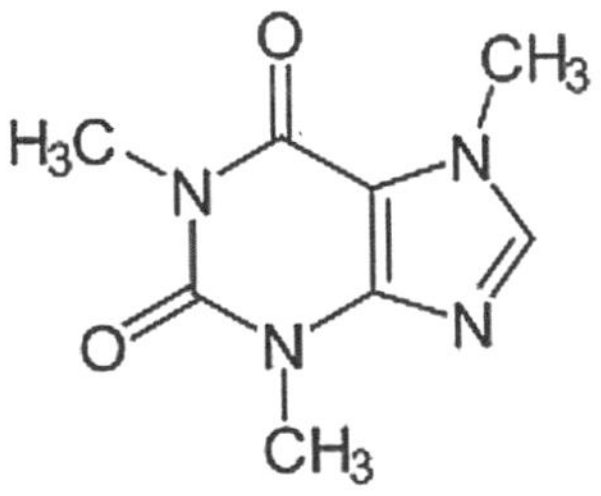

Figure 2 Structural formula of caffeine

There is considerable debate about the nature of the intermolecular interactions of carbon dioxide under conditions of extremely high pressure. Certain molecular modeling calculations suggest that oxygen lone-pairs on neighboring molecules begin to interact with the carbon atoms, causing the O-C-O angle to bend and the intramolecular C=O bonds to lengthen. The significance of this is related to proposals for the sequestration of carbon dioxide in deep geologic storage, in order to circumvent some of the greenhouse gas effects that are of concern when carbon dioxide from combustion of fossil fuels is released into the atmosphere.

6. Which of the following is closest to the O-Si-O bond angle in silica?
    A. 90°
    B. 109°
    C. 120°
    D. 180°

7. Carbon dioxide at 101 kPa and 100°C is in which phase?
    A. Solid
    B. Liquid
    C. Gas
    D. Super-critical fluid

8. Which of the following compounds would most likely NOT be extracted to any significant extent by supercritical carbon dioxide?
    A. 1,3,7-Trimethylpurine-2,6-dione
    B. Ammonium nitrate
    C. Methyl salicylate
    D. Benzaldehyde

9. Which of the following would represent the major solute/solvent intermolecular force in a methylene chloride solution of caffeine?
    A. London dispersion forces
    B. Dipole-dipole interactions
    C. Hydrogen bonding
    D. Ion-dipole interactions

Passage 3 (Questions 10-14)

Kidney stones are insoluble aggregate crystals that can form in the urine of certain people. One of the compounds that can contribute to the formation of kidney stones is calcium oxalate (CaC_2O_4, FW = 128.097 g/mol, K_{sp} = 2.3 x 10^{-9}). Oxalic acid is a naturally occurring diprotic acid, ($H_2C_2O_4$, pK_{a1} = 1.3 and pK_{a2} = 4.3) present in a number of foods, including rhubarb and spinach. Oxalic acid can be produced from oxaloacetate, which plays an important role in the citric acid cycle. Uric acid can also contribute to the formation of kidney stones and can also crystallize in the synovial fluid of the joints, producing inflammation and the painful symptoms associated with gout. In humans, uric acid is the final oxidation product of purine metabolism and like oxalic acid is also a diprotic acid ($H_2C_5H_2N_4O_3$, pK_{a1} = 5.4 and pK_{a2} = 10.3), but unlike oxalic acid, it is not completely ionized at pHs typical for urine.

If the urine becomes supersaturated, seed crystals can result in the formation of a large mass, or stone, in one of several possible locations, including the bladder, the ureters and the kidneys. In many cases, small stones (< 3 mm) are readily passed, however in some cases, large stones can cause obstruction and renal colic, or worse. In some cases ultrasound can be used to break up stones and facilitate their passing, however in extreme cases, surgery may be required.

Urine contains a number of natural chelating agents, one of which is citrate. These chelating agents are polydentate ligands (Lewis bases) that coordinate to a metal ion and form soluble coordination compounds that help prevent the nucleation and precipitation of calcium oxalate. Citric acid is a weak triprotic acid (pK_{a1} = 3.1, pK_{a2} = 4.8 and pK_{a3} = 6.4), whose structure is shown in Figure 1. The equilibrium constant at 37°C for the formation of the calcium citrate complex ion (Reaction 1) is 1.9 x 10^3. The calcium citrate complex has a residual negative charge that enhances its solubility in aqueous solution.

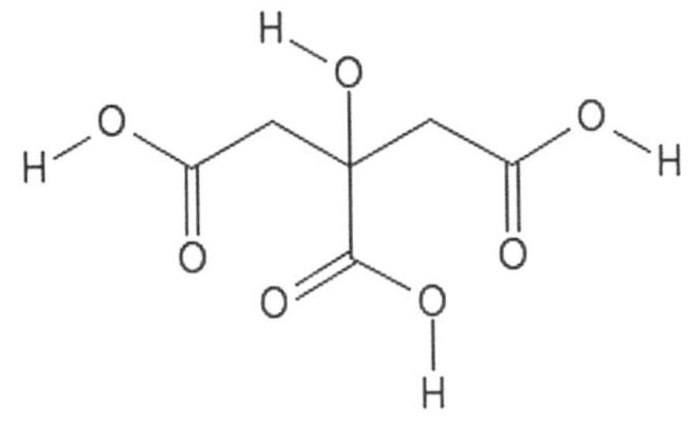

Figure 1 The structure of citric acid, $H_3C_6H_5O_7$

Reaction 1 Ca^{2+} (aq) + $C_6H_5O_7^{3-}$ (aq) → $CaC_6H_5O_7^{-}$ (aq)

10. Which of the following formulas best represents the predominant form that exists in solution when citric acid is dissolved in normal urine whose pH is approximately 7?
    A. $H_3C_6H_5O_7$
    B. $H_2C_6H_5O_7^-$
    C. $HC_6H_5O_7^{2-}$
    D. $C_6H_5O_7^{3-}$

11. In the passage, the equilibrium constant for the formation of the calcium citrate complex is quoted as being at 37°C. Which of the following temperatures on the Fahrenheit scale corresponds to this temperature?
    A. 32° F
    B. 75° F
    C. 99° F
    D. 212° F

12. Based on information in the passage, what is the equilibrium constant for the following reaction?

$$CaC_2O_4 \text{ (s)} + C_6H_5O_7^{3-} \text{ (aq)} \leftrightarrows CaC_6H_5O_7^- \text{ (aq)} + C_2O_4^{2-} \text{ (aq)}$$

    A. 4.3×10^8
    B. 1.9×10^3
    C. 4.4×10^{-6}
    D. 2.3×10^{-9}

13. If equal molar solutions of oxalic acid, uric acid, citric acid and urea are prepared, which solution will have the lowest pH?
    A. Oxalic acid, because the first acid dissociation constant is the largest of the three acids.
    B. Uric acid, because its pK_{a2} value is the largest of the three acids.
    C. Citric acid, because it is a triprotic acid.
    D. Urea because it is a basic compound.

14. DNA is made of nucleotides, some of which contain purine groups that interact by way of non-covalent interactions, such as hydrogen bonding, to form base-pairs. Which of the following nucleotides could produce uric acid as a result of metabolism?
    I.   Adenine
    II.   Guanine
    III.   Glucose

    A. I only
    B. II only
    C. I and II only
    D. I, II and III

These questions are NOT related to a passage.

15. The chemical formula of calcium phosphate is:
    A. $CaPO_4$
    B. Ca_3PO_4
    C. $Ca_2(PO_4)_3$
    D. $Ca_3(PO_4)_2$

16. Acetic acid, $HC_2H_3O_2$, has a pK_a of 4.8. What is the pH of a 0.10 M solution of sodium acetate?
    A. 2.9
    B. 7.0
    C. 8.9
    D. 13.0

17. Which of the following compounds has the highest boiling point?
    A. CH_4
    B. NH_3
    C. H_2O
    D. HF

18. The polypeptide NH_2-Trp-Glu-Gly-Arg-Tyr-Pro-Lys-Pro-Trp-COO^- was treated with the active form of three peptidases: trypsin, which cleaves peptide bonds after non-terminal Arg and Lys residues unless followed by Pro, endopeptidase V8, which cuts after non-terminal Glu residues, and carboxypeptidase A, which cleaves the peptide linkage immediately prior to C-terminal aromatic or aliphatic amino acid residues. What is the most likely combination of fragments obtained by this treatment?
    A. Gly-Arg, Tyr-Pro-Lys, Trp-Glu, and Pro-Trp
    B. Trp-Glu-Gly-Arg, Tyr-Pro-Lys, Pro, and Trp
    C. Trp-Glu, Gly-Arg, and Tyr-Pro-Lys-Pro-Trp
    D. Tyr-Pro-Lys, Pro, Gly-Arg, Trp-Glu, and Trp

THIS PAGE LEFT

INTENTIONALLY BLANK

Passage 4 (Questions 19-23)

Students in a biophysics class used the experimental setup shown in Figure 1 to simulate a human arm. The apparatus consisted of a horizontal beam having a length (L) of 0.50 m and a mass (M_b) of 2.0 kg, was attached to a frictionless hinge, which was also attached to a vertically oriented beam having a frictionless wheel at the top. An essentially massless string was initially attached in the middle of the horizontal beam at a distance from the center of the pivot point of the hinge. The string was draped over the wheel and then attached to a standard brass mass (M_1). The angle formed between the string and the horizontal beam was 60°. A second standard 1.0 kg brass mass (M_2) was then attached at the end of the horizontal beam. The weight of the mass hanging from the string (M_1) was adjusted until the two beams once again formed a right angle.

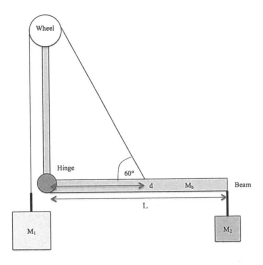

Figure 1 A schematic diagram of the experimental setup used to simulate a human arm. Note that sin 30° = cos 60° = 0.5, sin 60° = cos 30° = 0.866, tan 30° = 0.577, tan 60° = 1.732. The drawing is not to scale.

19. When the system in the passage is at equilibrium, what is the length of the string between where it is attached to the horizontal beam and the point where it comes in contact with the wheel?
    A. 0.35 m
    B. 0.50 m
    C. 0.70 m
    D. 1.0 m

20. What is the mass of the brass weight hanging from the end of the string when the system is at equilibrium?
    A. 2.3 kg
    B. 3.0 kg
    C. 4.6 kg
    D. 6.0 kg

21. What is the horizontal force that the beam exerts on the hinge?
    A. 9.8 N
    B. 17 N
    C. 23 N
    D. 34 N

22. What is the tension in the string when the system is at equilibrium as described in the passage?
    A. 3 N
    B. 23 N
    C. 29 N
    D. 45 N

23. Which anatomical part of the human body is NOT simulated in the experimental setup described in the passage?
    A. Ligaments
    B. Triceps
    C. Humerus
    D. Radius

Passage 5 (Questions 24-28)

Natural gas production in the United States has recently increased dramatically. This has been the result of the development of hydraulic fracturing techniques that release trapped natural gas from rock layers that were previously inaccessible using other techniques. This process involves drilling and subsequent pumping of proprietary aqueous based fluids into a sedimentary rock layer, often a shale deposit, under high pressure. The natural gas that is produced is mostly methane, but also contains small amounts of other hydrocarbons, such as ethane and propane. The use of natural gas as an energy source has considerable advantages over other fossil fuels, in that it produces much more energy and less carbon dioxide per carbon atom than fuels such as petroleum or coal. In addition, natural gas does not contain significant amounts of impurities, like the sulfur in coal that can contribute to air pollution and acid rain. One of the downsides of this increased production of natural gas is the inadvertent release of methane into the atmosphere. Like carbon dioxide, methane is a potent greenhouse gas and methane concentrations in the atmosphere have been steadily increasing over time. Methane can also be produced biologically under anaerobic conditions by bacteria. In fact, industrial production of animal protein from poultry flocks, as well as swine and cattle herds is thought to be a major contributor to changes in the methane concentrations in the earth's atmosphere. Table 1 compares the heats of reaction for methane to several other potential organic fuels that are major contributors to the world's energy supply.

Table 1 Heats of reaction at 25°C and 1 atm pressure for the complete combustion of various carbon based fuels.

Formula	Heat (kJ/mol)	Density at 25°C (kg/m^3)
CH_4 (g)	-890	0.71
C_3H_8 (l)	-2220	493
C_8H_{18} (l)	-5470	703
C_2H_5OH (l)	-1370	789
$C_6H_{12}O_6$ (s)	-2800	1540
C (s) amorphous	-390	~2000

24. Propane can be purchased liquefied, in 10kg tanks and is used for cooking. A person wants to take a pot containing 4.0 kg of water at 25°C and raise its temperature to the boiling point of the water, which has a specific heat of 4.18 J/g°C. Which of the following is closest to the amount of propane that would be required to heat the water?
   A. 10 g
   B. 25 g
   C. 60 g
   D. 80 g

25. Which of the fuels given below produces the LEAST energy per carbon dioxide molecule produced when used as a fuel to produce electricity?
   A. CH_4 (g)
   B. C_2H_5OH (l)
   C. $C_6H_{12}O_6$ (s)
   D. C_8H_{18} (l)

26. Coal is a complicated mixture of substances. One of the downsides of using coal as a fuel is the production of gases that can contribute to acid rain. Which of the following elements found in coal would NOT produce an oxide that contributes to acid rain?
   A. Sulfur
   B. Calcium
   C. Phosphorus
   D. Nitrogen

27. Which of the following regions of the infrared spectrum would be most useful in detecting methane in the atmosphere?
   A. 1600 - 1900 cm^{-1}
   B. 1900 - 2100 cm^{-1}
   C. 2700 - 3000 cm^{-1}
   D. 3000 - 3800 cm^{-1}

28. There is considerable interest in the use of biofuels as renewable sources of energy that would be essentially carbon neutral, because the carbon used to make the fuel ultimately comes from the carbon dioxide in the air. Which of the following are potentially biofuels?
   I. Methane
   II. Ethanol
   III. Cellulose

   A. I only
   B. I and II only
   C. II and III only
   D. I, II and III

These questions are NOT related to a passage.

29. The azimuthal quantum number corresponds to which of the following?
    A. The potential energy of the electron
    B. Approximate radial size of an electron cloud
    C. Approximate geometric shape of the orbital
    D. Number of valence electrons orbiting a nucleus

30. Presbyopia is diagnosed when the lens of the eye focuses incoming light rays to a position between the retina and the choroid. Which type of lens should be placed in front of the eye to focus light on the retina and correct this condition?
    A. Flat
    B. Spherical
    C. Diverging
    D. Converging

31. Which of the following compounds or ions has the same carbon-oxygen bond order, but a longer bond length, than carbon dioxide?

    I. Carbon monoxide
    II. Formaldehyde
    III. Carbonate

    A. I only
    B. II only
    C. II and III only
    D. I, II and III

THIS PAGE LEFT

INTENTIONALLY BLANK

Passage 6 (Questions 32-35)

Cyclic adenosine monophosphate, also known as cAMP, or (4aR,6R,7R,7aS)-6-(6-aminopurin-9-yl)-2-hydroxy-2-oxo-4a,6,7,7a-tetrahydro-4H-furo[3,2-d][1,3,2]dioxaphosphinin-7-ol in the IUPAC nomenclature, is a well-characterized second messenger derived from ATP and commonly found in the human body.

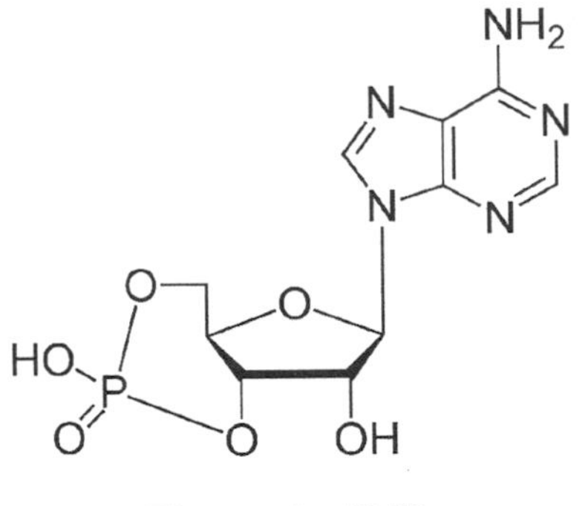

Figure 1 cAMP

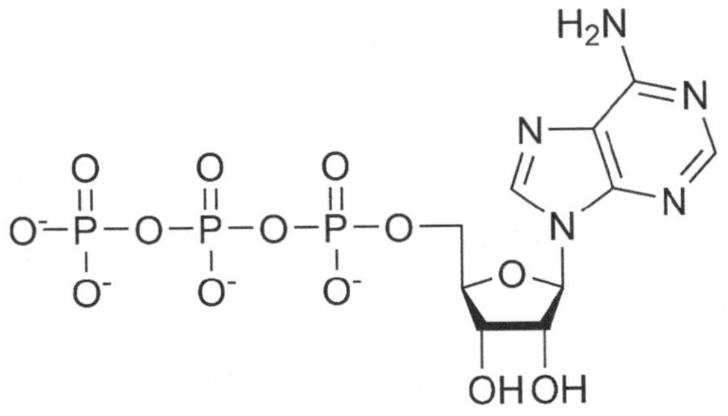

Figure 2 ATP

Second messengers, as one of the chief precipitators of intracellular signal transduction cascades, play an important biological role in processes such as apoptosis or cell differentiation. cAMP plays a role in the use of ion channels in the cell, the activation of protein kinases, and the intracellular effects of hormones such as glucagon or epinephrine. Aberrant activities in cAMP-mediated cellular pathways are linked to abnormal cell growth and proliferation, particularly in some cancers.

cAMP is an example of a nucleotide, or an organic compound comprised of a nitrogenous base, a ribose or deoxyribose sugar, and a minimum of one phosphate group. Nucleotides form the basic building blocks of nucleic acids, such as DNA or RNA, and also serve as the metabolic precursors for nucleosides, nucleobases, ribose, deoxyribose, the various nitrogenous bases, or (deoxy)ribose-1-phosphate.

32. Which of the following facts related to the "cyclic" portion of cyclic adenosine monophosphate (cAMP) is/are NOT true?

    I. The ring is principally formed by the nucleophilic attack on the primary phosphate's oxygen by the penultimate ring carbon on the pentose sugar.

    II. The ring is principally formed by the nucleophilic attack by the primary phosphate's oxygen on the penultimate ring carbon on the pentose sugar.

    III. The presence of a polar, protic solvent when reproducing the ring formation in vitro exhibits a retarding effect on the formation of desired product.

    A. I only
    B. II only
    C. I and III only
    D. I, II, and III

33. Which of the following is LEAST likely to be an evolutionary advantage gained from utilization of intracellular signal transduction cascades?
    A. The ability to "amplify" the signaling effect of one molecule, by increasing the number of triggered biological compounds at each step of the cascade
    B. The ability to have a variety of biochemical triggers precipitate a single downstream action within the cell
    C. The ability to have a single biochemical trigger precipitate a variety of downstream actions within the cell
    D. The ability to degrade or corrupt signal transduction at multiple points of biochemical interaction throughout the entirety of the transduction cascade

34. In which of the following biological compounds, *in vivo*, would a researcher be most likely to observe similar cyclic structures to cAMP?
    A. Monosaccharides
    B. Triacylglycerols
    C. Gonadotropins
    D. Kinases

35. The versatility lent by the sugar-phosphate backbone to the structure of biologically-relevant nucleic acids permits which of the following in nature?
    A. The formation of a double helix of grooves or voids adjacent to bound base pairs, providing binding sites to intercalating compounds such as histones
    B. The structural stability of dsDNA
    C. The ability of the cell to selectively induce either positive or negative supercoiling (e.g., through the action of topoisomerases)
    D. The looped conformation of the DNA backbone in G-quadraplexes, most notably found in telomeres.

Passage 7 (Questions 36-39)

Maintenance of proper pH levels in various parts of the human body is vitally important for a number of different reasons, among them prevention of tissue degradation due to excessive acidity or basicity, and creation of an internal environment in which biochemical reactions can proceed at appropriate times and rates.

Systems and processes which can help to partially stabilize pH levels include respiratory feedback mechanisms, which can decrease the level of CO_2 in blood plasma and hence can avoid an excessive concentration of carbonic acid, H_2CO_3. Other mechanisms for doing so include a buffer system catalyzed by carbonic anhydrase enzymes and involving both carbonic acid (H_2CO_3) and bicarbonate (HCO_3^-). One such buffer system was replicated in vitro and a titration procedure was applied, measuring pH as a function of what percentage of buffer was in the form of bicarbonate. The measurements from this system are graphed in Figure 1.

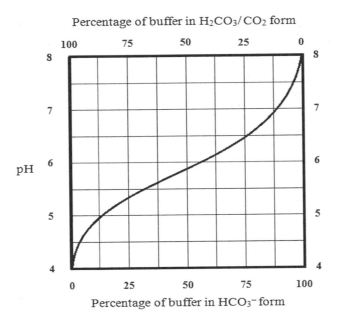

Figure 1 pH level as a function of buffer component percentage

Yet another system involves regulation of blood acidity by the kidneys, which can excrete either H^+ ions or bicarbonate ions, depending on which direction the chemical concentrations in the buffer system must shift to reach a safe blood plasma pH range. Excreting a substantial amount of bicarbonate will cause a significant number of the remaining carbonic acid molecules to separate into an H^+ ion and a bicarbonate ion.

36. If respiratory function is interrupted at a time when excessive CO_2 is in the bloodstream, then the pH of the blood plasma will:
    - **A.** increase, because increased CO_2 means increased acidity.
    - **B.** decrease, because excessive CO_2 will cause elevated levels of carbonic acid.
    - **C.** remain constant, because CO_2 will simply convert itself into H_2CO_3 by combining with water.
    - **D.** remain constant, because CO_2 does not have a hydrogen atom and hence cannot affect pH level.

37. pOH is a number obtained by taking the negative logarithm of $[OH^-]$ concentration within water. When pOH is equal to pH under conditions of 25°C and 1 atm of atmospheric pressure, the number representing each will be:
    - **A.** 7, because the product of $[H^+]$ and $[OH^-]$ in these circumstances can only match the K_W constant if each of these two concentrations equals 1×10^{-7}.
    - **B.** 8, because the sum of pH and pOH must always be 16.
    - **C.** 9, because the K_W constant will equal both pH and pOH if the two are equal, and K_W is always at a level of 9 under conditions of 25°C and 1 atm of atmospheric pressure.
    - **D.** pH and pOH do not apply to a situation in which $[H^+]$ equals $[OH^-]$, as each ion will immediately combine with the other to form H_2O, reducing the concentration of each to zero.

38. Figure 1 indicates that the rate of change of pH level is high as a function of bicarbonate concentration between the pH ranges of 7 and 8. What might account for this?
    - **A.** Increased HCO_3^- levels resulting in the donation of more $[OH^-]$ ions, causing a basic mixture of H_2O and OH^- to form
    - **B.** Ionization of water
    - **C.** The fact that titration occurred in the laboratory caused more inefficient functioning of the buffer system compared to how it would have operated in a living specimen.
    - **D.** Exhaustion of carbonic acid levels which could otherwise help to neutralize increased basicity.

39. Titration of potassium acetate in solution was conducted in a further attempt to determine a superior buffer system. The equation describing the reactions preceding titration appears below:

$$KCH_3COO + H_2O \rightarrow K^+ + CH_3COO^- + H_2O \rightleftharpoons CH_3COOH + OH^-$$

    What best describes what occurs in this process?
    - **A.** An acidic salt is hydrolyzed.
    - **B.** A basic salt is hydrolyzed.
    - **C.** A weak acid is dissolved.
    - **D.** A strong acid is dissolved.

These questions are NOT related to a passage.

40. Which of the following compounds has polar covalent bonds but no molecular dipole moment?
    A. Ammonia
    B. Formaldehyde
    C. Carbon dioxide
    D. Methane

41. It is possible to categorize amino acids based on the nature of the groups attached to the alpha carbon as being acidic, basic, nonpolar (hydrophobic) and polar (hydrophilic). Which of the following is most likely a nonpolar amino acid?

    A.

    B.

    C.

    D.

42. What is the energy, in joules, of a photon with a wavelength of 6.5×10^{-7} m, if $c = 3.0 \times 10^8$ m/s and $h = 6.62 \times 10^{-34}$ kg m^2 s^{-1}?
    A. 4.6×10^{14} J
    B. 4.6×10^{5} J
    C. 3.0×10^{-19} J
    D. 3.0×10^{-28} J

43. An object is fired at an initial speed of 30 m/s at an angle of 60°. 1.5 seconds after the ball has launched, the approximate total horizontal distance traveled is:
    A. 22.5 m
    B. 31.8 m
    C. 38.9 m
    D. 45.0 m

THIS PAGE LEFT

INTENTIONALLY BLANK

Passage 8 (Questions 44 - 47)

There are two types of covalent bonds found in biologically important molecules, non-polar and polar covalent bonds. In chemistry, the distinction between these types of bonds is based on differences in electronegativity between the nonmetal atoms involved in sharing pairs of electrons. If the difference in electronegativity between the two elements is less than 0.5, the bond is considered nonpolar and if the difference is greater than 0.5, but less than 2.0, the bond is considered polar. If the difference in electronegativity is greater than 2.0, the bond is no longer considered covalent. Listed in Table 1 are the electronegativity values for selected nonmetal elements.

Table 1 Electronegativity values for selected second period elements

Atomic Symbol	Electronegativity (Pauling scale)
H	2.2
C	2.6
N	3.0
O	3.4
F	4.0

Unequal sharing of electrons in a covalent bond, due to differences in electronegativity, imparts a degree of ionic character to the bond. Specifically, the more electronegative atom will gain a partial negative charge ($-\delta$) and the atom that is less able to attract the shared electrons will gain an equal amount of positive partial charge ($+\delta$). These bond dipoles represent electric fields with vector properties. Having polar covalent bonds is a necessary requirement for a molecule to have a molecular dipole moment, but, if the bond dipole moments do not combine to give a net dipole moment, the molecule will be nonpolar. Table 2 lists the experimentally determined molecular dipole moments for selected compounds.

Table 2 Molecular dipole moments, measured in debyes (D)

Formula	Name	Molecular Dipole (D)
CH_4	methane	0
NH_3	ammonia	1.47
H_2O	water	1.85
H_2CO	methanal	2.33
CO_2	carbon dioxide	0
CH_3COH	ethanal	2.7
$(CH_3)_2CO$	propanone	2.91
C_2H_6	ethane	0
N_2H_4	hydrazine	1.85
H_2O_2	hydrogen peroxide	2.26
CH_3NH_2	methyl amine	1.31
CH_3OH	methanol	1.69
$(CH_3)_2O$	dimethyl ether	1.30

44. Which of the following is the best estimate of an O-H bond dipole moment in water? Note that sin 109° = 0.95; sin 55° = 0.82; cos 109° = -0.33; and cos 55° = 0.57.
    A. 0.97 D
    B. 1.13 D
    C. 1.50 D
    D. 3.24 D

45. Which of the following compounds has the smallest molecular dipole moment?
    A. Methanol
    B. Dimethyl ether
    C. Methyl amine
    D. Dimethyl amine

46. Shown below is drawing representing the most stable conformation of hydrogen peroxide. Which of the following vectors best represents the direction of electric field generated by the dipole moment of hydrogen peroxide based on this drawing?

    A.  ↓
    B.  ↑
    C.  ↘
    D.  ↙

47. Which of the following compounds would most likely have the highest boiling point?
    A. Formaldehyde
    B. Acetaldehyde
    C. Acetone
    D. Ethane

Passage 9 (Questions 48-51)

Diffraction experiments can be particularly useful for indirectly determining information about the structure of objects that are too small to be observed by the human eye. In order for diffraction to be useful there must be a regular repeating pattern associated with the object or material and the wavelength of radiation used in the experiment must be comparable to the size of the spaces between the objects. In a commonly performed introductory physics experiment, students are asked to determine the spacing between parallel lines on a diffraction grating using a red (λ = 650 nm) laser pointer, Figure 1. When the laser is focused on a diffraction grating whose parallel lines are oriented horizontally, a vertical series of bright red spots are observed on a screen at some distance (L) from the diffraction grating. The angle θ can be determined from L and the distance between the bright spots. In order for constructive interference to occur, the diffracted light rays must travel integral multiples of the wavelength. The Fraunhofer equation (Equation 1) can be used to calculate the spacing between parallel lines on the diffraction grating. The orientation of the series of bright spots is always perpendicular to the orientation of the parallel lines. If the diffraction grating is rotated 90°, a horizontal series of bright spots will be observed. Particularly interesting two-dimensional diffraction patterns can be observed if there are two-dimensional patterns of shapes on the diffraction grating. Babinet's principle states that the observed diffraction pattern will be the same as the diffraction pattern of an aperture of the same shape. Thus, a diffraction grating consisting of two sets of parallel lines intersecting at some angle α, would produce two sets of bright spots also intersecting at that same angle.

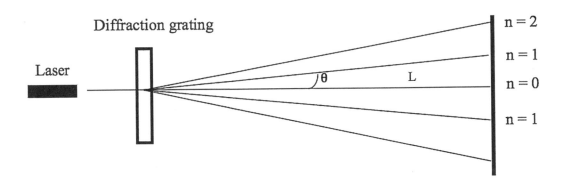

Figure 1 A schematic of a laser diffraction experiment.

Equation 1 $$d \sin \theta = n \lambda$$

This forms the basis for the analysis of perhaps the most important diffraction experiment of all time. In 1952 Gosling and Franklin used X-ray diffraction to help determine the structure of a crystalline form of deoxyribonucleic acid (DNA). After performing numerous experiments, they were able to orient the crystal such that the long axis of the unit cell was perpendicular to the path of the X-ray beam. In her notes she (Franklin) wrote, "The results suggest a helical structure (which must be very closely packed) containing 2, 3 or 4 co-axial nucleic acid chains per helical unit, and having the phosphate groups near the outside." This was well before Watson and Crick published their Nobel award winning description of DNA, which was based in part on Franklin's experiments. This insight into the helical structure of crystalline DNA can be easily understood by analogy to the shape of a coiled spring. If one were to look closely at a spring held with the principle axis oriented vertically, you would see two sets of parallel straight lines, Figure 2 (ignoring the curved shapes that would be seen on the ends) forming an angle of 2α, where α represents the pitch angle of the helix. If one were to imagine a large number of springs (DNA molecules), all oriented vertically, the straight portions would form a series of intersecting diffraction grating lines, that would produce two series of intersecting bright diffraction spots.

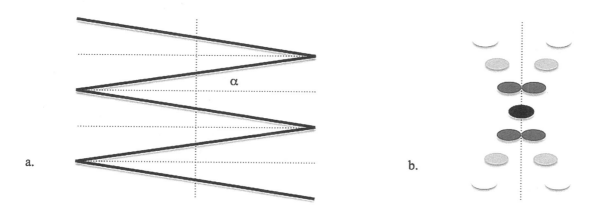

Figure 2   A side representation of a vertically oriented helical coil structure,
and the resulting diffraction pattern.

48. A student performed a diffraction experiment using an experimental set-up similar to that shown in Figure 1. If the distance between the laser pointer and the diffraction grating is increased, what happens to the distance between the bright spots on the screen?
    A. The distance between the bright spots increases, but the brightness of the spots remain the same.
    B. The distance between the bright spots decreases, but the brightness of the spots remain the same.
    C. The distance between the spots remains the same, and the brightness of the spots remains the same.
    D. The distance between the spots remains the same, but the size of the spots gets smaller.

49. A student performed a diffraction experiment using an experimental set-up similar to that shown in Figure 1, but instead of using a red laser, she used a blue laser. What happens to the spacing between the bright spots for the blue laser, as compared to the spacing between the bright spots of the red laser?
    A. The spacing gets bigger because the wavelength of blue light is longer than the wavelength of red light.
    B. The spacing gets smaller because the wavelength of blue light is longer than the wavelength of red light.
    C. The spacing gets bigger because the wavelength of blue light is shorter than the wavelength of red light.
    D. The spacing gets smaller because the wavelength of blue light is shorter than the wavelength of red light.

50. X-ray diffraction results from the scattering that occurs when electromagnetic radiation interacts with the electrons of atoms. Which of the following portions of crystalline nucleic acids would scatter x-rays the most?
    A. The phosphate groups
    B. The ribose sugar groups
    C. The purine bases
    D. The pyrimidine bases

51. Which of the following best describes what would happen to the diffraction pattern that would be observed for a spring similar to that shown in Figure 2, if a weight were suspended from the spring?
    A. The pitch angle α would decrease.
    B. The pitch angle α would increase.
    C. The spots would get brighter.
    D. The spots would get less bright.

Passage 10 (Questions 52 -55)

Keratin is the common name for a family of fibrous structural proteins, which are the key structural material making up the outer layer of human skin, as well as human hair, human nails, and many other natural structures in the animal kingdom. Keratin is formed from a series of monomers that assemble into bundles to form intermediate filaments. Its intermediate filaments are tough and insoluble and form strong "un-mineralized" tissues found in reptiles, birds, amphibians, and mammals. The reactions below summarize the generic in vitro lysing of disulfide bridges (induced either by hydrogen peroxide, acetic acid, or thioglycolic acid) formed in keratin.

Reactions 1(a) and 1(b): Generalized lysing of disulfide bridges formed in keratin

These disulfide bridges occur in addition to inter and/or intramolecular hydrogen bonds or interactions between charged functional groups in abnormal pH environments, due largely to keratins' relatively high concentration of sulfur-containing amino acids. Disulfide bridges are part of a larger family of crosslinks (covalent or ionic polymer bonds that link one polymer chain to another).These crosslinks contribute to the insolubility of keratins, except when in certain dissociating or reducing agents. Such crosslinks are important in generating mechanically stable structures such as keratinaceous formations in the human body.

The more flexible and elastic keratins of hair have fewer disulfide bridges than the keratins in mammalian fingernails, hooves and claws, which are harder and more like their analogues across the animal kingdom. Hair and other "α-keratins" consist of α-helically coiled single protein strands (with regular intra-chain H-bonding), which are then further twisted into so-called "superhelical" strands that may comprise a macro "coiled-coil" structure.

The β-keratins of reptiles and birds, on the other hand, are typically found in the scales, shells, and claws of reptiles, in the feathers, beaks, and claws of birds, and the quills of porcupines. Figure 1 below illustrates the typical structure of a β-keratin.

Figure 1 Generalized illustration of a β-keratin

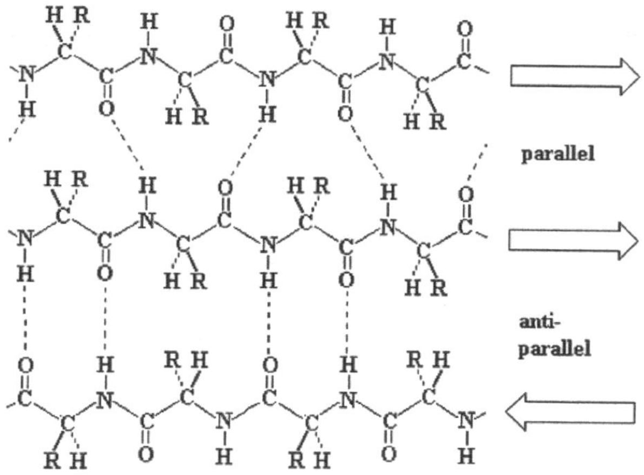

52. Which of the following is the correct reason why thioglycolic acid doesn't appear in the equation for K_{eq} of Reaction 1(b)? Assume the reaction takes place under normal biological conditions.
    A. Thioglycolic acid is a dilute solvent; its concentration can be reasonably approximated to equal to 1.
    B. Thioglycolic acid is a solid; its concentration can be reasonably approximated to equal to 1.
    C. Thioglycolic acid has no ionic activity; its concentration can be reasonably approximated to equal to 1.
    D. None of the above

53. Carbon-14 is frequently used by researchers in isotopic labelling of enzymes; however, under certain conditions, it can be subject to both β^- and β^+ decay. Which of the following isotopes might be observed if a sample of C-14 in use by a researcher were subjected to β^+ decay?
    A. Boron-14
    B. Nitrogen-15
    C. Nitrogen-14
    D. Boron-15

54. Disulfide bridges that form under natural conditions generally:
    A. stabilize proteins, because the energy absorbed by the formation of the intramolecular bond reduces the overall instability of the protein molecule.
    B. destabilize proteins, because the energy absorbed by the formation of the intramolecular bond reduces the overall instability of the protein molecule.
    C. stabilize proteins, because the energy released by the formation of the intramolecular bond reduces the overall instability of the protein molecule.
    D. destabilize proteins, because the energy released by the formation of the intramolecular bond reduces the overall instability of the protein molecule.

55. One popular means of real-time observation of enzyme-catalyzed crosslink formations is to introduce the use of radio-tagged enzymes. Researchers who use this method use enzymes that contain radioactive isotopes of biologically-common elements into *in vitro* reaction media to enable their direct observation via certain spectroscopic methods. Which of the following physical properties could these spectroscopic methods take advantage of in order to differentiate between radioactive isotopes and other elements in the reaction?
    I.   Mass
    II.   Vibrational Mode
    III. Nuclear Instability

    A. I only
    B. I and III only
    C. II and III only
    D. I, II, and III

These questions are NOT related to a passage.

56. Uric acid is thought to be acidic due to the following isomerization. Which of the following best describes the relationship between these structures?

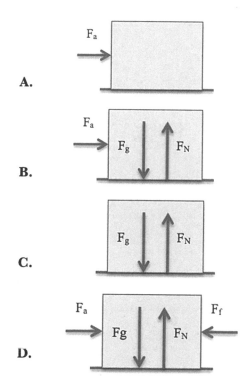

    A. These structures are tautomers.
    B. These structures are diastereomers.
    C. These structures are enantiomers.
    D. These structures are epimers.

57. Which of the following free-body-diagrams corresponds to a 1.0 N box sliding across a frictionless horizontal surface?

A. F_a

B. F_a F_g F_N

C. F_g F_N

D. F_a Fg F_N F_f

58. Second messengers are most distinguishable from so-called "first messengers" in the body by their ability to do which of the following?
    A. Engage in intracellular intermolecular bonding
    B. Engage in intercellular intermolecular bonding
    C. Engage in intracellular intramolecular bonding
    D. Engage in intercellular intramolecular bonding

59. A patient with disrupted kidney function has a limited ability to excrete HCO_3^-. How might the excess bicarbonate function according to the Brønsted-Lowry model?
    A. It will function as an acid because its negative charge can attract H^+ ions.
    B. It will function as an acid because it is an important component of a system which buffers against increased basicity.
    C. It will function as a base because it is an important component of a system which buffers against increased acidity.
    D. It will function as a base because it is capable of accepting an H^+ ion.

TIMED
SECTION 1
Answers and Explanations

Timed Section 1 Answer Key

Passage 1
1. A
2. D
3. B
4. A
5. A

Passage 2
6. B
7. C
8. B
9. B

Passage 3
10. D
11. C
12. C
13. A
14. C

Discrete Set 1
15. D
16. C
17. C
18. D

Passage 4
19. B
20. C
21. C
22. D
23. B

Passage 5
24. B
25. C
26. B
27. C
28. D

Discrete Set 2
29. C
30. D
31. B

Passage 6
32. A
33. D
34. A
35. C

Passage 7
36. B
37. A
38. D
39. B

Discrete Set 3
40. C
41. A
42. C
43. A

Passage 8
44. C
45. D
46. A
47. C

Passage 9
48. C
49. D
50. A
51. B

Passage 10
52. D
53. A
54. C
55. B

Discrete Set 4
56. A
57. C
58. A
59. D

Passage 1 Explanation

The structure of a **polypeptide** was determined beginning with the identification of its constituent **amino acids**. A purified sample of the polypeptide was denatured and then hydrolyzed by a strong acid at 110°C for 24 hours. The individual amino acids released by the treatment were then separated by **cation-exchange chromatography**. In this technique, amino acids bind to, with differing affinities, negatively charged groups attached to **resins** applied along the column.

Key terms: polypeptide, amino acids, cation-exchange chromatography, resins

Cause-and-Effect: primary structure of polypeptide determine begins with amino acid identification and quantitation; polypeptides are first denatured and hydrolyzed by strong acid; free amino acids are separated by cation-exchange chromatography

Following treatment with a series of **eluting solutions**, the separated amino acids contained in the eluate from the column were heated with **ninhydrin**—a reagent that forms the blue-purple compound **Ruhemann's Purple** with most amino acids, amines and ammonia.

Key terms: eluting solutions, ninhydrin, Ruhemann's Purple

Cause-and-Effect: column-bound amino acids are washed with elutant and the eluate then containing them was heated with ninhydrin; ninhydrin forms the blue-purple compound with Ruhemann's Purple

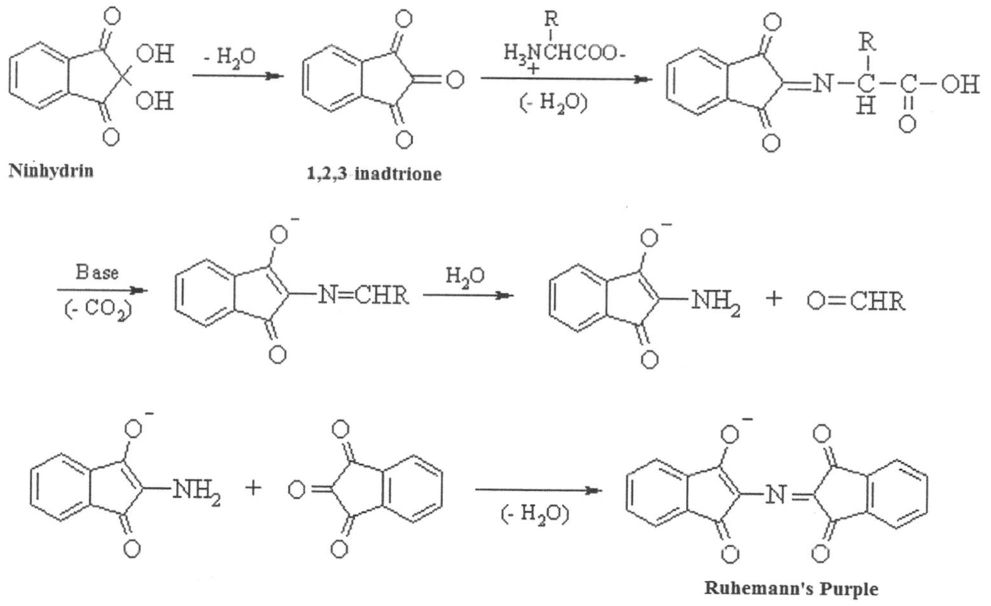

Figure 1. Ninhydrin dehydrates to form 1,2,3-indantrione which reacts with α-amino acid to form a Schiff base. After decarboxylation and hydration, a primary amine and aldehyde are formed. The primary amine condenses with a second molecule of 1,2,3-indantrione forming the chromophore, Ruhemann's Purple.

The amount of each amino acid present was then determined spectrophotometrically by measuring the amount of blue-purple light absorbed.

Key terms: spectrophotometrically

Cause-and-Effect: the amount of each amino acid present was determined spectrophotometrically.

The specific position of each amino acid in the polypeptide chain was also found. **Edman reagent (phenylisothiocyanate)** was used to label **a terminal residue** under mildly alkaline conditions, resulting in the formation of a **phenylthiocarbamoyl**. Under acidic conditions, the terminal amino acid of the polypeptide was cleaved, releasing free polypeptide and **phenylthiohydantoin (PTH)**, an amino acid derivative that can be identified. Edman reagent was applied repeatedly, shortening the peptide bond obtained following each cycle. The steps of the **Edman degradation** are shown in Figure 2.

Key terms: Edman reagent (phenylisothiocyanate), terminal residue, phenylthiocarbamoyl, phenylthiohydantoin (PTH), Edman degradation

Cause-and-Effect: the position of each amino acid in the polypeptide chain was found beginning with treatment with Edman reagent (phenylisothiocyanate); N-terminal residues were labeled to form a phenylthiocarbamoyl and was then cleaved to release free polypeptide and phenylthiohydantoin (PTH); the PTH-amino acid derivative was identified; Edman reagent was applied repeatedly, shortening the peptide obtained following each cycle

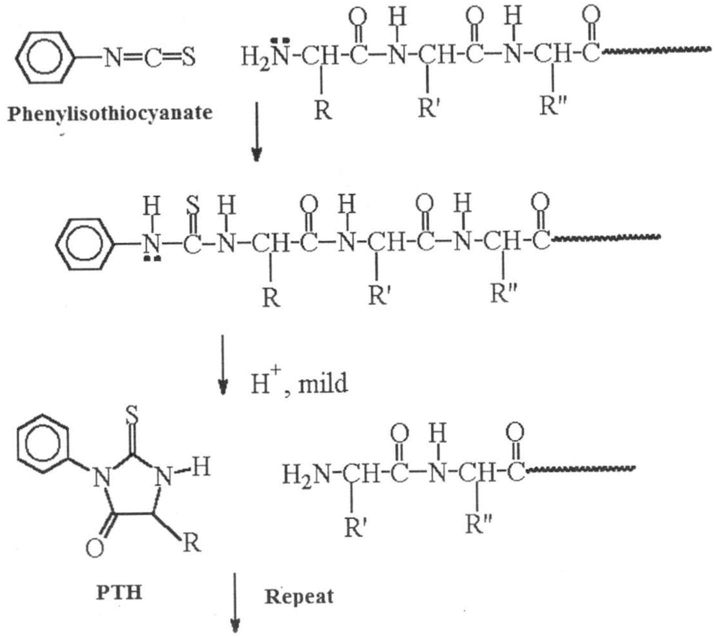

Figure 2. The steps of Edman degradation are shown. Phenylisothiocyanate is coupled to a polypeptide; the coupled phenylthiocarbamyol is cleaved producing PTH and the shortened polypeptide; the PTH-amino acid derivative is separated from the shortened polypeptide, and the shortened polypeptide is recycled for further coupling.

There are limits on the length of polypeptides that can be sequenced by this method. Over time, the yield of PTH-amino acid products decreases relative to the background level of PTH-amino acids. **Repetitive yield** is a measure of the percent of detectable material remaining after each turn of the cycle. Longer polypeptides can be sequenced from greater initial sample sizes and larger repetitive yields. They may also be cleaved by **peptidase enzymes** to create shorter polypeptides for sequencing.

Key terms: repetitive yield; peptidase enzymes

Cause-and-Effect: there are limits on the length of polypeptides that can be sequenced by this method; repetitive yield is a measure of the percent of detectable material remaining after each turn of the cycle; longer polypeptides can be sequenced from greater initial sample sizes and larger repetitive yields; longer polypeptides can also be cleaved by peptidase enzymes, creating shorter polypeptides, prior to sequencing.

1. The kinetics of the ninhydrin reaction were shown to be first order with respect to 1,2,3-indantrione and α-alpha amino acid, and second order overall. The reaction rate was shown to vary with solution pH. The initial reaction rate was greatest when the product of which two concentrations was maximized? (Note: $R=C_8H_4O_2$.)
    A. [RC=O⁺H], [H₂NCHRCOO⁻]
    B. [RC=O], [H₃⁺NCHRCOO⁻]
    C. [RC=O⁺H], [H₃⁺NCHRCOOH]
    D. [RC=O], [H₂NCHRCOOH]

Choice **A** is correct. The reaction between 1,2,3-indantrione and the α-alpha amino begins with attack by the nitrogen of the α-alpha amino acid's amino residue on a carbonyl carbon of 1,2,3-indantrione. The reaction requires an available lone pair on the amino nitrogen of the acid.

No lone pair is available in the protonated, quaternary amino nitrogen shown in choices B and C. The reaction rate will be maximized when the carbonyl oxygen of the carbonyl attacked in the reaction is activated to attack by protonation (choice A). Because of a more favorable resonance contributor in the protonated versus the unprotonated carbonyl, the electrophilicity of the carbonyl carbon, and the reaction rate, are increased when compared to the carbonyl carbon electrophilicity and reaction rate of the unprotonated carbonyl-oxygen (choice D).

2. Which of the following molecules is the product obtained at the end of the Edman degradation of the polypeptide H₂N-Ala-Gly-Arg-Met-COOH?
    A. PTH-Ala
    B. PTH-Gly
    C. PTH-Arg
    D. PTH-Met

Choice **D** is correct. According to the passage, the first residue labeled by reaction with phenylisothiocyanate is a terminal one. Figure 2 indicates that the N-terminal amino residue is specifically the first removed. The N-terminal residue of the polypeptide shown, alanine (Ala), will be isolated first (choice A). Choice B will be the second residue isolated. Choice C will be the third residue isolated. Choice D will be the final residue isolated.

A, B, C: The order of elution is described above.

3. What is most likely true of the eluant solutions used to recover free amino acids from the ion-exchange column employed?
    A. They are hydrophobic.
    B. They possess a characteristic salt concentration.
    C. They must be capable of denaturing disulfide linkages.
    D. They must contain digestive enzymes.

Choice **B** is correct. According to the passage, free amino acids bind negatively charged resins. Treatment with an eluant of increasing ionic strength and pH, such as those with differing salt concentrations, could disrupt the ionic bonding between polypeptide and column anions by influencing the charge state of the polypeptides, decreasing their likelihood of existing in the charged, cationic state.

A, C, D: As the concentration of protonated amino acid decreases, so too does the concentration of amino acids capable of interacting with negatively charged substrate (choice B). A hydrophobic wash would not directly lead to deprotonation of bound amino acids (choice A). Neither digestive enzymes, nor a denaturant would be relevant when considering free amino acids.

4.   Unfolding of the polypeptide in the presence of the denaturant preceded unimolecularly with rate constant, k. What are the units for this rate constant?
   A. s^{-1}
   B. $M \cdot s$
   C. $M^{-1} \cdot s^{-1}$
   D. $M \cdot s^{-1}$

Choice **A** is correct. If polypeptide unfolding precedes unimolecularly, the rate law for the reaction must be first order with respect to only the polypeptide and first order overall. The rate law for such a reaction is given by the expression R = k [polypeptide], where R represents the rate of the reaction, given in units of M/s. Rearranging the expression to solve for k, you find k = R/[polypeptide].

B, C, D: In terms of unit, $k = ([M]/[s])/[M] = 1/s$ (choice A). Choice B is incorrect because all rate constants include an inverse time term. Choice C gives the units of a second order rate constant. Choice D gives the units for a zeroth order rate constant, the units of an overall rate expression.

5.   Which of the following reaction types best describes the formation of the bond between phenylisothiocyanate and a polypeptide during the first reaction in Figure 2?
   A. **Addition**
   B. Dehydration
   C. Neutralization
   D. Elimination

Choice **A** is correct. The reaction of phenylisothiocyanate and the polypeptide is an addition reaction. In an addition reaction, the number of pi bonds declines, while the number of sigma bonds increases, as is the case in this reaction (choice A).

B, C, D: A dehydration reaction (choice B) involves the net loss of water. A neutralization reaction (choice C) occurs between an acid and base to form a salt and, in many cases, water. An elimination reaction (choice D), is the reverse of an addition reaction. During elimination, the number of pi bonds increases and the number of sigma bonds decreases.

Passage 2 Answers and Explanations

Carbon dioxide is a **molecular compound** with a linear structure and exists primarily in the gas phase under normal temperature and pressure conditions. The solid is often referred to as dry ice, **in which the molecular units form a trigonal unit-cell crystal structure, in which the O-C-O angle is essentially 180° and the C=O bond lengths of 1.16 Å are shorter than the C=O bond lengths observed in organic carbonyl compounds (1.23 Å)**, and only slightly longer than that observed in carbon monoxide (1.13 Å). As seen in the phase diagram shown in Figure 1, the liquid phase does not exist under **standard conditions** of temperature and pressure, and relatively high pressures are required to condense the gas to the liquid. Below the triple point pressure the gas will condense directly to the solid, or the solid will sublime directly to the gas. These properties are clearly the **result of the weak intermolecular** interactions, which stands in stark contrast to the properties of its silicon homolog, silica (SiO_2), which forms a network solid in which each silicon atom is bonded to four oxygen atoms. Supercritical carbon dioxide has received considerable interest as a solvent for the extraction of organic compounds from **complex matrices**, such as in the preparation of decaffeinated coffee as opposed to using chlorocarbon solvents such as chloroform ($CHCl_3$) or methylene chloride (CH_2Cl_2). The structure of caffeine is shown in Figure 2.

Key Terms: molecular compound, unit-cell, standard conditions, intermolecular, homolog and matrices

Cause and effect: The favorable π-overlap for the 2p atomic orbitals of carbon and oxygen favor multiple bonding and a linear molecular structure for carbon dioxide, resulting in the stability of the gas phase under normal conditions of temperature and pressure.

Contrast: Under condition of high pressure, carbon dioxide may begin to form a bent structure having a dipole moment that would account for its ability to act as a solvent for both nonpolar and slightly polar solutes under different conditions of pressure. Furthermore, under extreme pressures, carbon dioxide might form a network covalent type structure, similar to silica, rather than the linear molecular structure seen under normal conditions.

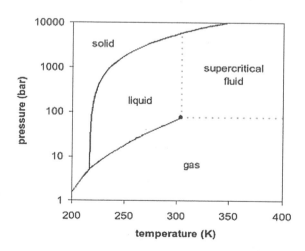

Figure 1 Phase diagram for carbon dioxide, (1.01 bar = 1 atm = 101 kPa)

Figure 1 The phase diagram for carbon dioxide in which the pressure is in bars and the temperature is on the Kelvin scale. The solid lines represent conditions of temperature and pressure in which there is a phase change. The dashed line indicates the approximate transition to the super-critical fluid state.

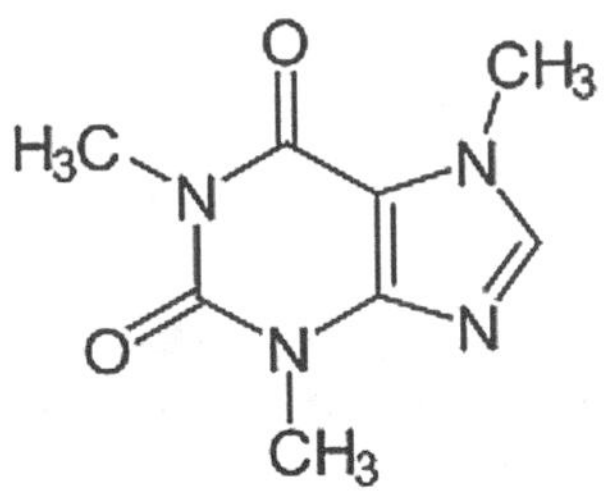

Figure 2 Structural formula of caffeine

Figure 2 The structure of caffeine, or 1,3,7-trimethylpurine-2,6-dione, is a purine based structure with resonance stabilization due to the ring π bonding system. Caffeine acts as a very weak base in aqueous solution due to the nitrogen of the imidazole ring.

There is considerable debate about the nature of the intermolecular interactions of carbon dioxide under conditions of extremely high pressure. Certain **molecular modeling** calculations suggest that oxygen lone-pairs on neighboring molecules begin to interact with the carbon atoms, causing the O-C-O angle to bend and the intramolecular C=O bonds to lengthen. The significance of this is related to proposals for the **sequestration** of carbon dioxide in deep geologic storage, in order to circumvent some of the **greenhouse gas** effects that are of concern when carbon dioxide from combustion of fossil fuels is released into the atmosphere.

Key Terms: molecular modeling, sequestration and greenhouse gas

Cause and effect: Carbon dioxide has an asymmetric O=C=O stretch that absorbs infrared radiation in a region of the spectrum that most other compounds do not absorb and when this energy is re-radiated into the atmosphere, it tends to help trap heat and leads to a warming of the atmosphere.

6. Which of the following is closest to the O-Si-O bond angle in silica?
   A. 90°
   B. 109°
   C. 120°
   D. 180°

Choice **B** is correct. As stated in the passage, the bonding of carbon dioxide "...stands in stark contrast to the properties of its silicon homolog, silica (SiO_2), which forms a network solid in which each silicon atom is bonded to four oxygen atoms." Silicon has four valence electrons and prefers to form single bonds, as opposed to carbon's preference for multiple bonds. The four oxygen atoms form a tetrahedral geometry around each of the silicon atoms, with an O-Si-O angle of 109°. Choice B is the correct answer.

7. In which phase is carbon dioxide at 101 kPa and 100°C?
   A. Solid
   B. Liquid
   C. Gas
   D. Super-critical fluid

Choice **C** is correct. Looking closely at Figure 1, the label for the y-axis indicates that the pressure is in units of bar and the x-axis label indicates that the temperature is in Kelvin (K = °C + 273). The caption for the figure indicates that "1.01 bar = 1 atm = 101 kPa". Therefore 101 kPa is 1.01 bar and the temperature of 100°C is 373 K. Finding this point on the phase diagram indicates that carbon dioxide will be in the gas phase. Choice C is the correct answer.

A, B, D: Without paying close attention to the unit of temperature, you might think that at 100 K the carbon dioxide would be solid. Alternatively, without converting the pressure unit, you might think that at 101 bar, carbon dioxide would be a supercritical fluid.

8. Which of the following compounds would most likely NOT be extracted to any significant extent by supercritical carbon dioxide?
   A. 1,3,7-Trimethylpurine-2,6-dione
   B. **Ammonium nitrate**
   C. Methyl salicylate
   D. Benzaldehyde

Choice **B** is correct. Looking closely at the structure in Figure 2, you should notice that 1,3,7-Trimethylpurine-2,6-dione is the IUPAC name for caffeine and the passage clearly indicates that caffeine can be extracted by supercritical carbon dioxide, "... in the preparation of decaffeinated coffee."

A, C, D: Choice A can be eliminated. Since carbon dioxide is a nonpolar molecule, it would be expected that relatively nonpolar organic compounds would be soluble in supercritical carbon dioxide. Methyl salicylate, is also known as aspirin, and is the methyl ester of salicylic acid. Aspirin is moderately soluble in nonpolar solvents, such as chloroform and methylene chloride, and therefore would be expected to be soluble in supercritical carbon dioxide as well. Choice C can be eliminated. Benzaldehyde is one of the flavorings in almond extract, and is also modestly soluble in chlorocarbon solvents and choice D can be eliminated. Ammonium nitrate (NH_4NO_3) is a water-soluble ionic compound, which is a key component in many fertilizers. Ammonium nitrate would not be expected to be soluble in nonpolar solvents or supercritical carbon dioxide. Thus, choice B is the correct..

9. Which of the following would represent the major solute/solvent intermolecular force in a methylene chloride solution of caffeine?
   A. London dispersion forces
   B. **Dipole-dipole interactions**
   C. Hydrogen bonding
   D. Ion-dipole interactions

Choice **B** is correct. Drawing the Lewis dot structures and determining the molecular shape of CH_2Cl_2, you can conclude that the molecule has a minimal molecular dipole, but is not capable of hydrogen bonding. Likewise from Figure 2, caffeine is also a polar molecule. Hence, the major type of intermolecular interaction between the solute, caffeine, and the solvent, methylene chloride, would be dipole-dipole interactions. Choice B is the correct answer.

A, C, D: These forces are either too small to be relevant or are non-existent.

Passage 3 Explanation

Kidney stones are insoluble **aggregate** crystals that can form in the urine of certain people. One of the compounds that can contribute to the formation of kidney stones is calcium oxalate (CaC_2O_4, FW = 128.097 g/mol, Ksp = 2.3×10^{-9}). Oxalic acid is a naturally occurring **diprotic acid**, ($H_2C_2O_4$, pK_{a1} = 1.3 and pK_{a2} = 4.3) present in a number of foods, including rhubarb and spinach. Oxalic acid can be produced from **oxaloacetate**, which plays an important role in the **citric acid cycle**. Uric acid can also contribute to the formation of kidney stones and can also crystalize in the **synovial fluid** of joints, producing inflammation and the painful symptoms associated with **gout**. In humans, uric acid is the final oxidation product of **purine** metabolism and like oxalic acid is also a diprotic acid ($H_2C_5H_2N_4O_3$, pK_{a1} = 5.4 and pK_{a2} = 10.3), but unlike oxalic acid, it is not **completely ionized at pHs** typical for urine.

Key terms: Aggregate, diprotic acid, oxaloacetate, citric acid cycle, synovial fluid, gout, and purine.

Cause-and-Effect: Since calcium oxalate and uric acid are relatively insoluble in aqueous solution they tend to form precipitates whose solubility is significantly affected by the pH of the solution.

Contrast: Both oxalic acid and uric acid are diprotic acids, but uric acid is a much weaker acid and tends not to be completely ionized under normal physiological pH conditions.

If the urine becomes **supersaturated**, seed crystals can result in the formation of a large mass, or stone, in one of several possible locations, including the bladder, the ureters and the kidneys. In many cases, small stones (< 3 mm) are readily passed. However, in some cases, large stones can cause obstruction and **renal colic**, or worse. In some cases **ultrasound** can be used to break up stones and facilitate their passing, however in extreme cases, surgery may be required.

Key terms: Supersaturated, bladder, ureters, kidneys, renal colic, and ultrasound.

Cause-and-Effect: In a supersaturated solution, the solution contains more solute than normally would exist at equilibrium, but the solute is unable to form a precipitate due to a large kinetic energy barrier. Often the introduction of a seed, or surface having a similar shape to that of the crystal lattice of the precipitate will cause the rapid formation of a crystal (or stone) centered around one particular site.

Urine contains a number of natural **chelating agents**, one of which is citrate. These chelating agents are **polydentate ligands** (Lewis bases) that coordinate to a metal ion and form soluble coordination compounds that help prevent the **nucleation and precipitation** of calcium oxalate. Citric acid is a weak triprotic acid (pK_{a1} = 3.1, pK_{a2} = 4.8 and pK_{a3} = 6.4), whose structure is shown in Figure 1. The equilibrium constant at 37°C for the formation of the calcium citrate complex ion (Reaction 1) is 1.9×10^3. The calcium citrate complex has a residual negative charge that enhances its solubility in aqueous solution.

Key terms: Chelating agents, polydentate ligands, nucleation, and precipitation

Cause-and-Effect: A chelating polydentate ligand can act as a Lewis base to a metal ion and help prevent the precipitation of calcium oxalate by removing free calcium ions from the solution.

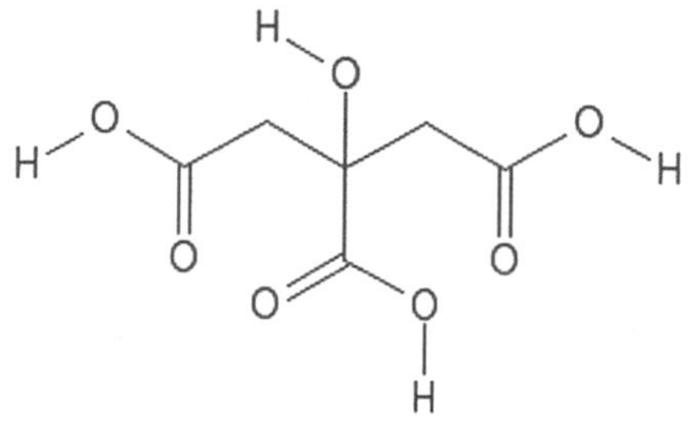

Figure 1 The structure of citric acid, $H_3C_6H_5O_7$.

Figure 1 The structure of citric acid contains three carboxylic acid groups, which are relatively easily ionized and a single hydroxyl group, which does not significantly ionize, but does form hydrogen bonds with water molecules and enhances the solubility of this compound in aqueous solutions.

Reaction 1 Ca^{2+} (aq) + $C_6H_5O_7^{3-}$ (aq) → $CaC_6H_5O_7^{-}$ (aq)

Reaction 1 This reaction gives the net ionic equation for the reaction between aqueous calcium ion and citrate ion, to form the negatively charge calcium citrate anion, which makes the amount of free calcium ion present in solution lower and reduces the possibility of the precipitation of calcium oxalate.

10. Which of the following formulas best represents the predominant form that exists in solution when citric acid is dissolved in normal urine whose pH is approximately 7?
    A. $H_3C_6H_5O_7$
    B. $H_2C_6H_5O_7^{-}$
    C. $HC_6H_5O_7^{2-}$
    D. <u>$C_6H_5O_7^{3-}$</u>

Choice **D** is correct. Given in the passage, the pK_as for citric acid are pK_{a1} = 3.1, pK_{a2} = 4.8 and pK_{a3} = 6.4, at a pH of 7, the first two carboxylate groups will be almost completely deprotonated. Since the pH of the solution is above the pKa of the third carboxylic acid pKa, more than half of the citrate ions present in the solution will be $C_6H_5O_7^{3-}$, with a smaller portion being in the $HC_6H_5O_7^{2-}$ form. Therefore, D represents the predominant form of citrate in solution at a pH of 7.

A, B, C: At this high a pH, given the pK_a, all three protons should be removed from most of the citric acid molecules.

11. In the passage, the equilibrium constant for the formation of the calcium citrate complex is quoted as being at 37°C. Which of the following temperatures on the Fahrenheit scale corresponds to this temperature?
    A. 32° F
    B. 75° F
    C. <u>**99° F**</u>
    D. 212° F

Choice **C** is correct. The temperature of 37 °C, corresponds to body temperature or 98.6 °F, which is choice C. Room temperature is 25 °C or approximately 75 °F (Choice and the freezing point of water is 0 °C or 32 °F (Choice A). The boiling point of water is 100 °C or 212 °F (Choice D).

A, B, D: These are a result of miscalculation or confusing the temperature scales.

12. Based on information in the passage, what is the equilibrium constant for the following reaction?

$$CaC_2O_4 \text{ (s)} + C_6H_5O_7^{3-} \text{ (aq)} \leftrightarrows CaC_6H_5O_7^{-} \text{ (aq)} + C_2O_4^{2-} \text{ (aq)}$$

    A. 4.3×10^8
    B. 1.9×10^3
    C. <u>**4.4×10^{-6}**</u>
    D. 2.3×10^{-9}

Choice **C** is correct. The reaction given in the question is the sum of solubility reaction for calcium oxalate and the formation reaction for calcium citrate (Reaction 1 in the passage). The corresponding equilibrium constants for these reactions are given in the passage.

$$CaC_2O_4 \text{ (s)} \leftrightarrows Ca_2+ \text{ (aq)} + C_2O_4^{2-} \text{ (aq)} \qquad\qquad K_{sp} = 2.3 \times 10^{-9}$$
$$Ca^{2+} \text{ (aq)} + C_6H_5O_7^{3-} \text{ (aq)} \leftrightarrows CaC_6H_5O_7^{-} \text{ (aq)} \qquad\qquad K_f = 1.9 \times 10^3$$
$$CaC_2O_4 \text{ (s)} + C_6H_5O_7^{3-} \text{ (aq)} + \cancel{Ca^{2+} \text{ (aq)}} \leftrightarrows CaC_6H_5O_7^{-} \text{ (aq)} + \cancel{Ca^{2+} \text{ (aq)}} + C_2O_4^{2-} \text{ (aq)} \quad K_{eq} = K_{sp} \times K_f$$

Canceling the calcium ion that appears on both sides of the reaction gives the reaction required in the question. Therefore, multiplying the two equilibrium constants, K_{sp} and K_f will give the equilibrium constant for the desired reaction.

$$K_{sp} \times K_f = (2.3 \times 10^{-9}) \times (1.9 \times 10^3) \sim 2 \times 10^{-9} \times 2 \times 10^3 = 4 \times 10^{-6}$$

A, B, D: These are a result of miscalculation.

13. If equal molar solutions of oxalic acid, uric acid, citric acid and urea are prepared, which solution will have the lowest pH?
    A. <u>**Oxalic acid, because the first acid dissociation constant is the largest of the three acids.**</u>
    B. Uric acid, because its pK_{a2} value is the largest of the three acids.
    C. Citric acid, because it is a triprotic acid.
    D. Urea because it is a basic compound.

Choice **A** is correct. Urea is a carbamide, which reduces the basicity of the nitrogen lone pairs and slightly increases the acidity of the hydrogen attached to the nitrogen atoms, but as it turns out this makes urea a relative neutral molecule as far as acid/base properties are concerned. However, it can undergo hydrolysis to break the carbon-nitrogen bond and produce ammonia, which has a distinct odor and produces a solution with a pH greater than 7.

Oxalic acid, uric acid and citric acid are all weak acids, the acidity of which can be measured by the first ionization constant or pK_{a1}. Of the choices and information presented in the passage, oxalic acid is the most acidic since it has the smallest pK_{a1} (thus the largest K_a) and would produce the lowest pH. Therefore choice A is the correct answer.

14. Which of the following could produce uric acid as a result of metabolism?
    I. Adenine
    II. Guanine
    III. Glucose

    A. I only
    B. II only
    C. <u>**I and II only**</u>
    D. I, II and III

Choice **C** is correct. Adenine and guanine are purines. A purine is a heterocyclic aromatic organic nitrogen-containing compound, consisting of a pyrimidine ring fused to an imidazole ring. III, Glucose is a carbohydrate and therefore does not contain nitrogen and can't be metabolized to uric acid. Choice C is the correct answer.

These questions are NOT related to a passage.

15. The chemical formula of calcium phosphate is:
    - **A.** $CaPO_4$
    - **B.** Ca_3PO_4
    - **C.** $Ca_2(PO_4)_3$
    - **D.** <u>$Ca_3(PO_4)_2$</u>

Choice **D** is correct. Calcium is in Group 2 of the periodic table and the only stable ion is 2^+. The phosphate ions charge is 3^-.

In order to achieve charge balance in the formula, there needs to be three calcium ions:

$3 \times 2^+ = 6^+$, and two phosphate ions, $2 \times 3^- = 6^-$. Choice D is the correct answer.

A, B, C: These are a result of miscalculation or mis-labeling the charge on phosphate or calcium.

16. Acetic acid, $HC_2H_3O_2$, has a pK_a of 4.8. What is the pH of a 0.10 M solution of sodium acetate?
    - **A.** 2.9
    - **B.** 7.0
    - **C.** <u>**8.9**</u>
    - **D.** 13.0

Choice **C** is correct. There are two ways to the correct answer. When sodium acetate dissolves in solution, it produces sodium ions and acetate ions. The former does not affect the pH of the solution because it is the conjugate of the strong base, NaOH. However, acetate is the conjugate of acetic acid, and therefore is a weak base. As a result, the pH of a sodium acetate solution should be >7. A pH of 13, would be the pH of a 0.1 M solution of a strong base, not a weak base. Therefore, choice C is the correct answer.

It is also possible to calculate the pH of the solution, but this is not recommended, since it will consume more time than it is worth. However, if you have to do it, the pK_b for acetate is $14 - pKa = 14\text{-}4.8 = 9.2 \sim 9$.

The hydrolysis of acetate is

$$C_2H_3O_2^- \text{ (aq)} + H_2O \text{ (l)} \leftrightarrows HC_2H_3O_2 \text{ (aq)} + OH^- \text{ (aq)}$$

The equilibrium expression is

$$K_b = [HC_2H_3O_2][OH^-]/[C_2H_3O_2^-]$$
$$10^{-9} = x^2/(0.1 - x)$$

Since x will be small compared with 0.1, you can approximate this quadratic equation and simplify

$$10^{-9} = x^2/0.1$$
$$10^{-10} = x^2$$
$$10^{-5} = x = [OH^-]$$

Calculating the pOH and pH gives

$$pOH = -\log(10^{-5}) = 5$$

$$pH = 14 - pOH = 14 - 5 = 9$$

All that, just to get the same result.

17. Which of the following compounds has the highest boiling point?
    A. CH_4
    B. NH_3
    C. $\underline{\textbf{H}_2\textbf{O}}$
    D. HF

Choice **C** is correct. Of the compounds listed, NH_3, H_2O and HF all have hydrogen bonding and the normal boiling points of these compounds are -33°C, 100°C, and 20°C, respectively. Water has an optimal ratio of covalently bonded hydrogen atoms to lone pairs (1:1) and therefore maximizes the degree of intermolecular forces between liquid water molecules.

A, B, D: These ratios for NH_3 and HF are 3:1 and 1:3 respectively, which means that on average, each molecule never forms more than one hydrogen bond per molecule. The normal boiling point for CH_4 is -164 °C (Choice A) and is due to very weak temporary dipoles created by the random movement of electrons, known as London dispersion forces.

18. The polypeptide NH_2-Trp-Glu-Gly-Arg-Tyr-Pro-Lys-Pro-Trp-COO^- was treated with the active form of three peptidases: trypsin, which cleaves peptide bonds after non-terminal Arg and Lys residues unless followed by Pro, endopeptidase V8, which cuts after non-terminal Glu residues, and carboxypeptidase A, which cleaves the peptide linkage immediately prior to C-terminal aromatic or aliphatic amino acid residues. What is the most likely combination of fragments obtained by this treatment?

    A. Gly-Arg, Tyr-Pro-Lys, Trp-Glu, and Pro-Trp
    B. Trp-Glu-Gly-Arg, Tyr-Pro-Lys, Pro, and Trp
    C. Trp-Glu, Gly-Arg, and Tyr-Pro-Lys-Pro-Trp
    D. **Tyr-Pro-Lys, Pro, Gly-Arg, Trp-Glu, and Trp**

Choice **D** is correct. Beginning with polypeptide NH_2-Trp-Glu-Gly-Arg-Tyr-Pro-Lys-Pro-Trp-COO^- and considering the action of the three peptidases individually.

Trypsin will cleave a non-terminal Arg-Tyr bond, but will not cleave Lys-Pro, giving two fragments: Trp-Glu-Gly-Arg and Tyr-Pro-Lys-Pro-Trp.

Endopeptidase V8 will cut the non-terminal Glu-Gly bond to give three fragments: Trp-Glu, Gly-Arg and Tyr-Pro-Lys-Pro-Trp.

Finally, carboxypeptidase will cleave a terminal peptide linkage if an aromatic or aliphatic amino acid is present. Cleavage of the Pro-Trp bond in Tyr-Pro-Lys-Pro-Trp will result in the formation of Tyr-Pro-Lys-Pro and Trp. Carboxypeptidase will further digest this fragment, producing Tyr-Pro-Lys and Pro. In summary, the fragments Tyr-Pro-Lys, Trp-Glu, Gly-Arg, Pro and Trp, choice D. Choice A shows an incorrect Pro-Trp fragment. Choice B shows an incorrect Trp-Glu-Gly-Arg fragment. Both fragments in choice C are incorrect.

A, B, C: see the cleavage steps above.

Passage 4 Answers and Explanations

Students in a biophysics class used the experimental setup shown in Figure 1 to simulate a human arm. The apparatus consisted of a horizontal **beam** having a length (L) of **0.50 m and a mass (M_b)of 2.0 kg**, was attached to a frictionless **hinge**, which was also attached to a vertically oriented beam having a frictionless wheel at the top. An essentially massless string was initially attached in **the middle of the horizontal beam** at a distance (from the center of the **pivot point** of the hinge. The string was draped over the wheel and then attached to a standard brass mass (M_1). **The angle** formed between the string and the horizontal beam was **60°**. A second standard **1.0 kg brass mass (M_2) was then attached at the end** of the horizontal beam. The weight of the mass hanging from the string (M_1) was adjusted until the two beams once again formed a right angle.

Key terms: Beam, hinge, pivot point and right angle

Cause-and-Effect: The human arm functions much like two beams connected by a hinge, in which application of the concepts of torque provides a satisfactory model.

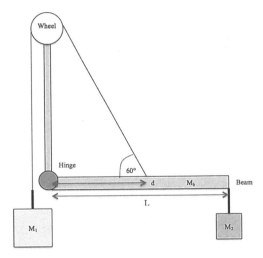

Figure 1 A schematic diagram of the experimental setup used to simulate a human arm. Note that sin 30° = cos 60° = 0.5, sin 60° = cos 30° = 0.866, tan 30° = 0.577, tan 60° = 1.732. The drawing is not intended to be to scale.

Figure 1 A diagram showing two beams connected by a hinge, in which a weight connected to a string provides tension, the vertical component of which creates an equilibrium situation between the clockwise and counter clockwise torques around the pivot point of the hinge. Whenever you see right triangles and trigonometric relationships given, you should begin to anticipate using them to calculate components of a vector.

19. When the system in the passage is at equilibrium, what is the length of the string between where it is attached to the horizontal beam and the point where it comes in contact with the wheel?
    A. 0.35 m
    B. **0.50 m**
    C. 0.70 m
    D. 1.0 m

Choice **B** is correct. The system shown in Figure 1 forms a right triangle in which the string is the hypotenuse and the horizontal beam is the side adjacent to the 60° angle. Since this is a special right triangle (30°, 60° and 90°), the length of the side of the triangle adjacent to the 60° angle is x and the length of the hypotenuse is 2x, where x = 0.25 m. Choice B is the answer.

A, C, D: Choice A can be eliminated. Choice C and D are double choice A and B, and could result from using the total length of the horizontal beam, which is 0.5 m.

20. What is the mass of the brass weight hanging from the end of the string when the system is at equilibrium?
    A. 2.3 kg
    B. 3.0 kg
    C. **4.6 kg**
    D. 6.0 kg

Choice **C** is correct. The sum of the torques acting on the horizontal beam must be zero to have the system be at equilibrium. Torque (τ) is a twisting force (F) applied at some distance (from a center of rotation, the so-called pivot point. In this case the pivot point is the hinge. The equation for torque is $\tau = rF\sin\theta$.

To a first order approximation, you must determine the clockwise (downward) torque acting on the horizontal beam.

The center of mass of the beam is located at the center of the beam, d = 0.25 m, from the pivot point. The force of gravity acting on the beam is 2.0 kg x (-9.8 m/s²) ~ -20 N, which is a torque of -5 N m. The other torque acting in the clockwise direction is the mass hung at the end of the horizontal beam, which creates a torque of 1.0 kg x (-9.8 m/s²) x 0.5 m which is a torque of -5 N m.

The total clockwise torque is -10 N m. Therefore, the counterclockwise torque (up) must be 10 = T(0.25) = +40 N m, which is provided by the vertical component of the tension in the string. The tension in the string is T = 40/sin 60° = 40/0.866 = 46 N. The mass of M_1 = 46/9.8 = 4.6 kg. Choice C is the answer.

A, B, D: These are a result of faulty calculations or the use of cosine instead of sine.

21. What is the horizontal force that the beam exerts on the hinge?
    A. 9.8 N
    B. 17 N
    C. **23 N**
    D. 34 N

Choice **C** is correct. The force the beam exerts on the hinge is simply the x component of the tension in the rope (since the other forces on the beam are gravity due to the mass of the beam and gravity due to M_2 and are both vertical). As shown in Question 20, the tension in the string is 46 N and the horizontal component of the tension is F_x = 46 N x cos 60° = 46 x 0.5 = 23 N.

A, B, D: These are a result of trigonometric error or miscalculation.

22. What is the tension in the string when the system is at equilibrium as described in the passage?
    A. 3 N
    B. 23 N
    C. 29 N
    D. 45 N

Choice **D** is correct. First, you must determine the clockwise (downward) torque acting on the horizontal beam. The center of mass of the beam is located at the center of the beam, d = 0.25 m, from the pivot point.

The force of gravity acting on the beam is 2.0 kg x (-9.8 m/s²) ~ -20 N, which is a torque of -5 N m.

The other torque acting in the clockwise direction is the mass hung at the end of the horizontal beam, which creates a torque of 1.0 kg x (-9.8 m/s²) x 0.5 m which is a torque of -5 N m.

The total clockwise torque is -10 N m. Therefore, the counterclockwise torque (up) must be 10 = T(0.25) = +40 N m, which is provided by the vertical component of the tension in the string. The tension in the string is cos 30 = 40/T, or T = 40/0.866 = 45 N. Choice D is the answer.

A, B, C: These are a result of trigonometric error or miscalculation.

23. Which of the following anatomical parts of the human body is NOT simulated in the experimental setup described in the passage?
    A. Ligaments
    B. Triceps
    C. Humerus
    D. Radius

Choice **B** is correct. The biceps are the muscles on the front side of the humerus that apply a force that reduces the angle between the lower and upper portion of the arm. The biceps are attached by tendons to the humerus near the shoulder and attached to the radius, in the forearm close to the elbow. The tension in the string is what exerts the force on the beams and simulates the biceps, not the triceps. The triceps are the muscles on the back of the humerus, opposing the biceps, providing a force (when the biceps relax) that extends the arm, and increasing the angle of the arm. Choice B is the answer.

A, C, D: The ligaments connecting the humerus and radius at the elbow are simulated in the experimental setup by the hinge, and choice A can be eliminated. The vertical and horizontal beams simulate the humerus and radius (and ulna as well). Choices C and D can be eliminated.

Passage 5 Answers and Explanations

Natural gas production in the United States has recently increased dramatically. This has been the result of the development of hydraulic fracturing techniques that release trapped natural gas from rock layers that were previously inaccessible using other techniques. This process involves drilling and subsequent pumping of proprietary aqueous based fluids into a sedimentary rock layer, often a shale deposit, under high pressure. **The natural gas that is produced is mostly methane**, but also contains small amounts of other hydrocarbons, such as ethane and propane. The use of natural gas as an energy source has considerable advantages over other fossil fuels, in that it **produces much more energy and less carbon dioxide per carbon atom than fuels such as petroleum or coal**. In addition, natural gas does not contain significant amount of **impurities, like the sulfur in coal that can contribute to air pollution and acid rain**. One of the downsides of this increased production of natural gas is the inadvertent release of methane into the atmosphere. **Like carbon dioxide, methane is a potent greenhouse gas** and methane concentrations in the atmosphere have been steadily increasing over time. **Methane can also be produced biologically under anaerobic conditions by bacteria**. In fact, industrial production of animal protein from poultry flocks, as well as swine and cattle herds is thought to be a major contributor to changes in the methane concentrations in the earth's atmosphere. Table 1 compares the heats of reaction for methane to several other potential organic fuels that are major contributors to the worlds energy supply.

Key terms: methane, hydrocarbons, ethane, propane, carbon dioxide, petroleum, coal, acid rain, greenhouse gas, anaerobic, and heats of reaction.

Contrast: Methane and carbon dioxide both act as greenhouse gases, because they absorb infrared energy radiated from the surface of the earth after absorbing sunlight. The IR radiation that methane absorbs is not in the same energy region as carbon dioxide, and therefore the two gases together are even more problematic than an increase in the concentration of just one of these gases in the earth's atmosphere.

Contrast: Methane produces more energy per carbon atom than other fuels because of its relatively high carbon to hydrogen ratio.

Cause-and-Effect: Increased natural gas production and use may slow the increase in carbon dioxide in the earth's atmosphere as compared with the production of the same amount of energy from fuels like coal.

Table 1 Heats of reaction at 25°C and 1 atm pressure for the complete combustion of various carbon based fuels.

Formula	Heat (kJ/mol)	Density at 25°C (kg/m^3)
CH_4 (g)	-890	0.71
C_3H_8 (l)	-2220	493
C_8H_{18} (l)	-5470	703
C_2H_5OH (l)	-1370	789
$C_6H_{12}O_6$ (s)	-2800	1540
C (s) amorphous	-390	~2000

Table 1 This table provides the heats of reaction for the complete combustion of a number of organic compounds that are used as fuels. Coal is primarily elemental carbon, so the heat of reaction of amorphous carbon approximates the value for coal. Note that the heats of reaction are all negative or exothermic. Also note that the amount of heat produced generally increases as the number of carbons in the formula increases. The density of the various fuels is also provided. Methane has an apparently low density compared with the other fuels, because it is a gas, whereas the compounds that are liquids and solids have significantly higher densities. Methane is sometimes transported in liquefied form, by placing it under high pressure.

24. Propane can be purchased liquefied, in 20 kg tanks and is used for cooking. A person wants to take a pot containing 4.0 kg of water at 25°C and raise its temperature to the boiling point of the water, which has a specific heat of 4.18 J/g°C. Which of the following is closest to the amount of propane that would be required to heat the water?
    A. 10 g
    B. 25 g
    C. 60 g
    D. 80 g

Choice **B** is correct. The balanced combustion reaction for propane, including the heat as a product, is

$$C_3H_8 \text{ (l)} + O_2 \text{ (g)} \rightarrow CO_2 \text{ (g)} + H_2O \text{ (g)} + 2220 \text{ kJ}$$

The molecular weight of propane is $3(12) + 8(1) = 44$ g/mol. The units for the specific heat can be used to calculate the heat required to raise the temperature of water 75°C, from 25°C to the boiling point of water, 100°C.

$$4.0 \text{ kg} \times (10^3 \text{ g/kg}) \times 75°C \times 4.18 \text{ J/g°C} \times (1 \text{ kJ}/10^3 \text{ J}) \times (1 \text{ mol } C_3H_8/2220 \text{ kJ}) \times (44 \text{ g/mol}) = 24.9 \text{ g } C_3H_8$$

Choice B is the answer.

25. Which of the fuels given below produces the LEAST energy per carbon dioxide molecule produced when used as a fuel to produce electricity?
    A. CH_4 (g)
    B. C_2H_5OH (l)
    C. $C_6H_{12}O_6$ (s)
    D. C_8H_{18} (l)

Choice **C** is correct. The number of carbon dioxide molecules produced by a fuel is directly related to the number of carbon atoms in the formula. If you take the heats of reaction given in Table 1 for each of the answer choices and divide by the number of carbons in the formula you get:

CH_4: 890/1 ~ 900 kJ per carbon
C_2H_5OH: 1370/2 ~ 700 kJ per carbon
$C_6H_{12}O_6$: 2800/6 ~ 450 kJ per carbon
C_8H_{18}: 5470/8 ~ 700 kJ per carbon

Therefore glucose, choice C, is the correct answer. Note that both methane and octane do not have oxygen in the formula, which reduces the heat of combustion significantly. The ratio of carbon to hydrogen in the formula is also an important contributor to the amount of energy per carbon dioxide formed. The ratio of carbon to hydrogen in methane is 1:4, whereas this ratio is about 1:2 in octane.
A, B, D: These would have a higher ratio than glucose.

26. Coal is a complicated mixture of substances. One of the downsides of using coal as a fuel is the production of gases that can contribute to acid rain. Which of the following elements found in coal would NOT produce an oxide that contributes to acid rain?
    A. Sulfur
    B. **Calcium**
    C. Phosphorus
    D. Nitrogen

Choice **B** is correct. Since coal is the remnants of decayed plants, all of the elements in the answer choices are found in coal. However, only the nonmetal elements will produce acidic oxides. When calcium is burned, it produces calcium oxide, CaO, which is commonly known as lime. Reacting lime with water produces calcium hydroxide, which is a strong base. Choice B is the correct answer.

A, C, D: For example, when elemental sulfur is burned, it produces SO_2 and SO_3, that react with water to produce sulfurous acid and sulfuric acid, respectively, and therefore choice A can be eliminated. When phosphorus is burned it can produce diphosphorus pentoxide, which reacts with water to produce phosphoric acid, eliminating choice C. When elemental nitrogen and its compounds are burned, the most common product is nitrogen dioxide, which reacts with water to form nitric acid, eliminating choice D.

27. Which of the following regions of the infrared spectrum would be most useful in detecting methane in the atmosphere?
    A. 1600 - 1900 cm^{-1}
    B. 1900 - 2100 cm^{-1}
    C. **2700 - 3000 cm^{-1}**
    D. 3000 - 3800 cm^{-1}

Choice **C** is correct. Methane has a formula of CH_4 and it adopts a tetrahcdral structure with four C-H bonds, which should have asymmetric stretching modes between 2700 and 3000 cm^{-1}, which is choice C.

A, B, D: Choice A represent the typical carbonyl region of the IR spectrum and methane does not have a C=O, so this choice can be eliminated. Choice B is the region where you might expect triple bonds such as in nitriles or carbon monoxide and can be eliminated. Choice D is where you might expect O-H or N-H stretches, often appearing as broad features due to hydrogen bonding in the liquid or solid state.

28. There is considerable interest in the use of biofuels as renewable sources of energy that would be essentially carbon neutral, because the carbon used to make the fuel, ultimately comes from the carbon dioxide in the air. Which of the following are potentially biofuels?
    I. Methane
    II. Ethanol
    III. Cellulose

    A. I only
    B. I and II only
    C. II and III only
    D. **I, II and III**

Choice **D** is correct. As stated in the passage, methane (I) can be produced by bacteria under anaerobic conditions and therefore could be used as a biofuel, since the methane is the result of the decay of plant material that recently removed carbon from the atmosphere. Some dairy farms actually use their manure to generate methane, which is used as an energy source for running machinery.

A, B, C: Choice C can be eliminated. Ethanol (II) is considered a biofuel, because it can be made by fermentation of corn. Choice A can be eliminated. Cellulose (III) is a polymer of glucose and is a major component of wood and other plants, which are considered biofuels. Cellulose can also be decomposed under acidic conditions to make glucose that can then be fermented into ethanol. The bacteria in the guts of ruminant animals (e.g. cows) can convert cellulose into forms that can be digested. Choice D is the correct answer.

These questions are NOT related to a passage.

29. The azimuthal quantum number corresponds to which of the following?
    A. The potential energy of the electron
    B. Approximate radial size of an electron cloud
    C. **Approximate geometric shape of the orbital**
    D. Number of valence electrons orbiting a nucleus

Choice **C** is correct. The azimuthal quantum number is a quantum number for an atomic orbital that determines its orbital angular momentum and describes the shape of the orbital.

A: This value is quantified by the principal quantum number, n.
B: This value is quantified by the principal quantum number, n.
D: This value is not quantified by any quantum number. The number of valence electrons orbiting a nucleus can only be obtained by examining the complete spectroscopic notation of the electron or the location of the atom on the periodic table.

30. Presbyopia is diagnosed when the lens of the eye focuses incoming light rays to a position between the retina and the choroid. Which type of lens should be placed in front of the eye to focus light on the retina and correct this condition?
    A. Flat
    B. Spherical
    C. Diverging
    D. **Converging**

Choice **D** is correct. The problem with presbyopia (farsightedness) is that the image is formed behind the retina rather than on the retina. A converging lens will converge light rays before they can pass the retina and focus light closer to the retina.

A: A flat lens will not cause the light rays to converge any sooner and will not correct presbyopia.
B: A spherical lens can be diverging or converging and may not cause the light rays to converge any sooner and will not correct presbyopia.
C: A diverging lens would spread out the light before it reaches the retina and will further exacerbate the problem. It will not correct presbyopia.

31. Which of the following compounds or ions has the same carbon-oxygen bond order, but a longer bond length, than carbon dioxide?
    I. Carbon monoxide
    II. Formaldehyde
    III. Carbonate

    A. I only
    B. **II only**
    C. II and III only
    D. I, II and III

Choice **B** is correct. You should draw the Lewis dot structures of the answer choices. The Lewis structure of formaldehyde, H_2CO, has a carbon-oxygen double bond and so does CO_2.

A, C, D: The best Lewis structure for carbon monoxide has a carbon-oxygen triple bond and choices A and D can be eliminated. Carbonate has a Lewis structure in which two of the oxygen atoms have carbon-oxygen single bonds and one has a carbon-oxygen double bond. This requires that there be a total of three resonance structures, with the resulting average carbon-oxygen bond order being 1.33, eliminating choices C and D.

Passage 6 Explanation

Cyclic adenosine monophosphate, also known as **cAMP**, or (4aR,6R,7R,7aS)-6-(6-aminopurin-9-yl)-2-hydroxy-2-oxo-4a,6,7,7a-tetrahydro-4H-furo[3,2-d][1,3,2]dioxaphosphinin-7-ol in the IUPAC nomenclature, is a well-characterized **second messenger derived from ATP** and commonly found in the human body.

Cause and effect: Here, the passage introduces the concept of a "second messenger". You should begin recalling, from our MCAT preparation, that second-messengers are compounds that allow a received signal from the cell membrane to be communicated elsewhere within the cell.

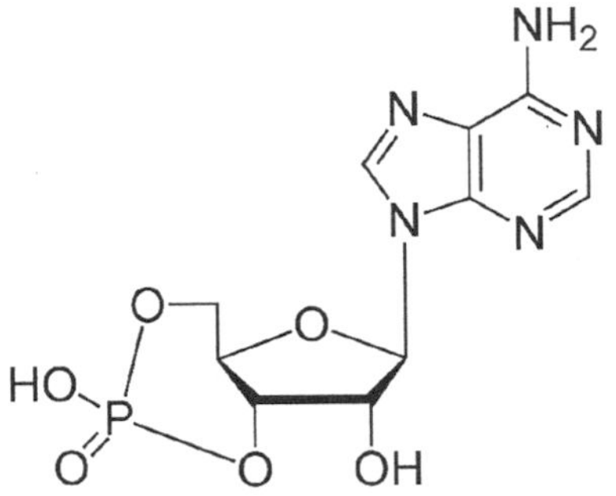

Figure 1 cAMP

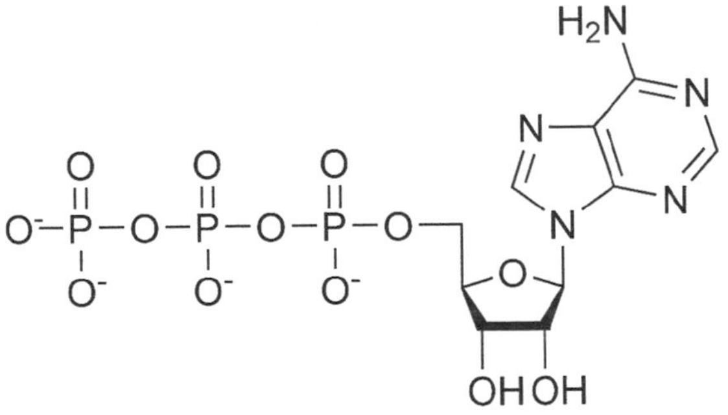

Figure 2 ATP

Second messengers, as one of the chief precipitators of **intracellular signal transduction cascades**, play an important biological role in processes such as apoptosis or cell differentiation. cAMP plays a role in the use of ion channels in the cell, the activation of protein kinases, and the intracellular effects of hormones such as glucagon or epinephrine. Aberrant activities in cAMP-mediated cellular pathways are **linked to abnormal cell growth and proliferation, particularly in some cancers**.

Keywords: intracellular signal transduction cascades, are linked to abnormal cell growth and proliferation particularly in some cancers.

Cause and effect: The passage here introduces the concept of intracellular signal transduction cascades. We're already familiar with the concept—biochemical compounds play an elaborate game of "tag", thereby allowing signaling mechanisms within the body to induce certain effects within a particular cell.

cAMP is an example of a nucleotide, or an organic compound comprised of a nitrogenous base, a ribose or deoxyribose sugar, and a minimum of one phosphate group. Nucleotides form the basic building blocks of nucleic acids, such as DNA or RNA, and also serve as the metabolic precursors for nucleosides, nucleobases, ribose, deoxyribose, the various nitrogenous bases, or (deoxy)ribose-1-phosphate.

Keywords : Nucleotide, serve as the metabolic precursors

Cause and effect: The passage here helpfully defines nucleotides, and gives a partial list of metabolic derivatives. You should definitely note this down; it's likely to be useful later.

32. Which of the following facts related to the "cyclic" portion of cyclic adenosine monophosphate (cAMP) is/are NOT true?
    I. The ring is principally formed by the nucleophilic attack on the primary phosphate's oxygen by the penultimate ring carbon on the pentose sugar.
    II. The ring is principally formed by the nucleophilic attack by the primary phosphate's oxygen on the penultimate ring carbon on the pentose sugar.
    III. The presence of a polar, protic solvent when reproducing the ring formation in vitro exhibits a retarding effect on the formation of desired product.
    A. I only
    B. II only
    C. I and III only
    D. I, II, and III

Choice **A** is correct. cAMP's cyclic portion is the analogue of a hemiacetal/hemiketal functional group, formed by nucleophilic attack of an electronegative O on a carbonyl carbon. Keep in mind that this is a NOT question—you want to scan the Roman numerals for false statements and ensure that our choices include them.

B, C, D: Just by doing a quick scan, you can see that I and II contradict. They cannot both be true/false, so you can immediately eliminate choice D.

Roman numeral I and II differ in which atom is the nucleophile and which the electrophile. The nucleophile must be the oxygen, which means that I is false and II is true. You therefore eliminate choice B, since you do NOT want true statements in our answer. You now have only to verify Roman numeral III.

Roman numeral III is a true statement: protic solvents can engage in hydrogen bonding with oxygen-containing nucleophiles, thereby "distracting" them from their electrophile targets. Since III is true, you do NOT want it in our answer, and can therefore eliminate choice C.

33. Which of the following is LEAST likely to be an evolutionary advantage gained from utilization of intracellular signal transduction cascades?
    A. The ability to "amplify" the signaling effect of one molecule, by increasing the number of triggered biological compounds at each step of the cascade
    B. The ability to have a variety of biochemical triggers precipitate a single downstream action within the cell
    C. The ability to have a single biochemical trigger precipitate a variety of downstream actions within the cell
    D. The ability to degrade or corrupt signal transduction at multiple points of biochemical interaction throughout the entirety of the transduction cascade

Choice **D** is correct. The reason why signal transduction cascades are called "cascades" is because at each step, the number of molecules signaled can increase dramatically. Molecule A can activate two of Molecule B, each of which can activate three of Molecule C, and so on. This is means wide change can be triggered throughout a variety of areas in the body using relatively few biochemical compounds.

A: Either Molecule A or B could trigger Molecule C, which goes on to trigger D, E, F, etc. Therefore, multiple triggers can induce a single downstream action (such as cell inflammation or apoptosis) via multiple inputs into the cascade. Having the ability to do the same thing in response to multiple different stimuli adds versatility to the organism (e.g. you might want a cell to self-destruct if it's old OR injured).

B: This is definitely likely to be an evolutionary advantage. Molecule A can trigger BOTH Molecule B and C, which each go on to precipitate their own respective downstream actions. One action (cell injury, for example) might need to induce several different responses (reconstruction, halting of metabolic breakdown, damage control).

C: An organism could have need to "degrade or corrupt" transduction cascades (what if they get triggered incorrectly?). However, that same ability also leads to natural openings for exploitation by viruses, bacteria, protozoans, etc. Furthermore, spontaneous degradation or corruption (perhaps in the case of certain cancers or inflammatory disorders for example) are also made possible due to this ability. Choice D isn't exactly an outright disadvantage, but it's definitely the most disadvantageous of the answer choices we're given, and so becomes the correct answer here.

34. In which of the following biological organic compounds, *in vivo*, would a researcher be most likely to observe similar cyclic structures to cAMP?
    A. <u>Monosaccharides</u>
    B. Triacylglycerols
    C. Gonadotropins
    D. Kinases

Choice **A** is correct. As you can see in Figure 1, cAMP has both purine (the adenosine base) and hemiacetal/ketal cyclic structures (the cyclic phosphate group). Monosaccharides form hemiacetals/ketals,

B, C, D: None of these molecules have the requisite groups to resemble cAMP in structure. Triacylglycerols typically have neither, gonadotropins have neither, and kinases only rarely contain purine functional groups. You can therefore conclude that the most likely place for a researcher to look to find similar cyclic structures to cAMP would be monosaccharides, making choice A the correct answer here.

35. The versatility lent by the sugar-phosphate backbone to the structure of biologically-relevant nucleic acids permits which of the following in nature?
    A. The formation of a double helix of grooves or voids adjacent to bound base pairs, providing binding sites to intercalating compounds such as histones
    B. The structural stability of dsDNA
    C. <u>The ability of the cell to selectively induce either positive or negative supercoiling (e.g., through the action of topoisomerases)</u>
    D. The looped conformation of the DNA backbone in G-quadraplexes, most notably found in telomeres.

Choice **C** is correct. The question is directly asking us to identify a cause-and-effect relationship, you can effectively throw out answer choices by searching for those that describe an effect with an inappropriate cause. Choice C describes supercoiling, or the "twisting" of the coils in the helix much like one might wind a rubber band. This is directly related to the sugar phosphate backbone, as such coiling or "uncoiling" (in the case of negative supercoiling, as performed by topoisomerases) leaves base-pairing and electrostatic interactions more or less intact. You should definitely keep this answer in consideration; it's thus far the strongest possibility.

The question specifically wants to know which of the answer choices describes an effect that has all of the following characteristics:
1) Correct
2) Positive
3) Derived from the sugar-phosphate backbone of nucleic acids

A: Describes the spaces between the sugar-phosphate backbone. Those spaces are affected more by the strength and stability of the base pairing within the nucleic acid's helix, so you can eliminate A.

B: Describes the structural stability of double-stranded DNA. This is also a direct effect of the DNA's base-pairing (for example, you should know from outside knowledge that C-G pairing is stronger than A-T or A-U pairing). You can eliminate B.

D: Describes the unique quadraplex structure that DNA forms in telomeres in eukaryotes, and other microbial or archaeal DNA structures. The quadraplex structure stems from base-pairing as well (specifically between C and G), and is therefore irrelevant to the sugar-phosphate backbone. You can eliminate D.

Passage 7 Explanation

Maintenance of proper pH levels in various parts of the human body is vitally important for a number of different reasons, among them prevention of tissue degradation due to excessive acidity or basicity, and creation of an internal environment in which biochemical **reactions can proceed** at appropriate times and rates.

Keywords: Maintenance of proper pH, reactions can proceed

Systems and processes which can help to partially **stabilize pH** levels include **respiratory feedback** mechanisms, which can decrease the level of CO_2 in blood plasma and hence can avoid an excessive concentration of carbonic acid, H_2CO_3. Other mechanisms for doing so include a **buffer system** catalyzed by **carbonic anhydrase** enzymes and involving both carbonic acid (H_2CO_3) and bicarbonate (HCO_3^-). One such buffer system was replicated in vitro and a titration procedure was applied, measuring pH as a function of what percentage of buffer was in the form of bicarbonate. The **measurements from this system** are graphed in Figure 1.

Keywords: Systems, stabilize pH, respiratory feedback, buffer system, carbonic anhydrase, measurements from this system

Cause and effect: The buffer system is mainly what this passage is concerned with. The respiratory feedback system will also be involved with a few of the questions below.

Figure 1 pH level as a function of buffer component percentage

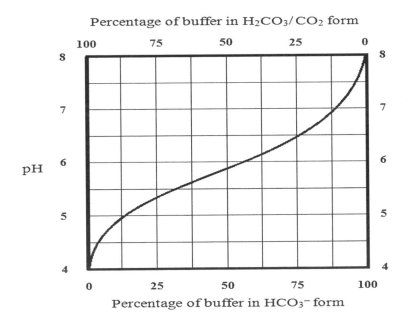

Cause and effect: Changes in the pH of a solution will occur when acid is added, or when a base is added. A buffer system, though, can help to slow the rate of this change. Figure 1 reveals that the rate of change of pH is slower when the percentage of bicarbonate (HCO_3^-) is similar to the percentage of H_2CO_3 / CO_2. This is when the buffer system has the most capability to resist pH changes.

Yet another system involves **regulation** of blood acidity **by the kidneys**, which can **excrete either H$^\pm$ ions** or **bicarbonate** ions, depending on which direction the chemical concentrations in the buffer system must shift to reach a safe blood plasma pH range. Excreting a substantial amount of bicarbonate will cause a significant number of the remaining carbonic acid molecules to separate into an H$^+$ ion and a bicarbonate ion.

Keywords: regulation, by the kidneys, excrete either H$^+$, bicarbonate

Cause and effect: Remember that carbonic acid is a weak acid – in other words, it will dissociate further if some of its conjugate base (bicarbonate, in this case) is removed from the solution. If it were a strong acid, it would dissociate completely from its H$^+$ component regardless of how much of its conjugate base were present.

36. If respiratory function is interrupted at a time when excessive CO_2 is in the bloodstream, then the pH of the blood plasma will:
    A. Increase, because increased CO_2 means increased acidity.
    B. **Decrease, because excessive CO_2 will cause elevated levels of carbonic acid.**
    C. Remain constant, because CO_2 will simply convert itself into H_2CO_3 by combining with a water molecule.
    D. Remain constant, because CO_2 does not have a hydrogen atom and hence cannot affect pH level.

Choice B is correct. CO_2 will combine with water, H_2O, to form carbonic acid, H_2CO_3. Increased carbonic acid means a more acidic solution because the acid will donate a proton, H$^+$, to other molecules in the surrounding environment. More acidic solutions have lower pH levels.

A: Increased acidity will result in a lower pH, not a higher one.
C: Although CO_2 will indeed combine with water to form H_2CO_3, this is the chemical formula for carbonic acid, which will make the blood plasma more acidic and lower its pH level.
D: Substances can react to form acids even though they themselves lack an H atom which can become an H$^+$ ion. The passage indicates that CO_2 is one of these substances because it can form carbonic acid.

37. pOH is a number obtained by taking the negative logarithm of [OH$^-$] concentration within water. When pOH is equal to pH under conditions of 25°C and 1 atm of atmospheric pressure, the number representing each will be:
    A. **7, because the product of [H$^\pm$] and [OH$^-$] in these circumstances can only match the K$_W$ constant if each of these two concentrations equals 1 x 10^{-7}.**
    B. 8, because the sum of pH and pOH must always be 16.
    C. 9, because the KW constant will equal both pH and pOH if the two are equal, and K$_W$ is always at a level of 9 under conditions of 25°C and 1 atm of atmospheric pressure.
    D. pH and pOH do not apply to a situation in which [H$^+$] equals [OH$^-$], as each ion will immediately combine with the other to form H_2O, reducing the concentration of each to zero.

Choice **A** is correct. K$_W$ is defined as the product of [H$^+$] and [OH$^-$]. The value of K$_W$ at 25°C and 1 atm is equal to 1 x 10^{-14}. Since it's been established that [H$^+$] = [OH$^-$] in this case, each can be calculated by taking the square root of K$_W$; this results in 1 x 10^{-7}. And since pH is defined as the negative logarithm of [H$^+$], the pH here will be 7. As such, (A) is the correct answer.
B: The sum of pH and pOH must always be 14, not 16. (This can be determined by taking the negative logarithm of both [H$^+$] and [OH$^-$], then adding the two.)
C: Neither part of this answer choice is accurate.
D: What actually occurs in pure water (an example of a situation where [H$^+$] equals [OH$^-$]) is that a very small number of H_2O water molecules will dissociate into [H$^+$] and [OH$^-$] ions; therefore, the concentration of each will never be completely zero.

38. Figure 1 indicates that the rate of change of pH level is high as a function of bicarbonate concentration between the pH ranges of 7 and 8. What might account for this?
    A. Increased HCO_3^- levels resulting in the donation of more $[OH^-]$ ions, causing a basic mixture of H_2O and OH^- to form.
    B. Ionization of water
    C. The fact that titration occurred in the laboratory caused more inefficient functioning of the buffer system compared to how it would have operated in a living specimen.
    D. **Exhaustion of carbonic acid levels which could otherwise help to neutralize increased basicity.**

Choice **D** is correct. Exhaustion of one of the two components of a buffer system will take away its ability to resist pH changes. In this case, depletion of carbonic acid will prevent the buffer's acid component from releasing hydrogen ions $[H^+]$ that could neutralize excessive basicity, i.e. prevent pH from rising too much. Figure 1 shows that the slope between the pH ranges 7 and 8 takes place when the concentration of carbonic acid (H_2CO_3) is low. (D) is therefore the correct answer.

A: No component of the chemical reaction involved in the specified buffer system involves donation of OH^- ions.
B: Ionization of water will occur in every solution, as well as pure water – it does not, by itself, explain the specific ineffectiveness of the buffer system at extreme pH ranges.
C: Buffer systems comprise fairly simple chemical reactions that do not operate differently in a laboratory setting than they would in a living organism.

39. Titration of potassium acetate in solution was conducted in a further attempt to determine a superior buffer system. The equation describing the reactions preceding titration appears below:

$$KCH_3COO + H_2O \rightarrow K^+ + CH_3COO^- + H_2O \rightleftharpoons CH_3COOH + OH^-$$

What best describes what occurs in this process?
    A. An acidic salt is hydrolyzed.
    B. **A basic salt is hydrolyzed.**
    C. A weak acid is dissolved.
    D. A strong acid is dissolved.

Choice **B** is correct. Potassium acetate is a basic salt – in other words, its components come from a strong base and a weak acid. In the specific case of potassium acetate, its K^+ component comes from a strong base (KOH, potassium hydroxide) and its CH_3COO^- component comes from a weak acid (CH_3COOH, acetic acid). Hydrolysis of this salt (hydrolysis being defined as separating the components through interaction with water) occurs when the salt is dissolved into K^+ and CH_3COO^-. Hence, (B) is the answer.

A: An acidic salt would have components which come from a strong acid and a weak base. Here, CH_3COO^- comes from a weak acid and K^+ comes from a strong base.
C, D: Potassium acetate does not qualify as an acid. After dissolution, neither the K^+ ion nor the CH_3COO^- acetate ion will donate an H^+ ion or accept an OH^- ion. (The reaction equation shows that the CH_3COO^- acetate ion can accept an H^+ ion, which means it is acting as a base, but it will not act as an acid.

These questions are NOT related to a passage.

40. Which of the following compounds has polar covalent bonds but no molecular dipole moment?
    A. Ammonia
    B. Formaldehyde
    C. <u>**Carbon dioxide**</u>
    D. Methane

Choice **C** is correct. The formula of carbon dioxide is CO_2. The shape of the molecule is linear and the symmetrical structure causes the bond dipole vectors to cancel, resulting in no net molecular dipole moment.

A: The formula of ammonia is NH_3. The electronegativity difference between nitrogen and hydrogen is 3.0 - 2.2 = 0.8 and the N-H bonds are polar covalent. The molecular shape of ammonia is pyramidal and the asymmetry results in a molecular dipole.

B: The formula for formaldehyde is $H_2C=O$. The C-H bonds are nonpolar, but the C=O bond has an electronegativity difference of 3.4 - 2.6 = 0.8 and therefore is polar covalent. The shape of the molecule is trigonal planar, but the asymmetry of having two hydrogen atoms and one oxygen atom in the trigonal positions results in a molecular dipole.

D: The formula of methane is CH_4, so you must first consider if a C-H bond is nonpolar or polar covalent. The electronegativity difference between the two atoms is 2.6 - 2.2 = 0.4, which is less than 0.5 and is therefore nonpolar.

41. It is possible to categorize amino acids based on the nature of the groups attached to the alpha carbon as being acidic, basic, nonpolar (hydrophobic) and polar (hydrophilic). Which of the following is most likely a nonpolar amino acid?

A.

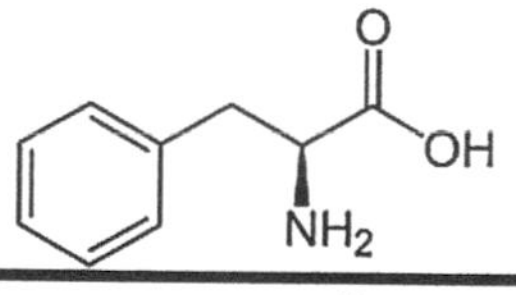

B.

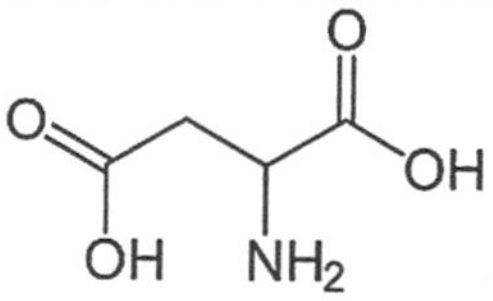

C.

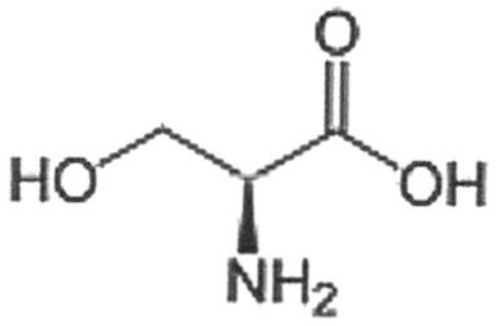

D.

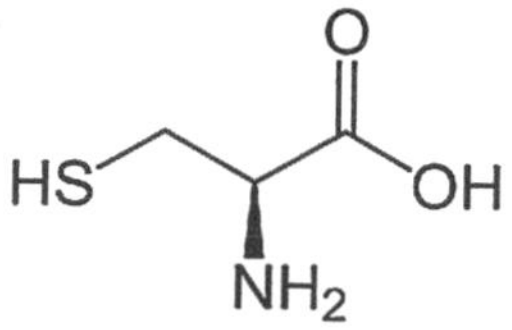

Choice **A** is correct. Phenylalanine is the only amino acid of the choices provided that has a side chain with only nonpolar covalent bonds, and choice A is the correct answer.

B, C, D: Aspartic acid (choice B), serine (choice C) and cysteine (choice D), have side chains with weakly acidic, polar and polar groups, respectively, and all can be eliminated.

42. What is the energy, in joules, of a photon with $\lambda = 6.5 \times 10^{-7}$, if $c = 3.0 \times 10^8$ m/s and $h = 6.62 \times 10^{-34}$ kg m^2 s^{-1}?
    A. 4.6×10^{14} J
    B. 4.6×10^5 J
    C. $\underline{\mathbf{3.0 \times 10^{-19}}}$ **J**
    D. 3.0×10^{-28} J

Choice **C** is correct. The equation that relates the frequency (f) and wavelength (λ) of electromagnetic radiation is c = fλ, and the energy (E) of a photon to the frequency is E = hf. Combining these equations gives E = hc/λ, which when substituting the wavelength, in meters, of a photon from the question and the values of the constants, gives

$$E = (3.0 \times 10^8)(6.62 \times 10^{-34})/(6.5 \times 10^{-7})$$
$$E = 3 \times 10^{-19} \text{ m s}^{-1} \text{ kg m}^2 \text{ s}^{-1} \text{ m}^{-1}$$
$$E = 3 \times 10^{-19} \text{ N m}$$
$$E = 3 \times 10^{-19} \text{ J}$$

A, B, D: These answers are a result of miscalculation.

43. An object is fired at an initial speed of 30 m/s at an angle of 60°. 1.5 seconds after the ball has launched, the approximate total horizontal distance traveled is (neglect air resistance):
    A. **22.5 m**
    B. 31.8 m
    C. 38.9 m
    D. 45.0 m

Choice **A** is correct. Horizontal distance is not affected by gravity (or by any force), so the equation you use is:

$d_x = v_x t$
$v_x = v_o \cos\theta$

Plugging in you get:

$d_x = (30)(\cos 60°)(1.5) = 30*0.5*1.5 = 15*1.5$

At this point, you can stop solving. 15 times 2 would be 30 but here we're only doing 15 times 1.5 so our answer will be less than 30. Looking at the answer choices, you see only choice A matches.

B, C, D: These answers are a result of miscalculation.

Passage 8 Answers and Explanations

There are **two types** of **covalent bonds** found in **biologically** important molecules, non-polar and polar covalent bonds. In chemistry, the distinction between these types of bonds is based on **differences in electronegativity** between **the nonmetal atoms** involved in sharing pairs of electrons. If the difference in electronegativity between the two elements is less than 0.5, the bond is considered nonpolar and if the difference is greater than 0.5, but less than 2.0, the bond is considered polar. If the difference in electronegativity is greater than 2.0, the bond is no longer considered covalent. Listed in Table 1 are the electronegativity values for selected nonmetal elements.

Key terms: covalent bonds, molecules, electronegativity, and nonmetal atoms

Cause-and-Effect: Nonmetal atoms with the same, or nearly the same, electronegativity share electrons in a bond and as a result do not have polarity.

Cause-and-Effect: Nonmetal atoms with significant differences in electronegativity do not share electrons equally and this results in a bond with a small degree of ionic character, known as a polar covalent bond.

Table 1 Electronegativity values for selected second period elements

Atomic Symbol	Electronegativity (Pauling scale)
H	2.2
C	2.6
N	3.0
O	3.4
F	4.0

Table 1 This table lists the Pauling electronegativities of the second period elements. Electronegativity is a value that measures an atom's ability to draw electrons to itself. Pauling first calculated these values based on bond energies and used a scale from approximately 1-4 in which fluorine had the highest value. The noble gases were originally not assigned electronegativity values because they were thought not to be able to form bonds, which you now know is not true for the heavier noble gases.

Unequal sharing of electrons in a covalent bond, due to differences in electronegativity, imparts a degree of **ionic character** to the bond. Specifically, the more electronegative atom will gain a partial negative charge ($-\delta$) and the atom that is less able to attract the shared electrons will gain an equal amount of positive partial charge ($+\delta$). These **bond dipoles** represent **electric fields** with **vector** properties. Having polar covalent bonds is a necessary requirement for a molecule to have a molecular dipole moment, but, if the bond dipole moments do not combine to give a net dipole moment, the molecule will be nonpolar. Table 2 lists the experimentally determined **molecular dipole** moments for selected compounds.

Key terms: ionic character, bond dipole, electric fields, vector, and molecular dipole

Cause-and-Effect: Nonmetal atoms do not always share electrons equally in covalent bonds, which causes the electrons within the bond to preferentially be drawn closer to the more electronegative atom, making this atom acquire some fraction of a charge, while the other atom acquires an equal fraction of positive charge.

Cause-and-Effect: The bond dipoles that have both magnitude and direction, therefore these vectors combine to determine the net molecular dipole.

Table 2 Molecular dipole moments, measured in debyes (D)

Formula	Name	Molecular Dipole (D)
CH_4	methane	0
NH_3	ammonia	1.47
H_2O	water	1.85
H_2CO	methanal	2.33
CO_2	carbon dioxide	0
CH_3COH	ethanal	2.7
$(CH_3)_2CO$	propanone	2.91
C_2H_6	ethane	0
N_2H_4	hydrazine	1.85
H_2O_2	hydrogen peroxide	2.26
CH_3NH_2	methyl amine	1.31
CH_3OH	methanol	1.69
$(CH_3)_2O$	dimethyl ether	1.30

Table 2 Experimentally determined molecular dipole moments, which are determined by placing the material between two charged plates and measuring the change in the capacitance.

44. Which of the following is the best estimate of an O-H bond dipole moment in water? Note that sin 109° = 0.95; sin 55° = 0.82; cos 109° = -0.33; and cos 55° = 0.57.
    A. 0.97 D
    B. 1.13 D
    C. 1.50 D
    D. 3.24 D

Choice **C** is correct. From Table 2, the molecular dipole of water is 1.85 D. To calculate the dipole moment of a single O-H bond, you must recognize that the direction of the molecular dipole in water bisects the H-O-H angle, which is approximately 109°. The O-H bond represents the hypotenuse of a right triangle where the side adjacent to the 55° angle is 1.85/2 = 0.925 D. Therefore

$$\cos 55° = 0.925/H$$
$$H = 0.925/\cos 55°$$
$$H = 0.925/0.57$$
$$H \sim 1.66 \text{ D}$$

The calculated bond dipole moment of O-H is slightly less than the value calculated above because the actual H-O-H angle in water is 104°, not an idealized tetrahedral angle of 109°, because the lone pairs of electrons on the oxygen actually occupy more space around the oxygen atom than the O-H bonding pairs of electrons.

A, B, D: These answers are a result of miscalculation.

45. Which of the following compounds has the smallest molecular dipole moment?
    A. Methanol
    B. Dimethyl ether
    C. Methyl amine
    D. <u>**Dimethyl amine**</u>

Choice **D** is correct. The molecular dipole moments for methanol, dimethyl ether and methyl amine can be found in Table 2.

A, B, C: It should be noted that dimethyl ether has a smaller molecular dipole moment than methanol, which can be understood by the fact that there is less of an electronegativity difference between carbon and oxygen than between hydrogen and oxygen. Likewise, methylamine has a lower molecular dipole moment than methanol, again due to the fact that there is less of an electronegativity difference between carbon and nitrogen than between carbon and oxygen. The molecular dipole moments of methyl amine and dimethyl ether are nearly the same. It would be reasonable to expect that the dipole moment of dimethyl amine would be lower than methyl amine, because the electronegativity difference between carbon and nitrogen is less than the electronegativity difference between nitrogen and hydrogen. Choice D is the correct answer.

46. Shown below is drawing representing the most stable conformation of hydrogen peroxide. Which of the following vectors best represents the direction of electric field generated by the dipole moment of hydrogen peroxide based on this drawing?

A.
B.
C.
D.

Choice **A** is correct. It should be noted that in its most stable conformation, as shown in the drawing, one of the hydrogen atoms comes out of the plane of the page slightly (wedge) and one H goes back behind the plane of the page slightly (ash). The dihedral angle is somewhere between 90° and 115°. This configuration is influenced by the repulsive interactions of the lone-pairs on the two oxygen atoms and by the maximization of dipole-dipole and hydrogen bonding interactions in the liquid and solid phases. The molecular dipole vector would be the three dimensional sum of the components of the O-H bond dipole moments. The resulting vector bisects the molecule, in the plane of the page, perpendicular to the O-O bond, with the arrow pointing in the direction of the electric field, δ+ to δ- as shown below.

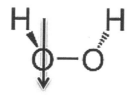

B, C, D: These are all improper vectors given the molecular geometry of H_2O_2. See the reasoning above.

47. Which of the following compounds would most likely have the highest boiling point?
    A. Formaldehyde
    B. Acetaldehyde
    C. **Acetone**
    D. Ethane

Choice **C** is correct. The boiling points of these compounds should correlate well with the molecular dipole moments, since dipole-dipole intermolecular forces should be the strongest intermolecular forces in these compounds. As seen in Table 2, acetone, also known as propanone, has the highest molecular dipole moment of the answer options, making choice C the correct answer.

A, B, D: The boiling points of ethane, methanal, ethanal and propanone are -89°C, -19°C, 20°C, and 56°C, respectively. Without knowing that (who does?) you can deduce that a greater degree of intermolecular forces will lead to higher boiling points. According to the table in the passage, These 3 molecules have a lower degree of IM forces compared to acetone.

Passage 9 Explanation

Diffraction experiments can be particularly useful for indirectly determining information about the structure of objects that are too small to be observed by the human eye. In order for diffraction to be useful there must be a regular repeating pattern associated with the object or material and the **wavelength of radiation** used in the experiment must be comparable to the size of the spaces between the objects. In a commonly performed introductory physics experiment, students are asked to determine the spacing between parallel lines on a **diffraction grating** using a red (λ = 650 nm) **laser** pointer, Figure 1. When the laser is focused on a diffraction grating whose parallel lines are oriented horizontally, a vertical series of bright red spots are observed on a screen at some distance (L) from the diffraction grating. The angle θ can be determined from L and the distance between the bright spots. In order for **constructive interference** to occur, the **diffracted light rays** must travel integral multiples of the wavelength. The Fraunhofer equation (Equation 1) can be used to calculate the spacing (between parallel lines on the diffraction grating. The orientation of the series of bright spots is always perpendicular to the orientation of the parallel lines. If the diffraction grating is rotated 90°, a horizontal series of bright spots will be observed. Particularly interesting two-dimensional diffraction patterns can be observed if there are two-dimensional patterns of shapes on the diffraction grating. Babinet's principle states that the observed diffraction pattern will be the same as the diffraction pattern of an **aperture** of the same shape. Thus, a diffraction grating consisting of two sets of parallel lines intersecting at some angle α, would produce two sets of bright diffraction spots also intersecting at that same angle.

Key terms: Diffraction, wavelength, radiation, diffraction grating, laser, constructive interference, light rays, and aperture

Cause-and-Effect: When electromagnetic radiation passes through an opening an apparent bending of the light rays occurs, which is called diffraction.

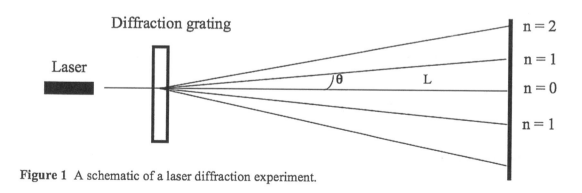

Figure 1 A schematic of a laser diffraction experiment.

Cause-and-Effect: The interference pattern that results from diffraction can provide information about distances and the shapes of objects that are too small to be seen by the naked eye.
Figure 1 The figures shows a laser beam passing through a diffraction grating, which causes the production of multiple orders of diffraction (n = 0, 1, 2, etc.) in which the rays are the result of constructive interference.

Equation 1 $d \sin \theta = n \lambda$

Equation 1 The Fraunhofer equation is derived from the trigonometric relationship in the right

triangle formed by the wavelength (n λ) of light being diffracted that results in constructive interference and the spacing (between the parallel lines on the diffraction grating, i.e. sin θ = λ/d. This forms the basis for the analysis of perhaps the most important diffraction experiment of all time. In 1952 Gosling and Franklin used **X-ray diffraction** to help determine the structure of a **crystalline** form of Deoxyribonucleic acid (DNA). After performing numerous experiments, they were able to orient the crystal such that the long axis of **the unit cell** was perpendicular to the path of the X-ray beam. In her notes she (Franklin) wrote, "The results suggest a **helical** structure (which must be very closely packed containing 2, 3 or 4 **co-axial nucleic** acid chains per helical unit, and having the **phosphate groups** near the outside." This was well before Watson and Crick published their Nobel award winning description of DNA, which was based in part on Franklin's experiments. This insight into the helical structure of crystalline DNA can be easily understood by analogy to the shape of a coiled spring. If one were to look closely at a spring held with the principle axis oriented vertically, you would see two sets of parallel straight lines, Figure 2 (ignoring the curved shapes that would be seen on the ends) forming an angle of 2α, where α represents the **pitch** angle of the helix. If one were to imagine a large number of springs (DNA molecules), all oriented vertically, the straight portions would form a series of intersecting diffraction grating lines, that would produce two series of intersecting bright diffraction spots.

Key terms: X-ray diffraction, crystalline, unit cell, helical, co-axial, phosphate groups, and pitch

Cause-and-Effect: The basic shape of the X-ray diffraction pattern for DNA resulted in our current understanding of the helical structure of nucleic acids.

Cause-and-Effect: The determination of the basic structure of DNA was such an important discovery that it lead to a Nobel prize for Crick and Watson, but unfortunately the importance of

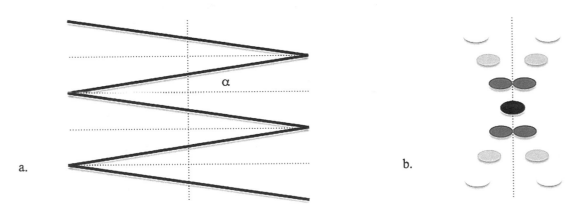

the contributions of Franklin and her student Gosling, were not recognized until recently.

Figure 2 (a) A side representation of a vertically oriented helical coil structure, and (b) the resulting diffraction pattern.

Figure 2 Looking at a coiled spring hanging vertically from some distance would appear like a vertically oriented sine function if you were unable to discern depth perception for the coil. If you ignore the curved portions on the left and right sides of the sine function, the coil would appear to be a zig-zag shape, resulting from connecting straight lines at some angle α with respect to the horizontal, which is referred to as the pitch angle. The more the spring is stretched, the greater the incline of the pitch. These straight portions of the coil can be thought of as intersecting diffraction grid lines (Figure 2a), which would produce an X-shaped diffraction pattern of bright spots (Figure 2if a focused beam of electromagnetic radiation of appropriate wavelength were to pass through

the coil perpendicular to the primary axis.

48. A student performed a diffraction experiment using an experimental set-up similar to that shown in Figure 1. If the distance between the laser pointer and the diffraction grating is increased, what happens to the distance between the bright spots on the screen?
    A. The distance between the bright spots increases, but the brightness of the spots remains the same.
    B. The distance between the bright spots decreases, but the brightness of the spots remains the same.
    C. **The distance between the spots remains the same, and the brightness of the spots remains the same.**
    D. The distance between the spots remains the same, but the size of the spots gets smaller.

Choice **C** is correct. Laser photons are highly coherent photons that do not significantly disperse over short distances. As a result the distance between the laser and the diffraction grating does not have a significant effect brightness or diameter of the laser beam. Based on Equation 1, the angle of diffraction is unaffected by the distance between the laser and the diffraction grating.

A,B, D: The distance between the laser and the diffraction grating does not have a significant effect brightness or diameter of the laser beam, eliminating choices A, B, D.

49. A student performed a diffraction experiment using an experimental set-up similar to that shown in Figure 1, but instead of using a red laser, she used a blue laser. What happens to the spacing between the bright spots for the blue laser, as compared to the spacing between the bright spots of the red laser?
    A. The spacing gets bigger because the wavelength of blue light is longer than the wavelength of red light.
    B. The spacing gets smaller because the wavelength of blue light is longer than the wavelength of red light.
    C. The spacing gets bigger because the wavelength of blue light is shorter than the wavelength of red light.
    D. **The spacing gets smaller because the wavelength of blue light is shorter than the wavelength of red light.**

Choice **D** is correct. Blue light has a shorter wavelength than red light, eliminating choices A and B. From Equation 1, there is a direct relationship between the wavelength of light and the sine of the angle of diffraction, causing the spacing between the diffraction spots to decrease.

50. X-ray diffraction results from the scattering that occurs when electromagnetic radiation interacts with the electrons of atoms. Which of the following portions of crystalline nucleic acids would scatter x-rays the most?
    A. **The phosphate groups**
    B. The ribose sugar groups
    C. The purine bases
    D. The pyrimidine bases

Choice **A** is correct. The phosphorus atom represents the atom with the greatest number of electrons and would scatter X-rays the most. Choice A is the correct answer.
B, C, D: the carbons, oxygens and hydrogens of ribose and the nitrogens of the nucleotides have fewer electrons than phosphorus.

51. Which of the following best describes what would happen to the diffraction pattern that would be observed for a spring similar to that shown in Figure 2, if a weight were suspended from the spring?

   A. The pitch angle α would decrease.
   B. <u>**The pitch angle α would increase.**</u>
   C. The spots would get brighter.
   D. The spots would get less bright.

Choice **B** is correct. As the spring is stretched the pitch angle will increase and the spacing between the parallel portions (of the helix will increase, but this will not have a significant effect on the brightness of the spots. Choice B is the correct answer.

Passage 10 Explanation

Keratin is the common name for a family of **fibrous structural proteins**, which are the key structural material making up the outer layer of human skin, as well as human hair, human nails, and many other natural structures in the animal kingdom. Keratin is formed from a **series of monomers** that assemble into bundles to form intermediate filaments. Its intermediate filaments are **tough and insoluble and form strong "un-mineralized" tissues** found in reptiles, birds, amphibians, and mammals. Reactions 1(a) and 1(b) below summarize the **generic in vitro lysing of disulfide bridges** (induced either by hydrogen peroxide, acetic acid, or thioglycolic acid formed in keratin.

Keywords: fibrous structural proteins, series of monomers, tough and insoluble and form strong "un-mineralized, tissues, generic in vitro lysing of disulfide bridges

Reactions 1(a) and 1(b): Generalized lysing of disulfide bridges formed in keratin

These disulfide bridges occur in addition to inter and/or intramolecular hydrogen bonds or interactions between charged functional groups in abnormal pH environments, due largely to keratins' relatively high concentration of sulfur-containing amino acids. Disulfide bridges are part of a larger family **of crosslinks (covalent or ionic) polymer bonds** that link one polymer chain to another). These crosslinks contribute to the insolubility of keratins, except when in certain dissociating or reducing agents. Such crosslinks are important in generating mechanically stable structures such as keratinaceous formations in the human body.

Keywords: crosslinks (covalent or ionic) polymer bonds

The more flexible and elastic **keratins of hair** have fewer **disulfide bridges** than the keratins in mammalian fingernails, hooves and claws, which are harder and more like their analogues across the animal kingdom. Hair and other "α-keratins" consist of α-helically coiled single protein strands (with regular intra-chain H-bonding), which are then further twisted into so-called "**superhelical**" strands that may comprise a macro "**coiled-coil**" structure.

Keywords: keratins of hair, fewer disulfide, superhelical, coiled-coil

The **"β-keratins" of reptiles and birds** on the other hand, are typically found in the scales, shells, and claws of reptiles, in the feathers, beaks, and claws of birds, and the quills of porcupines. Figure 1 below illustrates the typical structure of a β-keratin.

Keywords: β-keratins of reptiles and birds

Figure 1 Generalized illustration of a β-keratin

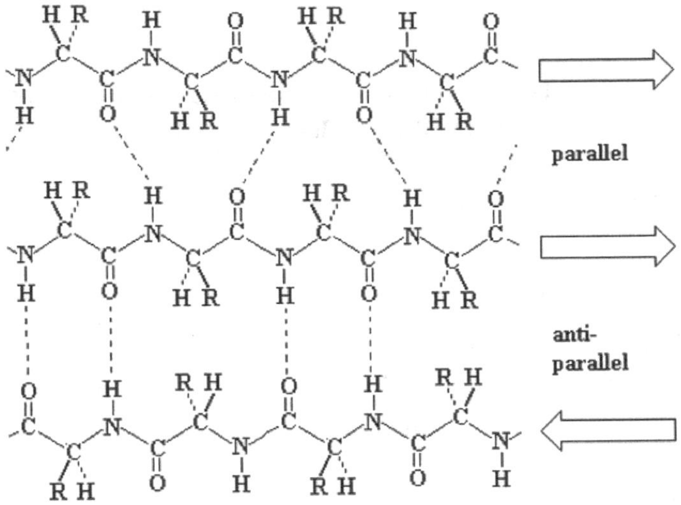

52. Which of the following is the correct reason why thioglycolic acid doesn't appear in the equation for K_{eq} of Reaction 1(b)? Assume the reaction takes place under normal biological conditions.

    A. Thioglycolic acid is a dilute solvent; its concentration can be reasonably approximated to equal to 1.
    B. Thioglycolic acid is a solid; its concentration can be reasonably approximated to equal to 1.
    C. Thioglycolic acid has no ionic activity; its concentration can be reasonably approximated to equal to 1.
    D. **None of the above**

Choice **D** is correct. Under normal biological conditions, thioglycolic acid would NOT be a solvent (one should always assume that water is the solvent for biological reactions unless explicitly told otherwise), and it would NOT be a solid. Though you have no explicit information as to the pK_a of thioglycolic acid, its structure is very similar to acetic acid, which you know to have ionic activity under normal biological conditions. You can therefore assume that it would indeed have ionic activity in the conditions described by the question (it, in fact, has a pK_a of 3.8, validating this assumption), eliminating answer choice C. Answer choice D must be the correct answer.

53. Carbon-14 is frequently used by researchers in isotopic labelling of enzymes; however, under certain conditions, it can be subject to both β^- and β^+ decay. Which of the following isotopes might be observed if a sample of C-14 in use by a researcher were subjected to β^+ decay?
    A. **Boron-14**
    B. Nitrogen-15
    C. Nitrogen-14
    D. Boron-15

Choice **A** is correct. Beta positive decay is the conversion of a proton to a positron and a neutron. This decreases the atomic number and maintains a constant mass number. Carbon-14 has an atomic number of 6 and a mass number of 14; our new element must have an atomic number of 5 and a mass number of 14. The correct answer must therefore be A (Boron-14).

B, C, D: Answer choices B and D incorrectly assert that beta decay alters the mass number, and answer choice C is the correct answer for β^- decay and not β^+ decay.

54. Disulfide bridges that form under natural conditions generally:

    A. stabilize proteins, because the energy absorbed by the formation of the intramolecular bond reduces the overall instability of the protein molecule
    B. destabilize proteins, because the energy absorbed by the formation of the intramolecular bond reduces the overall instability of the protein molecule
    C. <u>**stabilize proteins, because the energy released by the formation of the intramolecular bond reduces the overall instability of the protein molecule**</u>
    D. destabilize proteins, because the energy released by the formation of the intramolecular bond reduces the overall instability of the protein molecule

Choice **C** is correct. According to information in the passage, disulfide bridges stabilize proteins, which means you can immediately eliminate answer choices B and D. Under natural conditions (which in this case you can assume to mean spontaneous conditions), the formation of covalent bonds, whether intra- or inter-molecular, releases energy, which means you can eliminate answer choice A. Answer choice C must therefore be the correct answer.

55. One popular means of real-time observation of enzyme-catalysed crosslink formations is to introduce the use of "radio-tagged" enzymes. Researchers who use this method use enzymes that contain radioactive isotopes of biologically-common elements into in vitro reaction media to enable their direct observation via certain spectroscopic methods. Which of the following physical properties could these spectroscopic methods use in order to differentiate between radioactive isotopes and other elements in the reaction?
    I.   Mass
    II. Vibrational Mode
    III. Nuclear Instability

    A. I only
    B. <u>**I and III only**</u>
    C. II and III only
    D. I, II, and III

Choice **B** is correct. Isotopes are elements of the periodic table that deviate from the norm in mass number. This deviation from the mass number would certainly imply that spectroscopic methods could take advantage of mass, meaning that statement I is true.

You can eliminate answer choice C. If you look at the remaining choices, you can see that you should next look at statement II. If statement II is true, then the answer choice must be D by default, since it's the only answer choice that contains both statements I and II. Since (for the MCAT) you assume that vibrational mode is linked only to the elasticity/length of various covalent bonds in a molecule and not to the mass of the participating atoms in those bonds, you can eliminate statement II as false, thereby leaving us with only answer choice B.

These questions are NOT related to a passage.

56. Uric acid is thought to be acidic due to the following isomerization. Which of the following best describes the relationship between these structures?

   A. **These structures are tautomers.**
   B. These structures are diastereomers.
   C. These structures are enantiomers.
   D. These structures are epimers.

Choice **A** is correct. The movement of the double bonds and the hydrogen atoms is similar to that seen in ketones and is known as keto/enol tautomerization. This accounts for the relatively high acidity of the hydrogen atoms located on a-carbon atoms next to the carbonyl group in ketones.

B, C, D: Diastereomers, enantiomers and epimers all are isomers due to the presence of a chiral center. Uric acid does not have a chiral center and therefore, choice A is the correct answer.

57. Which of the following free-body-diagrams corresponds to a 1.0 N box sliding across a frictionless horizontal surface?

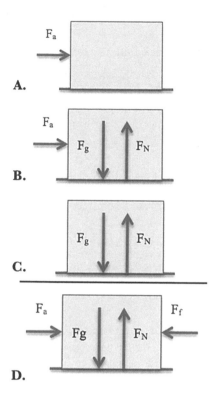

Choice **C** is correct. If the sum of all forces acting on an object do not equal zero, then the object will accelerate. The question indicates that the object has a weight of 1.0 N and choice A can be eliminated because there is not a force of gravity vector, which would have to be opposed by a normal force vector.

A, B: Choices A and B can be eliminated because the applied force in the horizontal direction will cause acceleration. The question states that the surface is frictionless.
D: While the box in choice D could be moving with constant velocity, the vector pointed to the left, labeled F_f, is a force of friction. Choice D can be eliminated.

58. Second messengers are most distinguishable from so-called "first messengers" in the body by their ability to do which of the following?
    A. **Engage in intracellular intermolecular bonding**
    B. Engage in intercellular intermolecular bonding
    C. Engage in intracellular intramolecular bonding
    D. Engage in intercellular intramolecular bonding

Choice **A** is correct. From outside knowledge, you know that second messengers take messages received from the cell membrane and transmit them elsewhere within the cell. The body uses them because many "first messengers" are too large or hydrophobic to move freely within the confines of the cell. This means that second messengers (as opposed to first messengers) can bond to other molecules (intermolecularly) within the cell (intracellularly). Answer choice A is therefore the correct answer here.
B, C, D: Second messengers (as opposed to first messengers) can bond to other molecules (intermolecularly) within the cell (intracellularly).

59. A patient with disrupted kidney function has a limited ability to excrete HCO_3^-. How might the excess bicarbonate function according to the Brønsted-Lowry model?

    A. It will function as an acid because its negative charge can attract H^+ ions.

    B. It will function as an acid because it is an important component of a system which buffers against increased basicity.

    C. It will function as a base because it is an important component of a system which buffers against increased acidity.

    D. <u>**It will function as a base because it is capable of accepting an $H^\pm$ ion.**</u>

Choice **D** is correct. The Brønsted-Lowry definition of a base is a molecule which can accept a proton.

A: Brønsted-Lowry acids will release an H^+ ion or ions, not attract them.

B, C: Although HCO_3^- (a.k.a. bicarbonate) participates in the buffer system described in the passage, this does not provide information about whether it is an acid or a base.

TIMED
SECTION 2
59 Questions, 95 Minutes

(Use the tear-out answer sheet provided in Appendix E)

Passage 1 (Questions 1-4)

A power stroke is a rapid change between two structural states of a protein that can be used to perform mechanical work in cells containing proteins such as myosin. If the binding or unbinding of a small molecule or a chemical change in a bound molecule converts a protein between two structural states separated by a distance d, then the power stroke can do work against an external load force of magnitude F_L, provided that $F_L d \leq \Delta G$, where ΔG is the decrease in free energy between the chemical states. Two mechanisms by which a chemical change can lead to a structural one have been proposed.

Mechanism 1

A chemical change strictly precedes structural change in the protein. A change in chemical bonds associated with a change in the ligand produces a strained conformation that relaxes into a final structural change. Application of an external load force will have little effect on the forward rate constant, k_{fr}, for this reaction.

Mechanism 2

A structural change in the protein precedes a chemical change. Because of thermal forces, a protein fluctuates from its initial state to its final state before being trapped by a resulting chemical change. An external load force will have a significant effect on the reaction's forward rate constant. The load dependence, ε, is defined as the ratio of the forward rate constant at a given load force, k_{fr}^*, to k_{fr} when no load is present. ε for mechanism 2 is related to an applied load force, F_L, according to Equation 1, where k_B is Boltzmann's constant, T the absolute temperature.

$$F_L = -\frac{k_B T}{d} \ln \varepsilon$$

Equation 1

The load dependence of rate constants for the power stroke of two molecular motor proteins was measured using atomic force microscopy at different applied load forces. Figure 1 shows the load dependence values of KIF2a, a kinesin class of motor proteins that travel along microtubule filaments, and bacteriophage T7 RNA polymerase (T7RNAP). T7RNAP is a single subunit enzyme that moves processively along DNA while performing its synthetic activity.

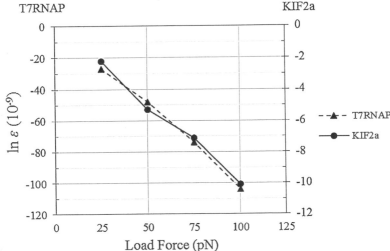

Figure 1: Load dependence of KIF2a and T7RNAP proteins

1. The load dependence measurements obtained by atomic force microscopy for the proteins tested most closely support:
    A. Mechanism 1, because a load force will minimally affect the chemical energy difference between the initial state and transition states of the protein.
    B. Mechanism 1, because a load force creates a large structural change and large increase in the energy of the protein transition state.
    C. Mechanism 2, because a load force will minimally affect the chemical energy difference between the initial state and transition states of the protein
    D. Mechanism 2, because a load force creates a large structural change and large increase in the energy of the protein transition state.

2. Based upon the results of the experiment performed, the magnitude of the change in the forward reaction rate of KIF2a is:
    A. greater than that of T7RNAP at equal external applied loads.
    B. smaller than that of T7RNAP at equal external applied loads.
    C. approximately equal to that of T7RNAP and non-zero at equal external applied loads.
    D. approximately equal to that of T7RNAP and near zero at equal external applied loads.

3. Assuming that the displacement of an actin filament during muscle myosin's power stroke is approximately 5 nm per ATP hydrolyzed ($\Delta G \approx 5 \times 10^{-20}$ J/ATP molecule), what is the maximum external load force against which it can perform work?
    A. 0.1 pN
    B. 0.25 pN
    C. 10 pN
    D. 25 pN

4. The kinetics of the binding reaction between myosin V and actin are depicted in the graph below, where M_u represents the concentration of unbound myosin V. Based upon this figure, what is the most likely rate law for this reaction, where k is the rate constant for the reaction and [actin] is the concentration of unbound actin?

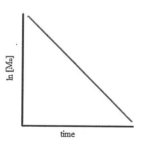

    A. k[actin]
    B. k[M_u]
    C. k[M_u][actin]
    D. k[M_u]^2

Passage 2 (Questions 5-8)

Typically saponification results from the base hydrolysis of triglycerides (Figure 1), to form glycerol and the corresponding sodium salts of fatty acids. Fats that have a high degree of saturation, as in many animal fats, tend to form amorphous solids at room temperature, whereas fats that contain a high degree of unsaturation, as in vegetable oils, tend to be liquids at room temperature. The production of soap can easily be accomplished on the small scale by individuals, in which the fat is heated and mixed with an appropriate amount of aqueous lye, (NaOH) or potash (KOH). Soap makers often will quote a "saponification number", which represents the number of milligrams of potassium hydroxide required to completely hydrolyze one gram of the fat with a particular average molar mass.

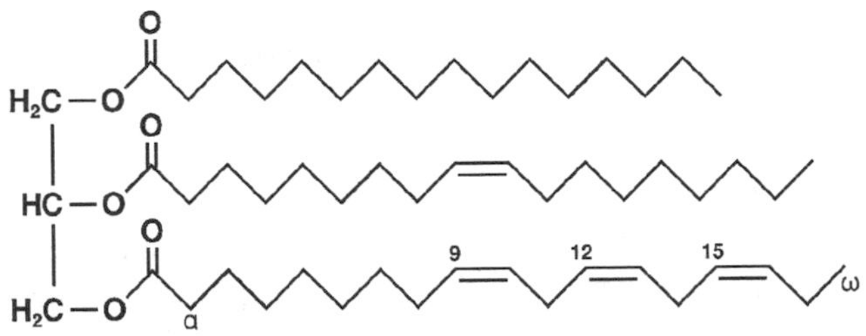

Figure 1 An example of a triglyceride in which one of the fatty acid esters is saturated, the second is unsaturated and the third is polyunsaturated. The chemical composition of a fat is typically not uniform and this is a hypothetical example, with a formula of $C_{55}H_{98}O_6$ (MW = 854 g mol^{-1}), and may not necessarily represent a naturally occurring fatty acid combination.

After combining the fat with the aqueous base solution, the resulting heterogeneous mixture is stirred to form an emulsion in which the reaction takes place at the interface between the aqueous phase and the liquid fat. The rate of the reaction is dependent upon the temperature and the interface surface area. The reaction is exothermic, so once the mixture begins to thicken, the external heat source is removed and the reaction is allowed to continue until the mixture "traces" when stirred. At that point, a fragrance is often added. Subsequently for bar soaps, the warm thick mixture is poured into molds and allowed to finish reacting and to cool for several hours. Interestingly enough, solid bar soap is usually made with sodium hydroxide, whereas potassium hydroxide tends to be used to make soft or liquid soaps.

5. What is the "saponification number" for the fat shown in Figure 1?
    A. 46
    B. 66
    C. 140
    D. 197

6. How many chiral atoms are present in the structure of the fat shown in Figure 1?
    A. 0
    B. 1
    C. 2
    D. 3

7. If a soap maker wanted to make a hard bar soap, which of the following fatty acids would be most desirable to be the major component of the fat?
    A. hexadecanoic acid
    B. (9Z)-Octadec-9-enoic acid
    C. (9E)-Octadec-9-enoic acid
    D. (9Z,12Z,15Z)-9,12,15-Octadecatrienoic acid

8. In the base catalyzed hydrolysis of fat, what is the most likely first step in the mechanism of the reaction?
    A. Protonation of an oxygen lone-pair of a carbonyl group.
    B. Electrophilic attack of sodium ion on the oxygen lone-pair of a carbonyl group.
    C. Nucleophilic attack on a carbonyl carbon by water.
    D. Nucleophilic attack on a carbonyl carbon by hydroxide.

Passage 3 (Questions 9-13)

Milk and various milk products have been used as food since antiquity. The major challenge was the preservation of milk in a form that retained its nutritional properties. The discovery of cheese is thought to have resulted from the use of the stomachs of slaughtered animals as bladders for the transportation and storage of milk produced from domesticated cattle, goats and sheep. The bladders contained residual protease enzymes that denatured the milk proteins, forming curds and whey. Separation of the liquid and solid components, followed by addition of salt, provided a convenient way to safely store this food for use during periods of scarcity. The subsequent discovery of bacteria that were also capable of acidifying milk by way of fermentation, imparted unique flavors and has led to the numerous dairy products that we enjoy today.

The major nutrients found in milk include: (1) Fats; (2) Proteins; (3) Carbohydrates; (4) Vitamins; and (5) Minerals. These components can be separated by taking advantage of differences in physical and chemical properties. Milk is an emulsion of milk fats, suspended in an aqueous solution. If fresh milk is allowed to stand undisturbed, the hydrophobic triglycerides form a layer on top of the aqueous solution, separation of which produces cream and skim milk. The milk fat is comprised of a complex mixture of triglycerides, containing both saturated and unsaturated fatty acids. The major saturated fatty acid in cow's milk is palmitic acid (31%, $CH_3(CH_2)_{14}CO_2H$) and the major unsaturated fatty acid is oleic acid (24%, $CH_3(CH_2)_7CH=CH(CH_2)_7CO_2H$). Homogenized milk can be prepared by breaking up the fat globules to form a colloidal suspension. Raw milk also contains various microbes, which are typically killed by heating the milk in a process known as pasteurization, in honor of the famous French scientist who first perfected this preservation method.

Cottage cheese can be prepared by the careful addition of vinegar to milk, which denatures the protein casein, whose isoelectric point is 4.6. The curds can easily be separated from the majority of the whey by filtration. The coagulation of the protein traps some of the milk fat and aqueous soluble components, like lactose, within the curd. The mild flavor, high protein content and potential low fat content of cottage cheese make it a popular food for people with certain dietary restrictions. The resulting whey contains lactose and additional proteins, like lactalbumin, as well as minerals that remain soluble in the mildly acidic aqueous solution. Neutralization and heating the whey causes the denaturing of the remaining proteins, which can be filtered after cooling the solution. Whey proteins are popular with certain athletes as nutritional supplements. The lactose in the remaining aqueous solution can be separated from the minerals by evaporating the water to produce a super-saturated solution, from which lactose will crystalize.

9. Which of the following types of reactions would convert an unsaturated fatty acid into a saturated fatty acid?
    A. Acetylation
    B. Hydrogenation
    C. Elimination
    D. Substitution

10. Which of the following hormones would most likely NOT significantly affect a lactating woman's production of milk?
    A. Epinephrine
    B. Progesterone
    C. Estrogen
    D. Oxytocin

11. What is the net charge of casein at a pH of 4.6?
    A. +4.6
    B. -4.6
    C. 2.5×10^{-5}
    D. 0

12. Which of the following enzymes is involved in the hydrolysis of peptide bonds?
    A. Pepsin
    B. Amylase
    C. Hexokinase
    D. Lactase

13. Which of the following structures are disrupted when a protein is heated to the point that it becomes denatured?
    I. Primary
    II. Secondary
    III. Tertiary
    IV. Quaternary

    A. I and II only
    B. III and IV only
    C. II, III, and IV only
    D. I, II, III and IV

These questions are NOT related to a passage. (Questions 14-17)

14. What is the primary intermolecular force that makes sucrose soluble in water?
    A. Van der Waals forces
    B. Dipole-dipole forces
    C. Hydrogen bonding
    D. Ion-dipole forces

15. A 5.0 kg object is completely submerged in water and experiences a buoyant force of 13 N. What is the approximate specific gravity of the object?
    A. 4
    B. 5
    C. 13
    D. 50

16. How many liters of carbon dioxide gas at 1 atm of pressure and 37°C can be produced by adding an excess of hydrochloric acid to 100 g of calcium carbonate? Note that R = 0.0821 L atm mol^{-1} K^{-1}.
    A. 100 L
    B. 50 L
    C. 25 L
    D. 10 L

17. In the circuit below, a 12 ohm resistor is connected to a 12 volt battery. A second identical resistor is attached in parallel to the first.

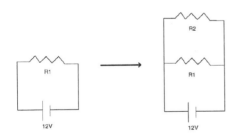

What happens to the current flowing through R$_1$?
    A. Current is reduced to ½ the original.
    B. Current remains unchanged.
    C. Current doubles.
    D. The change in current depends on the magnetic field which may vary.

THIS PAGE LEFT

INTENTIONALLY BLANK

Passage 4 (Questions 18-22)

In 1952, Urey and Miller conducted an experiment to simulate the conditions thought to be present in early earth's atmosphere, trying to produce the chemicals necessary for life. This relatively simple experiment used water, methane, ammonia and elemental hydrogen, sealed in a series of sterile glass flasks, connected by tubes, forming a closed loop. One of the flasks was half filled with liquid water and another flask contained electrodes. The liquid water was heated to produce water vapor and a voltage was applied across the electrodes to produce sparks, simulating energy input to the system from lightning. A portion of the apparatus contained a reflux condenser that cooled the gaseous mixture, simulating the process of precipitation. The condensate was allowed to trickle back into the original flask in a continuous cycle. Within a short period of time, the liquid became a darkly colored solution. Analysis of samples indicated the presence of a variety of organic compounds including amino acids and simple sugars. For the chiral amino acids, racemic mixtures were obtained. In addition to these compounds, a number of polycyclic aromatic compounds related to bitumen were formed.

It was originally thought that the primitive earth had an atmosphere that contained mostly ammonia and methane. However, geological evidence suggests that this primitive atmosphere might have been modified due to volcanic eruptions, which could have released carbon dioxide, nitrogen, hydrogen sulfide and sulfur dioxide into the atmosphere. Experiments using these gases, along with the ones in the original Urey-Miller experiment have produced an even more diverse mixture of molecules. In order to generate aromatic amino acids under primitive earth conditions it is necessary to use less hydrogen-rich reaction mixtures. At this point in time, most of the natural amino acids, and components of nucleotides, such as purines, pyrimidines, and sugars have been made in variants of the Urey-Miller experiment. Known reactions between the components of these modified Urey-Miller experiments can produce reactive intermediates such as formaldehyde, carbon monoxide, hydrogen cyanide (Reactions 1-4).

Reaction 1	$CO_2 + CH_4 \rightarrow 2\ CH_2O$
Reaction 2	$CH_4 + H_2O \rightarrow CO + 3\ H_2$
Reaction 3	$CO + NH_3 \rightarrow HCN + H_2O$
Reaction 4	$CH_4 + NH_3 \rightarrow HCN + 3\ H_2$

The formaldehyde, ammonia, and HCN can then react to form amino acids such as glycine, Reactions 5 through 7, as well as self-condensation of formaldehyde to produce ribose, Reaction 8.

Reaction 5	$CH_2O + NH_3 \rightarrow CH_2NH + H_2O$
Reaction 6	$CH_2NH + HCN \rightarrow NH_2CH_2CN$
Reaction 7	$NH_2CH_2CN + 2\ H_2O \rightarrow NH_3 + NH_2CH_2CO_2H$
Reaction 8	$5\ CH_2O \rightarrow C_5H_{10}O_5$

These experiments showed that under the early earth's atmospheric conditions, a "primordial soup" could be produced that would be conducive to the formation of even more complex biomolecules and potentially lead to the formation of primitive life forms.

18. Which of the following components of earth's current atmosphere was purposely excluded from the original Urey-Miller experiment?
    A. N_2
    B. O_2
    C. Ar
    D. CO_2

19. Which of the following amino acids formed by the Urey-Miller experiment would NOT have been a racemic mixture?
    A. Glycine
    B. Aspartic acid
    C. Serine
    D. Alanine

20. In Reaction 5, formaldehyde reacts with ammonia to form what type of organic compound?
    A. An amide
    B. An imide
    C. An imine
    D. An amine

21. Which of the following would be the LEAST reasonable substitute for an electric spark in a modified Urey-Miller experiment?
    A. Ultraviolet radiation
    B. Infrared radiation
    C. Microwave radiation
    D. Radio waves

22. Which of the following are components of nucleic acids formed in the modified Urey-Miller experiments?
    I. Purine
    II. Pyrimidine
    III. Ribose
    IV. Phosphate

    A. I and II only
    B. I and III only
    C. I, II and III only
    D. I, II, III and IV

Passage 5 (Questions 23-27)

The most commonly used model for understanding the physics associated with the human voice is the source-filter model, which is also used to understand certain musical instruments such as the slide trombone. Air forced out of the lungs causes the vocal cords to oscillate at various frequencies. Muscles in the larynx can adjust the tension of the vocal cords, thereby producing a periodic source of pressure waves that are harmonic in nature. This source of vibrations is then subject to resonance filtration in the vocal tract, the size and shape of which determines the ultimate sound signature of a person's voice. Since a human is able to change the size and shape of the vocal track, a wide variety of complex sounds can be produced. Changing the shape of your mouth has a significant effect on the pitch of the loudest resonance frequency. For example, if a person sings a particular note with their mouth only partially open and then suddenly opens their mouth, by dropping their jaw, the pitch of the sound drops to a lower resonance, without having changed the tension of the vocal cords or the position of their tongue. Alternatively, if the position of the jaw is held constant and the tongue is moved either forwards or backwards within the mouth, the length of the vocal track can be systematically changed, producing lower and higher pitched sounds, respectively.

Almost all information produced by human speech is in the 200 Hz to 8 kHz range, which happens to be well within the range of human hearing (20 Hz to 20 kHz). The pitch of a person's voice is determined more by the resonance amplification of the harmonic overtones than of the fundamental. Hence, there are few people that can sing bass in the choir, because their vocal tracks are not large enough to act as a resonance chamber for the lowest frequency vibrations produced by the vocal cords. In fact, a closed tube resonator whose length is about the same as the size of the human vocal track, i.e. 17 cm, produce overtone frequencies that closely approximate the optimal sensitivity range of human hearing, as seen in Figure 1. Note that the speed of sound in air is 334 m/s.

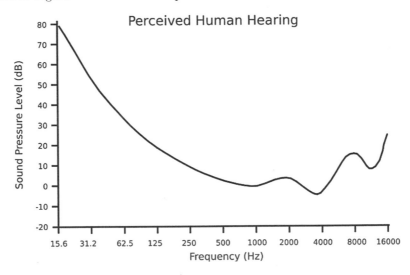

Figure 1 The minimum equal loudness plot for the range of human hearing

23. What is the wavelength of the highest pitched sound that the average person can hear?
    A. 21.8 m
    B. 17.0 m
    C. 0.021 m
    D. 0.017 m

24. What is the period of the fundamental vibration whose frequency is 500 Hz?
    A. 2×10^{-3} s
    B. 5×10^{-3} s
    C. 200 s
    D. 500 s

25. If the human vocal tract acts like a resonator closed at one end, which of the following frequencies represents a possible overtone?
    A. 500 Hz
    B. 1000 Hz
    C. 1500 Hz
    D. 2000 Hz

26. What happens to the length of the vocal tract, acting as the resonance filter, as a person moves their tongue towards the back of their mouth?
    A. The length of the vocal tract decreases, as the frequency of the sound increases.
    B. The length of the vocal tract decreases, as the frequency of the sound decreases.
    C. The length of the vocal tract increases, as the frequency of the sound increases.
    D. The length of the vocal tract increases, as the frequency of the sound decreases.

27. Which of the following frequencies have a minimum pressure for the perception of hearing that is 100 times greater than the pressure required at 3.8 kHz?
    I. 125 Hz
    II. 2.0 kHz
    III. 7.9 kHz

    A. I and II only
    B. II and III only
    C. I and III only
    D. I, II and III only

These questions are NOT based on a passage (Questions 28-31)

28. Which of the following potentially explains why acetone has a significantly higher boiling point and heat of vaporization than propane?

    I. Acetone has a molecular dipole.

    II. One of the tautomeric forms of acetone can form hydrogen bonds.

    III. Acetone can undergo self-aldol condensation.

    A. I only

    B. I and II only

    C. I and III only

    D. I, II, and III

29. Which of the following best describes sound and visible light?

    A. Sound is a longitudinal wave and light is a transverse wave.

    B. Sound is a transverse wave and light is a longitudinal wave.

    C. Sound and light are both transverse waves.

    D. Sound and light are both longitudinal waves.

30. Which of the following will NOT participate in hydrogen bonding when dissolved in aqueous solution?

    A. Ammonia

    B. Methanol

    C. Dimethyl ether

    D. Hydrogen

31. Which of the following best explains why we cannot see clear images under water with the naked eye?

    A. The refractive index of water is different from air.

    B. Water irritates the cornea.

    C. Water changes the index of refraction of the cornea.

    D. Water pressure changes the radius of curvature of the cornea.

THIS PAGE LEFT

INTENTIONALLY BLANK

Passage 6 (Questions 32-35)

The enthalpies of vaporization (ΔH_v) for some molecular compounds are given in Table 1. The magnitude of the enthalpy of vaporization is related to the strength of intermolecular forces holding molecules together in the liquid phase. In order to obtain the corresponding molecules in the gas phase, these intermolecular forces must be broken by adding energy, usually in the form of heat. However, in some cases, the intermolecular forces of attraction are strong enough to be retained in the gas phase to some extent, with hydrogen fluoride being a prime example. In order for a substance to boil, the vapor pressure of the liquid must equal the pressure of gas at the surface of the liquid. Cavitation within the liquid results in the formation of the bubbles characteristic of boiling. Normal boiling points are the temperature at which a liquid boils at one atmosphere of pressure. These boiling points can be elevated by dissolving a nonvolatile solute in the liquid to form a homogeneous solution. The boiling point change, ΔT, can be calculated using Equation 1, where m is the molality of the solution, n represents the number of moles of particles produced per mole of solute dissolved and K_b is a constant related to the strength of intermolecular forces, which can be calculated using Equation 2. The value of the gas constant is $8.14 \, J \, mol^{-1} \, K^{-1}$, T is the boiling point of the pure solvent, M is the molar mass (kg/mol) of the solvent and ΔH_v is the enthalpy of vaporization of the solvent.

Equation 1 $\qquad\qquad\qquad \Delta T = K_b \cdot n \, m$

Equation 2 $\qquad\qquad\qquad K_b = RT^2M/\Delta H_v$

Table 1 ΔH_v for various molecular compounds and elements.

Name	M (g/mole)	Normal Boiling Point (°C)	ΔH_v (kJ mol^{-1})	ΔH_v (kJ kg^{-1})
Methane	16	-163	8.2	480.6
Ammonia	17	-33	23.4	1371
Water	18	100	40.7	2260
Hydrogen Fluoride	20	20	-	-
Neon	20	-246	1.7	85
Methanol	32	65	35.3	1104
Ethanol	46	78	38.6	841
Phosphine	34	-88	14.6	429
Dimethyl ether	46	-24	19.3	420
Hydrogen	2	-252	0.46	452
Propane	44	-42	15.7	356
Propanone	58	57	31.3	539
Butane	58	-1	21.0	320

32. Based on the data presented in Table 1 which of the following values is most likely the enthalpy of vaporization of hydrogen fluoride?
    A. 20 kJ mol^{-1}
    B. 30 kJ mol^{-1}
    C. 40 kJ mol^{-1}
    D. 60 kJ mol^{-1}

33. At what temperature will boiling occur at sea level, if 5.8 g of sodium chloride are dissolved in 100 mL of water?
    A. 91 °C
    B. 101 °C
    C. 109 °C
    D. 118 °C

34. Which of the following compounds has the largest enthalpy of vaporization?
    A. Methanol
    B. Ethanol
    C. Ethylene glycol
    D. Glycerol

35. Which of the following compounds would have the LEAST effect on the boiling point of water, given solutions having equal molalities?
    A. Hydrofluoric acid
    B. Hydrochloric acid
    C. Hydrobromic acid
    D. Hydroiodic acid

Passage 7 (Questions 36-39)

The concept of bond energies can be very useful in predicting the enthalpy of various reactions that can not otherwise be determined experimentally. Bond energy is the heat required to break one mole of a particular type of chemical bond. Experimentally, this is done by determining the energy necessary to break all of the chemical bonds in one mole of a molecule in the gas phase into its component atoms. For example, the C-H bond energy can be determined by dividing the enthalpy of Reaction 1 for methane, by the number of C-H bonds in the molecule. The enthalpy of various other reactions can then be approximated by subtracting the sum of the bond energies of the products from the sum of the bond energies of the reactants. This information has provided chemists with considerable insight into the nature of chemical bonding. For example, selective comparisons of bond energies reveal subtle differences between purely covalent and polar covalent bonds with different bond orders.

Reaction 1 $\qquad CH_4 \text{ (g)} \rightarrow C \text{ (g)} + 4\,H \text{ (g)} \qquad \Delta H = +1652 \text{ kJ mol}^{-1}$

Table 1 Typical covalent bond energies

Single Bonds	ΔH (kJ mol^{-1})	Single Bonds	ΔH (kJ mol^{-1})	Double Bonds	ΔH (kJ mol^{-1})	Triple Bonds	ΔH (kJ mol^{-1})
H-H	432	C-C	347	C=C	614	C≡O	1072
H-C	413	N-N	160	N=N	418	C≡C	839
H-N	391	O-O	146	O=O	495	N≡N	941
H-O	467	C-N	305	C=O	745*	C≡N	891
H-F	565	C-O	358	C=N	615	P≡P	489

*Note that this is the bond energy for C=O in organic molecules such as formaldehyde and acetone. The C=O bond energy in carbon dioxide is 805 kJ mol^{-1}.

36. Which of the following represent the enthalpy for the complete combustion of one mole of methane gas?
    A. $+413$ kJ mol^{-1}
    B. $+1652$ kJ mol^{-1}
    C. -245 kJ mol^{-1}
    D. -880 kJ mol^{-1}

37. Which of the following is the most likely order of bond lengths?
    A. $C \equiv O > C = O > C\text{-}O$
    B. $C = O > C\text{-}O > C \equiv O$
    C. $C\text{-}O > C = O > C \equiv O$
    D. $C \equiv O > C\text{-}O > C = O$

38. Which of the following bonds would be expected to have the highest vibrational stretching frequency in the infrared spectrum?
    A. $C = C$
    B. $C\text{-}N$
    C. $C = O$
    D. $N\text{-}O$

39. Typically using bond energies to calculate heats of combustion (ΔH_c), underestimates the experimental values by 5-10%. Which of the following compounds would be expected to be an exception to this generalization?

    A. Methane, experimental $\Delta H_c = -880$ kJ mol^{-1}
    B. Methanol, experimental $\Delta H_c = -726$ kJ mol^{-1}
    C. Acetylene, experimental $\Delta H_c = -1300$ kJ mol^{-1}
    D. Benzene, experimental $\Delta H_c = -3270$ kJ mol^{-1}

These questions are NOT based on a passage (Questions 40-43)

40. Which of the following correctly describes the nature of polarized light waves?

   A. They are transverse waves in which the B field of one wave oscillates transverse to the B fields of other waves.
   B. They are light waves that have passed through a polarizing filter such that the velocity vector of each wave is unique.
   C. They are transverse waves in which the E fields of the waves oscillate along the same axis.
   D. They are light waves that have been passed through a polarizing filter to convert them from transverse into longitudinal waves.

41. In which of the following mediums does sound travel fastest?

   A. Air with no humidity
   B. Air at 90% humidity
   C. Water
   D. Steel

42. If a light wave A is in the visible spectrum and light wave B has a wavelength of 1500 nm. and $\frac{\text{Energy of B}}{\text{Energy of A}} = 1/3$, what color is light wave A?

Violet	380-450 nm
Blue	450-495 nm
Green	495-570 nm
Yellow	570-590 nm
Orange	590-620 nm
Red	620-750 nm

   A. Violet
   B. Orange
   C. Green
   D. Red

43. It is generally accepted that visible light has wavelengths between 400 and 800 nanometers. Which of the following wavelengths is most likely to be perceived as indigo?
   A. 420 nm
   B. 500 nm
   C. 750 nm
   D. 900 nm

THIS PAGE LEFT

INTENTIONALLY BLANK

Passage 8 (Questions 44-48)

Cardiologists often use stress tests to measure the ability of a patient's heart to deliver adequate volumes of blood during physical exertion. In some cases the stress is drug induced, rather than by way of actual exercise. The test compares coronary circulation while the patient is at rest to circulation during maximum exertion. Abnormal blood flows can indicate heart disease that might be caused by blockages in the coronary arteries and indicate the possibility of myocardial infarction. Perhaps the most common method for gauging the flow of blood to the heart is by way of nuclear imaging. This is done by injecting a sample of a radioisotope into the patient's blood, followed by imaging using a camera that is sensitive to the nuclear radiation produced.

The radioisotope of choice for imaging purposes has become technetium-99m, which is a gamma emitting meta-stable isotope having a short half-life of 6.01 hours. The product of the gamma emission is Tc-99, which is also radioactive, undergoing beta decay, with a half-life of 2.11×10^5 years. There are no stable isotopes of technetium, and all must be made in a nuclear reactor by transmutation. A Tc-99m generator that can easily be handled by appropriately trained medical technicians has been developed based on the decay of molybdenum-99, which has a half-life of 66 hours. Molybdenum-99 is produced by neutron activation of the stable isotope, molybdenum-98, which is the most abundant (24.14%) of the seven naturally occurring isotopes of molybdenum. The generator facilitates transport of the radiopharmaceutical from the source nuclear reactor, to the hospital or clinic where testing will occur. Reactions 1 and 2 summarize the nuclear processes that involve the meta-stable isotope of technetium.

Reaction 1 $^{99}\text{Mo} \rightarrow {}^{99m}\text{Tc} + \beta^-$

Reaction 2 $^{99m}\text{Tc} \rightarrow {}^{99}\text{Tc} + \gamma \ (140 \text{ keV})$

Technetium is in Group 7 of the periodic table and as such is a transition metal. It forms a stable pertechnitate ion, TcO_4^-, which has chemical properties similar to permanganate. In lower oxidation states, technetium ions form a variety of complexes with organic ligands that can be tailored to deliver the radioisotope to a particular organ of the body. This has led to breakthroughs in the treatment of parathyroid disorders and breast cancer.

44. Based on information presented in the passage, pertechnitate is expected to be a good:
    A. oxidizing agent.
    B. reducing agent.
    C. acid.
    D. base.

45. Molybdenum's naturally occurring stable isotopes have mass numbers between 92 and 100. If the atomic mass of molybdenum is 95.95 amu, which of the following must be true based on information presented in the passage?
    A. There must be more than one naturally occurring stable isotope of molybdenum with fewer than 54 neutrons.
    B. There must be more than one naturally occurring stable isotope of molybdenum with more than 56 neutrons.
    C. The most abundant naturally occurring isotope of molybdenum has 54 neutrons.
    D. All of the isotopes of molybdenum have 42 neutrons.

46. What is the product of the beta decay of Tc-99?
    A. Ru-99
    B. Ru-98
    C. Mo-99
    D. Mo-98

47. If it takes 24 hours for a technetium generator to be delivered from the nuclear reactor to a cardiologist's laboratory, by what percentage has the amount of Mo-99 gone down in the generator during the delivery time?
    A. < 1 %
    B. 22 %
    C. 78 %
    D. 94 %

48. Patients should be informed about the risks associated with any medical procedure. Which of the following pose a significant risk associated with radiopharmaceuticals?
    I. Internal exposure to radiopharmaceuticals can have a carcinogenic effect.
    II. Internal exposure to radiopharmaceuticals can have a mutagenic effect.
    III. Internal exposure to radiopharmaceuticals can have a teratogenic effect.

    A. I only
    B. II only
    C. I and II only
    D. I, II and III

Passage 9 (Questions 49-52)

Light is said to propagate through a medium in linear fashion. However, a change in medium or a curved lens will change the direction of light waves that pass through it. With medium changes, both refractive indices of the mediums are what determine the angles of directional changes. A positive lens will focus light rays on a spot behind the lens at a distance called the focal length. A negative lens will scatter an incoming light beam and have a negative focal length. The focal length is directly related to the radius of curvature of the lens. Figure 1 shows an example of a positive and negative lens.

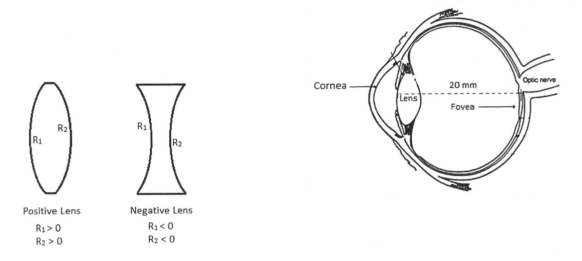

Figure 1 A positive and negative lens   **Figure 2** Diagram of human eye

All lenses actually have two radii of curvature at the front and back. The approximate equation relating focal length and radii of curvature is

Equation 1
$$\frac{1}{f} = (n-1)\left[\frac{1}{R_1} - \frac{1}{R_2}\right]$$

where f is the focal length, n is the refractive index of the lens material, and R_1 and R_2 are the front and back radii of curvature.

The human eye has a series of two convergent lenses whose overall effect is to focus images behind the lens to a point at the back of the eye called the fovea, about 20 mm from the eye lens. This is where all of the eye's rods and cones are concentrated. They are stimulated by the light coming through the eyes and send signals to the brain that are interpreted as our vision. The two lenses in the eye are the cornea and the eye lens, diagramed in Figure 2. The cornea has a fixed radius of curvature but the eye lens is under muscular control. When relaxed, the radius of curvature is at its largest. When focusing on nearby objects, the muscles around the lens contract and shorten the radius of curvature.

The relationship between a source of light, the focal length of a lens, and the distance to the image created by the lens is given by:

Equation 2
$$\frac{1}{o} + \frac{1}{i} = \frac{1}{f}$$

Where o is the distance from the object to the lens, and i is the distance from the lens to the image, or the distance at which the image will be clear. In humans, clear vision results when i is the distance from the lens to the fovea.

49. Given a lens with focal length 2 cm and a refractive index of 2, if $R_1 = 1$ cm, what is R_2?
    A. 2 cm
    B. 0.5 cm
    C. 1 cm
    D. -0.5 cm

50. Which of the following best describes why the radius of curvature must be shortened when looking at nearby objects?
    A. To maintain i at 20 mm when o decreases, f must increase.
    B. To maintain f at 20 mm when o decreases, i must increase.
    C. To maintain i at 20 mm when o decreases, f must also decrease.
    D. To maintain f at 20 mm when o decreases, i must also decrease.

51. Which of the following best explains why people have a hard time focusing on nearby objects with age?
    A. The shape of the eye lens flattens with age.
    B. The refractive index of the synovial fluid changes.
    C. The shape of the cornea flattens with age.
    D. Muscle weakness around the eye lens inhibits shortening the radius of curvature.

52. What will be the shape of a lens if $R_1 > 0$ and $R_2 < 0$?

    A.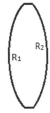

    C.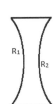

    B.

    D.

THIS PAGE LEFT

INTENTIONALLY BLANK

Passage 10 (Questions 53-56)

The hydrolysis of starch to sugars is catalyzed by β-amylase and is thought to be important in the ripening process of some fruits. The optimal pH for this enzyme was determined to be 4.5, at an enzyme to starch ratio of 200 U per gram of starch. The apparent rate constant, k (mol U^{-1}, min^{-1}), was determined by the method of initial rates at four different temperatures, ranging from 30° to 60°C. The least squares best-fit line of an Arrhenius plot, Figure 1 and Equation 1, was used to determine the activation energy (E_a) of the reaction. Once the reaction had reached equilibrium, the thermodynamic parameters for the reaction were determined from a van't Hoff plot, Figure 2 and Equation 2. The slope and intercept of the least squares fit of the data were used to determine the enthalpy (ΔH) and entropy (ΔS) changes for the reaction. The gas constant, R, is 8.314 J $mol^{-1}K^{-1}$.

Equation 1 $$\ln k = \ln A - (E_a/RT)$$
Equation 2 $$\ln K_{eq} = (\Delta S/R) - (\Delta H/RT)$$

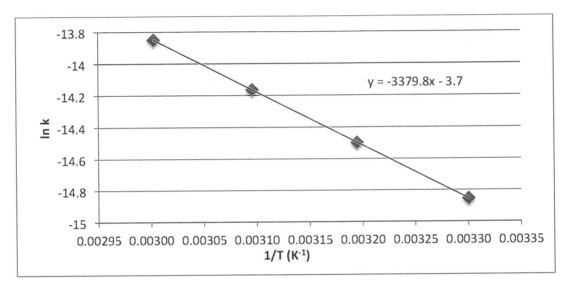

Figure 1 The Arrhenius plot of ln k versus 1/T for the hydrolysis of starch catalyzed by amylase.

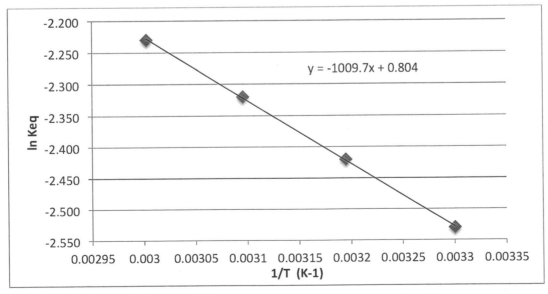

Figure 2 A van't Hoff plot of ln K_{eq} versus 1/T for the hydrolysis of starch catalyzed by amylase.

53. What is the value of the activation energy of the β-amylase catalyzed hydrolysis of starch described in the passage?
    A. 1.0 kJ/mol
    B. 3.4 kJ/mol
    C. 8.4 kJ/mol
    D. 28.1 kJ/mol

54. What are the values of the enthalpy and entropy changes for the β-amylase catalyzed hydrolysis of starch described in the passage?
    A. ΔH = -8.4 kJ/mol and ΔS = +6.7 J/mol K
    B. ΔH = +8.4 kJ/mol and ΔS = +6.7 J/mol K
    C. ΔH = +27.5 kJ/mol and ΔS = -30.1 J/mol K
    D. ΔH = -27.5 kJ/mol and ΔS = +30.1 J/mol K

55. Which of the following plots best describes the effect of substrate concentration on the rate of hydrolysis of starch by β-amylase?

A.

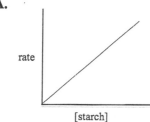

C.

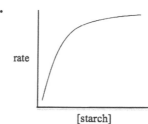

B.

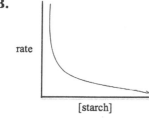

D.

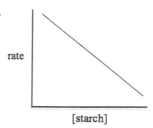

56. Which of the following accurately describes the hydrolysis of starch to sugars?
    I. The reaction is always spontaneous.
    II. The reaction is endothermic.
    III. The products are more disordered than the reactants.

    A. I only
    B. I and II only
    C. II and III only
    D. I, II and III

These questions are NOT related to a passage. (Questions 57-59)

57. Which of the following radioisotopes that are produced by nuclear fission would be most likely to cause thyroid cancer?
    A. I-131
    B. Pu-239
    C. U-235
    D. Sr-90

58. Which of the following convert mass into energy?
    I. Oxidation-Reduction reactions
    II. Combustion reactions
    III. Fusion reactions

    A. I only
    B. II only
    C. III only
    D. I and II only

59. Tritium is a man-made radioactive isotope of hydrogen that has a half-life of 12.32 years. Tritium is an essential component in modern thermonuclear weapons. It is estimated that there is about 4 grams of tritium per nuclear warhead in the U.S. arsenal of fusion-type nuclear weapons. As of 2001, the U.S. had about 9,600 thermonuclear warheads in its inventory. If the U.S. were to propose a method of arms control in which tritium is no longer manufactured worldwide, but existing stores could be recycled, approximately how long would it take before the U.S. had only one functional thermonuclear warhead?
    A. 12 years
    B. 36 years
    C. 163 years
    D. 246 years

TIMED
SECTION 2
Answers and Explanations

Timed Section 2 Answer Key

Passage 1
1. D
2. B
3. C
4. B

Passage 2
5. D
6. B
7. A
8. D

Passage 3
9. B
10. A
11. D
12. A
13. C

Discrete Set 1
14. C
15. A
16. C
17. B

Passage 4
18. B
19. A
20. C
21. D
22. C

Passage 5
23. D
24. A
25. C
26. A
27. C

Discrete Set 2
28. B
29. A
30. D
31. A

Passage 6
32. B
33. B
34. D
35. A

Passage 7
36. D
37. C
38. C
39. D

Discrete Set 3
40. C
41. D
42. C
43. A

Passage 8
44. A
45. A
46. A
47. B
48. D

Passage 9
49. A
50. C
51. D
52. B

Passage 10
53. D
54. B
55. C
56. C

Discrete Set 4
57. A
58. C
59. C

Passage 1 Explanation

A **power stroke** is a rapid change between two **structural states** of a protein that can be used to perform mechanical work. If the binding or unbinding of a small molecule or a chemical change in a bound molecule converts a protein between two structural states separated by a distance d, then the power stroke can do work against an **external load force** of magnitude F_L, provided that $F_L d \leq \Delta G$, where ΔG is the decrease in free energy between the chemical states. **Two mechanisms** by which a chemical change can lead to a structural one have been proposed.

Key terms: power stroke, structural states, external load force

Cause-and-Effect: power strokes are rapid changes between structural states of a protein that can perform work; the binding or unbinding of a small molecule or a chemical change converts a protein between two structural states; a power stroke can do work against an external load force if $F_L d \leq \Delta G$; two mechanisms by which a chemical change can cause this structural change have been proposed

Mechanism 1

A chemical change strictly precedes structural change in the protein. A change in **chemical bonds** associated with a change in the ligand produces a **strained conformation** that relaxes into a final structural change. Application of an external load force will have little effect on the **forward rate constant, k_{fr},** for this reaction.

Key terms: chemical bonds, strained conformation, forward rate constant

Cause-and-Effect: chemical changes precede structural changes in proteins; a change in chemical bonds associated with ligand changes produces a strained conformation that relaxes into a final structural change; external load forces have little effect on the forward reaction

Mechanism 2

A structural change in the protein precedes a chemical change. Because of **thermal forces**, a protein fluctuates from its initial to final state before being trapped by a resulting chemical change. An external load force will have a significant effect on the reaction's forward rate constant. The **load dependence, ε**, is defined as the ratio of the **forward rate constant at a given load force, k_{fr}*,** to k_{fr}, when no load is present. ε for mechanism 2 is related to an applied load force, F_L, according to Equation 1, where k_B is Boltzmann's constant, T the absolute temperature.

$$F_L = -\frac{k_B T}{d} \ln \varepsilon$$

Equation 1

Key terms: thermal forces, load dependence (ε) forward rate constant at a given load (k_{fr}*)

Cause-and-Effect: a structural change precedes a chemical one, wherein thermal forces cause protein fluctuations that lead to temporary structural changes; this fluctuation can cause a chemical change trapping the protein in its final state; load dependence is the ratio of the forward reaction rate constant with a load present to the forward reaction rate constant in the absence of load; equation 1 shows that load dependence decreases exponentially with applied load force.

The load dependence of rate constants for the power stroke of two molecular motor proteins was measured using **atomic force microscopy** at different applied load forces. Figure 1 shows the load dependence values of **KIF2a**, a member of the kinesin family of motor proteins that travel along **microtubule filaments**, and bacteriophage **T7 RNA polymerase (T7RNAP)**. T7RNAP is a single subunit enzyme that moves processively along DNA while performing its synthetic activity.

Key terms: atomic force microscopy, KIF2a, microtubule filaments, T7 RNA polymerase (T7RNAP)

Cause-and-Effect: load dependence was measured for KIF2a and T7RNAP for different applied load forces

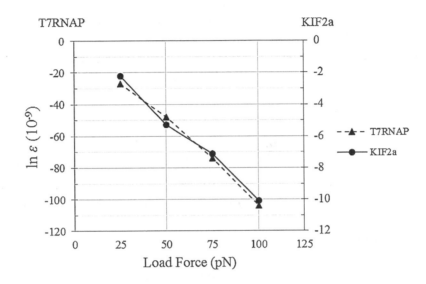

Figure 1. Load dependencies for KIF2a and T7RNAP are plotted as the natural logarithm of the load dependence versus load forces for different applied loads. For each applied load force, the magnitude of the load dependence of T7RNAP exceeds that of KIF2a

1. The load dependence measurements obtained by atomic force microscopy for the proteins tested most closely support:
    A. Mechanism 1, because a load force will minimally affect the chemical energy difference between the initial state and transition states of the protein.
    B. Mechanism 1, because a load force creates a large structural change and large increase in the energy of the protein transition state.
    C. Mechanism 2, because a load force will minimally affect the chemical energy difference between the initial state and transition states of the protein
    D. **Mechanism 2, because a load force creates a large structural change and large increase in the energy of the protein transition state.**

Choice **D** is correct. The load dependence measurements for the two proteins tested support Mechanism 2, as the load dependence (and thus the forward rate constant for the power stroke of each protein) decreased with increasing applied force (choices A and B are false). The forward reaction rate constant will decrease if the energy of the transition state, and thus the activation energy of the transition process, increases. This is consistent with choice D. While it is true that a load force is unlikely to change the chemical energy between the initial and transition states, Mechanism 2 describes a chemical change occurring due to a preceding structural change. The rate at which that structural change occurs should determine the rate of occurrence of the subsequence chemical change (choice D).

2. Based upon the results of the experiment performed, the magnitude of the change in the forward reaction rate of KIF2a is:
    A. greater than that of T7RNAP at equal external applied loads.
    B. <u>smaller than that of T7RNAP at equal external applied loads.</u>
    C. approximately equal to that of T7RNAP and non-zero at equal external applied loads.
    D. approximately equal to that of T7RNAP and near zero at equal external applied loads.

Choice **B** is correct. For a given transition, the load dependence, ε, should change proportionally to the forward reaction rate under a given external applied load, k_{fr}*. Figure 2 shows that that every load force along the x axis, the magnitude of ln ε, and accordingly ε, is less for KIF2a than T7RNAP (note the Y-axes).

3. Assuming that the displacement of an actin filament during muscle myosin's power stroke is approximately 5 nm per ATP hydrolyzed ($\Delta G \approx 5 \times 10^{-20}$ J/ATP molecule), what is the maximum external load force against which it can perform work?
    A. 0.1 pN
    B. 0.25 pN
    C. <u>10 pN</u>
    D. 25 pN

Choice **C** is correct. The passage states that power stroke can do work against an external load force of magnitude F_L, if $F_L d \leq \Delta G$. Using this equation, you find that the maximum external load force against which myosin can do work is $F_L = \Delta G / d = 5 \times 10^{-20} / 5 \times 10^{-9} = 10^{-11} = 10 \times 10^{-12} = 10$ pN (choice C).

A, B, D: All give the wrong maximum external load force. These answers are a result of miscalculation.

4. The kinetics of the binding reaction between myosin V and actin are depicted in the graph below, where M_u represents the concentration of unbound myosin V. Based upon this figure, what is the most likely rate law for this reaction, where k is the rate constant for the reaction and [actin] is the concentration of unbound actin?

    A. k[actin]
    B. <u>k[M_u]</u>
    C. k[M_u][actin]
    D. k[M_u]^2

Choice **B** is correct. The figure represents the change in concentration with time for a first order reaction. In such a reaction for some generic compound A, its change in concentration ln[A] should decrease linearly with time. This is consistent with the rate law of a reaction, which is first order only with respect to changes in concentration of unbound myosin, where rate = k[M_u] (choice B).

A, C, D: Choice A gives the rate expression for a reaction which is first order with respect to actin alone. Choices C and D give rate laws for second order reactions.

Passage 2 Explanation

Typically **saponification** results from the base hydrolysis of **triglycerides** (Figure 1), to form **glycerol** and the corresponding sodium salts of **fatty acids**. **Fats** that have a **high degree of saturation**, as in many animal fats, tend to form amorphous **solids** at room temperature, whereas fats that contain a high degree of **unsaturation,** as in vegetable oils, tend to be **liquids at room temperature**. The production of soap can easily be accomplished on the small scale by individuals, in which the fat is heated and mixed with an appropriate amount of aqueous lye, (NaOH) or potash (KOH). Soap makers often will quote a "saponification number", which represents the number of **milligrams of potassium hydroxide** required to completely **hydrolyze one gram of the fat** with a particular average molar mass.

Key Terms: Saponification, triglycerides, glycerol, fatty acids, fats, and molar mass

Cause and effect: The greater the number of carbon-carbon double bonds in a fatty acid, the greater the degree of unsaturation, which results in a lowering of the melting point of the fat by reducing the ability of the alkyl group to be flexible and wrap around other hydrophobic alkyl groups in neighboring triglyceride molecules.

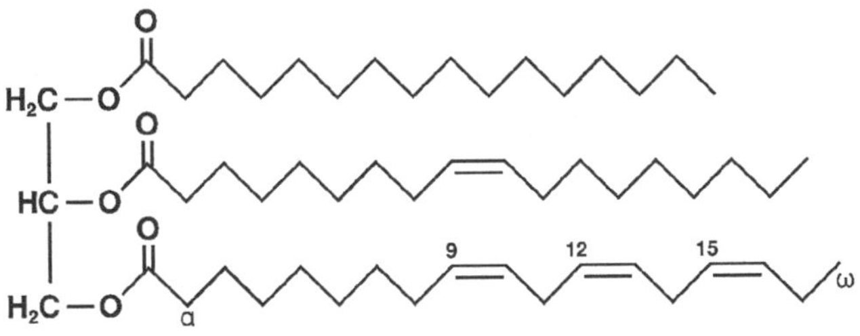

Figure 1 An example of a triglyceride in which one of the fatty acid esters is saturated, the second is unsaturated and the third is polyunsaturated. The chemical composition of a fat is typically not uniform and this is a hypothetical example, with a formula of $C_{55}H_{98}O_6$ (MW = 854 g mol⁻¹), and may not necessarily represent a naturally occurring fatty acid combination.

Figure 1 The structure of this hypothetical triglyceride, or fat, demonstrates three different types of fatty acids, with the greater number of carbon-carbon double bonds representing a higher degree of unsaturation. A key piece of information in the caption is the molecular weight.

After combining the fat with the aqueous base solution, the resulting **heterogeneous mixture** is stirred to form an **emulsion** in which the reaction takes place at the interface between the aqueous phase and the liquid fat. The rate of the reaction is dependent upon the temperature and the interface surface area. The reaction is **exothermic**, so once the mixture begins to thicken, the external heat source is removed and the reaction is allowed to continue until the mixture "traces" when stirred. At that point, a fragrance is often added. Subsequently for **bar soaps**, the warm thick mixture is poured into molds and allowed to finish reacting and to cool for several hours. Interestingly enough, solid bar soap is usually made with sodium hydroxide, whereas potassium hydroxide tends to be used to make soft or liquid soaps.

Key Terms: Heterogeneous, emulsion, and exothermic

Cause and effect: A potassium ion is larger than a sodium ion and this reduces the electrostatic interactions between the cation and the anionic carboxylate group, thereby lowering the melting point of the soap.

5. What is the "saponification number" for the fat shown in Figure 1?
    A. 46
    B. 66
    C. 140
    D. **197**

Choice **D** is correct. As stated in the passage, the "saponification number ... represents the number of milligrams of potassium hydroxide required to completely hydrolyze one gram of the fat with a particular average molecular mass." As stated in the caption for Figure 1, the molar mass of the fat depicted is 854 g/mol and the stoichiometry of the reaction is 3 moles of KOH for every one mole of fat. Therefore, the dimensional analysis is

$$1 \text{ g Fat} \times (1 \text{ mol}/854 \text{ g}) \times (3 \text{ KOH} / 1 \text{ Fat}) \times 56.1 \text{ g/mol} \times (10^3 \text{ mg}/ 1 \text{ g}) = 200$$

A, B, C: If you approximate 854 ~ 1000, then the number of mg of KOH needed per gram of fat is 3 x 56 ~ 168 mg, which is between choices C and D, but easily eliminates choices A and C. Remembering that the molar mass of the fat was approximated, the answer should be greater than 168, making choice D the correct answer.

You would get choice C if you used the molar mass of sodium hydroxide (40 g/mol) rather than the molar mass of potassium hydroxide. You would get choice B if you used a 1:1 molar ratio, rather than a 3:1 molar ratio.

6. How many chiral atoms are present in the structure of the fat shown in Figure 1?
    A. 0
    B. **1**
    C. 2
    D. 3

Choice **B** is correct. The only chiral carbon atom in the structure of the fat shown in Figure 1 is the central carbon of the glycerol. Choice B is the answer.

A, C, D: Only the central glycerol C is chiral.

7. If a soap maker wanted to make a hard bar soap, which of the following fatty acids would be most desirable to be the major component of the fat?
    A. **hexadecanoic acid**
    B. (9Z)-Octadec-9-enoic acid
    C. (9E)-Octadec-9-enoic acid
    D. (9Z,12Z,15Z)-9,12,15-Octadecatrienoic acid

Choice **A** is correct. As stated in the passage, fats containing saturated fatty acids tend to be higher melting and solids at room temperature, whereas fats containing unsaturated fatty acids tend to be lower melting and liquids at room temperature. These properties are related to the ability of the alkyl group to rotate around carbon-carbon bonds.

B, C, D: Choices B, C, and D all represent unsaturated fatty acids as denoted by the -enoic acid and can be eliminated. Hexadecanoic acid is a saturated fatty acid as denoted by the -anoic acid, and choice A is the correct answer.

8. In the base catalyzed hydrolysis of fat, what is the most likely first step in the mechanism of the reaction?
   A. Protonation of an oxygen lone-pair of a carbonyl group.
   B. Electrophilic attack of sodium ion on the oxygen lone-pair of a carbonyl group.
   C. Nucleophilic attack on a carbonyl carbon by water.
   D. <u>**Nucleophilic attack on a carbonyl carbon by hydroxide.**</u>

Choice **D** is correct. The concentration of hydrogen ions in the aqueous solution will be very low, since the solution is basic. Therefore, it is extremely unlikely that a carbonyl oxygen lone-pair would be protonated, as it might under acid catalyzed conditions.

A, B, C: Choice A can be eliminated. Sodium is an exceptionally poor electrophile and is unlikely to act as a Lewis acid. Choice B can be eliminated. While water could act as a nucleophile and attack a carbonyl carbon (choice C), water is not nearly as good a nucleophile as hydroxide. Choice D is the correct answer. This is the commonly accepted first step in the base-catalyzed hydrolysis of esters.

Passage 3 Explanation

Milk and various milk products have been used as food since antiquity. The major challenge was the preservation of milk in a form that retained its nutritional properties. The discovery of cheese is thought to have resulted from the use of stomachs of slaughtered animals as bladders for the transportation and storage of milk produced from domesticated cattle, goats and sheep. The bladders contained residual **protease enzymes that denatured** the milk **proteins**, forming **curds** and **whey.** Separation of the liquid and solid components, followed by addition of salt, provided a convenient way to safely store this food for use during periods of scarcity. The subsequent discovery of **bacteria** that were also capable of **acidifying** milk by way of **fermentation**, imparted unique flavors and has led to numerous dairy products that you enjoy today

Key terms: Protease enzymes, denatured, proteins, curds, whey, bacteria, acidifying, fermentation.

Cause-and-Effect: Domestication of certain animals provided the opportunity to take advantage of milk as a regular food source. The storage of milk in bladders made from the stomachs of large animals resulted in the formation of curds that were used to make cheese.

The **major nutrients** found in milk include: (1) **Fats**; (2) **Proteins**; (3) **Carbohydrates**; (4) **Vitamins**; and (5) **Minerals**. These components can be separated by taking advantage of differences in physical and chemical properties.

Key terms: Fats, proteins, carbohydrates, vitamins, minerals.

Cause-and-Effect: The physical and chemical properties of the various components of milk can be used as a basis for separations.

Milk is an **emulsion** of milk fats, suspended in an aqueous solution. If fresh milk is allowed to stand undisturbed, the **hydrophobic triglycerides** form a layer on top of the aqueous solution, separation of which produces cream and skim milk. The milk fat is comprised of a complex mixture of triglycerides, containing both **saturated and unsaturated fatty acids**. The major saturated fatty acid in cow's milk is palmitic acid (31%, $CH_3(CH_2)_{14}CO_2H$) and the major unsaturated fatty acid is oleic acid (24%, $CH_3(CH_2)_7CH=CH(CH_2)_7CO_2H$). **Homogenized** milk can be prepared by breaking up the fat globules, to form a **colloidal** suspension. Raw milk also contains various **microbes**, which are typically killed by heating the milk in a process known as pasteurization, in honor of the famous French scientist who first perfected this preservation method.

Key terms: Emulsion, hydrophobic, triglycerides, saturated, unsaturated, fatty acids, homogenized, colloidal, microbes.

Cause-and-Effect: Hydrophobic milk fats, or cream, will naturally separate from the aqueous solution that comprises the major portion of milk. Breaking up the fat globules can result in homogenized whole milk in which the cream remains evenly distributed throughout the aqueous solution.

Cottage cheese can be prepared by the careful addition of vinegar to milk, which **denatures** the protein casein, whose **isoelectric point** is 4.6. The curds can easily be separated from the majority of the whey by filtration. The **coagulation** of the protein traps some of the milk fat and aqueous soluble components, like lactose, within the curd. The mild flavor, high protein content and potential low fat content of cottage cheese make it a popular food for people with certain dietary restrictions. The resulting whey contains lactose and additional proteins, like lactalbumin, as well as minerals that remain soluble in the mildly acidic aqueous solution. **Neutralization** and heating the whey causes the denaturing of the remaining proteins, which can be filtered after cooling the solution. Whey proteins are popular with certain athletes as nutritional supplements. The lactose in the remaining aqueous solution can be separated from the minerals by evaporating the water to produce a **super-saturated** solution, from which lactose will crystalize.

Key terms: Denatures, isoelectric point, coagulation, neutralization, super-saturated.

Cause-and-Effect: Addition of acetic acid, or vinegar to lower the pH to the isoelectric point of casein, denatures the protein, which reduces its solubility in aqueous solution and causes the formation of the insoluble gelatinous curds.

Cause-and-Effect: The soluble protein components of the whey solution can also be separated from the aqueous soluble components by heat denaturation.

Cause-and-Effect: Lactose can be separated from the final aqueous solution by evaporating the water to produce a solution that is concentrated enough such that the lactose crystalizes and separates from the water and minerals.

9. Which of the following types of reactions would convert an unsaturated fatty acid into a saturated fatty acid?
   A. Acetylation
   B. **Hydrogenation**
   C. Elimination
   D. Substitution

Choice **B** is correct. The passage gives an example of both a saturated and an unsaturated fatty acid, palmitic acid and oleic acid, respectively. The unsaturated fatty acid contains a carbon-carbon double bond, whereas the saturated fatty acid only has carbon-carbon single bonds. Addition of hydrogen to the carbon-carbon double bond would convert the unsaturated fatty acid, into a saturated fatty acid, which often lowers the melting point, i.e. fats with saturated fatty acids are more likely to be solids at room temperature than unsaturated fatty acids. Hydrogenation is the addition of hydrogen to a carbon-carbon multiple bond. Choice B is the correct answer.

A, C, D: Acetylation would result in more C-C bonds, elimination would also cause additional C-C bonds, while substitution would not alter the saturation of the acid.

10. Which of the following hormones would most likely NOT significantly affect a lactating woman's production of milk?
    A. **Epinephrine**
    B. Progesterone
    C. Estrogen
    D. Oxytocin

Choice **A** is correct. You are looking for the hormone that does not affect milk production. Epinephrine, or adrenaline, is a fight or flight hormone released by the adrenal gland, which does not significantly affect milk production.

B, C: High levels of estrogen and progesterone inhibit the production of milk. Estrogen and progesterone levels drop after birth, helping stimulate the production of milk for the baby.
D: Oxytocin causes the contraction of smooth muscles in the uterus during labor and is essential for the release of milk from the alveoli through the nipple, to the baby.

11. What is the net charge of casein at a pH of 4.6?
    A. +4.6
    B. -4.6
    C. 2.5 x 10^{-5}
    D. 0

Choice **D** is correct. The isoelectric point is the pH at which a compound has no net charge. Since amino acids and proteins can act as Zwitterions, zero net charge comes from having the same amount of positively and negatively charged functional groups.

12. Which of the following enzymes is involved in the hydrolysis of peptide bonds?
    A. Pepsin
    B. Amylase
    C. Hexokinase
    D. Lactase

Choice **A** is correct. Pepsin is an enzyme released in the stomach that catabolizes proteins to smaller peptides and amino acids, which is the reaction of interest in this question.

B: Amylase is an enzyme that catalyzes the hydrolysis of starches to sugars and is produced by the salivary glands and pancreas.
C: Hexokinase is an enzyme that catalyzes the phosphorylation of sugars.
D: Lactase is an enzyme that catalyzes the hydrolysis of lactose to glucose and galactose.

13. Which of the following structures are disrupted when a protein is heated to the point that it becomes denatured?
    I.   Primary
    II. Secondary
    III. Tertiary
    IV. Quaternary

    A. I and II only
    B. III and IV only
    C. II, III, and IV only
    D. I, II, III and IV

Choice **C** is correct. Denaturing is when a protein (or nucleic acid) loses its quaternary, tertiary and secondary structures due to the breaking of non-covalent interactions, such as electrostatic interactions of oppositely charged groups, hydrogen bonding, dipole-dipole interactions and hydrophobic interactions of alkyl side chains. Denaturing can also break disulfide bonds between cysteine groups. Denaturing does not break peptide bonds to any significant extent, and therefore does not change the primary structure.

These questions are NOT related to a passage.

14. What is the primary intermolecular force that makes sucrose soluble in water?
    A. Van der Waals forces
    B. Dipole-dipole forces
    C. **Hydrogen bonding**
    D. Ion-dipole forces

Choice **C** is correct. Sucrose is a disaccharide comprised of the monosaccharides glucose and fructose. Like alcohols, sugars have hydroxyl groups that can hydrogen bond to water molecules.

A, B: While there will be van der Waals and dipole-dipole interactions, these intermolecular forces tend to be weaker than hydrogen bonding.
D: Sucrose is not ionic and does not have functionalities that will become significantly ionized in water.

15. A 5.0 kg object is completely submerged in water and experiences a buoyant force of 13 N. What is the approximate specific gravity of the object?
    A. **4**
    B. 5
    C. 13
    D. 50

Choice **A** is correct. The specific gravity of an object is the ratio of the density of that object to the density of water. The buoyant force is equal to the weight of water that was displaced by the object, and since the volume of water displaced is the same as the volume of the object, the specific gravity will be the ratio of the weight of the object to the buoyant force. The weight of the object is 5.0 kg x 10 m/s^2 = 50 N. The specific gravity will be (50 N)/(13 N) = 3.8 ~ 4. Choice A is the answer.

16. How many liters of carbon dioxide gas at 1 atm of pressure and 37°C can be produced by adding an excess of hydrochloric acid to 100 g of calcium carbonate? Note that R = 0.0821 L atm mol^{-1} K^{-1}.
    A. 100 L
    B. 50 L
    C. **25 L**
    D. 10 L

Choice **C** is correct. The formula for calcium carbonate is $CaCO_3$ and its formula weight is 40 + 12 + 3(16) = 100 g/mol. Therefore 100 g represents one mole. A rough approximation would be to use the volume of one mole of an ideal gas at STP, which would be 22.4 L. Since the temperature is above 0°C, the volume should be slightly larger, making choice C the correct answer. You could also plug the appropriate values into the ideal gas law and solve for the volume. The temperature must be in Kelvin and is 273 + 37 = 310 K.

$$V = nRT/P = (1\ mol)(0.0821\ L\ atm\ mol^{-1}K^{-1})(310\ K)/(1\ atm) = 25.4\ L$$

17. In the circuit below, a 12 ohm resistor is connected to a 12 volt battery. A second identical resistor is attached in parallel to the first.

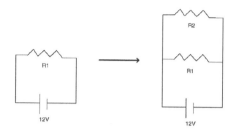

What happens to the current flowing through R_1?

    A. Current is reduced to ½ the original.
    B. <u>**Current remains unchanged.**</u>
    C. Current doubles.
    D. The change in current depends on the magnetic field which may vary.

Choice **B** is correct. Originally the current through R_1 is 1 amp:

$V = IR$
$12V = (I)(12\Omega)$
$1A = I$

When a second resistor is added in parallel, the total resistance of the circuit drops to 6 Ω:

$$1/R_{tot} = 1/R_1 + 1/R_2 = 1/12 + 1/12 = 2/12 = 1/6, \quad R_{tot} = 6 \ \Omega$$

Now, the total current is 2A:

$$V=IR \qquad\qquad 12V = (I)(6\Omega) \qquad\qquad 2A = I_{tot}$$

With 2 amps of current flowing through the circuit, half of it (1A) will flow through R_2 and half (1A) will flow through R_1, since they're equivalent resistors in parallel. Thus the current through R_1 remains unchanged.

Passage 4 Explanation

In 1952, Urey and Miller conducted an experiment to simulate the conditions thought to be present in early earth's atmosphere, trying to produce the chemicals necessary for life. This relatively simple experiment used water, methane, ammonia and elemental hydrogen, sealed in a series of **sterile** glass flasks, connected by tubes, forming a closed loop. One of the flasks was half filled with liquid water and another flask contained **electrodes**. The liquid water was heated to produce water vapor and a **voltage** was applied across the electrodes to produce sparks, simulating energy input to the system from lightning. A portion of the apparatus contained a **reflux condenser** that cooled the gaseous mixture, simulating the process of precipitation. The condensate was allowed to trickle back into the original flask in a continuous cycle. Within a short period of time, the liquid became a darkly colored solution. Analysis of samples indicated the presence of a variety of **organic compounds including amino acids** and simple **sugars**. For the **chiral** amino acids, racemic mixtures were obtained. In addition to these compounds, a number of **polycyclic aromatic compounds,** related to **bitumen** were formed.

Key terms: Sterile, electrodes, voltage, reflux condenser, organic compounds, amino acids, sugars, chiral, racemic, polycyclic aromatic compounds, and bitumen.

Cause-and-Effect: By combining simple compounds containing the elements necessary for life under mildly reducing conditions (elemental hydrogen, but definitely no elemental oxygen) and by providing energy in the form of a spark, biologically important molecules can be formed.

It was originally thought that the primitive earth had an atmosphere that contained mostly **ammonia** and **methane**. However, geological evidence suggests that this primitive atmosphere might have been modified due to volcanic eruptions, which could have released **carbon dioxide, nitrogen, hydrogen sulfide** and **sulfur dioxide** into the atmosphere. Experiments using these gases, along with the ones in the original Urey-Miller experiment have produced an even more diverse mixture of molecules. In order to generate **aromatic amino acids** under primitive earth conditions it is necessary to use less hydrogen-rich reaction mixtures. At this point in time, most of the natural amino acids, and components of nucleotides, such as purines, pyrimidines, and sugars have been made in variants of the Urey-Miller experiment. Known reactions between the components of these **modified Urey-Miller experiments can produce reactive intermediates** such as formaldehyde, carbon monoxide, hydrogen cyanide, (Reactions 1-4).

Key terms: Ammonia, methane, carbon dioxide, nitrogen, hydrogen sulfide, sulfur dioxide

Cause-and-Effect: Reactions between simple molecules present in the primordial atmosphere may have produced a variety of biologically important compounds by way of reactive intermediates such as carbon monoxide (CO), hydrogen cyanide (HCN) and formaldehyde (CH_2O).

Reaction 1	$CO_2 + CH_4 \rightarrow 2\ CH_2O$
Reaction 2	$CH_4 + H_2O \rightarrow CO + 3\ H_2$
Reaction 3	$CO + NH_3 \rightarrow HCN + H_2O$
Reaction 4	$CH_4 + NH_3 \rightarrow HCN + 3\ H_2$

Reaction 1. This reaction converts carbon dioxide and methane directly to formaldehyde by way of a comproportionation reaction in which carbon in its highest oxidation state (4^+ in CO_2) and its lowest oxidation state (4^- in CH_4) combine to produce carbon in an intermediate oxidation state (formally 0 in CH_2O). This reaction has been shown to occur separately, and is catalyzed by vanadium. This reaction could also proceed by way of the production of atomic oxygen from dissociation of the water in the electric discharge.

Reaction 2. This reaction is used in the chemical industry, with the resulting mixture known as "syngas." This is the primary source of elemental hydrogen used in the petrochemical industry.

Reaction 3 and 4 represent two methods for the production of hydrogen cyanide from ammonia. Reaction 3 uses carbon monoxide produced in Reaction 2, while Reaction 4 combines ammonia directly with methane. The formaldehyde, ammonia, and HCN then react to form amino acids (Reactions 5-7) as well as self-condensation of formaldehyde to produce ribose, Reaction 8.

The formaldehyde, ammonia, and HCN can then react to form amino acids such as **glycine**, Reactions 5 through 7, as well as self-condensation of formaldehyde to produce **ribose**, Reaction 8.

Key terms: Glycine and ribose.

Cause-and-Effect: Intermediate compounds containing reactive multiple bonds can combine to form amino acids and carbohydrates, which are important building blocks for more complex biological molecules, such as proteins and nucleic acids.

Reaction 5	$CH_2O + NH_3 \rightarrow CH_2NH + H_2O$
Reaction 6	$CH_2NH + HCN \rightarrow NH_2CH_2CN$
Reaction 7	$NH_2CH_2CN + 2 H_2O \rightarrow NH_3 + NH_2CH_2CO_2H$
Reaction 8	$5 CH_2O \rightarrow C_5H_{10}O_5$

Reactions 5-7. These three reactions combined are referred to as the Strecker synthesis of glycine.

Reaction 8. This reaction is known as the Formose reaction, and can be catalyzed by base and calcium ion. The proposed mechanism proceeds by formation of intermediates such as glycoaldehyde, glyceraldehyde, and dihydroxyacetone.

These experiments showed that under the early earth's atmospheric conditions, a "**primordial soup**" could be produced that would be conducive to the formation of even more complex **biomolecules** and potentially lead to the formation of primitive life forms.

Key terms: Primordial and biomolecules.

Cause-and-Effect: The production of a complex mixture of simple biological molecules can result in further combinations to produce the self-replicating molecules of life.

18. Which of the following components of earth's current atmosphere was purposely excluded from the original Urey-Miller experiment?
    A. N_2
    B. **O_2**
    C. Ar
    D. CO_2

Choice **B** is correct. Oxygen was purposefully excluded from the original Urey-Miller experiment for a couple of reasons. Oxygen was presumably not present in the atmosphere of early earth, since it is produced as a result of photosynthesis. Secondly, the introduction of oxygen to this mixture would have produced a potential explosion as soon as the spark was generated.

19. Which of the following amino acids formed by the Urey-Miller experiment would NOT have been a racemic mixture?
    A. **Glycine**
    B. Aspartic acid
    C. Serine
    D. Alanine

Choice **A** is correct. As stated in the passage, the chiral amino acids produced by the Urey-Miller experiment were racemic mixtures. However, glycine does not have a chiral carbon atom and therefore does not have optically active isomers.

B, C, D: Aspartic acid, serine and alanine all have chiral carbons that could potentially create a racemic mixture of enantiomers.

20. In Reaction 5, formaldehyde reacts with ammonia to form what type of organic compound?
    A. An amide
    B. An imide
    C. **An imine**
    D. An amine

Choice **C** is correct. The organic product of Reaction 5 is $CH_2=NH$, which is an imine.

A: An amide is an organic functional group in which the hydroxyl of an organic acid is replaced by a $-NR_2$ to give $R'CONR_2$.
B: An imide is where there are two amides attached to the same nitrogen, $(R'CO)_2NR$.
D: An amine is when an alkyl group is attached to a nitrogen, as in methyl amine, CH_3NH_2. There are primary $(R-NH_2)$, secondary (R_2NH) and tertiary (R_3N) amines.

21. Which of the following would be the LEAST reasonable substitute for an electric spark in a modified Urey-Miller experiment?
    A. Ultraviolet radiation
    B. Infrared radiation
    C. Microwave radiation
    D. **Radio waves**

Choice **D** is correct. All of the choices are different forms of electromagnetic radiation (EM). Radio waves are the lowest energy form of EM and not generally energetic enough to produce chemical reactions. Choice D is the correct answer.

A: Ultraviolet radiation was presumably a significant contributor to the possible sources of energy in the earth's early atmosphere, because there was not an ozone layer at that time.
B: Infrared radiation stimulates the vibrations of chemical bonds and is a form of heat, which could be used to promote chemical reactions.
C: Microwaves can also interact with aqueous solutions to produce heat and overcome the activation energies of chemical reactions.

22. Which of the following are components of nucleic acids formed in the modified Urey-Miller experiments?
    I. Purine
    II. Pyrimidine
    III. Ribose
    IV. Phosphate

    A. I and II only
    B. I and III only
    C. <u>I, II and III only</u>
    D. I, II, III and IV

Choice **C** is correct. As stated in the passage, purines, pyrimidines and sugars such as ribose were all produced by the modified Urey-Miller experiments and are components of nucleotide and nucleic acids. Phosphorus was not a component of these experiments (but is a component of nucleic acids) therefore it was not possible for phosphate (IV) to be formed.

Passage 5 Explanation

The most commonly used model for understanding the physics associated with the human voice, is the source-filter model, which is also used to understand certain musical instruments, such as the slide trombone. Air forced out of the lungs, causes the **vocal cords** to oscillate at various **frequencies**. Muscles in the **larynx can adjust the tension** of the vocal cords, thereby producing a **periodic** source of **pressure waves** that are **harmonic** in nature. This source of vibrations is then subject to **resonance** filtration in the vocal track, the size and shape of which determines the ultimate sound signature of a person's voice. Since a human is able to change the size and shape of the vocal track, a wide variety of complex sounds can be produced. Changing the shape of your mouth has a significant effect on the **pitch** of the loudest resonance frequency. For example, if a person sings a particular note with their mouth only partially open and then suddenly opens their mouth, by dropping their jaw, the pitch of the sound drops to a lower resonance, without having changed the tension of the vocal cords or the position of their tongue. Alternatively, if the position of the jaw is held constant and the tongue is moved either forwards or backwards within the mouth, the length of the vocal track can be systematically changed, producing lower and higher pitched sounds, respectively.

Key terms: vocal cords, frequencies, larynx, tension, periodic, pressure waves, harmonic, resonance, and pitch

Cause-and-Effect: Human vocal cords are capable of producing a variety of vibrations at various frequencies, which have overtones or harmonics in which the frequencies are multiples of the fundamental.

Almost all information produced by human speech is in the 200 Hz to 8 kHz range, which happens to be well within the range of human hearing (20 Hz to 20 kHz). The pitch of a person's voice is determined more by the resonance **amplification** of the harmonic **overtones**, than of the **fundamental**. Hence, there are few people that can sing bass in the choir, because their vocal tracks are not large enough to **act as a resonance chamber** for the lowest frequency vibrations produced by the vocal cords. In fact, a closed tube resonator whose length is about the same as the size of the human vocal track, i.e. 17 cm, produce overtone frequencies that closely approximate the optimal sensitivity range of human hearing, as seen in Figure 1. Note that the speed of sound in air is 334 m/s.

Key terms: amplification, overtones, fundamental, and resonance chamber

Cause-and-Effect: The human vocal tract has an adjustable size and shape such that certain overtones of the fundamental frequencies of the vocal cords can be amplified by resonance, producing the distinct qualities of a person's voice, such as pitch and timbre.

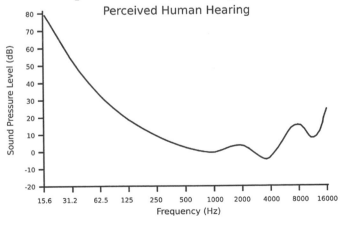

Figure 1 The minimum equal loudness plot for the range of human hearing.

Figure 1 This plot shows the sensitivity of the human ear to various frequencies. The ear is most sensitive to pressure waves having a frequency of 3.8 kHz. The sound pressure level at other frequencies is greater, with the minimum pressure required to be heard is measured in decibels, relative to the pressure required at the most sensitive frequency. The equation for decibels (dB) is based on a logarithmic scale

$$dB = 10 \log [I/I_o]$$

where I is the intensity and $I_o = 10^{-12}$ W/m².

23. What is the wavelength of the highest pitched sound that the average person can hear?
    A. 21.8 m
    B. 17.0 m
    C. 0.021 m
    D. 0.017 m

Choice **D** is correct. From the information provided in the passage, the highest frequency that an average person can hear is 20 kilohertz, or 20,000 s⁻¹. The equation relating frequency (f), wavelength (λ) and the speed (v) of sound is v = f λ, with the speed of sound in air being 334 m/s. Inserting these values into the equation in scientific notation gives

$$3.3 \times 10^2 = 2 \times 10^4 \, \lambda$$
$$(3.3/2) \times 10^{-2} = \lambda$$
$$1.15 \times 10^{-2} \, m = \lambda$$

24. What is the period of the fundamental vibration whose frequency is 500 Hz?
    A. 2 x 10⁻³ s
    B. 5 x 10⁻³ s
    C. 200 s
    D. 500 s

Choice **A** is correct. Period and frequency are inversely related. The frequency unit of hertz (Hz), is the same as a reciprocal second (s⁻¹), therefore, 1/500 = 1/5 x 10⁻² = 0.2 x 10⁻² = 2 x 10⁻³ s. Choice A is the answer.

25. If the human vocal tract acts like a resonator closed at one end, which of the following frequencies represents a possible overtone?
    A. 500 Hz
    B. 1000 Hz
    C. 1500 Hz
    D. 2000 Hz

Choice **C** is correct. For a closed tube resonator of length L, the wavelengths (λ) of harmonic vibrations corresponds to λ = (4/n) L, where n = 1, 3, 5, ... etc. or the odd harmonics. Therefore, the wavelength for the fundamental is when n = 1 and from information in the passage the length of the vocal track is 0.17 m, giving a wavelength of λ = 4(0.17) = 0.68 m. The frequency is equal to the speed of sound divided by the wavelength, f = v/λ = 334/0.68 ~ 3.3/6.8 x 10³ ~ 0.5 x 10³ ~ 500 Hz. Overtones can be the fundamental multiplied by any odd integer (so 1500 Hz, 2500 Hz, 3500 Hz, etc. would all be possible overtones).

A, B, D: Choice A is the fundamental and can be eliminated. If you multiply the frequency of the fundamental by the next possible overtone, n = 3, you get 1500 Hz. The even numbered n values are not observed for a closed tube resonator. Therefore choices B and D can be eliminated and choice C is the correct answer.

26. What happens to the length of the vocal tract, acting as the resonance filter, as a person moves their tongue towards the back of their mouth?
    A. **The length of the vocal tract decreases, as the frequency of the sound increases.**
    B. The length of the vocal tract decreases, as the frequency of the sound decreases.
    C. The length of the vocal tract increases, as the frequency of the sound increases.
    D. The length of the vocal tract increases, as the frequency of the sound decreases.

Choice **A** is correct. As stated in the passage, if "...the tongue is moved either forwards or backwards within the mouth, the length of the vocal track can be systematically changed, producing lower and higher pitched sounds, respectively." The latter corresponds to the situation in the question, producing a higher pitched sound, which also corresponds to a higher frequency.

B, C: Wavelength and frequency are inversely related so they could not both increase or both decrease.
D: To increase the length of the vocal tract, the tongue would need to be moved towards the front of the mouth.

27. Which of the following frequencies have a minimum pressure for the perception of hearing that is 100 times greater than the pressure required at 3.8 kHz?
    I. 125 Hz
    II. 2.0 kHz
    III. 7.9 kHz

    A. I and II only
    B. II and III only
    C. **I and III only**
    D. I, II and III only

Choice **C** is correct. The y-axis of Figure 1 is on the decibel scale (dB), where dB = 10 log (I/I_o). In this question I/I_o = 100, with dB = 10 log 10^2 = 20.

A, B, D: You are looking for frequencies that have dB values of approximately 20, corresponding to answer options I and III. It is estimated that the dB level for 2.0 kHz, answer option II, is 10 dB. Choices A, B, and D can be eliminated, and choice C is the correct answer.

These questions are NOT based on a passage

28. Which of the following potentially explains why acetone has a significantly higher boiling point and heat of vaporization than propane?
    I.   Acetone has a molecular dipole.
    II. One of the tautomeric forms of acetone can form hydrogen bonds.
    III. Acetone can undergo self-aldol condensation.

  A. I only
  B. **I and II only**
  C. I and III only
  D. 1, II, and III

Choice **B** is correct. Acetone, also known as propanone, has a carbonyl functional group and a trigonal planar structure that results in a molecular dipole, resulting in dipole-dipole intermolecular forces that are stronger than the London dispersion forces present in propane. Therefore, it does explain why acetone has a higher boiling point and ΔH_v than propane. Acetone is able to undergo a keto-enol tautomerization equilibrium, to a small extent. The enol form would be able to form hydrogen-bonding interactions and potentially helps to explain why acetone's boiling point and ΔH_v are higher than propane.

III is incorrect, because while acetone can undergo self aldol condensation,

$$2\ CH_3COCH_3 \rightarrow (CH_3)_2C{=}CH(CO)CH_3 + H_2O$$

This chemical reaction is not an intermolecular force that can be used to explain relative boiling points. III can be eliminated.

29. Which of the following best describes sound and visible light?
  A. **Sound is a longitudinal wave and light is a transverse wave.**
  B. Sound is a transverse wave and light is a longitudinal wave.
  C. Sound and light are both transverse waves.
  D. Sound and light are both longitudinal waves.

Choice **A** is correct. Sound result from vibrations that cause the compression and rarefaction of air, and is best described as a longitudinal wave. Light is a form of electromagnetic radiation that has wave properties best modeled by a transverse wave.

30. Which of the following will NOT participate in hydrogen bonding when dissolved in aqueous solution?
  A. Ammonia
  B. Methanol
  C. Dimethyl ether
  D. **Hydrogen**

Choice **D** is correct. To form hydrogen-bonding interactions a compound must have a hydrogen atom covalently bonded to one of three atoms (nitrogen, oxygen or fluorine) and there must be lone pairs of electrons that will act as the hydrogen bond acceptors. H_2, when dissolved in aqueous solution cannot therefore participate in hydrogen bonding with water molecules.

A, B: Ammonia and methanol can both be hydrogen bond donors and acceptors when dissolved in water.
C: While dimethyl ether can not be a hydrogen bond donor, because it does not have a hydrogen atom directly bonded to an oxygen atom, it does have lone pairs on the oxygen atom, which can act as hydrogen bond acceptors from the water molecules.

31. Which of the following best explains why you cannot see clear images under water with the naked eye?

    A. **The refractive index of water is different from air.**
    B. Water irritates the cornea.
    C. Water changes the index of refraction of the cornea.
    D. Water pressure changes the radius of curvature of the cornea.

Choice **A** is correct. The refractive index of a medium determines the angles of refraction when light travels from one medium to another. Therefore, the refractive index of water being different from that of air causes light to enter the eye at different angles and will prevent the eye from properly focusing the image on the retina.

Passage 6 Explanation

The **enthalpies of vaporization** (ΔH_v) for some **molecular compounds** are given in Table 1. The magnitude of the enthalpy of vaporization is related to the strength **of intermolecular forces** holding molecules together in the liquid phase. In order to obtain the corresponding molecules in the gas phase, these intermolecular forces must be broken by adding energy, usually in the form of heat. However, in some cases, the intermolecular forces of attraction are strong enough to be retained in the gas phase to some extent, with hydrogen fluoride being a prime example. In order for a substance to **boil**, the vapor pressure of the liquid must equal the pressure of gas at the surface of the liquid. **Cavitation** within the liquid results in the formation of the bubbles characteristic of boiling. Normal boiling points are the temperature at which a liquid boils at one atmosphere of pressure. These boiling points can be elevated, by dissolving a **nonvolatile solute** in the liquid, to form a **homogeneous solution**. The boiling point change, ΔT, can be calculated using Equation 1, where m is the molality of the solution, n represents the number of moles of particles produced per mole of solute dissolved and K_b is a constant related to the strength of intermolecular forces, which can be calculated using Equation 2. The value of the gas constant is $8.14 \, \text{J mol}^{-1} \, \text{K}^{-1}$, T is the boiling point of the pure solvent, M is the molar mass (kg/mol) of the solvent and ΔH_v is the enthalpy of vaporization of the solvent.

Key terms: Enthalpies of vaporization, molecular compounds, intermolecular forces, boil, vapor pressure, cavitation, nonvolatile solute, homogeneous solution, molality, solvent.

Cause-and-Effect: The nature of the intermolecular forces present in a particular molecular structure have a significant effect on the physical properties of that compound and can be observed in properties such at the normal boiling points and enthalpies of vaporization.

Cause-and-Effect: Dissolving a nonvolatile solute in a liquid cause the boiling to rise due to colligative properties.

Equation 1 $\qquad\qquad\qquad\qquad \Delta T = K_b \cdot n \, m$

Equation 2 $\qquad\qquad\qquad\qquad K_b = RT^2 M / \Delta H_v$

Equations 1 and 2. These equations can be used to calculate the boiling point change that results from dissolving a nonvolatile solute in a liquid solvent. The molality (m) is the moles of solute per kilogram of solvent and n is the number of particles per mole of solute dissolved, i.e. an ionic solid such as NaCl has a value of 2, since for every mole of NaCl dissolved there are two ions produced. The constant, K_b, depends upon the normal boiling point (T) of the solvent in Kelvin as well as the molar mass of the solvent in kilograms per mole and the enthalpy of vaporization in joules per mole.

Table 1 ΔH_v for various molecular compounds and elements.

Name	M (g/mole)	Normal Boiling Point (°C)	ΔH_v (kJ mol^{-1})	ΔH_v (kJ kg^{-1})
Methane	16	-163	8.2	480.6
Ammonia	17	-33	23.4	1371
Water	18	100	40.7	2260
Hydrogen Fluoride	20	20	-	-
Neon	20	-246	1.7	85
Methanol	32	65	35.3	1104
Ethanol	46	78	38.6	841
Phosphine	34	-88	14.6	429
Dimethyl ether	46	-24	19.3	420
Hydrogen	2	-252	0.46	452
Propane	44	-42	15.7	356
Propanone	58	57	31.3	539
Butane	58	-1	21.0	320

Table 1. This table presents data such as normal boiling points and enthalpy of vaporization as related to the magnitude of intermolecular forces for representative compounds and elements having hydrogen bonding, dipole-dipole forces and London dispersion forces.

32. Based on the data presented in Table 1 which of the following values is most likely the enthalpy of vaporization of hydrogen fluoride?
    A. 20 kJ mol^{-1}
    B. **30 kJ mol^{-1}**
    C. 40 kJ mol^{-1}
    D. 60 kJ mol^{-1}

Choice **B** is correct. It should be noted that there is a good correlation between the boiling points and enthalpies of vaporization for the compounds in Table 1. It should also be noted that the boiling point of hydrogen fluoride (20°) is somewhere between ammonia (-33°) and water (100°C). Therefore you would expect the enthalpy of vaporization of hydrogen fluoride to be somewhere between ammonia (23.4 kJ/mol) and water (40.7 kJ/mol).

33. At what temperature will boiling occur at sea level, if 5.8 g of sodium chloride are dissolved in 100 mL of water?
    A. 91 °C
    B. **101 °C**
    C. 109 °C
    D. 118 °C

Choice **B** is correct. You first need to calculate the K_b for water using equation 2, where R = 8.14 J mol^{-1} K^{-1}, T = 373 K, M = 0.018 kg mol^{-1} and ΔH_v = 40.7 kJ mol^{-1} = 40700 J mol^{-1}. If you use the ΔH_v = 2260 kJ kg^{-1}, the units will not cancel properly.

$$K_b = (8.14 \text{ J mol}^{-1} \text{ K}^{+})(373 \text{ K})(373 \text{ K})(0.018 \text{ kg mol}^{+})/(40700 \text{ J mol}^{+}) = 0.50 \text{ K kg mol}^{-1}$$

Then you calculate the molality of the solution, or the moles of solute per kilograms of solvent. The density of water is essentially 1 g/mL, so 100 mL = 0.10 kg.

$$\text{moles} = (5.8 \text{ g})/(58 \text{ g mol}^{-1}) = 0.10 \text{ mol}$$
$$m = (0.10 \text{ mol})/(0.10 \text{ kg}) = 1 \text{ mol kg}^{-1}$$

The using Equation 1, you can calculate the ΔT. For NaCl there are two ions per formula unit, n = 2.

$$\Delta T = (0.50 \text{ K kg mol}^{-1})(2)(1 \text{ mol kg}^{-1}) = 1 \text{ K}$$

Since the normal boiling point for water is 100°C, the correct answer is choice B.

34. Which of the following compounds has the largest enthalpy of vaporization?
    A. Methanol
    B. Ethanol
    C. Ethylene glycol
    D. **Glycerol**

Choice **D** is correct. Each of the answer options is capable of forming hydrogen bonds. From Table 1 you can see that the enthalpy of ethanol is greater than methanol, presumably due to an increase in molecular weight and greater London dispersion forces. Ethylene glycol, also known as 1,2-ethanediol, has two hydroxyl groups, increasing the extent of hydrogen bonding interactions per molecule, which would increase both the boiling point and enthalpy of vaporization as compared with ethanol. Finally, glycerol, or 1,2,3-propanetriol, has three hydroxyl groups and even stronger hydrogen bonding interactions than ethylene glycol.

35. Which of the following compounds would have the LEAST effect on the boiling point of water, given solutions having equal molalities?
    A. **Hydrofluoric acid**
    B. Hydrochloric acid
    C. Hydrobromic acid
    D. Hydroiodic acid

Choice **A** is correct. The boiling point of a solution depends upon the number of particles of solute present in solution. Hydrochloric acid, hydrobromic acid and hydroiodic acid are all strong acids that completely dissociate in aqueous solution, producing two moles of ions per mole of solute dissolved. Hydrofluoric acid is a weak acid that does not completely dissociate and would not produce as many particles in solution as a strong acid.

Passage 7 Explanation

The concept of **bond energies** can be very useful in predicting the **enthalpy** of various reactions that can not otherwise be determined experimentally. Bond energy is the heat required to break one mole of a particular type of **chemical bond**. Experimentally, this is done by determining the energy necessary to break all of the chemical bonds, in one **mole** of a molecule in the gas phase, into its component atoms. For example, the C-H bond energy can be determined by dividing the enthalpy of Reaction 1 for **methane**, by the number of C-H bonds in the **molecule**. The enthalpy of various other reactions can then be approximated by **subtracting the sum of the bond energies of the products from the sum of the bond energies of the reactants**. This information has provided chemists with considerable insight into the nature of chemical bonding. For example, selective comparisons of bond energies reveal subtle differences between purely covalent and polar covalent bonds with different bond orders.

Key Terms: Bond energy, enthalpy, heat, chemical bond, mole, methane, and molecule

Cause and effect: Chemical reactions involve breaking bonds in the reactants and making new bonds in the products, as a result bond energies can be used to predict the enthalpy of many reactions with relatively good accuracy.

Reaction 1 $CH_4 (g) \rightarrow C (g) + 4 H (g)$ $\Delta H = +1652$ kJ mol^{-1}

Reaction 1 This endothermic reaction produces energetically unstable isolated carbon and hydrogen atoms. Since there are four C-H bonds in methane, the enthalpy for this reaction is four times greater than the C-H bond energy in Table 1.

Single Bonds	ΔH (kJ mol^{-1})	Single Bonds	ΔH (kJ mol^{-1})	Double Bonds	ΔH (kJ mol^{-1})	Triple Bonds	ΔH (kJ mol^{-1})
H-H	432	C-C	347	C=C	614	C≡O	1072
H-C	413	N-N	160	N=N	418	C≡C	839
H-N	391	O-O	146	O=O	495	N≡N	941
H-O	467	C-N	305	C=O	745*	C≡N	891
H-F	565	C-O	358	C=N	615	P≡P	489

Table 1 Typical covalent bond energies

*Note that this is the bond energy for C=O in organic molecules such as formaldehyde and acetone. The C=O bond energy in carbon dioxide is 805 kJ mol^{-1}.

Table 1 This table provides bond energies for most of the common types of bonds found in organic molecules. One needs to be careful when using and interpreting these values, since they do not account for things like resonance stabilization. In addition the C=O bond energy given in the table is typical for aldehydes and ketones, which is lower than that seen in carbon dioxide, as stated in the footnote.

36. Which of the following represent the enthalpy for the complete combustion of one mole of methane gas?
    A. +413 kJ mol^{-1}
    B. +1652 kJ mol^{-1}
    C. -245 kJ mol^{-1}
    D. **-880 kJ mol^{-1}**

Choice **D** is correct. Combustion reactions are exothermic, with negative enthalpies. Choice A and B can be eliminated.

The balanced complete combustion reaction for methane is

$$CH_4 \text{ (g)} + 2 \, O_2 \text{ (g)} \rightarrow CO_2 \text{ (g)} + 2 \, H_2O$$

Drawing the Lewis dot structures for the reactants and products indicates that CH_4 has four C-H bonds, O_2 has a O=O bond, CO_2 has two C=O bonds, and water has two O-H bonds. It is important to read the footnote for the C=O bond energy in Table 1. The C=O bond energy of 745 kJ mol^{-1} is for organic compounds. The C=O bond energy in carbon dioxide, of 805 kJ mol^{-1}, is higher. Using the bond energies from Table 1, the calculated heat of combustion is

$$[4(C\text{-}H) + 2 \, (O=O)] - [2(C=O) + 4(O\text{-}H)] =$$
$$[4(413) + 2 \, (495)] - [2(805) + 4(467)] = -836 \text{ kJ mol}^{-1}$$

37. Which of the following is the most likely order of bond lengths?
    A. C≡O > C=O > C-O
    B. C=O > C-O > C≡O
    C. **C-O > C=O > C≡O**
    D. C≡O > C-O > C=O

Choice **C** is correct. Bond lengths are generally inversely related to bond energies and bond order. The longest carbon-oxygen bond should be the single bond, followed by the double bond and the shortest should be the triple bond, which is consistent with the bond energies in Table 1.

38. Which of the following bonds would be expected to have the highest vibrational stretching frequency in the infrared spectrum?
    A. C=C
    B. C-N
    C. **C=O**
    D. N-O

Choice **C** is correct. The higher the bond-order, the stronger the bond and the higher the vibrational stretching frequencies in the IR spectrum and therefore, double bonds should have higher stretching frequencies than single bonds. Choice B and D can be eliminated.

The stronger the bond the higher the vibrational stretching frequency, therefore examining the bond energies of the remaining answer options indicates that the C=O bond has a higher bond energy (745 kJ mol^{-1}) than the C=C bond energy (614 kJ mol^{-1}). The experimentally observed range of C=O vibrational frequencies of aldehydes and ketones in the IR spectrum are 1740 - 1710 cm^{-1}, whereas the C=C range in alkenes is 1680 - 1620 cm^{-1}.

39. Typically using bond energies to calculate heats of combustion (ΔH_c), underestimates the experimental values by 5-10%. Which of the following compounds would be expected to be an exception to this generalization?

    A. Methane, experimental ΔH_c = -880 kJ mol^{-1}
    B. Methanol, experimental ΔH_c = -726 kJ mol^{-1}
    C. Acetylene, experimental ΔH_c = -1300 kJ mol^{-1}
    D. <u>**Benzene, experimental ΔH_c = -3270 kJ mol^{-1}**</u>

Choice **D** is correct. The easiest way to answer this question is to recognize that benzene is the only molecule of the answer choices that should have a resonance stabilization, which should decrease the heat of combustion as compared to the prediction based on the bond energies of six C-H, three C-C and three C=C bonds. Choice D is the correct answer.

A, B, C: Draw the Lewis dot structures for all of the reactants and products to determine the number of bonds of each type. It is important to read the footnote for the C=O bond energy in Table 1. The C=O bond energy of 745 kJ mol^{-1} is for organic compounds. The C=O bond energy in carbon dioxide, of 805 kJ mol^{-1}, should be used in these calculations.

The balanced combustion reactions for one mole of the fuel and the calculated heats of combustion are

$$CH_4 \text{ (g)} + 2\ O_2 \text{ (g)} \rightarrow CO_2 \text{ (g)} + 2\ H_2O$$

$$[4(\text{C-H}) + 2\ (\text{O=O})] - [2(\text{C=O}) + 4(\text{O-H})] =$$
$$[4(413) + 2\ (495)] - [2(805) + 4(467)] = -836 \text{ kJ mol}^{-1}$$

$$CH_3OH \text{ (g)} + 1.5\ O_2 \text{ (g)} \rightarrow CO_2 \text{ (g)} + 2\ H_2O \text{ (g)}$$

$$[3(\text{C-H}) + (\text{C-O}) + (\text{O-H}) + 1.5(\text{O=O})] - [2(\text{C=O}) + 4(\text{O-H})] =$$
$$[3(413) + (358) + (467) + 1.5(495)] - [2(805) + 4(467)] = -671.5 \text{ kJ mol}^{-1}$$

$$C_2H_2 \text{ (g)} + 2.5\ O_2 \rightarrow 2\ CO_2 \text{ (g)} + H_2O \text{ (g)}$$

$$[2(\text{C-H}) + (\text{C}\equiv\text{C}) + 2.5(\text{O=O})] - [4(\text{C=O}) + 2(\text{O-H})] =$$
$$[2(413) + (839) + 2.5(495)] - [4(805) + 2(467)] = -1221.5 \text{ kJ mol}^{-1}$$

$$C_6H_6 \text{ (g)} + 7.5\ O_2 \rightarrow 6\ CO_2 \text{ (g)} + 3\ H_2O \text{ (g)}$$

$$[6(\text{C-H}) + 3(\text{C-C}) + 3(\text{C=C}) + 7.5(\text{O=O})] - [12(\text{C=O}) + 6(\text{O-H})] =$$
$$[6(413) + 3(347) + 3(614) + 7.5(495)] - [12(805) + 6(467)] = -3388.5 \text{ kJ mol}^{-1}$$

The calculation for benzene is the only value of the answer options that is more exothermic than the experimental value. Again choice D is the correct answer due to the resonance stabilization of the aromatic π system.

These questions are NOT based on a passage.

40. Which of the following correctly describes the nature of polarized light waves?
    A. They are transverse waves in which the B field of one wave oscillates transverse to the B fields of other waves.
    B. They are light waves that have passed through a polarizing filter such that the velocity vector of each wave is unique.
    C. <u>**They are transverse waves in which the E fields of the waves oscillate along the same axis.**</u>
    D. They are light waves that have been passed through a polarizing filter to convert them from transverse into longitudinal waves.

Choice **C** is correct. Light waves are transverse waves with E and B fields oscillating at right angles to each other. A polarizing filter only lets light through if the E field of the wave aligns with the openings in the filter. A, B, and D all fail to mention this effect on E fields.

41. In which of the following mediums does sound travel fastest?
    A. Air with no humidity
    B. Air at 90% humidity
    C. Water
    D. **Steel**

Choice **D** is correct. Since sound is a mechanical wave that relies on collision of adjacent molecules in the medium through which it travels, the closer together the molecules are the faster the waves travel. Thus choice D is correct because the molecules in any solid are closer together than in a liquid or gas.

42. If a light wave A is in the visible spectrum, light wave B has a wavelength of 1500 nm and (Energy of B)/(Energy of A) = 1/3, what color is light wave A?

Violet	380-450 nm
Blue	450-495 nm
Green	495-570 nm
Yellow	570-590 nm
Orange	590-620 nm
Red	620-750 nm

    A. Violet
    B. Orange
    C. **Green**
    D. Red

Choice **C** is correct. This question asks us to evaluate the relationship between wavelengths of light waves given the relationship between their energies. Since energy and wavelength are inversely related by $E = hf/\lambda$ where λ is wavelength. So that means that (Wavelength of B)/(Wavelength of A) = 3, so wavelength of A must be 500 nm. This means that it is green light so choice C is correct.

43. It is generally accepted that visible light has wavelengths between 400 and 800 nanometers. Which of the following wavelengths is most likely to be perceived as indigo?
    A. **420 nm**
    B. 500 nm
    C. 750 nm
    D. 900 nm

Choice **A** is correct. The colors of the visible spectrum are red, orange, yellow, green blue, indigo and violet (ROYGBIV), with shorter wavelengths corresponding to higher frequencies and energies. Violet light is the highest energy visible light and would correspond to a wavelength of 400 nm, with indigo being at a slightly longer wavelength.

Passage 8 Explanation

Cardiologists often use stress tests to **measure the ability** of a patient's heart to **deliver** adequate **volumes** of blood during physical exertion. In some cases the stress is drug induced, rather than by way of actual exercise. The test compares coronary circulation while the patient is at rest, to circulation during maximum exertion. Abnormal blood flows can indicate heart disease that might be caused by blockages in the **coronary arteries**, and indicate the possibility of **myocardial infarction**. Perhaps the most common method for gauging the flow of blood to the heart is by way of nuclear imaging. This is done by injecting a sample of a **radioisotope** into the patient's blood, followed by imaging using a camera that is sensitive to the **nuclear radiation** produced.

Key terms: Cardiologists, coronary arteries, myocardial infarction, radioisotope, nuclear radiation.

Cause-and-Effect: Blockage of coronary arteries can lead to myocardial infarction (heart attacks), therefore cardiologist use stress tests involving radioisotope imaging to diagnosis potential problems and prescribe possible remedies.

The radioisotope of choice for imaging purposes has become technetium-99m, which is a gamma emitting **meta-stable isotope** having a short half-life of 6.01 hours. The product of the **gamma emission** is **Tc-99**, which is also radioactive, undergoing **beta decay**, with a half-life of 2.11×10^5 years. There are no stable isotopes of technetium, and all must be made in a nuclear reactor **by transmutation**. A Tc-99m generator that can easily be handled by appropriately trained medical technicians has been developed based on the decay of molybedenum-99, which has a half-life of 66 hours. Molybdenum-99 is produced by **neutron activation** of the stable isotope, molybdenum-98, which is the most abundant (24.14 %) of the seven naturally occurring isotopes of molybdenum. The generator facilitates transport of the **radiopharmaceutical** from the source nuclear reactor, to the hospital or clinic where testing will occur. Reactions 1 and 2 summarize the **nuclear processes** that involve the meta-stable isotope of technetium.

Key terms: meta-stable isotope, half-life, gamma emission, beta decay, transmutation, neutron activation, radiopharmaceutical.

Cause-and-Effect: The meta stable isotope of technetium emits gamma photons which are easily used for imaging.

Cause-and-Effect: The use of technetium generators based on the beta decay of Mo-99 has made it possible to safely do stress tests in clinical settings.

Reaction 1 $\qquad\qquad ^{99}_{42}\text{Mo} \rightarrow \, ^{99m}_{43}\text{Tc} + \, ^{0}_{-1}\beta$

Reaction 2 $\qquad\qquad ^{99m}_{43}\text{Tc} \rightarrow \, ^{99}_{43}\text{Tc} + \gamma \ (140 \text{ keV})$

Reactions 1 & 2. These nuclear reactions show the conversion of Mo-99 into the meta-stable isotope of technetium and its gamma photon emission, which has 140 keV of energy. Note that the mass numbers of each isotope are the superscripts to the left of the atomic symbol, and that a small amount of mass is converted into the energy of the gamma photon in these nuclear reactions. The atomic numbers are the subscripts to the left of the symbol, except for the beta particle, where the subscript does not represent the number of protons, but represents the charge of the particle. Note that the sums of the subscripts on the reactant and product sides are equal.

Technetium is in Group 7 of the periodic table and as such is a **transition metal**. It forms a stable pertechnitate ion, TcO_4^-, which has chemical properties similar to **permanganate**. In lower **oxidations states**, technetium ions form a variety of complexes with organic **ligands** that can be tailored to deliver the radioisotope to a particular organ of the body. This has led to breakthroughs in the treatment of **parathyroid** disorders and breast cancer.

Key terms: Transition metal, permanganate, oxidation states, ligands, parathyroid.

Cause-and-Effect: Technetium is a transition metal with chemistry similar to that of manganese. As a result it can form coordination complexes with organic ligands that can direct the radioisotope to specific organs for specific imaging purposes.

44. Based on information presented in the passage, pertechnitate is expected to be a good:
    A. **oxidizing agent.**
    B. reducing agent.
    C. acid.
    D. base.

Choice **A** is correct. As stated in the passage, technetium is in the same group of the periodic table as manganese. Like permanganate (MnO_4^-), pertechnitate (TcO_4^-) is expected to be a very good oxidizing agent. Permanganate is essentially a neutral ion with respect to acid/base properties and pertechnitate would be expected to be similar.

45. Molybdenum's naturally occurring stable isotopes have mass numbers between 92 and 100. If the atomic mass of molybdenum is 95.95 amu, which of the following must be true based on information presented in the passage?
    A. **There must be more than one naturally occurring stable isotope of molybdenum with fewer than 54 neutrons.**
    B. There must be more than one naturally occurring stable isotope of molybdenum with more than 56 neutrons.
    C. The most abundant naturally occurring isotope of molybdenum has 54 neutrons.
    D. All of the isotopes of molybdenum have 42 neutrons.

Choice **A** is correct. Since Mo-92, Mo-98 and Mo-100 account for three of the seven isotopes, there must be four isotopes remaining. If three of these isotopes were Mo-99, Mo-97 and Mo-96, then the final isotope must be either Mo-93, Mo-94, or Mo-95, all of which have fewer than 54 neutrons, requiring that there is more than one isotope with less than 54 neutrons. Choice A is the correct answer.

The passage states that Mo-98 is the most abundant naturally occurring stable isotope of molybdenum. Subtracting the number of protons from the mass number of this isotope gives 56 neutrons, not 54 neutrons.

Choice D can be eliminated because isotopes of an element must have different numbers of neutrons. In fact, the atomic number of molybdenum is 42, so each isotope has 42 protons. Choice B can also be eliminated, because while choice B could be true, is not required to be true. Since the atomic mass (95.95 amu) is the weighted average of the isotopes of an element. The passage states that there are "seven naturally occurring isotopes of molybdenum", with Mo-98 being the most abundant, at 24.14%. The question indicates that the mass numbers (protons + neutrons) for the stable isotopes of molybdenum range from 92 to 100. Therefore, the percent abundances of Mo-92 and Mo-100 can not exceed 24% each. Since Mo-98 has 56 neutrons, it is possible for all of the remaining isotopes to have mass numbers less than 98, or less than 56 neutrons. For example if you assume that the percent abundances of Mo-92, Mo-98 and Mo-100 are all 24%, the sum of the percent abundances for remaining isotopes can not be more than 28%. You can also then assume that Mo-99 is not one of these isotopes. Writing the equation for the weighted average gives the following equation, with x representing a hypothetical isotope having a mass number which is the average of the remaining isotopes.

$$95.95 = (24/100)92 + (24/100)98 + (24/100)100 + (28/100)x$$
$$95.95 = 22.08 + 23.52 + 24 + 0.28x$$
$$26.35 = 0.28x$$
$$94.1 = x$$

This indicates that the average of the mass numbers of the four remaining isotopes must be about 94, which could be done with combinations of Mo-93, Mo-94, Mo-95, Mo-96, and Mo-97, all of which have fewer than 56 neutrons. Therefore, it is not required that Mo-99 is one of the seven stable naturally occurring isotopes of molybdenum.

46. What is the product of the beta decay of Tc-99?
    A. **Ru-99**
    B. Ru-98
    C. Mo-99
    D. Mo-98

Choice **A** is correct. A beta negative particle is the equivalent of an electron ejected from the nucleus. Beta negative decay converts a neutron into a proton and an electron. Beta decay causes the number of protons in the nucleus to increase by one, resulting in the production of an element one position to the right in the periodic table, without a change in the mass number. Therefore, the product of beta decay of Tc-99 should be the element with one additional proton and the same mass number, which is ruthenium-99.

47. If it takes 24 hours for a technetium generator to be delivered from the nuclear reactor to a cardiologist's laboratory, by what percentage has the amount of Mo-99 gone down in the generator during the delivery time?
    A. $< 1\,\%$
    B. **22 %**
    C. 78 %
    D. 94 %

Choice **B** is correct. As stated in the passage, the half-life of Mo-99 is 66 hours. The actual percentage can be calculated from the definition of half-life. A half-life is the time required for half the material to decay. After multiple half-lives (n), the fraction remaining will continue to be cut in half, as stated in the following equation

$$F = (\tfrac{1}{2})^n$$

where F is the fraction of the radioisotope remaining and n is the number of half-lives. In this case, the n = 24/66 = 0.36. The fraction remaining can be calculated as $(\tfrac{1}{2})^{0.36} = 0.78$ or 78%. Therefore 22% has decayed.

To make the mental math easier, if you approximate n = 24/66 ~ 0.5. The square root of ½ is approximately 0.7 (0.7 x 0.7 = 0.49 ~ 0.5). If the fraction remaining is 0.7, then 70% remains, meaning that approximately 30% has decayed, which is closest to choice B.

48. Patients should be informed about the risks associated with any medical procedure. Which of the following pose a significant risk associated with radiopharmaceuticals?

    I. Internal exposure to radiopharmaceuticals can have a carcinogenic effect.

    II. Internal exposure to radiopharmaceuticals can have a mutagenic effect.

    III. Internal exposure to radiopharmaceuticals can have a teratogenic effect.

    A. I only

    B. II only

    C. I and II only

    D. <u>I, II and III</u>

Choice **D** is correct. Nuclear radiation, sometimes known as ionizing radiation, can disrupt or break chemical bonds in important biological molecules, such as DNA. This can cause changes in genetic sequences that can cause abnormal mitosis and meiosis. A carcinogen is any substance that directly causes genetic changes that result in the formation of cancer. A mutagen is any substance that causes a genetic change and a teratogen is any substance that causes a malformation of an embryo. Therefore, unnecessary exposure to radioisotopes can cause all three effects.

Passage 9 Explanation

Light is said to propagate through a medium in linear fashion. However, a **change in medium** or a curved **lens** will change the direction of light waves that pass through it. With medium changes, both **refractive indices** of the mediums are what determine the angles of directional changes. A positive lens will focus light rays on a spot behind the lens at a distance called **the focal length**. A negative lens will scatter an incoming light beam and have a negative focal length. The focal length is directly **related to the radius of curvature** of the lens. Figure 1 shows an example of a positive and negative lens.

Key terms: Change in medium, lens, refractive indices, focal length,

Cause-and-Effect: focal length directly related to radius of curvature of lens, in the first paragraph we're told that light waves change direction in new mediums or encountering a curved lens. Focal length is the distance from the lens where the light rays converge.

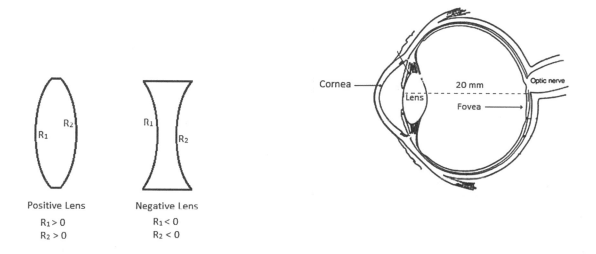

Figure 1 A positive and negative lens   **Figure 2** Diagram of human eye

Figure 1 shows a positive lens and a negative lens. The radii of curvature are given.

Figure 2 shows a diagram of the eye. The distance from the lens to the fovea is given. The cornea and eye lens are pointed out.

All lenses actually have **two radii of curvature** at the front and back. The approximate equation relating focal length and radii of curvature is

$$\frac{1}{f} = (n-1)\left[\frac{1}{R_1} - \frac{1}{R_2}\right]$$

Equation 1 shows the relationship between the radii of curvature of a lens, the refractive index, and the focal length.

where f is the focal length, n is **the refractive index** of the lens material, and R_1 and R_2 are the front and back radii of curvature.

Key terms: Radii of curvature, refractive index, you are told that a lens has two radii of curvature and that the refractive index of the lens material affects the focal length.

The human eye has a series of two convergent lenses whose overall effect is to focus images behind the lens to a point at the back of the eye called the fovea, about 20 mm from the eye lens. This is where most of the eyes rods and cones are concentrated. They are stimulated by the light coming through the eyes and send signals to the brain that are interpreted as our vision. The two lenses in the eye are the **cornea and the eye** lens, diagramed in Figure 2. The cornea has a fixed radius of curvature but the eye lens is under **muscular control**. When relaxed, the radius of curvature is at its largest. When focusing on nearby objects, the muscles around the lens contract and shorten the radius of curvature.

The relationship between a source of light, the focal length of a lens, and the distance to the image created by the lens is given by

$$\frac{1}{o} + \frac{1}{i} = \frac{1}{f}$$

Equation 2 shows the relationship between the distance from an object to the lens, the distance from the lens to the image, and the focal length.

Where o is the **distance** from the object to the lens, and i is the distance from the lens to the image, or the distance at which the image will be clear. In humans, **clear vision results** when i is the distance from the lens to the fovea.

Key terms: cornea, eye lens, muscular control, o, i, and f.

Cause and effect: In the last part of the passage you learn about the corena and eye lens and that the eye lens is under muscular control. You are reminded of the optics equation, equation 2. Lastly, you are told that in order for vision to be clear when viewing an object, i must be 20 mm.

49. Given a lens with focal length 2 cm and a refractive index of 2. If $R_1=1$ cm, what is R_2?
    A. **2 cm**
    B. 0.5 cm
    C. 1 cm
    D. -0.5 cm

Choice **A** is correct. This question is solved using Equation 1.

$$\frac{1}{2} = (2-1)\left[\frac{1}{1} - \frac{1}{R_2}\right] = (1)\left[1 - \frac{1}{R_2}\right]$$

So you end up with

$$-\frac{1}{2} = -\frac{1}{R_2}$$

So R_2 must equal 2 cm. and choice A is correct.

50. With regards to equation 2, which of the following best describes why the radius of curvature must be shortened when looking at nearby objects?
    A. To maintain i at 20 mm when o decreases, f must increase.
    B. To maintain f at 20 mm when o decreases, i must increase.
    C. **To maintain i at 20 mm when o decreases, f must also decrease.**
    D. To maintain f at 20 mm when o decreases, i must also decrease.

Choice **C** is correct. This question is asking us to analyze why the radius of curvature must be shortened when o is decreased. You know we're looking at equation 2. You also must recognize that shortening the radius of curvature means a decrease in focal length. Lastly, you must remember that i has to be maintained at a constant value, namely 20 mm. Therefore, the correct explanation starts with "in order to maintain i at 20 mm, when o decreases." Since you know there is a decrease in focal length, you know f must decrease so choice C is correct.

A: f is decreasing, not increasing,
B, D: i must remain constant.

51. Which of the following best explains why people have a hard time focusing on nearby objects with age?
    A. The shape of the eye lens flattens with age.
    B. The refractive index of the synovial fluid changes.
    C. The shape of the cornea flattens with age.
    D. **Muscle weakness around eye lens inhibits shortening the radius of curvature.**

Choice **D** is correct. This question is asking us how old age might affect our ability to see images clearly that are nearby. You must realize that moving an object closer means a decrease in o and an increase in 1/o. Therefore, 1/f must also increase to maintain i at 20 mm. This means that f must decrease, meaning the radius of curvature of the eye lens must decrease. Knowing that the eye lens radius of curvature is decreased by muscular control and that muscles weaken with age, choice D is correct.

A, B, C: There is no evidence of these statements in the passage nor are they supported by outside knowledge of the eye. The lens and cornea can change shape but this would not explain the consistent loss of focus on nearby objects mentioned. Both would cause more profound vision issues. Synovial fluid refractive index does not alter with age.

52. What will be the shape of a lens if $R_1 > 0$ and $R_2 < 0$.

A.

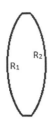

B.

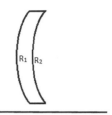

C.

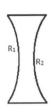

D.

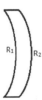

Choice **B** is correct. This question is asking us to glean from the passage, mostly from Figure 1, what a certain lens will look like. You learn from figure 1 that a positive R_1 means a convex front side. Also, from the figure of the negative lens you learn that a negative R_2 means a concave back side. Thus, choice B is correct.

Passage 10 Explanation

The hydrolysis of starch to sugars is catalyzed by β-amylase and is thought to be important in the ripening process of some fruits. The optimal pH for this enzyme was determined to be 4.5, at an enzyme to starch ratio of 200 U per gram of starch. The apparent rate constant, k (mol U^{-1}, min-1), was determined by the method of **initial rates** at four different temperatures, ranging from 30° to 60°C. The least squares best-fit line of an **Arrhenius plot**, Figure 1 and Equation 1, was used to determine the **activation energy** (E_a) of the reaction. Once the reaction had reached equilibrium, the thermodynamic parameters for the reaction were determined from a van't Hoff plot, Figure 2 and Equation 2. **The slope and intercept of the least squares fit of the data were used to determine the enthalpy (ΔH) and entropy (ΔS) changes for the reaction.** The gas constant, R, is 8.314 J $mol^{-1}K^{-1}$.

Key Terms: Initial rates, Arrhenius plot, activation energy, enthalpy and entropy

Cause and effect: The number of collisions with energy sufficient to form the activated complex is determined by the Boltzmann distribution of energies, which is temperature dependent, with higher temperatures having a greater number of effective collisions that will overcome the activation energy and give products.

Equation 1
$$\ln k = \ln A - (E_a/RT)$$

Equation 1 The rate constant (k) for a chemical reaction is temperature dependent, $k = Ae^{-Ea/RT}$ and the natural logarithmic form of the equation provides a linear plot of ln k versus 1/T, where the slope of the line is equal to -Ea/R.

Equation 2
$$\ln K_{eq} = (\Delta S/R) - (\Delta H/RT)$$

Equation 2 The van't Hoff relationship can be derived from the Gibbs Free energy equation, and demonstrates a linear relationship between the natural logarithm of the equilibrium constant and 1/T, where the slope of the plot is equal to -ΔH/R and the y-intercept is equal to ΔS/R.

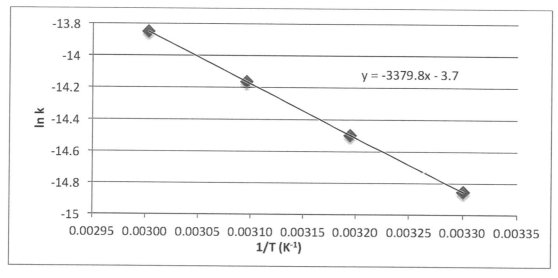

$$y = -3379.8x - 3.7$$

Figure 1 The Arrhenius plot of ln k versus 1/T for the hydrolysis of starch catalyzed by amylase.

Figure 1 The linear Arrhenius plot for the hydrolysis of starch catalyzed by β-amylase, produces a best fit line in which the slope of -3380 = -E$_a$/R.

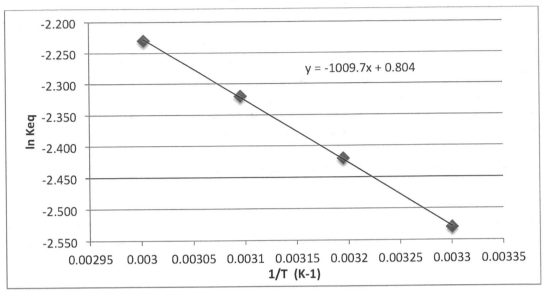

Figure 2 A van't Hoff plot of ln K$_{eq}$ versus 1/T for the hydrolysis of starch catalyzed by amylase.

Figure 2 A linear van't Hoff plot results in a best fit line in which the slope of -1010 = -ΔH/R and the intercept of 0.804 = ΔS/R.

53. What is the value of the activation energy of the β-amylase catalyzed hydrolysis of starch described in the passage?
    A. 1.0 kJ/mol
    B. 3.4 kJ/mol
    C. 8.4 kJ/mol
    D. <u>**28.1 kJ/mol**</u>

Choice **D** is correct. The best fit line for the plot in Figure 1, is y = -3379.8x - 3.7. The variable plotted on the y-axis is ln k and the variable on the x-axis is 1/T. Comparing this to Equation 1, you can see that the slope is equal to -E$_a$/R. Therefore,

$$-3379.8 = -E_a/R$$

Since the value of R is 8.314 J mol^{-1} K^{-1} and approximating the values in scientific notation

$$(3 \times 10^3)(8) = R$$
$$24 \times 10^3 = R$$
$$2.4 \times 10^4 \text{ J mol}^{-1} \text{ or } 24 \text{ kJ mol}^{-1}$$

Choice **D** is the correct answer.

54. What are the values of the enthalpy and entropy changes for the β-amylase catalyzed hydrolysis of starch described in the passage?

    A. $\Delta H = -8.4$ kJ/mol and $\Delta S = +6.7$ J/mol K
    B. $\underline{\Delta H = +8.4}$ kJ/mol and $\underline{\Delta S = +6.7}$ J/mol K
    C. $\Delta H = +27.5$ kJ/mol and $\Delta S = -30.1$ J/mol K
    D. $\Delta H = -27.5$ kJ/mol and $\Delta S = +30.1$ J/mol K

Choice **B** is correct. Using the equation for the linear best-fit line from Figure 1, the slope = $-\Delta H/R$, which using approximate values to simplify the math, gives

$$-1010 = -\Delta H/(8.314)$$
$$(1000)(8) \sim \Delta H$$
$$\Delta H \sim 8000 \text{ J/mol or } 8 \text{ kJ/mol}$$

The intercept = $\Delta S/R$ and using approximate values to simplify the math gives

$$0.8 = \Delta S/(8)$$
$$0.8(8) = \Delta S$$
$$\Delta S = 6.4 \text{ J/mol}$$

55. Which of the following plots best describes the effect of substrate concentration on the rate of hydrolysis of starch by β-amylase?

A.

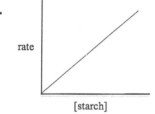

C.

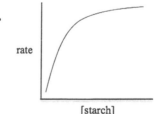

B.

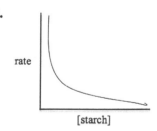

D.

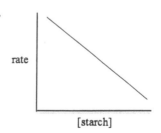

Choice **C** is correct. As the concentration of the starch increases, the rate of the reaction should increase. However, at some point the active sites of the enzyme will become saturated and the rate of the overall reaction will be limited by the concentration of the enzyme, causing the rate of reaction to plateau at some level of substrate.

56. Which of the following accurately describes the hydrolysis of starch to sugars?

    I. The reaction is always spontaneous.

    II. The reaction is endothermic.

    III. The products are more disordered than the reactants.

    A. I only

    B. I and II only

    C. **II and III only**

    D. I, II and III

Choice **C** is correct. Based on the least squares fit in Figure 2 and based on the information in Equation 2, you can evaluate the enthalpy and entropy of the reaction. The slope of the van't Hoff plot is negative, which is equal to $-\Delta H/R$, therefore the enthalpy must be positive and the reaction is endothermic. Choice A can be eliminated. The intercept of the van't Hoff plot is positive, which is equal to $\Delta S/R$, therefore the entropy is also positive and the products are more disordered than the reactants. Choice B can be eliminated. The Gibbs Free Energy equation is $\Delta G = \Delta H - T\Delta S$. If the temperature is sufficiently high, the $-T\Delta S$ term will cause the ΔG to be negative and the reaction will be spontaneous. However, at low temperatures the positive enthalpy will dominate and cause the reaction to be nonspontaneous. Therefore, the reaction is not always spontaneous, and choices A, B, and D can be eliminated. Choice C is the correct answer.

These questions are NOT related to a passage.

57. Which of the following radioisotopes that are produced by nuclear fission would be most likely to cause thyroid cancer or dysfunctions?

    A. **I-131**

    B. Pu-239

    C. U-235

    D. Sr-90

Choice **A** is correct. Since iodine is an essential element associated with thyroid function, internal exposure to radioactive iodine (I-131), a beta emitter, ($T_{1/2} = 8$ days) can cause the death of thyroid cells (high doses) or cancer (low doses).

58. Which of the following convert mass into energy?

    I. Oxidation-Reduction reactions

    II. Combustion reactions

    III. Fusion reactions

    A. I only

    B. II only

    C. **III only**

    D. I and II only

Choice **C** is correct. All chemical reactions obey the Law of Conservation of Mass. Fusion reactions are a type of nuclear reaction in which atoms of small atomic mass are converted to atoms of heavier atomic mass. The sum of the mass of the reactant nuclei is slightly greater than the mass of the product nuclei, and the difference in mass accounts for the production of the massive amounts of energy in fusion reactions.

59. Tritium is a man-made radioactive isotope of hydrogen that has a half-life of 12.32 years. Tritium is an essential component in modern thermonuclear weapons. It is estimated that there is about 4 grams of tritium per nuclear warhead in the U.S. arsenal of fusion type nuclear weapons. As of 2001, the U.S. had about 9,600 thermonuclear warheads in its inventory. If the U.S. were to propose a method of arms control in which tritium is no longer manufactured worldwide, but existing stores could be recycled, approximately how long would it take before the U.S. had only one functional thermonuclear warhead?

    A. 12 years
    B. 36 years
    C. **163 years**
    D. 246 years

Choice **C** is correct. The mass of tritium per nuclear warhead is not required information in this question. Half-life is defined as the time required for half of the radioactive material to decay. If you start with 9,600 warheads, the whole numbers of warheads after each half-life will be

$$9600 \rightarrow 4800 \rightarrow 2400 \rightarrow 1200 \rightarrow 600 \rightarrow 300 \rightarrow 150 \rightarrow 75 \rightarrow 38 \rightarrow 19 \rightarrow 9 \rightarrow 5 \rightarrow 3 \rightarrow 2 \rightarrow 1$$

with each arrow representing a half-life of 12 years. It takes approximately 14 half-lives to reach the equivalent of one warhead. Therefore 14 x 12 = 168 years, which is close enough to choice C.

TIMED

SECTION 3

59 Questions, 95 Minutes

(Use the tear-out answer sheet provided in Appendix E)

Passage 1 (Questions 1-4)

The production of nitrogen oxides by internal combustion engines is an important environmental health concern, because of their role as part of photochemical smog and air pollution. In addition to pollution from nitrogen oxides, the production of hydrocarbon radicals from incomplete combustion also contributes to unhealthy levels of photochemical smog and ozone in large urban areas. Elemental nitrogen is the major gas in the earth's atmosphere (78 %) and oxygen represents the majority of the remainder (20.8%). Normally elemental nitrogen is very stable and does not react with the oxygen in the air, but the elevated temperatures inside an engine provide more than enough activation energy for Reaction 1. The rate of reaction between nitrogen monoxide and elemental oxygen, Reaction 2, has been studied using the method of initial rates and selected data are presented in Table 1, with the initial rate being measured in terms of the change in the concentration of elemental oxygen.

Reaction 1 $N_2 (g) + O_2 (g) \rightarrow 2\ NO\ (g)$

Reaction 2 $2\ NO\ (g) + O_2 (g) \rightarrow 2\ NO_2\ (g)$

Table 1 Initial rate data for Reaction 2

Experiment Number	Initial Rate $(M\ s^{-1})$	Initial $[O_2]$ (M)	Initial $[NO]$ (M)
1	6.81×10^{-4}	6.50×10^{-3}	7.80×10^{-3}
2	2.04×10^{-3}	1.95×10^{-2}	7.80×10^{-3}
3	6.13×10^{-3}	6.50×10^{-3}	2.34×10^{-2}
4	5.44×10^{-3}	1.30×10^{-2}	1.56×10^{-2}

1. Based on the data in Table 1, what is the overall order of Reaction 2?
   A. Reaction 2 is first order with respect to O_2, second order with respect to NO and first order overall.
   B. Reaction 2 is second order with respect to O_2, first order with respect to NO and first order overall.
   C. Reaction 2 is first order with respect to O_2, second order with respect to NO and third order overall.
   D. Reaction 2 is second order with respect to O_2, first order with respect to NO and third order overall.

2. Which of the following is the rate constant for Reaction 2?
   A. 1.7×10^3 M^{-2} s^{-1}
   B. 2.2×10^1 M^{-2} s^{-1}
   C. 6.7×10^1 M^{-2} s^{-1}
   D. 5.4×10^5 M^{-2} s^{-1}

3. Which of the following is NOT a radical?
   A. CH_3
   B. N_2
   C. NO
   D. NO_2

4. The following mechanisms have been proposed for Reaction 2. Which of these mechanisms can be eliminated based on the data in Table 1?

   I. $2\,NO\,(g) \rightleftharpoons N_2O_2\,(g)$ (fast)
        $N_2O_2\,(g) + O_2\,(g) \rightarrow 2\,NO_2\,(g)$ (slow)

   II. $NO\,(g) + O_2\,(g) \rightarrow NO_2\,(g) + O\,(g)$ (slow)
        $NO\,(g) + O\,(g) \rightarrow NO_2\,(g)$ (fast)

   III. $2\,NO\,(g) + O_2\,(g) \rightarrow 2\,NO_2\,(g)$ (slow)

   A. I only
   B. II only
   C. II and III only
   D. I and III only

Passage 2 (Questions 5-9)

Shown in Figure 1 are the linear forms of three naturally occurring monosaccharides, as well as the corresponding ring structures of two of these compounds, and a disaccharide. The ring structures are formed by addition of a hydroxyl group to the carbonyl group, to form either a five- or a six-membered ring.

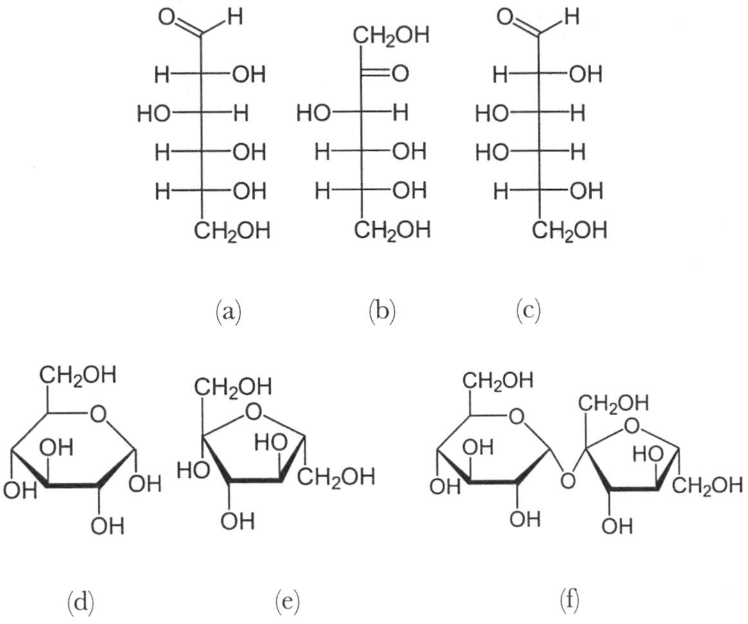

Figure 1 The linear forms of (a) glucose, (b) fructose, and (c) galactose. Also shown are the ring structures of (d) glucose and (e) fructose, as well as the disaccharide, (f) sucrose.

5. Glucose and galactose are which of the following types of stereoisomers?
    A. Enantiomers
    B. Rotomers
    C. Epimers
    D. Constitutional isomers

6. Which of the following types of reactions are involved in the formation of sucrose, from glucose and fructose?
    A. Hydrolysis
    B. Dehydration
    C. Esterification
    D. Addition

7. A student in an organic chemistry class was given a sample of an unknown monosaccharide and was asked to identify the compound. The student initially performed an elemental analysis and found that the sample was 40.0 % carbon, 6.7 % hydrogen and 53.3 % oxygen. Which of the following monosaccharides could be the unknown based on this experiment?

    I. Glucose
    II. Galactose
    III. Fructose

    A. I only
    B. II only
    C. I and II only
    D. I, II, and III

8. Which of the following is the source of the oxygen atoms in pyruvate that is formed by glycolysis?
    A. Elemental oxygen
    B. Glucose
    C. Carbon dioxide
    D. Hexokinase

9. The disaccharide maltose, shown below, is composed of which of the following monosaccharides?

    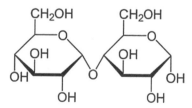

    I. Glucose
    II. Galactose
    III. Fructose

    A. I only
    B. II only
    C. I and II only
    D. I and III only

Passage 3 (Questions 10-14)

An experiment was conducted to study Newton's 2nd law. A nearly frictionless cart was placed on a track and a string was used to connect the cart to a 5.0g mass hanger that was strung over a wheel, providing tension due to the weight of the hanger, as shown in Figure 1. Four standard 20g brass masses were placed on the cart. An ultrasonic motion detector, interfaced with a computer, was used to determine the position of the cart as a function of time. Initially, the students were asked to calibrate the software by placing the cart at a position on the track such that there was 1.000 m between the cart and the motion detector and collecting data without the cart moving. Individual trials of the experiment were performed in which the cart was held relatively close to the motion detector and then released. After data collection was completed for a trial, the computer provided the students with two graphs of the data, a position versus time graph and a velocity versus time graph, and least-squares fit equations were displayed. The students recorded the acceleration of the cart for three trials, and then moved one of the standard brass masses from the cart and placed it on the hanger, thereby increasing the force applied to the system, without changing the total mass of the system. Three additional trials were performed, and the process was repeated until each individual mass was transferred from the cart to the hanger. The data for one of the students is shown in Figure 1. The students were then asked to take the cart and place it on an electronic balance to determine the gravitational mass of the cart. Students then used the data collected in this experiment to determine the inertial mass of the system and subsequently the inertial mass of the cart, which was then compared with the gravitational mass.

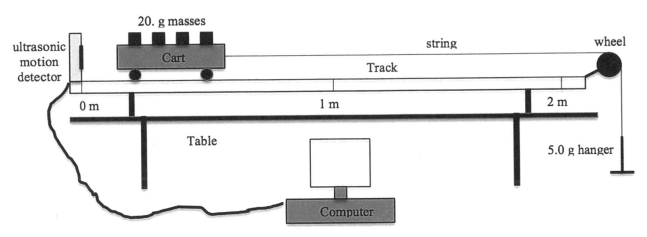

Figure 1 Experimental set up for determining the inertial mass of a cart based on Newton's Second law.

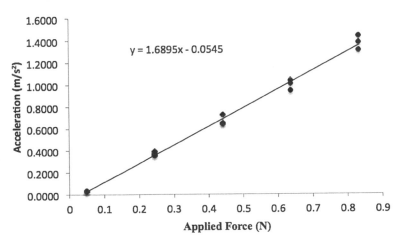

Figure 2 Acceleration versus applied force collected by a student using the experimental set-up shown in Figure 1 and described in the passage. Note that the least-squares best fit line for the data is displayed on the graph.

10. What is the magnitude of weight of the hanger used for the first three trials of the experiment?
    A. 0.005 N
    B. 0.05 N
    C. 0.25 N
    D. 0.45 N

11. Based on the student's data and best fit line shown in Figure 2, what is the inertial mass of the system that is being accelerated in the experiment described in the passage?
    A. 0.085 kg
    B. 0.457 kg
    C. 0.542 kg
    D. 1.845 kg

12. The commonly accepted range of human hearing is from 20 Hz to 20 kHz and the speed of sound in air is 340 m/s. During the calibration portion of the experiment, what is the minimum sampling time between when the ultrasonic device produces the sound and when it is detected?
    A. 5×10^{-5} s
    B. 3×10^{-3} s
    C. 6×10^{-3} s
    D. 5×10^{-2} s

13. If the student measured the gravitational mass of the cart to be 503 g, what is the absolute value of the percent error between the gravitational mass of the cart and the inertial mass of the cart from the experiment?
    A. 1 %
    B. 12 %
    C. 20 %
    D. 53 %

14. Which of the following are true for the experiment described in the passage?
    I. Force is the independent variable and acceleration is the dependent variable.
    II. The mass of the cart is the inverse of the slope of the acceleration versus applied force graph.
    III. An unlevel track would introduce a systematic error into the experiment affecting the apparent mass of the system.

    A. I and II only
    B. I and III only
    C. II and III only
    D. I, II, and III

These questions are NOT based on a passage. (Questions 15-17)

15. Benedict's solution, aqueous basic Cu^{2+}, is used to test for aldehydes and α-hydroxyketones. Which of the following will act as a reducing sugar and give a positive Benedict's test?

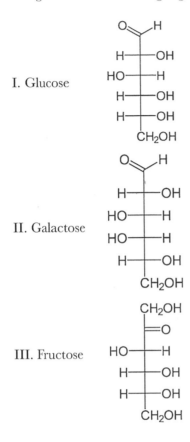

   A. I only
   B. II only
   C. I and II only
   D. I, II and III

16. If an object has a gravitational mass of 50 kg on the surface of the earth, what is the gravitational mass of that same object on the surface of the moon, where the acceleration due to gravity is 1/6 the acceleration due to gravity on the earth?
   A. 50 kg
   B. 8.3 kg
   C. 490 N
   D. 82 N

17. Which of the following compounds does NOT have an empirical formula of CH_2O?
   A. Glucose
   B. Acetic acid
   C. Formic acid
   D. Glyceraldehyde

THIS PAGE LEFT

INTENTIONALLY BLANK

Passage 4 (Questions 18-21)

Both glucose and galactose enter glycolysis through a common intermediate, glucose-6-phosphate (G-6-P). Glucose is acted upon either by hexokinase or by one of its isoforms to yield G-6-P in a single step. The multi-step conversion of galactose to glucose-6-phosphate requires the action of several enzymes.

It has long been observed that in certain tumor cell lines grown in glucose-containing medium, lactic acid is produced rapidly. When the same cells are grown in galactose-containing medium, the cells exhibits only moderately elevated lactic acid production, but equal growth rates. Hepatoma cells are one such rapidly dividing cancerous cell type. It has been hypothesized that mitochondria in cancerous cells are either defective or are less able to compete with glycolytic enzymes for common intermediates. As a result, nearly all hexoses imported into the cell enter glycolysis, but relatively few are oxidatively phosphorylated. In order to investigate mitochondria's involvement in the altered, largely anaerobic metabolism of some tumor cells, three experiments were performed on cultured hepatoma cells established from rat hepatoma cell lines.

Experiment 1

^{14}C labeled hexose transport by intact hepatoma cells was measured at physiological temperature and pH for ^{14}C-glucose, ^{14}C-galactose, and 3-O-methyl-^{14}C-glucose (a non-metabolizable sugar derivative). Transport rates for the three sugars were found to be nearly identical, indicating cells import hexoses at equal rates. However, when measurements were made in a repeat experiment over a much longer period of time, glucose uptake was found to be greater than galactose uptake.

Experiment 2

Hexokinase specific activity was determined photometrically for control rat liver homogenates, regenerating rat liver homogenates and hepatoma cells at various assay G-6-P concentrations. The assay glucose concentration for the hepatoma cells was 0.5 mM, while that for control and regenerating liver was 13 mM. The hexokinase activity of liver homogenate at 0.5 mM glucose concentrations was negligible. Hexokinase activity was found to be approximately constant and elevated more than 20-fold in hepatoma cells versus activities found in both control and regenerating rat liver at G-6-P concentrations of up to 0.6 mM.

Experiment 3

Respiration rates of isolated hepatoma mitochondria were measured using an oxygen electron in a closed container. Elevated glucose levels were found to significantly stimulate the respiration of coupled hepatoma mitochondria, a result that should be obtained only if the hexokinase reaction (glucose + ATP → G-6-P + ADP) consumed mitochondrially synthesized ATP. The glucose-stimulated respiration of hepatoma cells was found to lack inhibition by G-6-P up to 0.6 mM. However, when added, glucose was unable to stimulate respiration of mitochondria from control and regenerating rat liver. When tumor mitochondria were added to respiring normal mitochondria, cell respiration was again stimulated by the presence of glucose, indicating coupling of glycolysis and mitochondrial oxidative phosphorylation.

In a separate series of experiments, the researchers demonstrated that in hepatoma cells at least 50% of the cellular hexokinase is associated with the mitochondrial fraction and that the mitochondrial hexokinase activity is four times higher than any other subcellular fraction.

18. Na^+/K^+ ATPases pump sodium from the cells of the proximal tubule of the nephron into the blood. SGLT proteins found in the plasma membrane of the same cells import glucose against its concentration from the tubular filtrate into the cell while exporting sodium down its concentration gradient. The action of SGLT proteins correctly represents which form of protein transport?
    A. Primary active transport
    B. Symport
    C. Secondary active transport
    D. Facilitated diffusion

19. A test of the respiratory response by regenerating rat liver to glucose stimulation was most likely included in Experiment 3 in order to:
    A. determine whether high activity levels of mitochondrially bound hexokinase are present in the neoplastic state.
    B. show that enhanced hexokinase response to glucose in hepatoma cells is not a property of the tissue of origin.
    C. test whether glucose-stimulated hexokinase activity is also a function of rapidly dividing normal liver cells.
    D. demonstrate that glucose is unable to stimulate the respiration of control rat liver.

20. Which of the following findings, if true, would most strongly challenge a finding or conclusion of the experiments presented in the passage?
    A. Transport rates of ^{14}C-ribose exceed those of ^{14}C-glucose or ^{14}C-galactose.
    B. Tumor mitochondria, when included in samples of normal mitochondria, significantly increase oxygen consumption due to their own basal rate of respiration.
    C. Non-specific trapping of hexoses equally decreases the real hexose transport rate for both glucose and galactose versus that which was measured spectrophotometrically.
    D. Enzyme activity measured in control and regenerating rat liver was exerted by the high-K_m enzyme glucokinase

21. Glucokinase regulatory protein (GKPR) is a fully competitive inhibitor of glucokinase. According to the Michaelis-Menten description of enzyme kinetics, what effect does the presence of GKPR have on the glucokinase kinetics?
    A. K_m is unchanged and V_{max} increases
    B. K_m decreases and V_{max} is unchanged
    C. K_m increases and V_{max} is unchanged
    D. K_m is unchanged and V_{max} decreases

Passage 5 (Questions 22-25)

An introductory chemistry laboratory involved the study of various reactions that produced precipitates when aqueous solutions were combined. Students were given a total of nine different solutions in dark brown glass bottles and asked to mix equal portions of these solutions in reaction wells, using pipets. The students were asked to record their observations for appropriate combinations in tabular form, including formation of precipitates, bubbling, color changes or any other observations they thought were relevant. One of the student's results are shown in Table 1. In order to prevent any hydrolysis of the Cu^{2+} or Fe^{3+} ions, the professor added a small amount of acid to these two solutions. The professor asked the students to perform some of these reactions in a fume hood to prevent being exposed to potentially noxious fumes. The professor noted that the dark brown bottles can help prevent reactions with light common to transition metals in the fifth period and below.

	NaCl colorless	NaOH colorless	Na$_2$S colorless	Na$_2$CO$_3$ colorless
KNO$_3$ colorless	NR	NR	NR	NR
AgNO$_3$ colorless	White precipitate	Beige precipitate	Black precipitate	White precipitate
Ca(NO$_3$)$_2$ colorless	NR	White precipitate	White precipitate	White precipitate
Cu(NO$_3$)$_2$ blue	NR	Pale blue gel	Black precipitate	Blue-green precipitate
Fe(NO$_3$)$_3$ orange	NR	Orange gel	Black precipitate	Orange precipitate

Table 1 Observations related to mixing known aqueous solutions. NR stands for "no reaction".

Subsequently, the students were given an unknown solution in test tubes. The students were told that the unknown contained two of the solutions used in the first part of the experiment. The students were also told that the unknown solution would always contain sodium nitrate. It was the student's job to identify the other ions present in the unknown by reacting the unknown solution with the known solutions and comparing their results to the previously obtained results. Student A was given 20 mL of a colorless unknown solution. Unfortunately, he ran out of his unknown solution and had to ask the professor for additional solution. Surprisingly to this student, silver nitrate was the only solution that caused the formation of a precipitate with his unknown. He correctly reported the ions present in his unknown solution to the professor. Student B was given 20 mL of an orange unknown solution. She reacted her unknown with a small amount of only one of the known solutions and found that no precipitate formed. Having identified the ions present in the unknown solution, she reported her results to the professor.

22. What is the formula of the precipitate formed by combining the iron (III) nitrate solution with the sodium sulfide solution?
    A. FeS
    B. FeS_2
    C. Fe_2S_3
    D. Fe_3S_2

23. In aqueous solution Fe^{3+} will undergo a hydrolysis reaction to form an orange gelatinous precipitate. Which of the following reactions best describes the formation of this precipitate?
    A. $Fe^{3+} (aq) \rightarrow FeOH^{2+} (s) + H^+ (aq)$
    B. $Fe^{3+} (aq) \rightarrow Fe(OH)_3 (s) + 3 H^+ (aq)$
    C. $Fe^{3+} (aq) + NO_3^- (aq) + 2 H^+ (aq) \rightarrow Fe(OH)_2 (s) + NO (g)$
    D. $Fe^{3+} (aq) + 2 H_2O (l) \rightarrow Fe(OH)_2 (s) + H_2 (g)$

24. When the copper (II) nitrate and iron (III) nitrate solutions were reacted with the sodium carbonate solution, some bubble formation was observed by certain students. What was the most likely identity of the bubbles?
    A. Carbon dioxide
    B. Carbon monoxide
    C. Elemental nitrogen
    D. Nitrogen monoxide

25. Student C was given an unknown wrapped in aluminum foil. The student asked the professor why his unknown was the only one wrapped in aluminum foil and the professor responded, "To prevent light from causing an unwanted side reaction". Which of the following was most likely in the unknown solution?
    A. Copper (II) nitrate, because exposure to light causes the solution to turn blue.
    B. Silver nitrate, because exposure to light can cause the formation of a black precipitate of elemental silver.
    C. Sodium sulfide, because exposure to light cause the formation of the smell of rotten eggs.
    D. Sodium carbonate, because exposure to produces carbon dioxide gas.

Passage 6 (Questions 26-30)

The elements in Group 18 of the periodic table, the so-called Noble Gases, are perhaps the most under-appreciated elements. This stems from the general misunderstanding that their physical, chemical and nuclear properties (Table 1) are already completely understood and that further study is unlikely to produce any new information.

Helium was first discovered in 1868, not on earth, but from the analysis of the spectral lines produced by the sun. During this analysis, it became clear that most of the spectral lines were due to the element hydrogen, which was previously discovered on earth. The remaining solar spectral lines were ascribed to a previously unknown substance that was given the name helium. We now recognize helium as a misnomer, but tradition prevails, preventing a name change to "hellion", which would be consistent with the suffix for the other elements in the family. We now know that helium is the product of nuclear fusion of hydrogen isotopes, which results in production of enormous amounts of energy. In contrast, helium's extremely low boiling point has made it the liquid of choice for cryogenic applications, such as in superconducting magnets used in high field nuclear magnetic resonance.

Both helium and neon are less dense than air (1.225 kg/m^3), with the former's noncombustible nature making it the preferred gas for use in lighter than air ships, also known as dirigibles. Perhaps surprisingly, argon is the third most abundant gas in earth's atmosphere ($\sim 1\%$). The other Group 18 elements have increasing densities in the gas phase, due to their increasing atomic mass. This is somewhat problematic for radon, which is radioactive, decaying by way of an alpha process, with a half-life of 3.8 days. Radon is part of the ^{238}U decay sequence and can collect in homes, particularly basements, built in areas where the soils may have high levels or uranium. Exposure to radon is thought to be the second leading source of lung carcinomas.

The relative chemical inertness of the group 18 elements stems from their completely filled s and p subshells. The stability of these elements is reflected in their relatively high first ionization energies. There are no known compounds of helium or neon. The reactivity of the heavier elements, krypton and xenon, with highly electronegative elements such as fluorine has been known for quite some time, and evidence for an argon compound has recently been presented. The xenon compounds XeF_2, XeF_4 and XeF_6 are often cited as part of the power of Valence Shell Electron Pair Repulsion (VSEPR) theory for predicting the structures of main-group compounds.

Table 1 Some properties of the Group 18 elements

Symbol	Boiling Point (K)	Melting Point (K)	Enthalpy of Vaporization (kJ/mol)	Atomic Number	Atomic Radius (Å)	First Ionization Energy (kJ/mol)
He	4	1	0.1	2	0.31	2370
Ne	27	25	1.7	10	0.38	2080
Ar	87	84	6.5	18	0.71	1520
Kr	122	116	9.1	36	0.88	1350
Xe	167	162	12.7	54	1.08	1170
Rn	212	202	18.1	86	1.20	1040

26. Which of the following best explains the periodic trend in first ionization energies for the Noble Gases as atomic number increases.
    A. The core charges increase as the number of shells increases.
    B. The core charges remain the same as the number of shells increases.
    C. The core charges decreases as the number of shells increases.
    D. The core charges increase as the number of shells decreases.

27. What is the density of radon at STP?
    A. 1.0 kg/m^3
    B. 1.225 kg/m^3
    C. 9.7 kg/m^3
    D. 22.4 kg/m^3

28. The suffix of helium suggests that the person that originally named this element thought it was which of the following types of elements?
    A. A non-metal
    B. A metal
    C. A liquid
    D. A gas

29. Which of the following ions does NOT have a Noble Gas electron configuration?
    A. Na^+
    B. Fe^{2+}
    C. O^{2-}
    D. F^-

30. Which of the following are the molecular shapes of XeF_2, and XeF_4 (respectively) as predicted by VSEPR theory?
    I. Linear
    II. Bent
    III. Tetrahedral
    IV. Square planar

    A. I and II
    B. II and III
    C. III and IV
    D. I and IV

These questions are NOT based on a passage (Questions 31-34)

31. For a blindfolded person, which of the following situations is indistinguishable from that person sitting in a car that is at rest on a level road?
    A. A blindfolded person riding in a car driving on a level straight road at a constant speed of 75 m/s.
    B. A blindfolded person riding in a car driving on a level straight road, but the car's peed changes from 50 m/s to 100 m/s in 20 seconds.
    C. A blindfolded person riding in a car driving on a level straight road, but the car's speed changes from 100 m/s to 50 m/s in 20 seconds.
    D. A blindfolded person riding in a car driving on a level road at a constant speed of 50 m/s going around a curve whose radius is 100 m.

32. A major source of glucose for glycolysis is liver glycogen, the hydrolysis of which is catalyzed by the enzyme glycogen phosphorylase. Non-phosphorylated glycogen phosphorylase is allosterically regulated by AMP, ATP and G-6-P. Which of the following statements regarding this regulation is likely to be true?
    A. ATP down-regulates glycogen phosphorylase activity by binding to and blocking a portion of the enzyme active site.
    B. AMP's binding alters the conformation of the enzyme active site.
    C. G-6-P binds to and competes with glucose at the glycogen phosphorylase active site.
    D. Phosphorylated glycogen phosphorylase activity is stimulated by AMP binding.

33. If a 0.1 kg object is dropped from a very tall cliff and reaches terminal velocity, what is the magnitude of the object's net acceleration and the net force acting on the object at terminal velocity?
    A. 0 m/s^2 and 0 N
    B. 9.8 m/s^2 and 0 N
    C. 0 m/s^2 and 0.98 N
    D. 9.8 m/s^2 and 0.98 N

34. Which of the following will cause the largest buoyant force on an object floating in the liquid at 25°C?
    A. Water (specific gravity = 1.0)
    B. Ethanol (specific gravity = 0.79)
    C. Diethyl ether (specific gravity = 0.71)
    D. Acetone (specific gravity = 0.78)

THIS PAGE LEFT

INTENTIONALLY BLANK

Passage 7 (Questions 35-39)

We have all seen them, those liquid-filled cylinders that have colored liquid filled glass bulbs that float or sink depending upon the temperature. A so-called Galileo's thermometer is constructed such that the small glass bulbs are partially filled with liquids that function as weights and the colors are purely decorative. Once the bulbs have been sealed, their densities are adjusted by attaching metal tags with temperature labels. Each glass bulb and metal tag has a predetermined density within the range of densities for the liquid in which they are immersed. The clear liquid in which the bulbs are submerged can be water, but more often is an organic liquid, such as ethanol (Figure 1), which has a significantly bigger temperature dependent variation in density. It is the buoyancy effect of this liquid and the weight of the individual glass bulbs that determines if a particular bulb will sink or float.

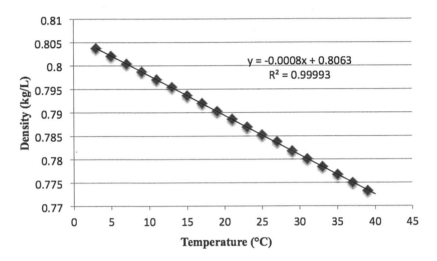

Figure 1 A plot of density versus temperature for pure ethanol, including the equation for the best-fit line. The melting and boiling points for pure ethanol are -114°C and 78°C, respectively.

Often times the temperature will be such that there will be a number of bulbs floating at the top of the liquid, as well as a few bulbs that sink to the bottom, but one bulb will seem to be suspended in the middle of the liquid. The question becomes, how is that possible? The most plausible explanation involves slight pressure differences (ΔP) acting on the bulbs, that are dependent upon the density (ρ) of the liquid, the acceleration due to gravity (g) and the depth (h) of the surfaces of the bulb submerged within the liquid, according to $\Delta P = \rho g h$.

35. What is the approximate weight of a glass bulb suspended in the middle of a Galileo's thermometer whose temperature is 298 K, assuming that the bulb can be approximated as a sphere and the diameter of the bulb is 2.0 cm?
    A. 0.032 N
    B. 0.041 N
    C. 0.13 N
    D. 0.16 N

36. What is the net force acting on a glass bulb suspended in the middle of a Galileo's thermometer whose temperature is 298 K?
    A. 0 N
    B. +0.032 N
    C. -0.032 N
    D. -0.041 N

37. Based on information in the passage, which of the following must be true concerning the buoyant force and the weight of a bulb that is suspended in the middle of the surrounding fluid of a Galileo's thermometer?
    A. The magnitude of the force of gravity acting on the bulb is greater than the magnitude of the buoyant force acting on the bulb.
    B. The magnitude of the force of gravity acting on the bulb is less than the magnitude of the buoyant force acting on the bulb.
    C. The magnitude of the force of gravity acting on the bulb is equal to the magnitude of the buoyant force acting on the bulb.
    D. There is no way to predict the relative magnitudes of the force of gravity acting on the bulb compared with the buoyant force acting on the bulb.

38. An alternative design for a Galileo's thermometer involves using hollow metal cubes with the length of a side being 1.0 cm. What is the pressure difference at 25°C that the ethanol exerts on the top-side, as compared with the bottom-side of the cube, when the center of mass of the cube is located 10.0 cm below the surface. The diameter of the thermometer is 3.0 cm and the total height is 25.0 cm. Note that 1 Pascal (Pa) of pressure is equivalent to a Newton per square meter.
    A. 77 Pa
    B. 231 Pa
    C. 730 Pa
    D. 807 Pa

39. What fraction of a bulb will be above the surface of ethanol at 7 °C, if the density of the bulb is 1.000 kg/L?
    A. 0
    B. 0.1
    C. 0.2
    D. 0.8

Passage 8 (Questions 40-43)

In order for divers to survive underwater, they must inhale highly compressed air in deep water, resulting in more gases than normal being dissolved in their blood and tissues. If the diver returns to the surface too rapidly, the dissolved gas forms bubbles, much like what happens when the cap of a soda bottle is removed, causing pain and possibly death. This condition is commonly known as "the bends." To prevent this condition, a diver must return to the surface slowly, allowing the dissolved gases to slowly adjust to the changes in pressure. Rather than breathing compressed air, the diver may breathe a mixture of compressed helium and oxygen, known as heliox, thereby avoiding the bends, because helium is much less soluble in water than nitrogen, which is the major gas (79%) found in air and nitrox mixtures. The solubility of gases in aqueous solution is dependent upon temperature and pressure. The solubility (C) of a gas directly depends on the pressure (P) of the gas on the surface of the liquid, and is known as Henry's Law, Equation 1, with selected proportionality constants, k, provided in Table 1. It should be noted that most gases are much more soluble in cold water than in hot water.

Equation 1
$$C = k\,P$$

Table 1 Henry's Law constants, k, at 25°C for aqueous solutions of selected gases

Formula	k (M atm^{-1})
N_2	6×10^{-4}
He	4×10^{-4}
Ne	5×10^{-4}
Ar	1×10^{-3}
CO	1×10^{-3}
CO_2	3×10^{-2}

In addition, narcosis can occur while scuba diving, which results in an alteration in consciousness at depth, caused by the anesthetic effect of certain gases at high pressure. This sensation is similar to the intoxication that results from consumption of alcoholic beverages. All gases have varying degrees of effect, with a higher lipid solubility seeming to correlate well with the degree of narcosis. At extreme depth, this mental impairment can be life threatening. Divers can learn to cope with some of these effects, but it is impossible to completely eliminate them. With the apparent exception of helium, most of the noble gases, as well as other gases such as elemental nitrogen, and carbon dioxide, have been shown to alter mental function at various levels. This effect is distinctly different than that caused by asphyxiation. Interestingly, the heavy noble gases are more narcotic than nitrogen at a given pressure, and xenon has such a high degree of activity that it has been used at standard pressures as an anesthetic during surgery. The precise mechanism of narcosis is not well understood, but appears to correlate to the solubility of the gas in the lipid bilayer of nerve membranes. Some of these effects may also be similar to the mechanism of nonpolar anesthetics such as chloroform, diethyl ether, and nitrous oxide. The production of these effects by the very chemically unreactive noble gases suggests a mechanism unrelated to chemical reactivity. A physical effect based on intermolecular forces may cause a change in membrane volume, thereby affecting the transport of ions through channels in the membranes of nerve cells.

40. Which of the following lipid soluble compounds has a nonzero dipole moment?
    A. Argon
    B. Elemental nitrogen
    C. Chloroform
    D. Carbon dioxide

41. Based on information in the passage, which of the following best explains the increase in anesthetic properties of the noble gases as the atomic number increases?
    A. The polarizability of the atoms increases.
    B. The number of protons in the nucleus increases.
    C. The number of neutrons in the nucleus increases.
    D. The size of the atoms decreases.

42. Which of the following best describes the effect of increasing temperature on the value of the Henry's law constant for a gas?
    A. Since the solubility of gases generally decrease with an increase in average kinetic energy, the value of the Henry's law constant increases.
    B. Since the solubility of gases generally decrease with an increase in average kinetic energy, the value of the Henry's law constant decreases.
    C. Since the solubility of gases generally increase with an increase in average kinetic energy, the value of the Henry's law constant decreases.
    D. Since the solubility of gases generally increase with an increase in average kinetic energy, the value of the Henry's law constant increases.

43. Which of the following gas mixtures is LEAST likely to cause the bends for a scuba diver?
    A. Compressed air
    B. Nitrox
    C. Heliox
    D. Neonox

These questions are NOT based on a passage (Questions 44-47)

44. Which of the following are fluids?
    I. Air
    II. Water
    III. Blood

    A. I only
    B. II only
    C. II and III only
    D. I, II and III

45. Which of the following is the formula for nitrous oxide?
    A. N_2O
    B. NO
    C. NO_2
    D. N_2O_4

46. The earth's atmosphere is comprised primarily of elemental nitrogen, which is unreactive. Certain nitrogen fixing bacteria have developed a symbiotic relationship with certain plants, and are able to convert elemental nitrogen to ammonia. Which of the following best explains why elemental nitrogen is so unreactive?
    A. Elemental nitrogen is diatomic, having a triple bond, being diamagnetic and reduction must occur to obtain ammonia.
    B. Elemental nitrogen is diatomic, having a triple bond, being paramagnetic and reduction must occur to obtain ammonia.
    C. Elemental nitrogen monatomic, having a double bond, being diamagnetic and oxidation must occur to obtain ammonia.
    D. Elemental nitrogen is monatomic, diamagnetic and oxidation must occur to obtain ammonia.

47. Which of the following represents the hybridization of the nitrogen atoms in N_2?
    A. sp
    B. sp^2
    C. sp^3
    D. sp^3d

THIS PAGE LEFT

INTENTIONALLY BLANK

Passage 9 (Questions 48-52)

Valence bond (VB) theory has been successful at explaining numerous aspects of bonding in simple inorganic and organic molecules. It is assumed that the direct overlap of hybridized atomic orbitals results in the formation of sigma type covalent bonds, and that multiple bonding can result from the sideways overlap of pure p-type atomic orbitals and the formation of p-type bonds. As a result, VB theory has proven to be quite useful in predicting molecular shapes and other physical properties such as bond lengths and strengths. However, explaining the properties of molecular oxygen proved to be a significant challenge. Specifically, VB theory predicts that molecular oxygen should have a double bond and be diamagnetic. While the experimentally observed bond length and strength of O_2 is consistent with a double bond, molecular oxygen is known to be paramagnetic.

Molecular orbital (MO) theory has proven to be a significant improvement over VB theory in explaining many of the physical properties of molecules. The basic premise of MO theory is that atomic orbitals have wave properties, and like waves, they can interact with one another to form constructive and destructive interference. Therefore, when two atomic orbitals interact, there will always be two molecular orbitals that result, one being an energetically stabilized bonding interaction and a destabilized out of phase anti-bonding interaction. MO theory takes advantage of the directionality of atomic orbitals and symmetry to predict the resulting energy differences between molecular orbitals, based partly on the concepts of hybridization and orbital overlap. As a result, theoretical chemists have been very successful at using MO theory to explain spectroscopic properties and chemical reactivity. Shown in Figure 1 is an example of a MO energy diagram used to predict the bonding of the second period diatomic elements. The bond order between the diatomic elements can be determined from the MO diagram, by: (1) Placing the total number of valence electrons in the various orbitals in order of increasing energy, following Hund's rules for degenerate orbitals; (2) Subtract the number of electrons in anti-bonding orbitals from the number of electrons in bonding type orbitals; and (3) Divide by two. In certain cases it is possible to have fractional bond orders.

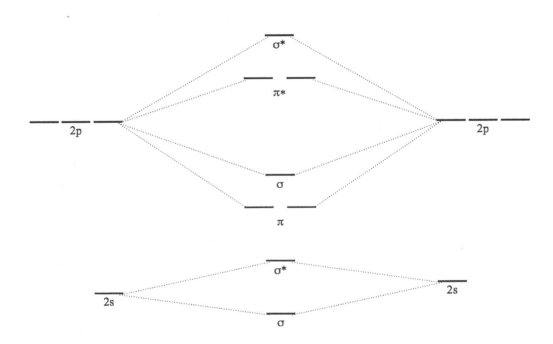

Figure 1 A generalized molecular orbital energy diagram for second period diatomic elements, using second order mixing of the 2s and 2p$_z$ orbitals to form the sigma-bonding (σ) and anti-bonding (σ^*) type orbitals.

48. Based on the MO energy diagram in Figure 1, what is the bond order between oxygen atoms in O_2?
    A. 1
    B. 2
    C. 2.5
    D. 3

49. Super oxide, O_2^-, is formed by the one electron reduction of elemental oxygen and is an especially reactive species which can cause a variety of problems for cells and has been implicated in the aging process. Superoxide dismutases rapidly convert superoxide into elemental oxygen and the peroxide ion. Which of the following sets of distances would be consistent with the bond orders in elemental oxygen, superoxide and peroxide?
    A. 1.21 Å, 1.28 Å and 1.49 Å respectively
    B. 1.49 Å, 1.28 Å and 1.21 Å respectively
    C. 1.21 Å, 1.49 Å and 1.28 Å respectively
    D. 1.28 Å, 1.49 Å and 1.21 Å respectively

50. Based on the MO energy diagram in Figure 1, which of the following diatomic elements would have unpaired electrons?
    A. Nitrogen
    B. Oxygen
    C. Fluorine
    D. Chlorine

51. Which of the following does NOT have π-type bonds?
    A. Acetic acid
    B. Propanol
    C. Propanal
    D. Propanone

52. Which of the following is/are isoelectronic with elemental nitrogen?
    I. Carbon monoxide
    II. Hydrogen peroxide
    III. Acetylene

    A. I only
    B. I and II only
    C. II and III only
    D. I and III only

Passage 10 (Questions 53-55)

An MD associated with Doctors Without Borders was working in West Africa at a clinic and discovered that a critical piece of electronic equipment had malfunctioned due to a problem with the electrical generator that was used by the clinic. The equipment was essential for monitoring several patients that may well recover as long as they received the appropriate care. It was determined that it would take several days to replace the equipment and in the meantime the doctor decided that he would try to repair the equipment, by replacing any burned out resistors or capacitors. The clinic had a battery operated digital multimeter and a supply of various resistors and capacitors. On the inside of the box of resistors there was a color code (Table 1) and two examples (Figure 1) for a 4-band and a 5-band resistor. In some cases there was not the equivalent resistor or capacitor to the ones that had burned out and the doctor had to figure out appropriate combinations to use for replacement.

Table 1 Color code for 4-band and 5-band resistors

Color	Digit	Multiplier	Tolerance (%)
Black	0	10^0	
Brown	1	10^1	1
Red	2	10^2	2
Orange	3	10^3	
Yellow	4	10^4	
Green	5	10^5	0.5
Blue	6	10^6	0.25
Violet	7	10^7	0.1
Grey	8	10^8	
White	9	10^9	
Gold		10^{-1}	5
Silver		10^{-2}	10
(none)			20

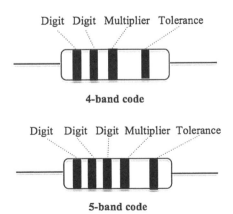

Figure 1 Examples of how to read resistor color codes. A 4-band resistor colored Yellow-Violet-Orange-Gold would be 47 kΩ with a tolerance of +/- 5%, and a 5-band resistor colored Brown-Green-Grey-Silver-Red would be 1.58 Ω with a tolerance of +/- 2%.

53. The broken instrument had an AC to DC power converter. The doctor needed to use the digital multimeter shown below to check the voltage drop for the resistors and identify the resistor(s) that had failed. To make this measurement the doctor inserted the plug for the black probe into the black common connection and inserted the plug for the red probe into the red voltage connection labeled 124, and:

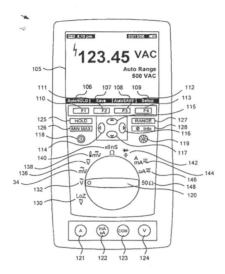

    A. turn the dial to the setting labeled 136 and connect the probes in parallel with the resistor that needs to be checked.

    B. turn the dial to the setting labeled 144 and connect the probes in parallel with the resistor that needs to be checked.

    C. turn the dial to the setting labeled 136 and connect the probes in series with the resistor that needs to be checked.

    D. turn the dial to the setting labeled 132 and connect the probes in series with the resistor that needs to be checked.

54. The doctor determined that the color bands of one of the burned out resistors was Brown-Gold-Black-Red. What was the resistance and tolerance of this resistor?

    A. $2.0\,\Omega \pm 1\,\%$

    B. $0.2\,\Omega \pm 2\,\%$

    C. $1\,\Omega \pm 2\,\%$

    D. It is not possible to determine the resistance of this resistor.

55. The doctor determined that a single 100 mF capacitor had failed. Which of the following combinations of capacitors could NOT be used to replace this capacitor?

    A. Two 200 mF capacitors

    B. Two 50 mF capacitors

    C. Three 100 mF capacitors

    D. One 200 mF and two 400 mF capacitors

These questions are NOT based on a passage (56-59)

56. An object is dropped from the top of a 125 m tall building. What is the object's speed right before hitting the ground, assuming wind resistance is negligible?
    A. 50 m/s
    B. 100 m/s
    C. 250 m/s
    D. 2500 m/s

57. Some students complained about the smell of rotten eggs when they mixed some of their solutions with acid at their lab bench. Which of the following combinations might be responsible for the smell of rotten eggs?
    A. Copper (II) nitrate plus sodium carbonate
    B. Iron (III) nitrate plus sodium sulfide
    C. Potassium nitrate plus sodium chloride
    D. Calcium nitrate plus sodium hydroxide

58. Which of the following types of bonding is NOT significant for ethanol?
    A. Covalent bonding
    B. Ionic bonding
    C. Hydrogen bonding
    D. Polar covalent bonding

59. If a liquid is flowing through a large diameter tube and then suddenly reaches a smaller diameter section, what happens to the pressure and velocity of the liquid?
    A. The pressure decreases and the velocity increases.
    B. The pressure increases and the velocity decreases.
    C. Both the pressure and the velocity increase.
    D. Both the pressure and the velocity decrease.

TIMED
SECTION 3
Answers and Explanations

Timed Section 3 Answer Key

Passage 1
1. C
2. A
3. B
4. B

Passage 2
5. C
6. B
7. D
8. B
9. A

Passage 3
10. B
11. C
12. C
13. A
14. B

Discrete Set 1
15. D
16. A
17. C

Passage 4
18. C
19. C
20. B
21. C

Passage 5
22. C
23. B
24. A
25. B

Passage 6
26. B
27. C
28. B
29. B
30. D

Discrete Set 2
31. A
32. B
33. A
34. A

Passage 7
35. A
36. A
37. A
38. A
39. A

Passage 8
40. C
41. A
42. B
43. C

Discrete Set 3
44. D
45. A
46. A
47. A

Passage 9
48. B
49. A
50. B
51. B
52. D

Passage 10
53. A
54. A
55. C

Discrete Set 4
56. A
57. B
58. B
59. A

Passage I Explanation

The production of nitrogen oxides by internal **combustion** engines is an important environmental health concern, because of their role as part of photochemical smog and air pollution. In addition to the **pollution from nitrogen oxides, the production of hydrocarbon radicals** from incomplete combustion also contributes to unhealthy levels of photochemical smog and ozone in large urban areas. Elemental nitrogen is the major gas in the earth's atmosphere (78 %) and oxygen represents the majority of the remainder (20.8%). Normally elemental nitrogen is very stable and does not react with the oxygen in the air, but the elevated temperatures inside an engine provide more than enough **activation energy** for Reaction 1. The rate of reaction between nitrogen monoxide and elemental oxygen, Reaction 2, has been studied using the method of **initial rates** and selected data are presented in Table 1, with the initial rate being measured in terms of the change in the concentration of elemental oxygen.

Key terms: Combustion, radicals, activation energy, and initial rates

Reaction 1 $$N_2 (g) + O_2 (g) \rightarrow 2 NO (g)$$

Reaction 1 **The overall reaction between elemental nitrogen and elemental oxygen, produces nitrogen monoxide, which has a very high activation energy, but the reaction is thermodynamically favorable.**

Reaction 2 $$2 NO (g) + O_2 (g) \rightarrow 2 NO_2 (g)$$

Reaction 2 **The reaction of nitrogen monoxide with elemental oxygen has a rate law that is first order with respect to oxygen and second order with respect to nitrogen monoxide.**

Experiment Number	Initial Rate ($M\,s^{-1}$)	Initial [O_2] (M)	Initial [NO] (M)
1	6.81×10^{-4}	6.50×10^{-3}	7.80×10^{-3}
2	2.04×10^{-3}	1.95×10^{-2}	7.80×10^{-3}
3	6.13×10^{-3}	6.50×10^{-3}	2.34×10^{-2}
4	5.44×10^{-3}	1.30×10^{-2}	1.56×10^{-2}

Table 1 Initial rate data for Reaction 1

Table 1 **The general rate law for reaction 2 can be determined from the initial rate data in table 1. In comparing experiments number 1 and 2, it should be noted that the concentration of nitrogen monoxide does not change, whereas the concentration of oxygen is approximately tripled, resulting in a three-fold increase in the rate. This indicates that the reaction is first order in oxygen.**

Comparing experiments 1 and 3, it should be noted that the concentration of oxygen remains constant, but the concentration of nitrogen oxide increases by a factor of three, causing the rate of the reaction to increase by a factor of 0.0061/0.00068 ~ 9 which is 32. The reaction order in terms of nitrogen monoxide is second order. The overall order for this reaction is third order.

1. Based on the data in Table 1, what is the overall order of Reaction 2?
    A. Reaction 2 is first order with respect to O_2, second order with respect to NO and first order overall.
    B. Reaction 2 is second order with respect to O_2, first order with respect to NO and first order overall.
    C. Reaction 2 is first order with respect to O_2, second order with respect to NO and third order overall.
    D. Reaction 2 is second order with respect to O_2, first order with respect to NO and third order overall.

Choice **C** is correct. The general rate law for reaction 2 can be determined from the initial rate data in table 1.

In comparing experiments number 1 and 2, it should be noted that the concentration of nitrogen monoxide does not change, whereas the concentration of oxygen is approximately tripled, resulting in a three-fold increase in the rate. This indicates that the reaction is first order in oxygen. Then comparing experiments 1 and 3, it should be noted that the concentration of oxygen remains constant, but the concentration of nitrogen oxide increases by a factor of three, causing the rate of the reaction to increase by a factor of $0.0061/0.00068 \sim 9$ which is 3^2. The reaction order in terms of nitrogen monoxide is second order. The overall order for this reaction is third order. Choice C is the correct answer.

A, B, D: These answers are a result of miscalculation or mis-reading of the experimental data.

2. Which of the following is the rate constant for Reaction 2?
    A. $1.7 \times 10^3 \, M^{-2} \, s^{-1}$
    B. $2.2 \times 10^1 \, M^{-1} \, s^{-1}$
    C. $6.7 \times 10^1 \, M^{-1} \, s^{-1}$
    D. $5.4 \times 10^5 \, M^{-1} \, s^{-1}$

Choice **A** is correct. From the data in Table 1, the rate law for Reaction 2 is

$$\text{Rate} = k \, [O_2][NO]^2$$

Selecting the rate and concentrations for one of the experiments, i.e. number 1, inserting these values into the rate law and rearranging for the rate constant, gives

$$k = \text{Rate}/[O_2][NO]^2$$
$$k = (6.8 \times 10^{-4})/[6.5 \times 10^{-3}][7.8 \times 10^{-3}]^2$$

Using approximate values gives

$$k \sim (7 \times 10^{-4})/[7 \times 10^{-3}][8 \times 10^{-3}]2$$
$$k \sim 1/64 \times 10^5$$
$$k \sim 1/6 \times 10^4$$
$$k \sim 0.15 \times 10^4$$
$$k \sim 1.5 \times 10^3$$

Choice **A** is the correct answer.

An alternative method would be to insert the answer choices as the rate constant in the rate law, along with the rate and concentration values from one of the experiments and see which choice gives the equality.

B,C, D: These answers are a result of miscalculation.

3. Which of the following is NOT a radical?
    A. CH_3 (g)
    B. <u>**N_2 (g)**</u>
    C. NO (g)
    D. NO_2 (g)

Choice **B** is correct. A radical is a species with one or more unpaired electrons. Generally for this to be true there needs to be an odd number of valence electrons. Elemental nitrogen has $2(5) = 10$ valence electrons. The Lewis dot structure indicates that there is a triple bond between the nitrogen atoms and no unpaired electrons. Choice B is the correct answer.

The number of valence electrons in CH_3 is $4 + 3(1) = 7$. Six of the electrons are used to form the three single bonds between the carbon and hydrogens. The remaining electrons on the carbon represent the unpaired electrons and CH_3 is a radical. Choice A can be eliminated. Nitrogen monoxide has $5 + 6 = 11$ valence electrons. Drawing the Lewis dot structure, it can be concluded that the unpaired electron is on the nitrogen atom and NO is a radical. Choice C can be eliminated. Nitrogen dioxide has $5 + 2(6) = 17$ valence electrons. Again drawing the Lewis dot structure, it can be concluded that the unpaired electron is on the nitrogen atom and NO_2 is a radical. Choice D can be eliminated.

4. The following two-step mechanisms have been proposed for Reaction 2. Which of these mechanisms can be eliminated based on the data in Table 1?

I. $2\ NO\ (g) \rightleftharpoons N_2O_2\ (g)$ (fast)
        $N_2O_2\ (g) + O_2\ (g) \rightarrow 2\ NO_2\ (g)$ (slow)

II.   <u>**$NO\ (g) + O_2\ (g) \rightarrow NO_2\ (g) + O\ (g)$ (slow)**</u>
        <u>**$NO\ (g) + O\ (g) \rightarrow NO_2\ (g)$ (fast)**</u>

III. $2\ NO\ (g) + O_2\ (g) \rightarrow 2\ NO_2\ (g)$ (slow)

    A. I only
    B. <u>**II only**</u>
    C. II and III only
    D. I and III only

Choice **B** is correct. The data in Table 1 indicates that the Reaction 2 is first order in oxygen and second order in nitrogen monoxide.

For answer option I, the rate of the forward and reverse reactions for the first step, which is a fast equilibrium, will be equal. Writing the rate law for both the forward and reverse reactions gives

$$Rate_f = k_1\ [NO]^2$$
$$Rate_r = k_{-1}\ [N_2O_2]$$

Setting the two equations equal to each other gives

$$k_1\ [NO]^2 = k_{-1}\ [N_2O_2]$$

Rearranging for the $[N_2O_2]$ gives

$$[N_2O_2] = k_1/k_{-1} \, [NO]^2$$

Writing the rate law for the second slow step, which is the rate determining step, gives

$$\text{Rate} = k_2 \, [N_2O_2][O_2]$$

Combining these two equations gives

$$\text{Rate} = k_2 \, k_1/k_{-1} \, [NO]^2[O_2]$$
$$\text{Rate} = K \, [NO]^2[O_2]$$

This mechanism would be second order in nitrogen monoxide and first order for oxygen, which is consistent with the data in Table 1. Choices A and D can be eliminated.

The rate law for mechanism II would be the rate law for the first slow step, $\text{Rate} = k_1 \, [NO][O_2]$, which would be first order in both nitrogen monoxide and oxygen, which is not consistent with, the data in Table 1. This mechanism can be eliminated, and eliminates choices A and D.

The rate law for mechanism III, which is a slow one step reaction, would be

$$\text{Rate} = K \, [O_2][NO]^2$$

This rate law is consistent with the data in Table 1, and eliminates choices C and D.

Choice **B** is the correct answer.

Passage 2 Explanation

Shown in Figure 1 are **the linear forms** of three naturally occurring monosaccharides, as well as the corresponding ring structures of two of these compounds, and a disaccharide. The ring structures are **formed by addition** of a hydroxyl group to the carbonyl group, to form either a five- or a six-membered ring.

Key terms: monosaccharides, disaccharide, hydroxyl, and carbonyl

Cause-and-Effect: The intramolecular reaction between a hydroxyl group and the carbonyl of the linear form of monosaccharides, results in the formation of ring structures, which can undergo dehydration to combine monosaccharides to form disaccharide by way of ether linkages.

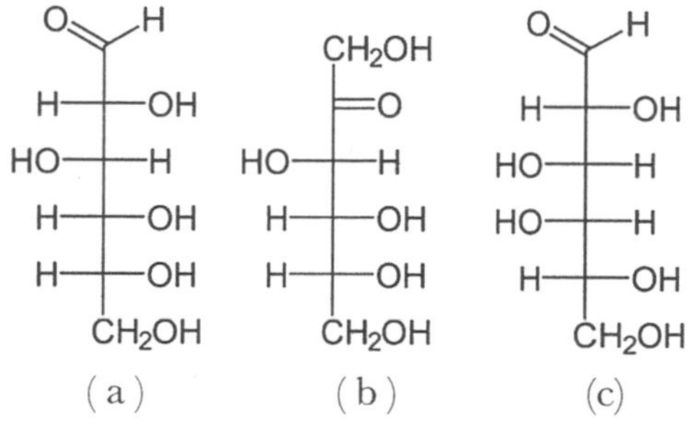

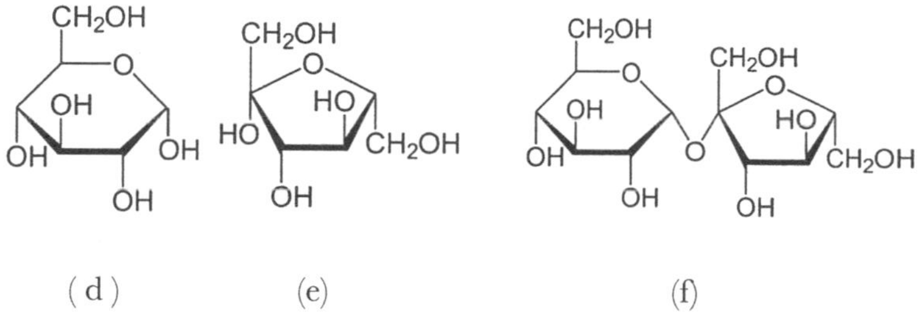

Figure 1 The linear forms of (a) glucose, (b) fructose, and (c) galactose. Also shown are the ring structures of (d) glucose and (e) fructose, as well as the disaccharide, (f) sucrose.

Figure 1 Saccharides can form either linear or ring structures, with the later being thermodynamically more stable. The ring structures are either five or six membered rings in which one of the atoms of the ring is an oxygen, forming a cyclic ether. The ring structures can combine by way of a dehydration reaction between the hydroxyl groups of adjacent saccharides to form an ether linkage. In the ring structures, each of the carbon atoms has a hydroxyl group, imparting the solubility properties of alcohols due to intermolecular hydrogen bonding interactions. The linear forms have carbonyl groups, making it possible to classify them as either aldehydes or ketones, both of which are capable of undergoing keto-enol tautomerization and rearrangements. Saccharides containing aldehyde groups are capable of being oxidized to carboxylate groups, which forms the basis for Benedict's test, in which basic aqueous solutions of azure Cu^{2+} gets reduced to insoluble Cu^+ compounds.

5. Glucose and galactose are which of the following types of stereoisomers?
    A. Enantiomers
    B. Rotomers
    C. **Epimers**
    D. Constitutional isomers

Choice **C** is correct. Looking closely at Figure 1 (a and c), shows that the only difference between glucose and galactose is the stereochemical arrangement of groups on C(4). Note that the aldehyde carbon establishes the order of numbering. Epimers are stereoisomers that differ by the stereochemistry of a single chiral center. Choice C is the correct answer.

Enantiomers are stereoisomers that are mirror image structures. For compounds with multiple chiral centers, each chiral atom would have opposite configurations to be enantiomers. Choice A can be eliminated. Rotomers result from different rotational conformations that can exist. Glucose and galactose are not rotomers and choice B can be eliminated. Constitutional isomers are also known as structural isomers, which occurs when two compounds have the same formula, but atoms have different connectivity. Stereoisomers are not constitutional isomers and choice D can be eliminated.

6. Which of the following types of reactions are involved in the formation of sucrose, from glucose and fructose?
    A. Hydrolysis
    B. **Dehydration**
    C. Esterification
    D. Addition

Choice **B** is correct. When sucrose is formed from glucose and fructose, essentially an ether group is formed from two alcohols by loss of a water molecule. Choice B is the correct answer.

Hydrolysis is when water is added to a compound and choice A can be eliminated. Esterification is when an organic acid and an alcohol are combined by way of dehydration, to form an ester. Choice C can be eliminated. As stated in the passage, addition typically occurs when an unsaturated molecule, such as an aldehyde, ketone or alkene becomes saturated. Choice D can be eliminated.

7. A student in an organic chemistry class was given a sample of an unknown monosaccharide and was asked to identify the compound. The student initially performed an elemental analysis and found that the sample was 40.0 % carbon, 6.7 % hydrogen and 53.3 % oxygen. Which of the following monosaccharides could be the unknown based on this experiment?
    I. Glucose
    II. Galactose
    III. Fructose

    A. I only
    B. II only
    C. I and II only
    D. **I, II, and III**

Choice **D** is correct. There are two basic ways to answer this question. The longer method would be to assume that you have 100 g of the unknown and then determine the mole ratio by dividing the resulting mass of carbon, hydrogen and oxygen by the corresponding atomic masses.

A potentially more efficient method would require a student to notice that glucose, fructose and galactose all have the same molecular formulas, $C_6H_{12}O_6$, and the same empirical formula, CH_2O. Right away, the only reasonable answer is choice D. If you must do the calculation to be sure, first determine the empirical weight, $12 + 2(1) + 16 = 30$, then determine the percentage of carbon, hydrogen and oxygen.

$$(12/30) \times 100 = 40\%$$
$$(2/30) \times 100 = 7\%$$
$$(16/30) \times 100 = 53\%$$

A, B, C: These answers are a result of miscalculation. Glucose, galactose and fructose ALL have the formula $C_6H_{12}O_6$, and would satisfy the student findings.

8. Which of the following is the source of the oxygen atoms in pyruvate that is formed by glycolysis?
    A. Elemental oxygen
    B. <u>**Glucose**</u>
    C. Carbon dioxide
    D. Hexokinase

Choice **B** is correct. Glycolysis is the metabolic pathway that converts glucose into pyruvate. The free energy released is used to form the high energy compounds namely ATP & NADH (reduced nicotinamide adenine dinucleotide). Glycolysis occurs with variation in nearly all organisms, both aerobic and anaerobic. The source of oxygen atoms in pyruvate is the substrate glucose. Choice B is the correct answer.

Glycolysis is an anaerobic process, therefore elemental oxygen is not involved and choice A can be eliminated. Carbon dioxide is a product of aerobic respiration and choice C can be eliminated. Hexokinase is the enzyme that phosphorylates glucose, which is an important step in glycolysis, but hexokinase is not the source of oxygen atoms in pyruvate. Choice D can be eliminated.

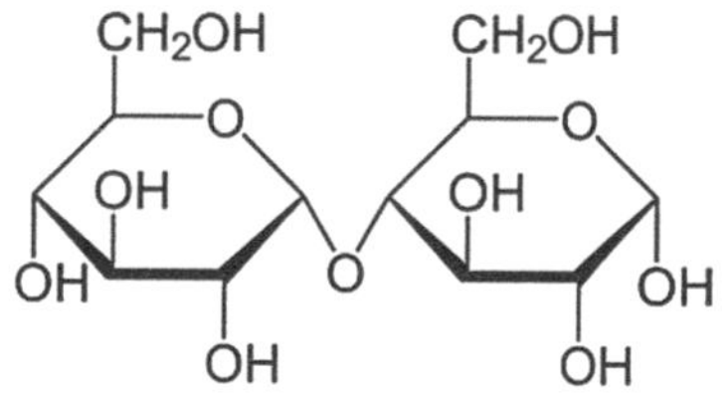

9. Shown below is the structure of the disaccharide maltose, which is composed of which of the following monosaccharides?
    I. Glucose
    II. Galactose
    III. Fructose

    A. <u>**I only**</u>
    B. II only
    C. I and II only
    D. I and III only

Choice **A** is correct. If you now look closely at the orientation of the hydroxyl groups in the maltose, you see that the orientations are the same, eliminating choice C. You now can compare the orientations of the hydroxyl groups in the maltose to the sucrose, which is comprised of glucose and fructose. Notice that the six membered ring structure in

Glucose   Galactose   Fructose

sucrose is identical to the six-membered ring on the left in the structure of maltose. Therefore maltose is comprised of two glucose molecules, connected by an ether link at the 1,4 positions of the rings. Choice A is the correct answer. II – The rings shown are not galactose. III - Looking closely at the ring structure of the maltose, shows that there are six atoms in the rings, eliminating fructose as one of the component monosaccharides.

Passage 3 Explanation

Students in an introductory physics class were asked to do an experiment to study Newton's second law. A **nearly frictionless cart** was placed on a track and a string was used to connect the cart to a 5. g mass hanger that was strung over a wheel, providing tension due to the weight of the hanger, as shown in Figure 1. Four standard 20 g brass masses were placed on the cart. An ultrasonic motion detector, interfaced with a computer, was used to determine the position of the cart as a function of time. Initially, the students were asked to calibrate the software by placing the cart at a position on the track such that there was **1.000 m between the cart and the motion detector** and collecting data without the cart moving. Individual trials of the experiment were performed in which the cart was held relatively close to the motion detector and then released. After data collection was completed for a trial, the computer provided the students with two graphs of the data, a position versus time graph and a velocity versus time graph, and least-squares fit equations were displayed. The **students recorded the acceleration of the cart for three trials**, and then moved one of the standard brass masses from the cart and placed it on the hanger, thereby **increasing the force applied to the system**, without changing the total mass of the system. Three additional trials were performed, and the process was repeated until each individual mass was transferred from the cart to the hanger. The data for one of the students is shown in Figure 1. The students were then asked to take the cart and place it on an electronic balance to **determine the gravitational mass of the cart**. Students then used the data collected in this experiment to determine the **inertial mass of the system** and subsequently the inertial mass of the cart, which was then compared with the gravitational mass.

Key terms: Newton's second law, frictionless, tension, weight, ultrasonic, calibrate, acceleration, force, gravitational mass, and inertial mass.

Cause-and-Effect: The gravitational force acting vertically on the mass hanging on the end of the string causes the acceleration of the entire system.

Contrast: Moving a brass mass from the cart to the hanger, increases the acceleration of the system, without changing the total mass of the system.

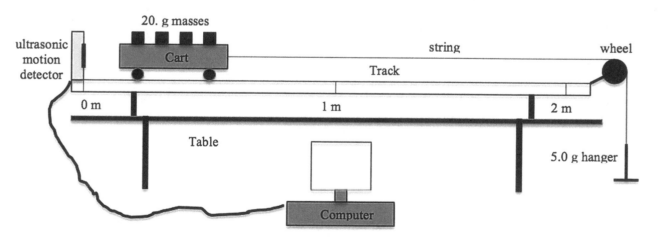

Figure 1 Experimental set up for determining the inertial mass of a cart based on Newton's Second law.

Figure 1 A schematic diagram of the experimental set-up used to study Newton's second law by systematically changing the acceleration without changing the total mass of the system. This is achieved by transferring mass from the cart to the hanger. The ultrasonic motion detector sends out sound pulses that reflect off the cart and return to the detector to determine the position of the cart.

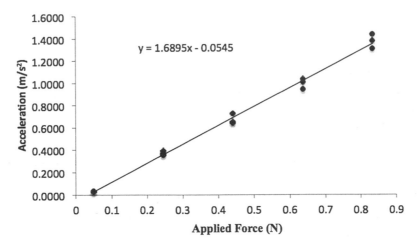

Figure 2 Acceleration versus applied force collected by a student using the experimental set-up shown in Figure 1 and described in the passage. Note that the least-squares best fit line for the data is displayed on the graph.

Figure 2 An example plot of applied force versus measured acceleration. There are three trials for each applied mass, as indicated by each individual data point for an applied mass. The random error of the experiment is reflected by the differences in the trials for a given applied mass. The slope of the plot is equal to the inverse of the total mass of the system.

10. What is the magnitude of weight of the hanger used for the first three trials of the experiment?
    A. 0.005 N
    B. 0.05 N
    C. 0.25 N
    D. 0.45 N

Choice **B** is correct. Weight is a force resulting for the acceleration of gravity acting on an object with mass. The mass of the hanger, from the passage, is 5 g or 0.005 kg. Multiplying this mass by the acceleration due to gravity, 9.8 m/s², gives 0.0050 x 9.8 = 0.05 kg m/s² = 0.05 N and choice B is the correct answer.

A, C, D: These answers are a result of miscalculation.

11. Based on the student's data and best-fit line shown in Figure 2, what is the inertial mass of the system that is being accelerated in the experiment described in the passage?
    A. 0.085 kg
    B. 0.507 kg
    C. 0.592 kg
    D. 1.690 kg

Choice **C** is correct. Newton's second law is F = ma, which can be compared with the equation of a straight line, y = mx + b. If force is plotted on the y-axis and acceleration is plotted on the x-axis, the slope of this graph would be equivalent to the mass of the system. However, in the experiment described in the passage, the acceleration is plotted on the y-axis, because of the convention of plotting the independent and dependent variables of an experiment on the x- and y-axes, respectively. In this case, you need to rearrange Newton's second law to give, a = (1/m)F and compare it to y = mx + b. In this case, plotting the force on the x axis and acceleration on the y-axis, gives a graph in which the slope is equal to the inverse of the mass of the system. From the equation of the best-fit line in Figure 2, the slope is 1.6895 = 1/m, or m = 1/1.6895 = 0.5919 kg. Choice C is the correct answer.
A, B, D: These answers are a result of miscalculation.

12. The commonly accepted range of human hearing is from 20 Hz to 20 kHz and the speed of sound in air is 340 m/s. During the calibration portion of the experiment, what is the minimum sampling time between when the ultrasonic device produces the sound and when it is detected?
    A. 5×10^{-5} s
    B. 3×10^{-3} s
    C. 6×10^{-3} s
    D. 5×10^{-2} s

Choice **C** is correct. During the calibration portion of the experiment, the cart was placed 1.0 m away from the motion detector. The ultrasound produced by the device must be reflected off the cart and go back to the detector, traveling a total of 2.0 m. Dividing this distance by the speed of sound, gives $2.0/340 \sim 2/3 \times 10^{-2} \sim 0.6 \times 10^{-2} \sim 6 \times 10^{-3}$ s. Choice C is the correct answer.

A, B, D: These answers are a result of miscalculation.

13. If the student measured the gravitational mass of the cart to be 503 g, what is the absolute value of the percent error between the gravitational mass of the cart and the inertial mass of the cart from the experiment?
    A. 1 %
    B. 12 %
    C. 20 %
    D. 53%

Choice **A** is correct. Note that the passage states that there is a "nearly frictionless cart". The inverse of the slope of the graph shown in Figure 2, is the mass of the entire system that is accelerating, therefore $1/1.6895 \sim 1/1.7 \sim 1/2 \sim 0.5$ kg, which is close to 500 g or 0.500 kg. If you stop here you will get the right answer, but for the wrong reason. Remember, that you must subtract the mass of the brass standards and the hanger, to get the mass of the cart. You must also remember that the real value of $1/1.6895$ is slightly greater than 0.5, i.e. 0.592 kg. You must then subtract the mass of the brass standard weights and the hanger, totaling 85 g, or 0.085 kg. This gives a mass close to 0.507 kg, which is very close to the gravitational mass of the cart. Choice A is the correct answer.

B, C, D: These answers are a result of miscalculation.

14. Which of the following are true for the experiment described in the passage?

    I. Force is the independent variable and acceleration is the dependent variable in the experiment described in the passage.
    II. The mass of the cart is the inverse of the slope of the acceleration versus applied force graph.
    III. An unlevel track would introduce a systematic error into the experiment affecting the apparent mass of the system.

    A. I and II only
    B. I and III only
    C. II and III only
    D. I, II, and III

Choice **B** is correct. Force is the variable controlled by the student, and is the independent variable, making I true (Eliminate choice C).
I - Force is the variable plotted on the x-axis (indep) and acceleration is the measured or dependent value plotted on the y-axis of the graph in Figure 2. Choice C can be eliminated.

II - The inverse of the slope of the graph in Figure 2, is the total mass of the system, not just the mass of the cart. Choices A and D can be eliminated.

III - The net force is the sum of all forces acting on the system in the horizontal direction. If the track is not level, there will be a component of the weight, which is in the vertical direction. If the track is tipped towards the end with the pulley (to the right in Figure 2), the acceleration will be slightly greater than expected, and if the track is tipped in the other direction, the acceleration of the system will be less than expected. This systematic error would cause the slope to be slightly greater or less than the theoretical value, and hence affects the calculated mass of the system. Thus III is true. Choice B is the correct answer. A systematic error is an error that causes a deviation in the experimental data in a specific way, and usually can be identified and corrected. Random error results in a statistically normal distribution of trial results around an accepted value and is inherent to the measuring devices used in the experiment.

A, C, D: See reasoning above. Only I and III are true.

These questions are NOT based on a passage

15. Benedict's solution, aqueous basic Cu^{2+}, is used to test for aldehydes and α-hydroxyketones. Which of the following will act as a reducing sugar and give a positive Benedict's test?

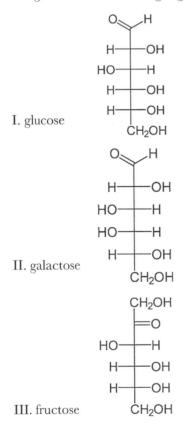

I. glucose

II. galactose

III. fructose

    A. I only
    B. II only
    C. I and II only
    D. <u>I, II and III</u>

Choice **D** is correct. As stated in the question, Benedict's test will give positive results for aldehydes. As seen in the structures shown in the answer options, glucose and galactose are both aldehydes, making I and II true and eliminating choices A and B. The other class of compounds that will give a positive Benedict's test are α-hydroxy-ketones, which is a ketone with a hydroxyl group on a carbon next to the ketone. Fructose is an α-hydroxy-ketone and will give a positive Benedict's test, because of the possibility of undergoing a keto-enol tautomerization, which could result in a rearrangement in the structure, producing glucose under the basic conditions of the test. Benedict's test involves the oxidation of the aldehyde group by the blue Cu^{2+} ion, which gets reduced and forms insoluble Cu^+ compounds. Choice D is the correct answer.

A, B, C: See reasoning above.

16. If an object has a gravitational mass of 50 kg on the surface of the earth, what is the gravitational mass of that same object on the surface of the moon, where the acceleration due to gravity is 1/6 the acceleration due to gravity on the earth?
    A. **50 kg**
    B. 100 kg
    C. 490 N
    D. 82 N

Choice **A** is correct. The mass, in kilograms, of an object does not change depending upon its location in the universe and proximity to other objects having mass, i.e. the earth, or the moon. Choice A is the correct answer. The weight of an object is the force of gravity due to the acceleration caused by the attractive force between two objects having mass. Weight, in newtons (N), does change depending upon an object's location in the universe.

According to Newton's laws, mass cannot change based upon location. Only physically changing the object can alter its mass.

17. Which of the following compounds does NOT have an empirical formula of CH_2O?
    A. Glucose
    B. Acetic acid
    C. **Formic acid**
    D. Glyceraldehyde

Choice **C** is correct. An empirical formula is the lowest whole number ratio of atoms in a formula. The molecular formula of formic acid is CH_2O_2, which is also the empirical formula, and choice C is the correct answer.

Glucose has a molecular formula of $C_6H_{12}O_6$, acetic acid has a molecular formula of $C_2H_4O_2$ and glyceraldehyde has a molecular formula of $C_3H_6O_3$, all of which have CH_2O as the empirical formula. Choices A, B and D can be eliminated

Passage 4 Explanation

Both glucose and galactose enter glycolysis through a common intermediate, glucose-6-phosphate (G-6-P). Glucose is acted upon either by hexokinase or by one of its isoforms to yield G-6-P in a single step. The multi-step conversion of galactose to glucose-6-phosphate requires the action of several enzymes.

Key terms: glucose, galactose, glucose-6-phosphate (G-6-P), hexokinase

Cause-and-Effect: glucose and galactose enter glycolysis through a common intermediate; glucose is converted to G-6-P by hexokinase or a hexokinase isoform in a single step; galactose is converted to G-6-P through a multi-step pathway.

It has long been observed that in certain tumor cell lines grown in glucose-containing medium, lactic acid is produced rapidly. When the same cells are grown in galactose-containing medium, the cells exhibits only moderately elevated lactic acid production, but equal growth rates. Hepatoma cells are one such rapidly dividing cancerous cell type. It has been **hypothesized** that **mitochondria in cancerous** cells are either **defective** or are **less able to compete** with glycolytic enzymes for common intermediates. As a result, nearly all **hexoses imported** into the cell enter glycolysis, but **relatively few are oxidatively phosphorylated**. In order to investigate **mitochondria's involvement** in the altered, largely anaerobic metabolism of some tumor cells, **three experiments** were performed on cultured hepatoma cells established from rat hepatoma cell lines.

Key terms: lactic acid, hepatoma cells, mitochondria, anaerobic, oxidatively phosphorylated

Cause-and-Effect: some cancer cells, including hepatoma cells, produce more lactic acid in glucose-containing media than in galactose-containing media and grow equally well when cultured in media containing either sugar; mitochondrial dysfunction or inability to outcompete glycolytic enzymes for common intermediates may be responsible.

Experiment 1

^{14}C labeled hexose transport by intact hepatoma cells was measured at physiological temperature and pH for ^{14}C-glucose, ^{14}C-galactose, and 3-O-methyl-^{14}C-glucose (a non-metabolizable sugar derivative). **Transport rates for the three sugars** were found to be nearly identical, indicating cell import hexoses at equal rates. However, when measurements were made in a repeat experiment over a much longer period of time, glucose uptake was found to be greater than galactose uptake.

Key terms: ^{14}C labeled hexose, ^{14}C-glucose, ^{14}C-galactose, 3-O-methyl-^{14}C-glucose, transport rates

Cause-and-Effect: transport rates in all ^{14}C labeled hexoses were approximately equal; over longer periods of time, glucose uptake exceeded galactose uptake by tested cells.

Experiment 2

Hexokinase specific activity was determined **photometrically** for **control rat liver homogenates, regenerating rat liver homogenates** and hepatoma cells at various assay G-6-P concentrations. The assay glucose concentration for the hepatoma cells was 0.5 mM, while that for control and regenerating liver was 13 mM. The hexokinase activity of liver homogenate at 0.5 mM was negligible. Hexokinase activity was found to be approximately constant and **elevated more than 20-fold in hepatoma cells** versus activities found in both control and regenerating rat liver at G-6-P concentrations of up to 0.6 mM.

Key terms: hexokinase specific activity, control rat liver homogenates, regenerating rat liver homogenates

Cause-and-Effect: hexokinase activity was determined at varying G-6-P concentrations; glucose concentration in hepatoma cell assays was lower than glucose concentration in control and regenerating liver assays; hexokinase activity at G-6-P concentrations up to 0.6 mM was elevated 20-fold when compared to the activities of control and regenerating liver samples.

Experiment 3

Respiration rates of isolated **hepatoma mitochondria** were measured using an oxygen electron in a closed container. Elevated glucose levels were found to significantly stimulate the respiration of coupled hepatoma mitochondria, a result that should be obtained only if the hexokinase reaction (glucose + ATP → G-6-P + ADP) **consumed mitochondrially synthesized ATP.** The glucose-stimulated respiration of **hepatoma cells was found to lack inhibition** by G-6-P up to 0.6 mM. However, when added, glucose was unable to stimulate respiration of mitochondria from control and regenerating rat liver. When tumor **mitochondria** were added to respiring normal mitochondria, cell **respiration was** again **stimulated** by the presence of glucose, indicating coupling of glycolysis and mitochondrial oxidative phosphorylation.

Key terms: mitochondrially stimulated ATP

Cause-and-Effect: more glucose stimulated respiration in the coupled mitochondria because the hexokinase reaction consumed mitochondrially synthesized ATP; this process was uninhibited by G-6-P concentrations up to 0.6 mM; glucose was unable to stimulate increased respiration of mitochondria in control and regenerating rat liver, but was able to stimulate increased mitochondrial respiration when mitochondria from hepatoma cells were added to normal mitochondria, indicating coupling of glycolysis and mitochondrial aerobic respiration.

In a separate series of experiments, the researchers demonstrated that in hepatoma cells at least 50% of cellular hexokinase is associated with the mitochondrial fraction and that the mitochondrial hexokinase activity is four-times higher than any other subcellular fraction.

Key terms: mitochondrial hexokinase

Cause-and-Effect: 50% of cellular hexokinase is associated with the mitochondrial fraction of hepatoma cells; mitochondrial hexokinase activity is 4-times higher than any other subcellular fraction.

18. Na^+/K^+ ATPases pump sodium from the cells of the proximal tubule of the nephron into the blood. SGLT proteins found in the plasma membrane of the same cells import glucose against its concentration from the tubular filtrate into the cell while exporting sodium down its concentration gradient. The action of SGLT proteins correctly represents which form of protein transport?

    A. Primary active transport
    B. Symport
    C. **Secondary active transport**
    D. Facilitated diffusion

Choice **C** is correct. Secondary active transport (co-transport) requires the input of energy to transport molecules across a membrane, but unlike in primary active transport, there is no direct coupling of ATP. The electrochemical potential difference created by pumping ions from the cell via primary active transport, thereby establishing a concentration gradient, is allows a molecule to flow down its concentration gradient.

SGLT proteins are specifically an example of secondary active transport antiport, in which two species are pumped in opposite directions across a membrane and down their concentration gradient (choice A). In the proximal tubule cells of the nephron, the Na^+/K^+ ATPase establishes the Na^+ gradient used in antiport via primary active transport (choice A). In symport, the other form of secondary active transport tested on the MCAT, both molecules are transported across a membrane in the same direction. Facilitated diffusion is the passive transport of solute down a concentration gradient through specific transmembrane protein channels (choice D).

19. A test of the respiratory response by regenerating rat liver to glucose stimulation was most likely included in Experiment 3 in order to:

    A. determine whether high activity levels of mitochondrially bound hexokinase are present in the neoplastic state.
    B. show that enhanced hexokinase response to glucose in hepatoma cells is not a property of the tissue of origin.
    C. **test whether glucose-stimulated hexokinase activity is also a function of rapidly dividing normal liver cells.**
    D. demonstrate that glucose is unable to stimulate the respiration of control rat liver.

Choice **C** is correct. The tests in experiment 3 determined that hexokinases of hepatoma cells are coupled to the oxidative phosphorylation system of mitochondria, and that this coupling is characteristic of cells in the neoplastic state. The inclusion of regenerating rat liver was intended as a control to show that this coupling is exclusively present in neoplastic cells (choice C).

The inclusion of tumor mitochondria in Experiment 3 was intended to demonstrate choice A. Testing the mitochondrial respiratory response of normal liver tissue was more specifically intended to test the statements made in choices B and D.

20. Which of the following findings, if true, would most strongly challenge a finding or conclusion of the experiments presented in the passage?

    A. Transport rates of ^{14}C-ribose exceed those of ^{14}C-glucose or ^{14}C-galactose.
    B. <u>**Tumor mitochondria, when included in samples of normal mitochondria, significantly increase oxygen consumption due to their own basal rate of respiration.**</u>
    C. Non-specific trapping of hexoses equally decreases the real hexose transport rate for both glucose and galactose versus that which was measured spectrophotometrically.
    D. Enzyme activity measured in control and regenerating rat liver was exerted by the high-K_m enzyme glucokinase

Choice **B** is correct. Experiment 3 demonstrates that oxygen consumption in the presence of glucose is increased in tumor mitochondria, but not in normal mitochondria. If that increase in oxygen consumption is due to basal levels of tumor mitochondrial respiration and not oxygen stimulation, then the finding that glycolysis and mitochondrial oxidative phosphorylation are coupled would be challenged (choice B).

Experiment 1 tests and subsequently makes a claim regarding only the rate of hexose transport—ribose is a pentose sugar (choice A). Non-specific hexose trapping would decrease the measured transport rate for both glucose and galactose and not impact the validity of the claim made in Experiment 1 regarding their equal transport rates (choice C). If the levels of enzyme activity measured in control and regenerating rat liver, which are assumed in Experiment 2 to be due to hexokinase activity, are found to be due to glucokinase, rather than hexokinase, then the claim made in 2 that the rate of hexokinase activity in tumor mitochondria is 20 times greater than in control and regenerating rat liver would represent a slight underestimate of the magnitude of the activity difference. However, the fundamental relationship between the activity levels would still be supported (choice D).

21. Glucokinase regulatory protein (GKPR) is a fully competitive inhibitor of glucokinase. According to the Michaelis-Menten description of enzyme kinetics, what effect does the presence of GKPR have on the glucokinase kinetics?

    A. K_m is unchanged and V_{max} increases
    B. K_m decreases and V_{max} is unchanged
    C. <u>**K_m increases and V_{max} is unchanged**</u>
    D. K_m is unchanged and V_{max} decreases

Choice **C** is correct. Competitive inhibitors compete with substrate for the active site of enzymes. V_{max} for such reactions is unchanged, as at high substrate concentrations, there is sufficient substrate present to outcompete inhibitor for access to the active site. At non-saturating substrate concentrations, competitive inhibitors meaningfully impact the rate of the catalyzed reaction. This leads to an increased K_m value—a measure of the substrate concentration required to reach the half-maximal reaction velocity (choice C).

See reasoning above. Choices A, B and D do not correspond to the predicted changes in V_{max} and K_m described.

Passage 5 Explanation

An introductory chemistry laboratory involved the study of various **reactions** that **produced precipitates** when aqueous solutions are combined. Students were given a total of nine different solutions in dark brown glass bottles and asked to mix equal portions of these solutions in reaction wells, using pipets. The students were asked to record their observations for appropriate combinations in tabular form, including formation of precipitates, bubbling, color changes or any other observations they thought were relevant. One of the student's **results are shown in Table 1**. In order to **prevent any hydrolysis** of the Cu^{2+} or Fe^{3+} ions, the professor added a small amount of **acid** to these two solutions. The professor asked the students to perform some of these reactions in a **fume hood** to **prevent** being exposed to potentially **noxious fumes**. The professor noted that the dark brown bottles can help prevent reactions with light common to transition metals in the fifth period and below.

Key terms: Precipitates, hydrolysis, ions, acid, fume hood, and noxious fumes.

Cause-and-Effect: If, when aqueous solutions of soluble ionic compounds result in a combination of cation and anion that is not soluble in aqueous solution, a precipitate will form.

Cause-and-Effect: Adding acid to an aqueous solution of acidic cations, such as Cu^{2+} or Fe^{3+} ions, prevents the hydrolysis reaction, which can cause the formation of the corresponding insoluble hydroxides, $Cu(OH)_2$ and $Fe(OH)_3$ respectively.

	NaCl colorless	NaOH colorless	Na₂S colorless	Na₂CO₃ colorless
KNO_3 colorless	NR	NR	NR	NR
$AgNO_3$ colorless	White precipitate	Beige precipitate	Black precipitate	White precipitate
$Ca(NO_3)_2$ colorless	NR	White precipitate	White precipitate	White precipitate
$Cu(NO_3)_2$ blue	NR	Pale blue gel	Black precipitate	Blue-green precipitate
$Fe(NO_3)_3$ orange	NR	Orange gel	Black precipitate	Orange precipitate

Table 1 Observations related to mixing known aqueous solutions. NR stands for "no reaction".

Table 1 Each cell of the table represents observations concerning the combination of solutions shown in the corresponding column and row labels.

Subsequently, the students were given an **unknown solution** in test tubes. The students were told that the unknown **contained two of the solutions** used in the **first part** of the experiment. The students were also told that the unknown solution would **always contain sodium nitrate**. It was the student's job to **identify the other ions**

present in the unknown by reacting the unknown solution with the known solutions and comparing their results to the previously obtained results. **Student A** was given 20 mL of a **colorless** unknown solution. This student wanted to combine his unknown with all of the known solutions to be sure that he would get the right answer. Unfortunately, he ran out of his unknown solution and had to ask the professor for additional solution. Surprisingly to this student, **silver nitrate was the only** solution that caused the formation of a precipitate with his unknown. He correctly reported the ions present in his unknown solution to the professor. **Student B** was given 20 mL of an orange unknown solution. She reacted her unknown with a small amount of only one of the known solutions and found that no precipitate formed. Having identified the ions present in the unknown solution, she reported her results to the professor.

Key terms: Experiment, sodium nitrate, colorless, and silver nitrate

Cause-and-Effect: By making insightful observations and selectively mixing their unknown solutions with the known solutions, students were able to determine the ions that were present in solution with a minimal use of unknown.

22. What is the formula of the precipitate formed by combining the iron (III) nitrate solution with the sodium sulfide solution?
    A. FeS
    B. FeS_2
    C. **Fe_2S_3**
    D. Fe_3S_2

Choice **C** is correct. Iron (III), Fe^{3+}, and sulfide, S^{2-}, combine to give an equal number of positive and negative charges, hence there are two Fe^{3+} ions and three S^{2-} ions in the formula, Fe_2S_3, with choice C be the answer.

These molecules are Iron II sulfide, Iron disulfide/persulfide, which is arranged Fe-S-S, and Fe_3S_2 is formed in response to very high pressures, which are not described in this passage and is unlikely to form.

23. In aqueous solution Fe^{3+} will undergo a hydrolysis reaction to form an orange gelatinous precipitate. Which of the following reactions best describes the formation of this precipitate?
    A. Fe^{3+} (aq) → $FeOH^{2+}$ (s) + H^+ (aq)
    B. **Fe^{3+} (aq) → $Fe(OH)_3$ (s) + 3 H^+ (aq)**
    C. Fe^{3+} (aq) + NO_3^- (aq) + 2 H^+ (aq) → $Fe(OH)_2$ (s) + NO (g)
    D. Fe^{3+} (aq) + 2 H_2O (l) → $Fe(OH)_2$ (s) + H_2 (g)

Choice **B** is correct. Choice B appears not to be balanced with respect to hydrogen and oxygen atoms, but you must remember that the Fe^{3+} (aq) has water molecules acting as Lewis bases and that coordinate to the Fe^{3+} ion. The ion is electron withdrawing and makes the polar covalent bond of these coordinated water molecules, even more polarized, resulting is dissociation of hydrogen ions and producing iron (III) hydroxide as the "orange gelatinous precipitate." This precipitate is consistent with the observations observed in Table 1, when the iron (III) nitrate solution is combined with the sodium hydroxide solution. Choice B is the correct answer.

Choice A is not reasonable, since cations, such as $FeOH^{2+}$, cannot form solids, and must be associated with anions of equal charge to form species with no net charge in the solid state. Choice A can be eliminated. The reactions shown in choices C and D are not balanced with respect to charge and can be eliminated.

24. When the copper (II) nitrate and iron (III) nitrate solutions were reacted with the sodium carbonate solution, some bubble formation was observed by certain students. What was the most likely identity of the bubbles?
    A. **Carbon dioxide**
    B. Carbon monoxide
    C. Elemental nitrogen
    D. Nitrogen monoxide

Choice **A** is correct. Since the professor added a small amount of acid to the copper (II) nitrate and iron (III) nitrate solutions, when combined with the sodium carbonate solution, the acid reacted with the carbonate ion to generate carbon dioxide gas. Choice A is the correct answer.

$$2 H^+ (aq) + CO_3^{2-} (aq) \rightarrow H_2O (l) + CO_2 (g)$$

To produce the gases in choices B, C and D, the metal ions would have to be very good reducing agents. Both Cu^{2+} and Fe^{3+} are already in their highest commonly observed oxidations states, and are unlikely to be oxidized further under these conditions.

25. Student C was given an unknown wrapped in aluminum foil. The student asked the professor why his unknown was the only one wrapped in aluminum foil and the professor responded, "To prevent light from causing an unwanted side reaction". Which of the following was most likely in the unknown solution, such that the professor wanted to keep it from being exposed to light?
    A. Copper (II) nitrate, because exposure to light causes the solution to turn blue.
    B. **Silver nitrate, because exposure to light can cause the formation of a black precipitate of elemental silver.**
    C. Sodium sulfide, because exposure to light cause the formation of the smell of rotten eggs.
    D. Sodium carbonate, because exposure to produces carbon dioxide gas.

Choice **B** is correct. One of the characteristic reactions of most silver salts is the production of finely divided silver metal when exposed to light. This formed the basis for the photographic industry for many years. The colloidal silver does not reflect light efficiently like crystalline silver metal and appears black, because it absorbs all of the wavelengths of visible radiation. Choice B is the correct answer.

Copper (II) solutions are blue because they absorb all other colors in the visible spectrum, due to electronic transitions of the Cu^{2+} ion. Choice A can be eliminated. Sodium sulfide, can produce the rotten egg smell of H_2S, if reacted with an acid, but will not undergo this reaction due to exposure to light. Choice C can be eliminated. Sodium carbonate will produce carbon dioxide gas if reacted with an acid, but not by exposure to light. Choice D can be eliminated.

Passage 6 Explanation

The elements in **Group 18 of the periodic table**, the so-**called Noble Gases**, are perhaps the most under appreciated **elements** of the 115 currently known. This stems from the general misunderstanding that their physical, chemical and nuclear properties (Table 1) are already completely understood and that further study is unlikely to produce any new information.

Key terms: Group, periodic table, and elements

Cause-and-Effect: The perceived lack of chemical reactivity of the Noble Gases produces a general lack of appreciation of this family of elements.

Helium was first discovered in 1868, not on earth, but from the analysis of the **spectral lines** produced by the sun. During this analysis, it became clear that most of the spectral lines were due to the element hydrogen, which was previously discovered on earth. The remaining solar spectral lines were ascribed to a previously unknown substance that was given the name helium, which was derived from the Greek name for the sun. You now recognize helium as a **misnomer**, but tradition prevails, preventing a name change to "hellion", which would be consistent with the **suffix** for the other elements in the family. You now know that helium is the product of **nuclear fusion** of hydrogen isotopes, which results in production of enormous amounts of energy. In contrast, helium's extremely low boiling point has made it the liquid of choice for cryogenic applications, such as in superconducting magnets used in high field nuclear magnetic resonance.

Key terms: Spectral lines, misnomer, suffix, and nuclear fusion

Cause-and-Effect: Spectral lines that are associated with the movement of electrons from one energy level to another can be used to identify the elemental composition of a star.

Both helium and neon are **less dense than air** (1.225 kg/m³), with the former's noncombustible nature making it the preferred gas for use in lighter than air ships, also known as dirigibles. Perhaps surprisingly, argon is the third most abundant gas in earth's atmosphere (~1%). The other Group 18 elements have increasing densities in the gas phase, due to their increasing **atomic mass**. This is somewhat problematic for radon, which is radioactive, decaying by way of an **alpha** process, with a **half-life** of 3.8 days. Radon is part of the ^{238}**U decay sequence** and can collect in homes, particularly basements, built in areas where the soils may have high levels or uranium. Exposure to radon is thought to be the second leading source of lung **carcinomas**.

Key terms: dense, atomic mass, alpha process, half-life, decay sequence, and carcinomas

Cause-and-Effect: Radon is a radioactive gas that is denser than air, causing it to collect in poorly ventilated homes and increasing the owner's risk of getting lung cancer.

The relative chemical **inertness** of the group 18 elements stems from their completely **filled s and p subshells**, which has formed the basis for the so-called **octet rule**. The stability of these elements is reflected in their relatively high **first ionization energies**. There are no known compounds of helium or neon. The reactivity of the heavier elements, krypton and xenon, with highly **electronegative** elements such as fluorine has been known for quite some time, and evidence for an argon compound has recently been presented. The xenon compounds XeF_2, XeF_4 and XeF_6 are often cited as part of the power of Valence Shell Electron Pair Repulsion (**VSEPR**) theory for predicting the structures of main-group compounds.

Key terms: Inertness, s and p subshells, octet rule, ionization energies, electronegative, VSEPR

Cause-and-Effect: The presence of low lying d-orbitals allows the heavier group 18 elements to form stable compounds when reacted with very strongly oxidizing and electronegative species, like fluorine.

Cause-and-Effect: The amount of space occupied by lone-pairs as compared with bonding pairs of electrons can be used (VSEPR theory) to predict the molecular shapes of the stable Group 18 compounds.

Table 1 Some properties of the Group 18 elements

Symbol	Boiling Point (K)	Melting Point (K)	Enthalpy of Vaporization (kJ/mol)	Atomic Number	Atomic Radius (Å)	First Ionization Energy (kJ/mol)
He	4	1	0.1	2	0.31	2370
Ne	27	25	1.7	10	0.38	2080
Ar	87	84	6.5	18	0.71	1520
Kr	122	116	9.1	36	0.88	1350
Xe	167	162	12.7	54	1.08	1170
Rn	212	202	18.1	86	1.20	1040

Table 1 The table includes data for a variety of physical properties of the Group 18 elements. It should be noted that there is a periodic trend in each of these properties.

26. Which of the following best explains the periodic trend in first ionization energies for the Noble Gases as atomic number increases?
    A. The core charges increase as the number of shells increases.
    B. <u>**The core charges remain the same as the number of shells increases.**</u>
    C. The core charges decreases as the number of shells increases.
    D. The core charges increase as the number of shells decreases.

Choice **B** is correct. The core charge of an atom is determined by adding the charges of the protons to the negative charges of the non-valence or inner shell electrons. The core charge for helium is 2+, but the core charge for all the other elements in Group 18 are +8. The valence shell electrons do not shield each other very well and each essentially feels the same amount of core charge. However, with each period, the valence electrons are placed into a new shell, which is further from the nucleus. According to Coulombs Law ($F = kQq/r^2$), the increase in the distance between the valence shell and the positive charge makes it easier to remove a valence electron and hence a lower first ionization energy. Choice B is the correct answer.

Coulomb's law states that $F = KQq/r^2$, which shows a direct relationship between F and charge, and an inverse-squared relationship between radius and F.

27. What is the density of radon at STP?
    - **A.** 1.0 kg /m^3
    - **B.** 1.225 kg/m^3
    - **C.** **9.7 kg/m^3**
    - **D.** 22.4 kg/m^3

Choice **C** is correct. At STP one mole of an ideal gas occupies 22.4 L. From the periodic table, the atomic mass of radon is 222 g/mole. Dividing the atomic mass by the molar volume gives:
222/22.4 ~ 10 g/L.

There are 1000 grams in a kilogram and 1000 L in a cubic meter, so:

10 g/L = 10 kg/m^3. Choice C is the correct answer.

A, B, D: These answers are a result of miscalculation.

28. The suffix of helium suggests that the person that originally named this element thought it was which of the following types of elements?
    - **A.** A non-metal
    - **B.** **A metal**
    - **C.** A liquid
    - **D.** A gas

Choice **B** is correct. The –ium suffix implies that the element is a metal. Many, but not all, of the names of the metals have this suffix, i.e. sodium, titanium, beryllium, etc. Scientists thought that the spectral lines that were not associated with hydrogen, must have been the metallic component of the sun, and thus used the –ium suffix, rather than the –on suffix, which means "one", for monoatomic. Choice B is the correct answer.

A, C, D: -ium is a standard suffix for a metal, not nonmetals, liquids or gases.

29. Which of the following ions does NOT have a Noble Gas electron configuration?
    - **A.** Na$^+$
    - **B.** **Fe^{2+}**
    - **C.** O^{2-}
    - **D.** F$^-$

Choice **B** is correct. Iron has eight valence electrons, with an electron configuration of [Ar]4s^{2}3d^6. The Fe^{2+} ion is formed by losing the two electrons in the s-orbital, producing a [Ar]3d^6 which is not a Noble Gas configuration. Choice B is the correct answer.

Elemental sodium is in Group 1 of the periodic table. The one valence electron is removed when the cation is formed, resulting in a closed-shell Noble Gas configuration, and choice A can be eliminated. Oxygen is in Group 16 and has six valence electrons. Forming the 2- oxide ion, produces a closed shell octet equivalent to neon, and choice C can be eliminated. Fluorine is in Group 17 and has seven valence electrons. Adding an electron to form the fluoride ion, also produces a closed shell octet equivalent to neon, and choice D can be eliminated.

30. Which of the following are the molecular shapes of XeF_2, and XeF_4 (respectively) as predicted by VSEPR theory?
    I.   Linear
    II. Bent
    III. Tetrahedral
    IV. Square planar

    A. I and II
    B. II and III
    C. III and IV
    D. <u>**I and IV**</u>

Choice **D** is correct. XeF_2 has a central xenon with a fluoride on either side. Each fluoride is single-bonded to the Xe and has a full octet. The Xe has an additional 3 lone pairs. The lone pairs adopt a trigonal planar arrangement, with the F sticking straight out above and below the flat triangle. This is an electronic geometry of a trigonal bipyramid arrangement. The question asks for molecular geometry, however, so we ignore the lone pairs and just look at the straight line, 180° angle between F-Xe-F.

Similarly, XeF_4 has a central Xe atom surrounded by four F atoms arranged in a square planar configuration. There are also two lone pairs, one sticking straight up out of the square and one out the bottom. Thus, the electronic geometry is octahedral but the molecular geometry is square planar.

These questions are NOT based on a passage

31. For a blindfolded person, which of the following situations is indistinguishable from that person sitting in a car that is at rest on a level road?

    A. **A blindfolded person riding in a car driving on a level straight road at a constant speed of 75 m/s.**

    B. A blindfolded person riding in a car driving on a level straight road, but the car's speed changes from 50 m/s to 100 m/s in 20 seconds.

    C. A blindfolded person riding in a car driving on a level straight road, but the car's speed changes from 100 m/s to 50 m/s in 20 seconds.

    D. A blindfolded person riding in a car driving on a level road at a constant speed of 50 m/s going around a curve whose radius is 100 m.

Choice **A** is correct. Newton's first law, the law of inertia, states that an object having a constant velocity, will only accelerate if a net force acts on that object. An object at rest has a constant velocity of zero, and an object moving with a constant speed and not changing direction, also has a constant velocity. A person's proprioceptive nervous system can detect changes in pressure due to applied forces that cause acceleration.

B, C, D: These choices all involve some sort of significant acceleration, which is detectable by the human senses, and can be eliminated.

32. A major source of glucose for glycolysis is liver glycogen, the hydrolysis of which is catalyzed by the enzyme glycogen phosphorylase. Non-phosphorylated glycogen phosphorylase is allosterically regulated by AMP, ATP and G-6-P. Which of the following statements regarding this regulation is likely to be true?

    A. ATP down-regulates glycogen phosphorylase activity by binding to and blocking a portion of the enzyme active site.

    B. **AMP's binding alters the conformation of the enzyme active site.**

    C. G-6-P binds to and competes with glucose at the glycogen phosphorylase active site.

    D. Phosphorylated glycogen phosphorylase activity is inhibited by AMP binding.

Choice **B** is correct. Allosteric modulators regulate enzyme activity by binding at a site other than a protein's active site (choices A and C are wrong). Allosteric site binding often modulates activity by inducing a conformational change in the enzyme active site. The question states that AMP, ATP and G-6-P all are allosteric regulators of non-phosphorylated glycogen phosphorylase. Choice B is consistent with such a role and is the correct answer. The question stem specifically addresses the role of allosteric modulation of non-phosphorylated glycogen, making choice D an unlikely correct answer unless all other answer choices can be eliminated.

33. If a 0.1 kg object is dropped from a very tall cliff and reaches terminal velocity, what is the magnitude of the object's net acceleration and the net force acting on the object at terminal velocity?

    A. **0 m/s^2 and 0 N**

    B. 9.8 m/s^2 and 0 N

    C. 0 m/s^2 and 0.98 N

    D. 9.8 m/s^2 and 0.98 N

Choice **A** is correct. If the object has reached terminal velocity, then the wind resistance is creating an upward force equal to the downward gravitational force, causing the net force acting on the object to be zero.

Choice C and D can be eliminated. If the net force acting on the object is zero, then based on Newton's second law, the net acceleration of the object must be zero and the object is fall with a constant negative velocity. Choice B can be eliminated and choice A is the correct answer.

34. Which of the following will cause the largest buoyant force on an object floating in the liquid at 25°C?
    A. **Water (specific gravity = 1.0)**
    B. Ethanol (specific gravity = 0.79)
    C. Diethyl ether (specific gravity = 0.71)
    D. Acetone (specific gravity = 0.78)

Choice **A** is correct. The fluid with the greatest density will create the greatest buoyant force, which is equivalent to the weight of the liquid displaced by the object. A higher specific gravity (the ratio of the substances' density to water's density) indicated a higher density and thus, a higher buoyant force.

B, C, D; Each of these answers has a lower specific gravity and thus, a lower density, than choice A.

Passage 7 Explanation

You have all seen them, those liquid-filled cylinders that have colored liquid filled glass bulbs that float or sink depending upon the temperature. A so-called **Galileo's thermometer** is constructed such that the small glass bulbs are partially filled with liquids that function as weights and the colors are purely decorative. Once the bulbs have been sealed, their densities are adjusted by attaching metal tags with temperature labels. Each glass bulb and metal tag has a predetermined **density within the range of densities for the liquid in which they are immersed**. The clear liquid in which the bulbs are submerged can be water, but more often is an organic liquid, such as ethanol (Figure 1), which has a significantly bigger temperature dependent variation in density. **It is the buoyancy effect of this liquid and the weight of the individual glass bulbs that determines if a particular bulb will sink or float.**

Key terms: Thermometer, density, and buoyancy

Cause-and-Effect: If the density of an individual glass bulb is greater than the density of the surrounding fluid, the bulb will sink; if the density of an individual bulb is less than the surrounding fluid, then the bulb will float; and if the density of an individual bulb is nearly the same as, but slightly more than the surrounding fluid, the bulb will be suspended in the middle of the fluid.

Cause-and-Effect: By having a series of bulbs with densities that match the temperature dependent range of densities of the surrounding fluid, the temperature can be determined by observing which bulbs float versus which bulbs sink.

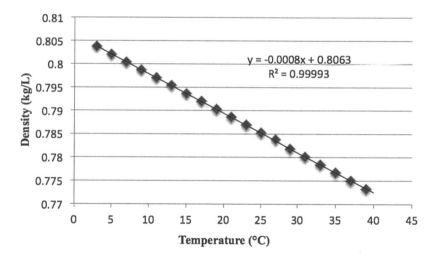

Figure 1 A plot of density versus temperature for pure ethanol, including the equation for the best fit line. The melting and boiling points for pure ethanol are -114°C and 78°C, respectively.

Figure 1 The density of ethanol decreases linearly as the temperature increases, with a slope of -8 x 10^{-4} kg/L°C and a y-intercept of 0.8063 kg/L.

Often times the temperature will be such that there will be a number of bulbs floating at the top of the liquid, as well as a few bulbs that sink to the bottom, but one bulb will seem to be suspended in the middle of the liquid. The question becomes, how is that possible? **The most plausible explanation involves slight pressure differences (ΔP) acting on the bulbs,** that are dependent upon the density (ρ) of the liquid, the **acceleration** due to **gravity** (g) and the **depth** (h) of the surfaces of the bulb submerged within the liquid, according to $\Delta P = \rho g h$.

Key terms: Pressure, acceleration, gravity and depth

Cause-and-Effect: A bulb with a density slightly less than the density of the surrounding liquid at a particular temperature, will appear to be suspended motionless within the liquid, because the pressure of the fluid on the lower half of the bulb will be slightly greater than the pressure of the fluid on the upper half of the bulb, such that the sum of the upward forces, buoyancy and upward pressure, will equal the downward forces, of weight and downward pressure.

35. What is the approximate weight of a glass bulb suspended in the middle of a Galileo's thermometer whose temperature is 298 K, assuming that the bulb can be approximated as a sphere and the diameter of the bulb is 2.0 cm?
    A. **0.032 N**
    B. 0.041 N
    C. 0.13 N
    D. 0.16 N

Choice **A** is correct. The volume of a sphere is $4/3 \, \pi r^3$ and the radius of the bulb is 1.0 cm, giving a volume of $4/3(3.14)(1)^3 \sim 4$ cm^3. Using Figure 1, the estimated density of ethanol at 25°C (273 + 25 = 298 K) is 0.785 kg/L or 0.785 g/cm^3, which is about 0.8 g/cm^3. If the bulb is suspended in the ethanol, the density of the bulb must be essentially the same as the liquid. The mass of the bulb can be determined from using the density, 0.8(4) = 3.2 g. To determine the weight you must convert the mass to kilograms and multiply by the acceleration of gravity, 0.0032(10) ~ 0.032 N. Choice A is the correct answer.

B,C, D: These answers are a result of miscalculation. If you simply use the volume, and don't use the density, you would get choice B, which is not correct. If you use the diameter of 2.0 cm in the volume equation, you might get choices C or D, which are not correct.

36. What is the net force acting on a glass bulb suspended in the middle of a Galileo's thermometer whose temperature is 298 K?
    A. **0 N**
    B. +0.032 N
    C. -0.032 N
    D. -0.041 N

Choice **A** is correct. If the bulb is "suspended in the middle" of the thermometer, the bulb is not accelerating and the sum of all the forces acting on the bulb must equal zero. Choice A is the correct answer.

B, C, D: Choices B and C would be approximately the buoyant force and the force of gravity acting on the bulb, but not the net force. D is a result of miscalculation.

37. Based on information in the passage, which of the following must be true concerning the buoyant force and the weight of a bulb that is suspended in the middle of the surrounding fluid of a Galileo's thermometer?

    A. The magnitude of the force of gravity acting on the bulb is greater than the magnitude of the buoyant force acting on the bulb.

    B. The magnitude of the force of gravity acting on the bulb is less than the magnitude of the buoyant force acting on the bulb.

    C. The magnitude of the force of gravity acting on the bulb is equal to the magnitude of the buoyant force acting on the bulb.

    D. There is no way to predict the relative magnitudes of the force of gravity acting on the bulb compared with the buoyant force acting on the bulb.

Choice **A** is correct. For a bulb suspended in the middle of the fluid (ethanol), the net force in the vertical direction must equal zero. The passage indicates that there will be a pressure difference that the fluid exerts on the top and bottom surfaces of the bulb, with the latter being slightly greater than the former. Therefore, the upward pressure is slightly greater than the downward pressure, then the upward buoyant force must be slightly less than the downward weight of the bulb. Choice A is the correct answer.

B, C, D: These answers are a result of miscalculation. If choices B and C were true, taking into account the differences in pressure acting upward and downward, the bulb should float to the surface of the surrounding fluid. Choice D can be eliminated, since an analysis of the forces of pressure, buoyancy and weight can make satisfactory predictions.

38. An alternative design for a Galileo's thermometer, involves using hollow metal cubes with the length of a side being 1.0 cm. What is the pressure difference at 25°C that the ethanol exerts on the top-side, as compared with the bottom-side of the cube, when the center of mass of the cube is located 10.0 cm below the surface. The diameter of the thermometer is 3.0 cm and the total height is 25.0 cm. Note that 1 Pascal (Pa) of pressure is equivalent to a Newton per square meter.

    A. 77 Pa

    B. 231 Pa

    C. 730 Pa

    D. 807 Pa

Choice **A** is correct. The difference in height from the top to the bottom of the cube is 1.0 cm or 0.01 m. From Figure 1, the density of the ethanol at 25°C is 0.785 kg/L, which is 785 kg/m³ (10^3 L = 1 m³). Inserting the variables into Equation 1 gives, $\Delta P = (785)(9.8)(0.01) = 77$ N/m². Choice A is the answer.

B, C, D: These answers are a result of miscalculation.

39. What fraction of a bulb will be above the surface of ethanol at 7 °C, if the density of the bulb is 1.000 kg/L?
    A. **0**
    B. 0.1
    C. 0.2
    D. 0.8

Choice **A** is correct. From Figure 1, the density of the bulb (1.000 kg/L) is greater than the density of the ethanol (0.800 kg/L) at 7°C. The bulb will sink and be completely submerged in the ethanol. Choice A is the correct answer. If the density of the bulb and the density of the fluid are confused, then you might think that the bulb will float, which would give some fraction of the bulb above the surface which is related to the ratio of the densities. The bulb would only have a portion of its volume below the surface, such that the weight of liquid displaced equals the weight of the bulb.

A, B, C: See reasoning above. If the density of the bulb and the density of the fluid are confused, then you might think that the bulb will float, which would give some fraction of the blub above the surface which is related to the ratio of the densities. The bulb would only have a portion of its volume below the surface, such that the weight of liquid displaced equals the weight of the bulb.

Passage 8 Explanation

In order for divers to survive underwater, they must inhale highly compressed air in deep water, resulting in more gases than normal being dissolved in their blood and tissues. If the diver returns to the surface too rapidly, the dissolved gas forms bubbles, much like what happens when the cap of a soda bottle is removed, causing pain and possibly death. This condition is commonly known as "the bends." To prevent this condition, a diver must return to the surface slowly, allowing the dissolved gases to slowly adjust to the changes in **pressure**. Rather than breathing compressed air, the diver may breathe a mixture of compressed helium and oxygen, known as heliox, thereby avoiding the bends, because helium is much less soluble in water than nitrogen, which is the major gas (79%) found in air and nitrox mixtures. The **solubility** of gases in **aqueous solution** is dependent upon temperature and pressure. The solubility (C) of a gas directly depends on the pressure (P) of the gas on the surface of the liquid, and is known as Henry's Law, Equation 1, with **selected proportionality constants**, k, provided in Table 1. It should be noted that most gases are much more soluble in cold water, than in hot water.

Key terms: pressure, solubility, aqueous solution, and proportionality constant

Cause-and-Effect: The more gas dissolved in an aqueous solution under pressure, the more likely that bubbles form when the pressure is released, potentially creating a serious problem for a diver.

Equation 1
$$C = k P$$

Equation 1 This equation, known as Henry's Law, is a simple direct relationship between the pressure (P) of a gas on the surface of a liquid and the concentration (C, in units of mol/L) of that gas dissolved in the liquid. The proportionality constant, k, is unique to the nature of the intermolecular and chemical interactions of the gas and the liquid, with similarities of intermolecular forces generally favoring the formation of the solution.

Table 1 Henry's Law constants at 25°C for aqueous solutions of selected gases

Formula	k (M atm^{-1})
N_2	6×10^{-4}
He	4×10^{-4}
Ne	5×10^{-4}
Ar	1×10^{-3}
CO	1×10^{-3}
CO_2	3×10^{-2}

Table 1 This table presents the Henry's Law constants at 25°C for a few nonpolar gases that are relevant to underwater diving as related to the bends and narcosis. Since the solubility of a gas in aqueous solution generally decreases with an increase in temperature, the values of the constant also generally decrease with temperature. Note that the solubility of the noble gas elements increases as the size and polarizability associated with increases in the van der Waals forces of attraction.

In addition, **narcosis** can occur while scuba diving, which results in an **alteration in consciousness** at depth, caused by the **anesthetic** effect of certain gases at high pressure. This sensation is similar to the **intoxication** that results from consumption of alcoholic beverages. All gases have varying degrees of effect, with a higher **lipid** solubility seeming to **correlate** well with the degree of narcosis. At extreme depth, this mental impairment can be life threatening. Divers can learn to cope with some of these effects, but it is impossible to completely eliminate them. With the apparent exception of helium, most of the **noble gases**, as well as other gases such as elemental nitrogen, and carbon dioxide, have been shown to alter mental function at various levels. This effect is distinctly different than that caused by asphyxiation. Interestingly, the heavy noble gases are more narcotic than nitrogen at a given pressure, and xenon has such a high degree of activity that it has been used at standard pressures as an anesthetic during surgery. The precise **mechanism** of narcosis is not well understood, but appears to **correlate to the solubility** of the gas in the lipid bilayer of nerve membranes. Some of these effects may also be similar to the mechanism of nonpolar anesthetics such as, chloroform, diethyl ether and nitrous oxide. The production of these effects by the very chemically unreactive noble gases suggests a mechanism **unrelated to chemical reactivity**. A **physical effect** based on intermolecular forces may cause a change in membrane volume, thereby affecting the transport of ions through channels in the membranes of nerve cells.

Key terms: narcosis, consciousness, anesthetic, intoxication, lipid, correlate, noble gases, surgery, lipid bilayer, nonpolar, chemical reactivity, and physical effect

Cause-and-Effect: The lipid solubility of a gas affects the ability of the ion channels of nerve cells to transport ions in and out of a nerve cell, reducing the ability of the cell to produce an action potential, thereby resulting in a reduction in nerve sensations.

40. Which of the following lipid soluble compounds has a nonzero dipole moment?
    A. Argon
    B. Elemental nitrogen
    C. Chloroform
    D. Carbon dioxide

Choice **C** is correct. To have a dipole, there must be polar covalent bonds and an asymmetric molecular structure. Chloroform, $CHCl_3$ has three polar covalent C-Cl bonds forming a pyramidal like structure that does produce a net dipole moment and choice C is the correct answer.

Argon, choice A, can be eliminated because it is monatomic. Elemental nitrogen, N_2, does not have a polar covalent bond, and choice B can be eliminated. Carbon dioxide does have polar covalent bonds, but the symmetrical linear structure does not produce a net dipole moment and choice D can be eliminated.

41. Based on information in the passage, which of the following best explains the increase in anesthetic properties of the noble gases as the atomic number increases?
    A. The polarizability of the atoms increases.
    B. The number of protons in the nucleus increases.
    C. The number of neutrons in the nucleus increases.
    D. The size of the atoms decrease.

Choice **A** is correct. The passage suggests that the anesthetic properties of the noble gases result from their degree of lipid solubility, which would be related to the van der Waals interactions. Generally as the size of an atom or molecule increases, it becomes easier to create temporary dipoles, which increase the intermolecular forces associated with the interactions of molecules. Choice A is the correct answer.

While the number of protons and neutrons in the nucleus (choices B and C) do increase with an increase in the atomic number, all of the noble gases have closed shell electron configurations and generally do not form covalent bonds. As the atomic number of the noble gases increases, the number of electron shells increases and as a result the size of the atom increases, not decreases. Choice D can be eliminated. It is the size and polarizability of an atom or molecule that affects the Van der Waals intermolecular forces the most. Choice B and C do not explain the trend in intermolecular forces for the noble gases and can also be eliminated. Choice A is the correct answer.

42. Which of the following best describes the effect of increasing temperature on the value of the Henry's law constant for a gas?
    A. Since the solubility of gases generally decrease with an increase in average kinetic energy, the value of the Henry's law constant increases.
    B. **Since the solubility of gases generally decrease with an increase in average kinetic energy, the value of the Henry's law constant decreases.**
    C. Since the solubility of gases generally increase with an increase in average kinetic energy, the value of the Henry's law constant decreases.
    D. Since the solubility of gases generally increase with an increase in average kinetic energy, the value of the Henry's law constant increases.

Choice **B** is correct. As stated at the end of the first paragraph of the passage, "...most gases are much more soluble in cold water, than in hot water." Increasing the temperature should therefore decrease the solubility of a gas in aqueous solution, which is directly related to the magnitude of the Henry's law constant, k. Temperature is a measure of the average kinetic energy of a system. Choice B is the correct answer.

A, C, D: See reasoning above. Gas solubility is inversely proportional to temperature.

43. Which of the following gas mixtures is LEAST likely to cause the bends for a scuba diver?
    A. Compressed air
    B. Nitrox
    C. **Heliox**
    D. Neonox

Choice **C** is correct. As indicated in the first paragraph of the passage, air is about 79% elemental nitrogen, with elemental oxygen representing about 20% and the remaining portion is made up of other gases such as water vapor, argon, carbon dioxide, methane and a variety of other trace gases. Nitrox is a synthetic mixture of elemental nitrogen (79%) and elemental oxygen. Likewise heliox and neonox are similar synthetic mixtures of oxygen, combined with helium and neon, respectively. The passage indicates that helium is much less soluble in aqueous solution than nitrogen and based on the Henry's law constants in Table 1, helium is much less soluble than neon as well. Therefore, since there will be less dissolved gas in the blood and tissues of a diver that was breathing heliox, this person is much less likely to experience the formation of bubbles and experience the "bends" when returning to the surface. Choice C is the correct answer.

These questions are NOT based on a passage

44. Which of the following are fluids?
    I. Air
    II. Water
    III. Blood

    A. I only
    B. II only
    C. II and III only
    D. <u>**I, II and III**</u>

Choice **D** is correct. A fluid is a substance that can flow and/or change the shape of its volume. Both liquids and gases are considered fluids and therefore air, water and blood all have properties of fluids. Choice D is the answer.

A, B, C: All of the elements presented meet the definition of a fluid.

45. Which of the following is the formula for nitrous oxide?
    A. <u>**N_2O**</u>
    B. NO
    C. NO_2
    D. N_2O_5

Choice **A** is correct. Nitrous oxide is an older name for dinitrogen monoxide, N_2O, making choice A the correct answer. The suffix –ous indicates a lower oxidation state. Nitric oxide is the older name for nitrogen monoxide, NO. Nitrogen dioxide is NO_2 and dinitrogen pentoxide is N_2O_5, the latter is sometimes called nitrogen pentoxide.

B, C, D: These are nitric oxide, nitrite, and dinitrogen pentoxide, respectively.

46. The earth's atmosphere is comprised primarily of elemental nitrogen, which is unreactive. Certain nitrogen fixing bacteria have developed a symbiotic relationship with certain plants, and are able to convert elemental nitrogen to ammonia. Which of the following best explains why elemental nitrogen is so unreactive?
    A. <u>**Elemental nitrogen is diatomic, having a triple bond, being diamagnetic and reduction must occur to obtain ammonia.**</u>
    B. Elemental nitrogen is diatomic, having a triple bond, being paramagnetic and reduction must occur to obtain ammonia.
    C. Elemental nitrogen monatomic, having a double bond, being diamagnetic and oxidation must occur to obtain ammonia.
    D. Elemental nitrogen is monatomic, diamagnetic and oxidation must occur to obtain ammonia.

Choice **A** is correct. Elemental nitrogen (N_2) is one of the diatomic elements and the Lewis dot structure as well as molecular orbital theory predicts a triple bond, with no unpaired electrons, making it diamagnetic, and electrons must be added to reduce the oxidation number from 0 to 3-, in order to make ammonia. Choice A is the correct answer.

B: Nitrogen is diamagnetic, not paramagnetic.
C, D: Elemental nitrogen is diatomic. A mnemonic for the diatomic elements is "Have No Fear Of Ice Cold Beer", indicating that H, N, F, O, Cl, and Br are all diatomic elements.

47. Which of the following represents the hybridization of the nitrogen atoms in N_2?
    A. <u>**sp**</u>
    B. sp^2
    C. sp^3
    D. sp^3d

Choice **A** is correct. Two of nitrogen's four valence orbitals mix to form two new hybridized orbitals. The unhybridized p-orbitals are used for π bonding which would have sp hybridization and linear geometry. Another way of spotting this is the fact that two pi bonds are present hence the atom is said to be sp hybridized. Choice A is the correct answer.

B: The nitrogen atom can hybridize in the sp^3 arrangement, but differs from carbon in that there is a "lone pair" of electrons left on the nitrogen that does not participate in the bonding. The geometry about nitrogen with three bonded ligands is therefore trigonal pyramidal.

C: Nitrogen will also hybridize sp^2 when there are only two atoms bonded to the nitrogen (one single and one double bond). Just as for sp^3 nitrogen, a pair of electrons is left on the nitrogen as a lone pair. The resulting geometry is bent with a bond angle of 120 degrees.

D: Nitrogen is not capable of sp^3d (5 total ligands) hybridization.

Passage 9 Explanation

Valence bond (VB) theory has been successful at explaining numerous aspects of bonding in simple inorganic and organic molecules. It is assumed that the direct overlap of **hybridized atomic orbitals** results in the formation of **sigma (σ) type covalent bonds**, and that **multiple bonding** can result from the sideways overlap of pure **p-type atomic orbitals** and the formation of **π-type bonds**. As a result, VB theory has proven to be quite useful in predicting **molecular shapes** and other physical properties such as bond lengths and strengths. However, explaining the properties of molecular oxygen proved to be a significant challenge. Specifically, VB theory predicts that molecular oxygen should have a **double bond** and be diamagnetic. While the experimentally observed bond length and strength of O_2 is consistent with a double bond, molecular oxygen is known to be **paramagnetic**.

Key terms: Valence bond theory, inorganic, organic, hybridized atomic orbitals, sigma type covalent bonds, multiple bonding, p type atomic orbitals, p-type bonds, molecular shapes, double bond, diamagnetic and paramagnetic.

Contrast: Valence bond theory does a reasonably good job of explaining the bond order of the second period diatomic elements, N_2, O_2, F_2, but does not do a good job in predicting the number of unpaired electrons in elemental oxygen and the resulting magnetic properties.

Molecular orbital (MO) theory has proven to be a significant improvement over VB theory in explaining many of the physical properties of molecules. The basic premise of MO theory is that atomic orbitals have wave properties, and like waves, they can interact with one another to form **constructive and destructive interference.** Therefore, when two atomic orbitals interact, there will always be two molecular orbitals that result, one being an energetically stabilized bonding interaction and a destabilized out of phase anti-bonding interaction. MO theory takes advantage of the directionality of atomic orbitals and **symmetry** to predict the resulting energy differences between molecular orbitals, based partly on the concepts of hybridization and orbital overlap. As a result, theoretical chemists have been very successful at using MO theory to explain **spectroscopic properties** and chemical reactivity. Shown in Figure 1 is an example of a MO energy diagram used to predict the bonding of the second period **diatomic elements**. The **bond order** between the diatomic elements can be determined from the MO diagram, by: (1) Placing the total number of valence electrons in the various orbitals in order of increasing energy, following **Hund's rules for degenerate orbitals**; (2) Subtract the number of electrons in anti-bonding orbitals from the number of electrons in bonding type orbitals; and (3) Divide by two. In certain cases it is possible to have fractional bond orders.

Key terms: Molecular orbital theory, constructive and destructive interference, symmetry, spectroscopic properties, energy diagram, diatomic elements, bond order, Hund's rules, and degenerate orbitals.

Cause-and-Effect: MO theory does an excellent job of predicting both the bond order and number of unpaired electrons for the second period diatomic elements.

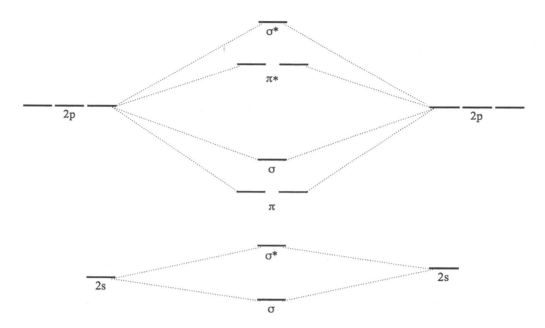

Figure 1 A generalized molecular orbital energy diagram for second period diatomic elements, using a second order mixing of the 2s and 2p$_z$ orbitals to form the sigma-bonding (σ) and anti-bonding (σ*) type orbitals.

Figure 1 The MO energy diagram shown below includes the shapes of the atomic and resulting molecular orbitals for the σ and σ*-type molecular orbitals. In phase combinations are bonding and out of phase combinations are anti-bonding (denoted by a *). The shaded portions of atomic orbitals can be considered to have positive amplitudes and the un-shaded portions can be considered to have negative amplitudes.

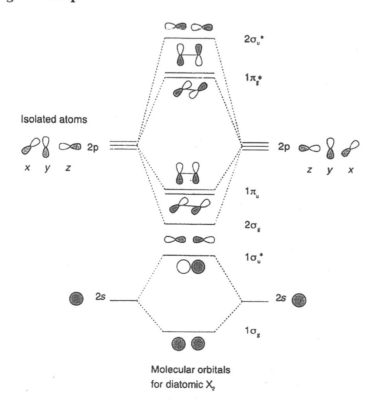

48. Based on the MO energy diagram in Figure 1, what is the bond order between oxygen atoms in O_2?
    A. 1
    B. **2**
    C. 2.5
    D. 3

Choice **B** is correct. The MO diagram predicts a double bond based on the fact that there are twelve valence electrons, with eight of these electrons being in bonding type MOs and the remaining four electrons in anti-bonding MOs. As stated in the last paragraph of the passage, subtracting the number of anti-bonding electrons from the bonding electrons and dividing by 2, gives the bond order, BO = (8-4)/2 = 2. Therefore O_2 has a double bond, consistent with the Lewis dot structure. Choice B is the correct answer.

A,C, D: These answers are a result of miscalculation.

49. Super oxide, O_2^-, is formed by the one electron reduction of elemental oxygen and is an especially reactive species which can cause a variety of problems for cells and has been implicated in the aging process. Superoxide dismutases rapidly convert superoxide into elemental oxygen and the peroxide ion. Which of the following sets of distances would be consistent with the bond orders in elemental oxygen, superoxide and peroxide?
    A. **1.21 Å, 1.28 Å and 1.49 Å respectively**
    B. 1.49 Å, 1.28 Å and 1.21 Å respectively
    C. 1.21 Å, 1.49 Å and 1.28 Å respectively
    D. 1.28 Å, 1.49 Å and 1.21 Å respectively

Choice **A** is correct. As explained for question #1, O_2 has a double bond. Superoxide has a total of thirteen valence electrons, with eight in bonding MOs and five in anti-bonding MOs, BO = (8-5)/2 = 1.5. Therefore O_2^- has a bond order of one and a half. As stated in the passage, it is possible to have fractional bond orders.

Peroxide has a total of fourteen valence electrons, with eight in bonding MOs and six in anti-bonding MOs, BO = (8-6)/2 = 1. Therefore, O_2^{2-} has a single bond, consistent with the Lewis dot structure.

The higher the bond order the shorter the bond length. Choice A is the correct answer.

50. Based on the MO energy diagram in Figure 1, which of the following diatomic elements would have unpaired electrons?
    A. Nitrogen
    B. **Oxygen**
    C. Fluorine
    D. Chlorine

Choice **B** is correct. O_2 has a total of 12 valence electrons. Placing these electrons in the MO diagram gives two electrons in the σ* orbitals, which are energetically degenerate, so following Hund's rules, putting one electron in each of the two σ* type orbitals, results in two unpaired electrons. This is consistent with the statement in the passage that "molecular oxygen is known to be paramagnetic", which results from oxygen having unpaired electrons.

A, C, D: Nitrogen, fluorine and chlorine (14, 16, 32 electrons) will have no unpaired electrons according to the MO model.

51. Which of the following does NOT have π-type bonds?
    A. Acetic acid
    B. **Propanol**
    C. Propanal
    D. Propanone

Choice **B** is correct. Propanol is an alkane alcohol and does not have a multiple bonds and is the correct answer.

Multiple bonds between second period elements will have π -bonds. Acetic acid has a C=O and therefore has a π -bond, eliminating choice A. Propanal and propanone are an aldehyde and a ketone respectively and have C=O bonds, and therefore also have π -bonds, eliminating choices C and D. Propanol is an alcohol and does not have a multiple bond and choice B is the correct answer.

52. Which of the following is(are) isoelectronic with elemental nitrogen?
    I.   Carbon monoxide
    II. Hydrogen peroxide
    III. Acetylene

    A. I only
    B. I and II only
    C. II and III only
    D. **I and III only**

Choice **D** is correct. Isoelectronic compounds have the same number of electrons. Elemental nitrogen, N_2, has a total of 14 electrons. Carbon monoxide, CO, has $6 + 8 = 14$ electrons as well, eliminating choice C. Hydrogen peroxide, H_2O_2 has, $2(1) + 2(8) = 18$ electrons and is not isoelectronic with N_2, eliminating choice B. Acetylene, C_2H_2, has $2(6) + 2(1) = 14$ electrons and is isoelectronic with N_2, eliminating choice A. Choice D is the correct answer. It should be noted that the Lewis dot structure of N_2 predicts a triple bond. Likewise CO and acetylene both have triple bonds.

Passage 10 Explanation

An MD associated with Doctors Without Borders was working in West Africa at a clinic and discovered that a critical piece of electronic equipment had malfunctioned due to a problem with the electrical generator that was used by the clinic. The equipment was essential for monitoring several patients that may well recover as long as they received the appropriate care. It was determined that it would take several days to replace the equipment and in the meantime the doctor decided that he would try to repair the equipment, by replacing any burned out **resistors** or **capacitors**. The clinic had a battery operated digital **multimeter** and a supply of various resistors and capacitors. On the inside of the box of resistors there was a color code (Table 1) and two examples (Figure 1) for a **4-band and a 5-band resistor**. In some cases there was not the equivalent resistor or capacitor to the ones that had burned out and the doctor had to figure out appropriate combinations to use for replacement.

Key Terms: Resistors, capacitors, and multimeter.

Cause and effect: The equivalent resistance (R_{eq}) of resistors in series is the sum of the resistances of the individual resistors ($R_{eq} = R_1 + R_2$ ...) and for resistors in parallel, the inverse of the equivalent resistance is equal to the sum of inverse resistances of the individual resistors ($1/R_{eq} = 1/R_1 + 1/R_2$ ...).

Cause and effect: The equivalent capacitance (C_{eq}) of capacitors in parallel is the sum of the capacitances of the individual capacitors ($C_{eq} = C_1 + C_2$ ...) and for capacitors in series, the inverse of the equivalent capacitance is equal to the sum of the inverse capacitances of the individual capacitors ($1/C_{eq} = 1/C_1 + 1/C_2$ ...).

Table 1 Color code for 4-band and 5-band resistors

Color	Digit	Multiplier	Tolerance (%)
Black	0	10^0	
Brown	1	10^1	1
Red	2	10^2	2
Orange	3	10^3	
Yellow	4	10^4	
Green	5	10^5	0.5
Blue	6	10^6	0.25
Violet	7	10^7	0.1
Grey	8	10^8	
White	9	10^9	
Gold		10^{-1}	5
Silver		10^{-2}	10
(none)			20

Table 1 This table can be used to determine the resistance of a resistor based on the colors of the bands as described in the caption for Figure 1.

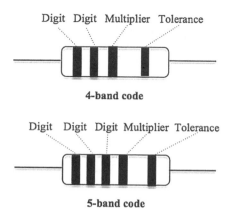

4-band code

5-band code

Figure 1 Examples of how to read resistor color codes. A 4-band resistor colored Yellow-Violet-Orange-Gold would be 47 kΩ with a tolerance of +/- 5%, and a 5-band resistor colored Brown-Green-Grey-Silver-Red would be 1.58 Ω with a tolerance of +/- 2%.

Figure 1 It is important to read the resistor correctly from left to right with the band indicating the tolerance on the right, slightly separated from the other bands. In some cases, if the resistor is turned around and read in the reverse order, the combination will not give a logical value with the appropriate number of digits for the resistance.

53. The broken instrument had an AC to DC power converter. The doctor needed to use the digital multimeter shown below to check the voltage drop for the resistors and identify the resistor(s) that had failed. To make this measurement the doctor inserted the plug for the black probe into the black common connection and inserted the plug for the red probe into the red voltage connection labeled 124, and:

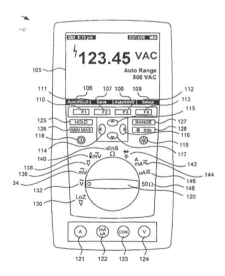

A. **turn the dial to the setting labeled 136 and connect the probes in parallel with the resistor that needs to be checked.**

B. turn the dial to the setting labeled 144 and connect the probes in parallel with the resistor that needs to be checked.

C. turn the dial to the setting labeled 136 and connect the probes in series with the resistor that needs to be checked.

D. turn the dial to the setting labeled 132 and connect the probes in series with the resistor that needs to be checked.

Choice **A** is correct. Since the equipment has an AC to DC power converter, the circuit in the equipment is run using direct current and voltage. To measure DC voltage the dial on the multimeter should be set on the position labeled 136. The straight bar over the V indicates direct voltage.

B, C, D: These answers are a result of miscalculation. Choices B and D can be eliminated. A voltage drop for a resistor must be measured with the meter in parallel to the resistor. Current, or amperage, is measured in series. Choices C and D can be eliminated. Choice A is the correct answer.

54. The doctor determined that the color bands of one of the burned out resistors was Brown-Gold-Black-Red. What was the resistance and tolerance of this resistor?
    A. **2.0 Ω ± 1 %**
    B. 0.2 Ω ± 2 %
    C. 1 Ω ± 2 %
    D. It is not possible to determine the resistance of this resistor.

Choice **A** is correct. If the resistor is read in the order given as a 4-band resistor, the first digit (Brown) is 1, but Gold does not have a digit value. This is because the doctor has the resistor turned around and misread the order of bands. The order of bands should be read Red-Black-Gold-Brown. Read this way, the first digit is 2, the second digit is 0, the multiplier is 10^{-1} and the tolerance is 1%. This gives $20 \times 10^{-1} \pm 1\%$, which is equivalent to choice A, which is the answer.

B, C, D: These answers are a result of miscalculation or failure to realize that gold cannot be read as the 2nd band in an accurate reading.

55. The doctor determined that a single 100 mF capacitor had failed. Which of the following combinations of capacitors could NOT be used to replace this capacitor?
    A. Two 200 mF capacitors
    B. Two 50 mF capacitors
    C. **Three 100 mF capacitors**
    D. One 200 mF and two 400 mF capacitors

Choice **C** is correct. There are two possible ways to combine multiple capacitors: in parallel or in series. The equivalent capacitance (C_{eq}) of capacitors in parallel is the sum of the capacitances of the individual capacitors $(C_{eq} = C_1 + C_2 ...)$ and for capacitors in series, the inverse of the equivalent capacitance is equal to the sum of the inverse capacitances of the individual capacitors $(1/C_{eq} = 1/C_1 + 1/C_2 ...)$.

Choice A can be eliminated because connecting the two capacitors in series, gives

$$1/C_{eq} = (1/200) + (1/200)$$
$$1/C_{eq} = 2/200 = 1/100$$
$$C_{eq} = 100 \text{ mF}$$

Choice B can be eliminated because connecting the two capacitors in parallel, gives

$$C_{eq} = 50 + 50 = 100 \text{ mF}$$

Choice D can be eliminated because connecting the three resistors in series, gives

$$1/C_{eq} = (1/400) + (1/400) + (1/200)$$
$$1/C_{eq} = (2/400) + (2/400)$$
$$1/C_{eq} = 4/400$$
$$C_{eq} = 100 \text{ mF}$$

At this point you need to confirm that choice C is the answer. Having all of the capacitors in parallel, gives

$$C_{eq} = 100 + 100 + 100 = 300 \text{ mF}$$

Which is not the desired capacitance.

Having all of the capacitors in series, gives

$$1/C_{eq} = (1/100) + (1/100) + (1/100)$$
$$1/C_{eq} = 3/100$$
$$C_{eq} = 100/3$$
$$C_{eq} = 33 \text{ mF}$$

Which is not the desired capacitance.

Having two of the capacitors in series and parallel with the third, gives

$$1/C_{eq} = (1/100) + (1/100)$$
$$1/C_{eq} = 2/100$$
$$C_{eq} = 50 \text{ mF}$$

$$C_{eq} = 50 + 100 = 150 \text{ mF}$$

Which is not the desired capacitance. Indeed, choice C is the correct answer.

These questions are NOT based on a passage

56. An object is dropped from the top of a 125 m tall building. What is the object's speed right before hitting the ground, assuming wind resistance is negligible?
    A. **50 m/s**
    B. 100 m/s
    C. 250 m/s
    D. 2500 m/s

Choice **A** is correct. The known variables are displacement (d = -125 m), acceleration (a = -9.8 m/s^2) and initial velocity (V_i = 0 m/s), with the final velocity (V_f = ?) being the variable of interest. The appropriate kinematic equation is $V_f^2 = V_i^2 + 2ad$ and substituting the variables into the equation gives

$$V_f^2 = 0^2 + 2(-9.8)(-125)$$
$$V_f^2 \sim 2500$$
$$V_f = 50 \text{ m/s}$$

57. Some students complained about the smell of rotten eggs when they mixed some of their solutions with acid at their lab bench. Which of the following combinations might be responsible for the smell of rotten eggs?
    A. Copper (II) nitrate plus sodium carbonate
    B. **Iron (III) nitrate plus sodium sulfide**
    C. Potassium nitrate plus sodium chloride
    D. Calcium nitrate plus sodium hydroxide

Choice **B** is correct. Acidic solutions will react with sulfide to produce H_2S gas, which produces the noxious smell of rotten eggs.

A, C, D: These answers are a result of miscalculation. Mixing the copper (II) nitrate and sodium carbonate solution probably produced carbon dioxide gas, but CO_2 is a colorless and odorless gas. Choice A can be eliminated. Choices C and D should not result in any kind of reaction that gives off noxious fumes and can be eliminated.

58. Which of the following types of bonding is NOT significant for ethanol?
    A. Covalent bonding
    B. **Ionic bonding**
    C. Hydrogen bonding
    D. Polar covalent bonding

Choice **B** is correct. Ionic bonding occurs due to electrostatic charge interactions between ions. Ethanol (C_2H_5OH) is not an ionic compound. Choice B is the correct answer.

59. If a liquid is flowing through a large diameter tube and then suddenly reaches a smaller diameter section, what happens to the pressure and velocity of the liquid?
    A. **The pressure decreases and the velocity increases.**
    B. The pressure increases and the velocity decreases.
    C. Both the pressure and the velocity increase.
    D. Both the pressure and the velocity decrease.

Choice **A** is correct. The continuity equation for the velocity of a fluid states that the volume flow rates, $Q = V/t$, in the two sections of the tube must be equal. The volume (V_1) of fluid that moves past a certain point in a unit of time (t), for the large diameter section must be equal to the surface area (A_1) times the length (L_1) of the cylinder, as shown below. Likewise, the volume (V_2) of fluid that moves past a certain point in the small diameter section, must be the surface area (A_2) times the length (L_2) of the cylinder in this section. Since the length of the cylinders divided by time is the velocity (v) of the fluid, you can obtain the continuity equation for the two sections.

$$Q_1 = Q_2$$
$$V_1/t = V_2/t$$
$$A_1L_1/t = A_2L_2/t$$
$$A_1v_1 = A_2v_2$$

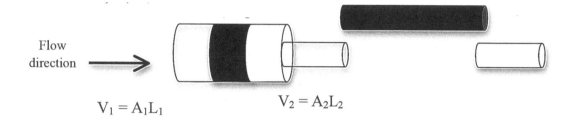

Flow direction

$$V_1 = A_1L_1 \qquad V_2 = A_2L_2$$

From the continuity equation you can see that if the diameter of the tube decreases, this causes A_2 to be less than A_1 and requires that v_2 be proportionally greater than v_1. Choice B and D can be eliminated.

You can now turn your attention to the pressure. Using Bernoulli's equation

$$P_1 + \rho gh_1 + 1/2\, \rho v_1^2 = P_2 + \rho gh_2 + 1/2\, \rho v_2^2$$

Where the variables are pressure (P), density (ρ), acceleration due to gravity (g), height (h) of the tube, and velocities (v) in the two different sections of the tube. If the height is the same, then this equation simplifies to

$$P_1 + 1/2\, \rho v_1^2 = P_2 + 1/2\, \rho v_2^2$$

Now, if you select some simple values to use to investigate the effect that changing the velocity of the fluid has on the pressure, using easy number to do the math with, you can say that $P_1 = 1$, $\rho = 1$, $v_1 = 1$ m/s and $v_2 = 1.5$ m/s, gives

$$1 + 1/2\,(1)(1^2) = P_2 + 1/2\,(1)(1.5^2)$$
$$1 + 0.5 = P_2 + 1/2\,(2.25)$$
$$1.5 = P_2 + 1.125$$
$$1.5 - 1.125 = P_2$$
$$0.375 = P_2$$

The pressure $(P_2 < P_1)$ goes down if the velocity of the fluid increases. Choices B and C can be eliminated and choice A is the correct answer.

B, C, D: These answers are a result of miscalculation. Don't confuse this situation with the Boyles law for an ideal gas, where if the volume of the container of a gas decreases, the pressure increases. In this case, the volume of the liquid does not change, but it is the velocity that is changing.

TIMED
SECTION 4

59 Questions, 95 Minutes

(Use the tear-out answer sheet provided in Appendix E)

Passage 1 (Questions 1-5)

There are over 90 different radioisotopes commonly used in medical diagnosis. Radioisotopes can be inhaled, swallowed, or injected. Imaging techniques using radioisotopes are similar to traditional X-ray photographs in that they require technicians to record varying intensities of radiation. However, rather than emitting this radiation from a source on one side of the person being examined, and detecting radiation intensities on the other side, the radiation comes from inside the person's body, emitted by the material they've taken into their body.

Of the three main categories of radiation: alpha, beta, and gamma, only radioisotopes that emit the last two are used in medical applications. Alpha decay (the emission of a helium nucleus) would be too destructive to internal tissues. Gamma decay (the emission of a high-energy photon) is okay if the dose is not too high. Unlike the other two types of decay, gamma decay involves a drop in energy levels but no transformation of the isotope itself.

In beta decay, a neutron emits an electron (beta particle) and transforms into a proton, preserving both total charge and mass (a much smaller neutrino is also emitted). The following equation shows a parent isotope (X) decaying to a daughter isotope (Y) and emitting a beta particle (β^-). Since the number of protons changes, the chemical identity of the daughter is different from the parent. The atomic mass for the parent and daughter is approximately equal, however, since the mass of the emitted particles is very small, and the number of nucleons remains constant.

$$\ce{^{A}_{Z}X} \rightarrow \ce{^{A'}_{Z'}Y} + \beta^-$$

One beta-decaying radioisotope is iodine-131. Only 10 percent of the energy emitted by this material is in beta form, the other 90 percent being in useless (for imaging purposes) gamma radiation, which can cause tissue damage. The radioactive iodine is still deemed safe to use in small doses, and since it is very inexpensive compared to other radioisotopes, is used frequently in certain diagnoses, thyroid conditions being one prominent example. Iodine-131 has a half-life of about eight days. Other commonly used radioisotopes might have half-lives of only a few hours, so iodine tracers are much more low-powered, but also more long-lasting. Faster-decaying isotopes tend to be favored for nuclear medical treatment, as they will release all their energy quickly enough to be easily directed towards one target.

1. What is the product of the beta-decay of iodine-131?
   A. Iodine-131 at a lower energy level
   B. Iodine-127
   C. Tellerium-130
   D. Xenon-131

2. Uranium-238 will, over time, emit radiation, producing daughter isotopes of thorium-234 (itself radioactive). This is an example of which of the following?
   A. Alpha decay
   B. Beta decay
   C. Gamma decay
   D. A chemical reaction

3. A sample of 50 grams of iodine-131 is injected into a patient. Assuming that none of it is excreted from the body in that time, approximately how much of the sample will remain after 24 days?
   A. 2 g
   B. 6 g
   C. 17 g
   D. 25 g

4. Approximately 8 out of every 9 times, the beta decay of iodine-131 is followed almost immediately by a gamma emission with energy equal to 364 keV. 1 out of 9 times this photon emission does not occur. If a sample of iodine-131 emits a total of 730 MeV over the course of an eight-day period, what was the original size of the sample?
   A. 4 atoms of iodine-131
   B. 2005 atoms of iodine-131
   C. 4011 atoms of iodine-131
   D. 4512 atoms of iodine-131

5. Which of the following would be the most appropriate use of iodine-131 as a tracer?
   A. Imaging a system through which fluids must take several weeks to traverse, and which include cells that are highly sensitive to mutation by radiation
   B. Imaging a system which tends to flush out its fluids in a matter of minutes
   C. Imaging a system through which fluids will spend several weeks passing through, and which is relatively impervious to gamma radiation
   D. Imaging a system which is resilient against beta radiation and will pass its fluids in a couple of days

Passage 2 (Questions 6-10)

Organic acids and alcohols can undergo esterification by way of an equilibrium involving dehydration, Reaction 1. In general the equilibrium constants for these reactions are slightly greater than 1 and the equilibrium concentration of species are significantly affected by experimental conditions as predicted by Le Châtelier's principle. The reaction can be either acid or base catalyzed, increasing the rate at which the reaction reaches equilibrium. Interestingly enough, most esters are perceived as having pleasant odors, and are often used as fragrances, with subtle changes in the alkyl groups having significant effects on the smells we perceive. For example, n-butyl acetate has a smell similar to apples, whereas isoamyl acetate has a smell similar to ripe bananas. On the other hand, methyl butyrate produces a smell like strawberries. These pleasant smells are seemingly in sharp contrast to the smells of the corresponding organic acids, many of which are considered putrid. For example butyric acid, which can be produced by the anaerobic fermentation of milk, has a particularly unpleasant smell and taste, often associated with rancid butter, vomit, body odor and feces. Humans are able to detect butyric acid at levels as low as 10 ppm, whereas dogs are able to detect butyric acid at three orders of magnitude lower concentrations in air. It is interesting to speculate that the sense of smell in mammals may well have systematically developed in order to avoid ingestion of potentially harmful bacteria and other pathogens that may be present in potentially spoiled foods.

Reaction 1 $RCO_2H + R'OH \rightleftharpoons RCO_2R' + H_2O$

By employing special Lewis acid catalysts and solvent combinations, it is also possible to synthesize organic amides by a similar dehydration reaction between an organic acid and an amine. The equilibrium constants are much less favorable for formation of products and acidic conditions tend to protonate the amine, making it a much less effective nucleophile.

6. In the reaction between methanol and acetic acid, which of the following would NOT increase the amount of methyl acetate that is formed at equilibrium?
    A. Adding 1 M H_2SO_4 aqueous solution to the reaction mixture
    B. Adding fuming sulfuric acid to the reaction mixture
    C. Using glacial acetic acid as the solvent, rather than water
    D. Using methanol as the solvent, rather than water

7. Which of the following is the concentration of butyric acid in air that can be detected by a dog?
    A. 10 ppm
    B. 1 ppm
    C. 10 ppb
    D. 1 ppb

8. Esters react with amines, to form amides. What are the products of the reaction between methyl formate and dimethyl amine?
    A. Dimethyl formamide and methanol
    B. Dimethyl formamide and water
    C. Methyl acetamide and methanol
    D. Methyl acetamide and water

9. Which of the following best describes the equilibrium involved in forming an ester from an organic acid and an alcohol?
    A. $K_{eq} > 1$ and $\Delta G > 0$
    B. $K_{eq} > 1$ and $\Delta G < 0$
    C. $K_{eq} < 1$ and $\Delta G > 0$
    D. $K_{eq} < 1$ and $\Delta G < 0$

10. What is the most likely purpose of the acid catalyst in the mechanism for esterification?

    A. The hydrogen ion protonates the carbonyl oxygen, making the carbonyl carbon more susceptible to nucleophilic attack by the alcohol.
    B. The hydrogen ion protonates the oxygen of the -OH group of the organic acid, making it a better leaving group for substitution.
    C. The hydrogen ion protonates the alcohol, making it a better nucleophile to attach the carbonyl carbon.
    D. The hydrogen ion protonates the alcohol, making it a better leaving group for substitution.

Passage 3 (Questions 11-15)

A student was asked to identify an unknown colorless liquid and was told that the liquid was a component of gasoline. The student initially determined by wafting that the unknown had a familiar odor and a small sample of the liquid readily dissolved in water. When a test tube containing the liquid was placed in a brine ice/water bath at approximately -8°C, the unknown remained liquid. After discussing these results with his professor, the student was asked to determine the heating curve of the unknown using a modified melt-temp apparatus that could be cooled to 77 K. To calibrate the equipment the student first conducted an experiment using deionized (DI) water as a control to ensure that the amount of heat being supplied to the sample was accurate. The student placed 100 g of DI water in a newly purchased thick walled glass tube and inserted a thermal couple into the apparatus, followed by adding liquid nitrogen to a reservoir, cooling the sample below its freezing point. The student was able to watch the sample through a small magnifying window as the sample was being cooled. To the student's surprise, the water did not begin to freeze until it reached a temperature of - 41°C, at which point the sample slowly solidified. The student initially thought that there was a significant problem with the equipment, but continued on with the calibration experiment. Once the sample became completely solid, the remaining liquid nitrogen was drained from the apparatus, and the sample was slowly heated using the electrical resistor system. A plot of heat added versus temperature was obtained, as shown in Figure 1a. Then 100 g of unknown was placed in a separate thick walled glass tube and the experiment was repeated, producing the heating curve shown in Figure 1b. After discussing his observations with his professor, the student was told that his observation concerning the differences between the freezing point and melting point of DI water was normal. The professor then asked the student to do one additional experiment using tap water. When the student did the experiment with tap water, he observed that the sample both froze and melted at 0°C, as he would have expected. The professor asked the student to do some literature research in order to explain his observations concerning the differences between the freezing points of DI water and tap water.

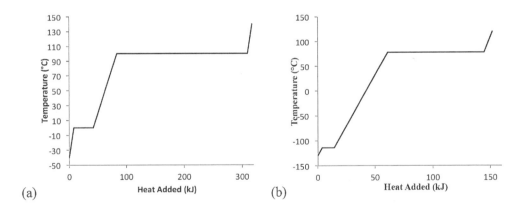

Figure 1 The heating curve for (a) DI water and (b) the unknown sample.

Finally the student was asked to determine the melting point, boiling points, heats of fusion (ΔH_f), specific heats (C_p) of the liquid and heats of vaporization (ΔH_v) for both his control sample and the unknown. The accepted values for water are given in Table 1.

Table 1 Literature values of constants related to the heating curve for water

Constant (unit)	Value
ΔH_f (J/g)	334
C_p (J/g°C)	4.18
ΔH_v (J/g)	2260

11. How much heat would be required to change the temperature of 100 g of water from 25°C to 75°C?
    A. 11 kJ
    B. 21 kJ
    C. 31 kJ
    D. 42 kJ

12. If the student measured the amount of heat required to vaporize the control water sample to be 230.0 kJ, what is the percent error in his measurement?
    A. 2%
    B. 10%
    C. 31%
    D. 98%

13. Based on the boiling point data and information in the passage, which of the following components of gasoline is most likely to be the unknown?
    A. Ethanol, BP is 78°C
    B. n-octane, BP is 125°C
    C. 2,2,4-trimethylpentane, BP is 99°C
    D. Methyl tert-butyl ether, BP is 55°C

14. In the heating curve for water, which of the following best describes the sample when the average kinetic energy is NOT changing?
    A. When the solid ice is going from -20°C to 0°C
    B. When the ice is melting
    C. When the liquid is going from 25°C to 50°C
    D. The average kinetic energy changes whenever heat is added.

15. As suggested by the professor, the student did some literature research concerning the melting point of DI water and found that it is possible to supercool pure water below its normal freezing point because the water molecules are in a metastable state and can not easily orient to form the crystalline solid state structure of ice. Which of the following changes in the experimental design would prevent this phenomenon from occurring?
    I. Using tap water
    II. Using an old, scratched thick walled glass tube
    III. Using distilled water

    A. I only
    B. II only
    C. I and II only
    D. I, II, and III

These questions are NOT based on a passage. (Questions 16-19)

16. The amount of ethanol in an alcoholic beverage is measure by its "proof". Liquors that are 100 proof are 50% ethanol by volume. When grain alcohol is distilled, it forms an azeotrope that is 5% water. What is the proof value of this distillate?
    A. 10 proof
    B. 95 proof
    C. 190 proof
    D. 200 proof

17. Which of the following components of gasoline would produce a broad absorption between 3000 and 3700 cm^{-1} in the infrared spectrum?
    A. Ethanol
    B. n-octane
    C. 2,2,4-trimethylpentane
    D. Methyl t-butyl ether

18. Which of the following would best describe what would happen to the melting point and boiling point of tap water if sodium chloride were dissolved in the solution?
    A. Both the boiling point and the melting point would increase.
    B. Both the boiling point and the melting point would decrease.
    C. The boiling point would increase and the melting point would decrease.
    D. The boiling point would decrease and the melting point would increase.

19. Which of the following compounds are considered radicals?
    I. Nitrogen monoxide
    II. Nitrogen dioxide
    III. Dinitrogen tetroxide
    IV. Ozone

    A. I and II only
    B. III and IV only
    C. I and III only
    D. II and IV only

THIS PAGE LEFT

INTENTIONALLY BLANK

Passage 4 (Questions 20-23)

Hydrocodone (4,5-α-epoxy-3-methoxy-17-methylmorphinan-6-one) is a commonly prescribed opioid chemically derived from codeine.

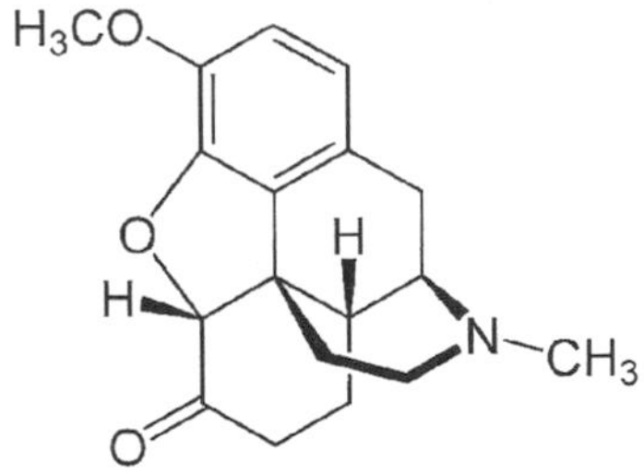

Figure 1 Hydrocodone

It's often administered in combination with ibuprofen (isobutyl propanoic phenolic acid, ((RS)-2-(4-(2-methylpropyl) phenyl)propanoic acid), or acetaminophen (N-(4-hydroxyphenyl)ethanamide).

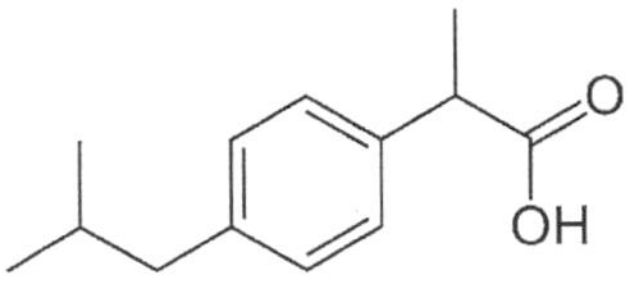

Figure 2 Ibuprofen

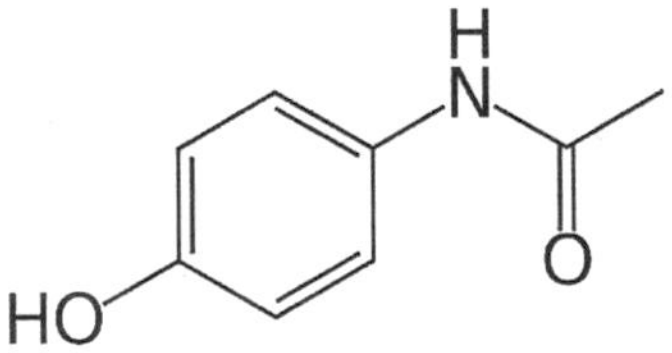

Figure 3 Acetaminophen

Hydrocodone reduces sensation of pain through a receptor-mediated neurochemical cascade triggered by binding of certain metabolites to opioid receptors in the central nervous system. The breakdown of hydrocodone to primary and secondary metabolites is a hepatic enzyme-mediated biotransformation, the principal pathway of which is approximately modelled by the following reaction:

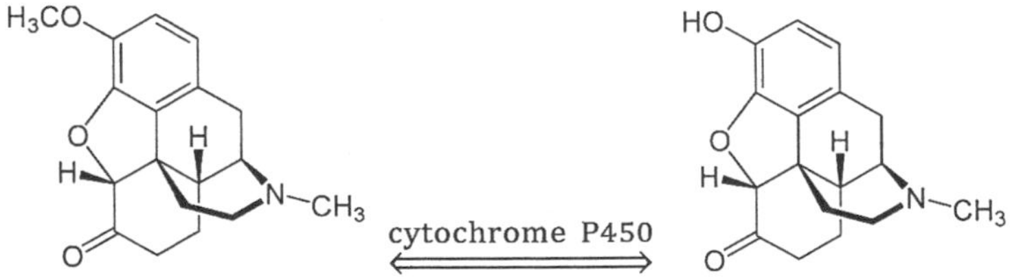

Equation 1   Enzyme-mediated conversion of hydrocodone to hydromorphone

Anecdotal evidence suggests that taking hydrocodone with grapefruit juice increases the sensation of any narcotic effects—this is theorized to occur due to competitive cytochrome P450 inhibition upon consumption of organic compounds in the juice.

20. Ibuprofen is usually synthesized from its immediate precursor via a mechanism known as palladium-catalyzed carbonylation, a process that adds carbon monoxide to the original organic substrate. It was developed as an alternative to a longer, six-step mechanism that, after a series of synthetic steps, produces ibuprofen from a nitrile. Which of the reactions below represents an illustration of the nitrile precursor to ibuprofen?

A.

B.

C.

D.

21. Two students intend to test the hypothesis that a linear increase in compound X, commonly found in grapefruit juice, leads to an exaggeration in observed impairment of test subjects dosed with hydrocodone. Which of the following graphical depictions of cytochrome p450 activity, if generated by the students' data, would appropriately support their hypothesis?

A.

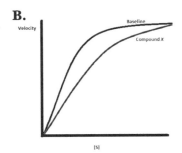

B.

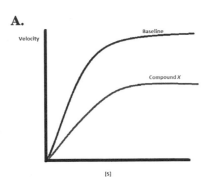

C.

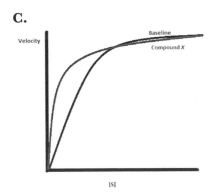

D.

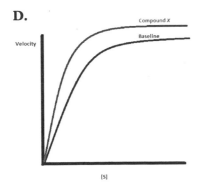

22. How many aromatic rings does hydrocodone have?
    A. 1
    B. 2
    C. 3
    D. 4

23. The enzymes belonging to the cytochrome p450 (CYP) family are collectively responsible for up to 75% of known xenobiotic (a substance foreign to living things or present in amounts much higher than normally found in living things) metabolic reactions in the human body. Certain substances, such as St. John's Wort, are known inhibitors of CYP activity. Which of the following metabolic pathways would be least affected by the consumption of a large amount of CYP inhibitors? Assume that cytochrome p450 enzymes are exclusively involved in xenobiotic metabolism.
    A. Steroidogenesis by the adrenal glands from fatty acids found in fish oil
    B. Benzo(α)pyrene toxification upon consumption of burnt meat
    C. Degradation of orally-ingested Vitamin D in the case of an infant's unintentional overdose.
    D. Metabolism of polycyclic aromatic hydrocarbons ingested via inhalation

Passage 5 (Questions 24-28)

Reactive oxygen species (ROS) and free radicals are oxidative byproducts of metabolism. Oxidative stress results when the production of free radicals exceeds the anti-oxidative capacity of the body. Direct free radical measurement is often inaccurate because of their brief half-lives, but may be measured indirectly by assessing their impact on lipids, proteins and DNA. Lipid peroxidation is a free radical mediated process resulting in the oxidation of polyunsaturated fatty acids (PUFAs) to one of several possible secondary products, as shown in Figure 1. The relative amounts of each secondary product produced depend upon conditions in the body.

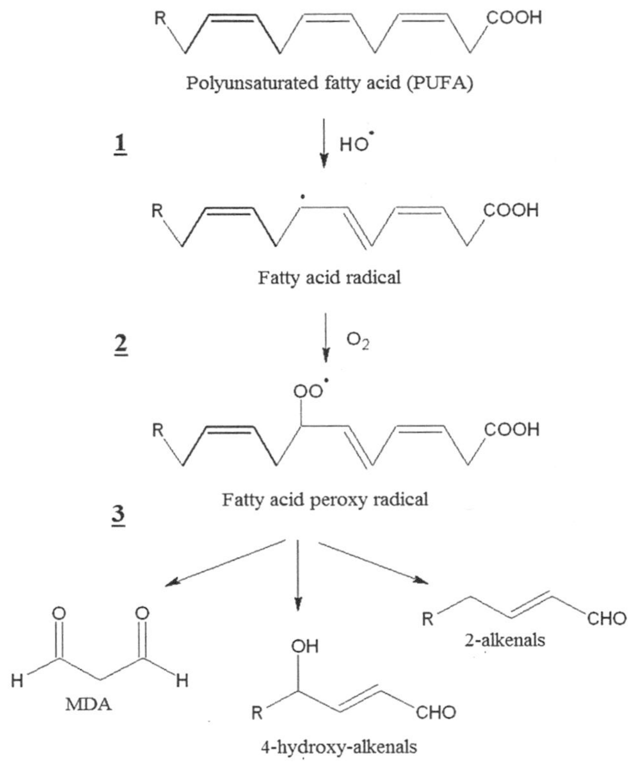

Figure 1 Lipid peroxidation

The presence of one such secondary product, malondialdehyde (MDA), is an indicator of oxidative damage to cells. A colorimetric detection method for MDA employing the Schiff reagent has long been known. In the presence of aldehydes, Schiff reagents undergo a color change. An alternative colorimetric method for assessing oxidative stress was used to measure urinary MDA concentrations in samples collected from healthy individuals. Thiobarbituric acid (TBA) was added to serially diluted urine samples, yielding the chromophoric product shown in Figure 2.

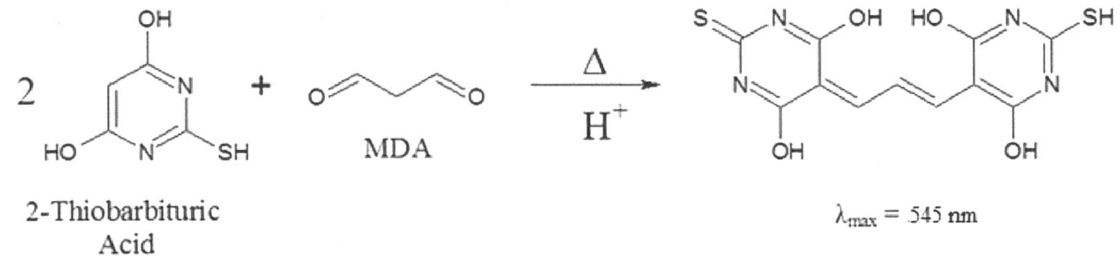

Figure 2 The reaction of 2-thiobarbituric acid and MDA

The absorbance of each solution was then measured spectrophotometrically. The absorbance curves obtained from the TBA assay for dilutions A-E are shown in Figure 3.

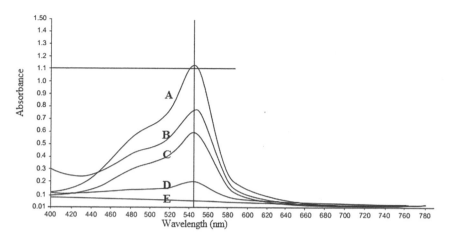

Figure 3 TBARS assay absorption curves at five MDA concentrations

Absorbance at 545 nm is plotted as a function of sample MDA concentration in Figure 4.

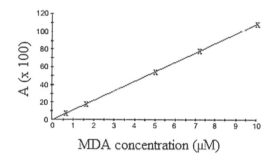

Figure 4 Absorbance at 545 nm versus sample MDA concentration

24. The concentration of MDA present in Dilution B is most nearly:
    A. 3 μM
    B. 5 μM
    C. 7 μM
    D. 10 μM

25. Which of the following PUFAs is most susceptible to lipid peroxidation by the pathway shown in Figure 1?
    A. *all-cis*-6,9,12,15,18,21-tetracosahexaenoic acid
    B. *all-cis*-8,11,14,17-eicosatetraenoic acid
    C. *all-cis*-9,12,15,18,21-tetracosapentaenoic acid
    D. *all-cis*-11,14,17-eicosatrienoic acid

26. All of the following are true of the reaction shown in step 1 of Figure 1 EXCEPT that:
    A. a hydrogen atom is abstracted from a PUFA reactant.
    B. a single electron is transferred to the hydroxyl radical.
    C. water is formed.
    D. the hydroxyl radical acts as a nucleophile.

27. An aqueous solution containing which of the following molecules will NOT undergo a color change upon addition of a Schiff reagent?

I.

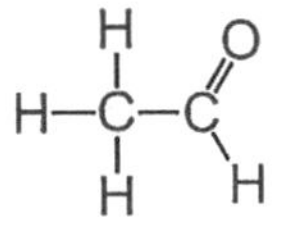

II.

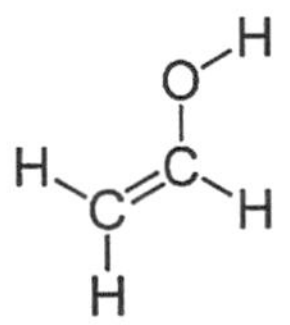

III.

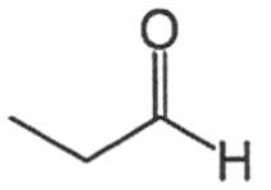

IV.

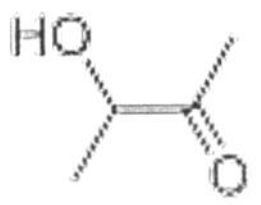

    A. IV only
    B. II and IV only
    C. I and III only
    D. III and IV only

28. Which statement reflects the most reasonable objection to using TBA assay absorbance at 545 nm as a measure of total cellular oxidative stress?
    A. Determining free radical concentration in the body is more direct measure of oxidative stress.
    B. Measurements only at 545 nm do not take into account TBA assay product absorbance at other wavelengths.
    C. MDA is produced cellularly as an end product of lipid peroxidation in variable quantities.
    D. Measured MDA may also be due to oxidation of urinary lipids by the hydrolytic conditions of the reaction.

These questions are NOT based on a passage (29-31)

29. Which of the following is an example of β^+ decay?

   A. Sodium-23 decays into magnesium-23.
   B. Carbon-11 decays into boron-11.
   C. Carbon-14 decays into carbon-12.
   D. Excited hydrogen decays into ground state hydrogen.

30. Sound is which type of wave?
   A. Sound is a transverse wave.
   B. Sound is a longitudinal wave.
   C. Sound is an electromagnetic wave.
   D. Sound is a wave pulse.

31. Which of the following lists of compounds and/or elements contains a substance that is NOT the product of a combustion reaction?
   A. CO_2 (g), O_2 (g) and H_2O (g)
   B. CO (g), CO_2 (g) and H_2O (g)
   C. C (s), CO_2 (g) and H_2O (g)
   D. C (s), CO (g) and CO_2 (g)

Passage 6 (Questions 32-35)

Carbon dioxide plays a pivotal role in many chemical, physical, geological, environmental and biological systems. In order to fully understand this central role, it is important to study the thermodynamic driving forces (Table 1) behind some of the most important physical and chemical reactions involving CO_2.

Carbon dioxide is the ultimate carbon-containing product of aerobic respiration. For most life, an important source of chemical energy is produced by plant photosynthesis. Overall, photosynthesis involves combining carbon dioxide, water and sunlight to produce a carbohydrate, such as glucose, along with elemental oxygen as a byproduct, Reaction 1. The reverse of this reaction is essentially a combustion reaction, which also happens to be the overall chemical reaction involved in aerobic respiration. Combustion reactions release stored chemical energy and can be considered redox reactions that proceed primarily by way of radical mechanisms. The carbon atoms of the reactants are oxidized to carbon's highest oxidation number by the electron acceptor, elemental oxygen. Incomplete combustion can lead to the formation of a variety of carbon containing byproducts, with carbon atoms in intermediate oxidation states, such as soot and carbon monoxide. Of course there is a significant difference between the process of combustion and the multistep processes of glycolysis and the Krebs cycle, that are used to produce useful amounts of energy in forms that can be used by living organisms.

In addition, the physical and chemical interactions of carbon dioxide and its associated ions in aqueous solution play a significant role in regulating a variety of biological processes. Carbon dioxide is a nonpolar molecule that is sparingly soluble in water at atmospheric pressure and room temperature. Increasing the pressure and decreasing the temperature dramatically improves the solubility of most gases in water and carbon dioxide is no exception. When dissolved in aqueous solution, carbon dioxide molecules undergo reaction with water to produce carbonic acid (Reactions 2 and 3), a weak diprotic acid that undergoes successive ionizations (Reaction 4 and 5) to produce bicarbonate and carbonate ions. Many metal cations, including calcium, react with carbonate to form precipitates (Reaction 6). Calcium and magnesium carbonate have solubility product constants of 5×10^{-9} and 5×10^{-6}, respectively. As most geologists know, these reactions can be reversed. For example, reaction of limestone with muriatic acid (concentrated aqueous HCl) causes vigorous bubbling and provides evidence for the origin of this class of sedimentary rock.

Reaction 1 $6\ CO_2\ (g) + 6\ H_2O\ (g) + photons\ \rightarrow C_6H_{12}O_6\ (s) + 6\ O_2\ (g)$

Reaction 2 $CO_2\ (g) + H_2O\ (l)\ \leftrightarrows\ CO_2\ (aq)$

Reaction 3 $CO_2\ (aq) + H_2O\ (l)\ \leftrightarrows\ H_2CO_3\ (aq)$ $K_{hyd} = 1.7 \times 10^{-3}$ at 25°C

Reaction 4 $H_2CO_3\ (aq)\ \leftrightarrows\ HCO_3^-\ (aq) + H^+\ (aq)$ $K_{a1} = 2.5 \times 10^{-4}$ at 25°C

Reaction 5 $HCO_3^-\ (aq)\ \leftrightarrows\ CO_3^{2-}\ (aq) + H^+\ (aq)$ $K_{a2} = 4.69 \times 10^{-11}$ at 25°C

Reaction 6 $Ca^{2+}\ (aq) + CO_3^{2-}\ (aq)\ \leftrightarrows\ CaCO_3\ (s)$

Table 1 Thermodynamic parameters for selected compounds and ions at 25°C.

Compound	Enthalpy of formation, $\Delta H°_f$ (kJ/mol)	Entropy of formation, $S°_f$ (J/mol K)
C (s, graphite)	0	5.74
CO (g)	-110.5	197.7
CO_2 (g)	-393.5	213.8
H_2O (l)	-285.8	69.9
H_2O (g)	-241.8	188.8
H_2CO_3 (aq)	-699.7	187.4
HCO_3^- (aq)	-692.0	91.2
CO_3^{2-} (aq)	-677.1	-56.9
Ca^{2+} (aq)	-542.8	-53.1
H^+ (aq)	0	0
$CaCO_3$ (s) (calcite)	-1206.9	92.9
$C_6H_{12}O_6$ (s)	-1268	-212
O_2 (g)	0	205.1

32. Based on the information in the passage, what is the most likely combination of signs for the enthalpy and entropy changes that occur when carbon dioxide gas dissolves in aqueous solution?
    A. ΔH is positive and ΔS is positive.
    B. ΔH is negative and ΔS is positive.
    C. ΔH is positive and ΔS is negative.
    D. ΔH is negative and ΔS is negative.

33. Based on information from Table 1 and the passage, what is the value of the equilibrium constant for the following reaction?

$$CO_2 \text{ (aq)} + H_2O \text{ (l)} + Ca^{2+} \text{ (aq)} \leftrightarrows CaCO_3 \text{ (s)} + 2\,H^+ \text{ (aq)}$$

    A. $K = 2 \times 10^5$
    B. $K = 2 \times 10^8$
    C. $K = 4 \times 10^{-9}$
    D. $K = 1 \times 10^{-25}$

34. What is the approximate Gibbs free energy change for the overall aerobic conversion of solid glucose to carbon dioxide and liquid water at body temperature (37° C)?
    A. +3000 kJ/mol
    B. +700 kJ/mol
    C. -3000 kJ/mol
    D. -200000 kJ/mol

35. Based on the data in Table 1, what is the heat of vaporization of water?
    A. +44 kJ/mole
    B. +2260 kJ/mole
    C. -241.8 kJ/mole
    D. -285.8 kJ/mole

THIS PAGE LEFT

INTENTIONALLY BLANK

Passage 7 (Questions 36-39)

The physician Luigi Galvani conducted experiments with static electricity and the triboelectric effect. While removing the skin of the frog, he accidentally touched a scalpel that had previously been electrically charged to the dead frog, resulting in a startling observation. The frog spontaneously moved as if it had come back to life. Galvani was able to reproduce this process numerous times, resulting in his investigations into "animal electricity." Frog tissue not only responded to electrical stimulation, but was also a conductor of charge. A number of experiments showed that the electrical conduction was not unique to animal tissue. For instance, Galvani obtained a similar result by simply soaking a paper towel in a brine solution, which he called an electrolyte. This lead to the discovery that different metals when in contact with brine soaked paper towels would produce similar effects, sparking a debate with Galvani concerning the nature of his "cells" that produced electricity. Scientists eventually were able to rank various metals to create the first electrochemical series (Table 1), and associated electromotive forces, based on the idea that various electrodes have a potential to cause charges to move in a conducting material. Subsequently, a mathematical relationship (Equation 1) was developed to predict the potentials for electrochemical cells.

$$E = E° - (RT/nF) \ln Q$$

Equation 1 The Nernst equation describes the relationship observed between the cell potential under nonstandard conditions to the potential under standard conditions, where $R = 8.314$ J K^{-1} mol^{-1}, T is the temperature in degrees Kelvin, n is the moles of electrons in the balanced reaction and F is Faraday's constant, 9.65×10^4 C mol^{-1}. Note that at 25°C [RT/nF] $\ln Q = (0.059/n) \log Q$

Table 1 Selected standard reduction potentials at 25°C.

Reduction Half-Reaction	E° (V)
F_2 (g) + 2 e$^-$ --> 2 F$^-$ (aq)	+ 2.87
MnO_4^- (aq) + 8 H$^+$ (aq) + 5 e$^-$ --> Mn^{2+} (aq) + 4 H_2O (l)	+ 1.51
$Cr_2O_7^{2-}$ (aq) + 14 H$^+$ (aq) + 6 e$^-$ --> 2 Cr^{3+} (aq) + 7 H_2O (l)	+ 1.33
O_2 (g) + 4 H$^+$ (aq) + 4 e$^-$ --> 2 H_2O (l)	+ 1.23
Ag$^+$ (aq) + e$^-$ --> Ag (s)	+ 0.80
O_2 (g) + 2 H_2O (l) + 4 e$^-$ --> 4 OH$^-$ (aq)	+0.40
Cu^{2+} (aq) + 2 e$^-$ --> Cu (s)	+0.34
2 H$^+$ (aq) + 2 e$^-$ --> H_2 (g)	0.00
Ni^{2+} (aq) + 2 e$^-$ --> Ni (s)	- 0.28
Cd^{2+} (aq) + 2 e$^-$ --> Cd (s)	-0.40
Zn^{2+} (aq) + 2 e$^-$ --> Zn (s)	- 0.76
2 H_2O (l) + 2 e$^-$ --> H_2 (g) + 2 OH$^-$ (aq)	- 0.83
Li$^+$ (aq) + e$^-$ --> Li (s)	-3.05

36. For an electrochemical cell based on the following redox reaction at 25°C, what is the cell potential when the concentration of Cu^{2+} (aq) is 10^8 times greater than the concentration of Zn^{2+} (aq)?

$$Cu^{2+} (aq) + Zn (s) \rightarrow Zn^{2+} (aq) + Cu (s)$$

   A. -0.18 V
   B. 1.10 V
   C. 1.34 V
   D. 1.57 V

37. Which of the following species is the best oxidizing agent?
   A. MnO^{4-} (aq)
   B. $Cr_2O_7^{2-}$ (aq)
   C. Zn (s)
   D. Li (s)

38. Which of the following combinations of unit symbols is NOT equivalent to a Volt?
   A. $A \cdot \Omega$
   B. $W\ A^{-1}$
   C. $J\ C^{-1}$
   D. $kg\ m\ s^{-2}$

39. Which of the following statements is true concerning a galvanic cell with a positive potential?
   I. The redox reaction is nonspontaneous because the Gibbs free energy is positive.
   II. Electrons flow through the circuit from the anode to the cathode.
   III. The anode is negatively charged.

   A. I only
   B. II only
   C. I and II only
   D. II and III only

Passage 8 (Questions 40-43)

Each person's voice has a unique quality, known as timbre, and is produced by a system designed to produce vibrations and filters based on a series of resonance chambers. As air is forced out of the lungs, the vocal cords that are stretched over the opening in the larynx vibrate to create pressure waves. Muscles associated with the vocal cords can adjust the tension of these membranes, affecting the fundamental frequencies of vibration. The sound waves are filtered, by changing the size and shape of the resonating cavities, which are the lungs, the larynx, the pharynx, the mouth and the sinuses. The frequencies of various harmonics, or overtones, having significant amplitudes also contribute to the timbre of the voice. A person can control the air pressure vibrating the vocal cords using the muscles of the diaphragm, abdomen and rib cage, thus affecting the loudness of the sound. The average person has a lung capacity of about 1200 cm³, with a trachea representing a tube having an average diameter of about 2 cm and a length of approximately 10 cm. A typical adult male will have a fundamental frequency from 85 to 180 Hz, and a typical adult female from 165 to 255 Hz. The amplitude of the overtones can be affected by manipulating the diameter of resonating chambers, i.e. the mouth, at the nodes and antinodes.

A surprisingly good model system for studying the fundamental resonance of the human voice is a bottle whistle. When air is blown over the opening of a bottle, air is forced into the cavity, creating a pressure slightly above atmospheric pressure. The system will respond like a spring, with air being pushed back out of the bottle, causing the pressure to decrease below atmospheric pressure. Air from outside then rushes back into the bottle and the process is repeated. Thus, the air will oscillate into and out of the container at some natural frequency. If air is gently blown over the opening, the sound that is produced is primarily due to the fundamental frequency of the resonating cavity. However, blowing air more forcefully can result in the production of one or more overtones as the principle source of the sound. The pitch of the fundamental frequency can be changed by adding water to the bottle. The fundamental frequency of a bottle with an irregular shape depends upon a number of variables, including the speed (v) of sound (in air v = 334 m/s), the area (of the opening), the volume (V) of the principle cavity of the bottle, and the length of the neck (l) of the tube. The relationship between frequency (f) and these variables is given in Equation 1. Figure 1 shows the pressure versus time plots for an empty bottle whistle and the same bottle with a small amount of water added, using a microphone to record the sound.

Equation 1

$$f = \frac{v}{2\pi}\sqrt{\frac{A}{Vl}}$$

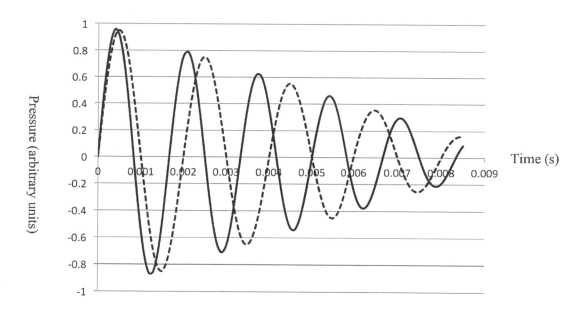

Figure 1 Pressure versus time plots for two different pitches of sound (F_1 = solid line and F_2 = dashed line) produced by a bottle whistle.

40. What is the frequency of the lowest pitched tone produced by the bottle whistle in Figure 1.
    A. 500 Hz
    B. 600 Hz
    C. 1000 Hz
    D. 1200 Hz

41. Using the information in the passage about the relationship between a bottle whistle and the resonating cavities of the human body what is the predicted frequency of the fundamental produced by the average person?
    A. 90 Hz
    B. 500 Hz
    C. 833 Hz
    D. 1500 Hz

42. Based on the information in Figure 1, what is happening to the pitch and loudness of the sounds over time?
    A. The pitches are getting higher and the loudness is staying the same.
    B. The pitches are staying the same and the loudness is decreasing.
    C. The pitches are decreasing and the loudness is increasing.
    D. Both the pitches and the loudness are remaining the same.

43. Which of the following describe the number of nodes and antinodes for a closed tube resonator?
    I. For the fundamental, there is a single node and a single antinode.
    II. For the third harmonic, there are two nodes and two antinodes.
    III. For the fifth harmonic, there are three nodes and three antinodes.

    A. I only
    B. II and III only
    C. I and III only
    D. I, II, and III

These questions are NOT based on a passage. (Questions 44-47)

44. Which of the following are considered carbohydrates?
    I.   Glucose
    II. Formaldehyde
    III. Acetic acid

    A. I only
    B. I and II only
    C. I and III only
    D. I, II and III

45. In cases of panic attacks and hyperventilation, the victim is sometimes asked to breath into a paper bag to slow the person's respiration rate. What does breathing into a paper bag do to the concentration of carbon dioxide and the pH of the blood?
    A. The concentration of carbon dioxide increases and pH both increase.
    B. The concentration of carbon dioxide increases and pH decreases.
    C. The concentration of carbon dioxide decreases and pH increases.
    D. The concentration of carbon dioxide and pH both decrease.

46. Which of the following best describes the complementary reactions of photosynthesis and combustion?
    A. Photosynthesis is endothermic and combustion is exothermic.
    B. Photosynthesis is exothermic and combustion is endothermic.
    C. Both photosynthesis and combustion are endothermic processes.
    D. Both photosynthesis and combustion are exothermic processes.

47. Which of the following best describes the bond angle in ozone?
    A. 90°
    B. 117°
    C. 135°
    D. 180°

Passage 9   (Questions 48-51)

Air pollution is a major contributor to public health issues for people living in urban regions. The major sources of air pollution are related to energy production and transportation. Recently there has been a significant change in how we produce energy in the United States, with the discovery and use of new natural gas reserves, which are replacing coal for electricity production. Burning coal, which can often contain relatively high amounts of sulfur, results in the formation of sulfur dioxide, which can contribute to particulate matter, as well as contributing to problems associated with acid rain. On the other hand, the use of internal combustion engines for transportation also contributes to the formation of air pollution from the release of volatile organic compounds, as well as the production of nitrogen oxides, both of which contribute to the production of photochemical smog which can produce dangerous concentrations of ozone.

Nitrogen oxides, both nitrogen monoxide and nitrogen dioxide, are formed when air is used as the source of oxygen in high temperature combustion reactions, such as in the internal combustion engine. The reaction between elemental nitrogen and elemental oxygen, Reaction 1, is thermodynamically favorable, but kinetically hindered.

Reaction 1 $\qquad\qquad$ $N_2 \text{ (g)} + O_2 \text{ (g)} \rightarrow 2 \text{ NO (g)}$

Nitrogen monoxide reacts further with elemental oxygen to form nitrogen dioxide. This reaction is thought to occur in a two step mechanism, in which two nitrogen monoxide molecules combine in a relatively fast pre-equilibrium, forming an intermediate species, dinitrogen dioxide, which then reacts in a slow step with an equivalent of elemental oxygen to form two nitrogen dioxide molecules, Reaction 2 and 3.

Reaction 2 $\qquad\qquad$ $2 \text{ NO (g)} \leftrightarrows N_2O_2 \text{ (g)} \qquad$ fast

Reaction 3 $\qquad\qquad$ $N_2O_2 \text{ (g)} + O_2 \text{ (g)} \rightarrow 2 \text{ NO}_2 \text{ (g)} \quad$ slow

Nitrogen dioxide is a brown gas and establishes equilibrium with the colorless gas dinitrogen tetroxide, Reaction 4. The color of nitrogen dioxide is a ubiquitous characteristic of seasonal smog episodes in cities such as Los Angeles.

Reaction 4 $\qquad\qquad$ $2 \text{ NO}_2 \text{ (g)} \leftrightarrows N_2O_4 \text{ (g)} + 57 \text{ kJ}$

48. Which of the following best describes the thermodynamic changes associated with the equilibrium between nitrogen dioxide and dinitrogen tetroxide?
    - **A.** The enthalpy change is positive and the entropy change is negative.
    - **B.** The enthalpy change is negative and the entropy change is positive.
    - **C.** Both the enthalpy and entropy changes are positive.
    - **D.** Both the enthalpy and entropy changes are negative.

49. Which of the following best describes the season during which air pollution in Los Angeles most likely has a brown color?
    - **A.** Air pollution has a brown color in the summer due to the increased amounts of nitrogen dioxide that is formed at high temperatures, because the reaction is exothermic.
    - **B.** Air pollution has a brown color in the summer due to the increased amounts of dinitrogen tetroxide that is formed at high temperatures, because the reaction is endothermic.
    - **C.** Air pollution has a brown color in the winter due to the increased amounts of nitrogen dioxide that is formed at low temperatures, because the reaction is exothermic.
    - **D.** Air pollution has a brown color in the winter due to the increased amounts of dinitrogen tetroxide that is formed at low temperatures, because the reaction is endothermic.

50. Which of the following energy diagrams best describes Reaction 1?

A.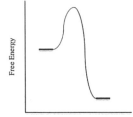

B.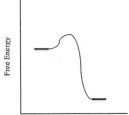

C.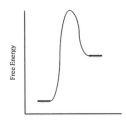

D.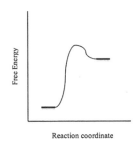

51. If sulfur dioxide is the major oxide of sulfur initially formed when coal is burned, which of the following acids will be formed when sulfur dioxide reacts with water?
    A. Sulfonic acid
    B. Sulfurous acid
    C. Sulfuric acid
    D. Hydrosulfuric acid

THIS PAGE LEFT

INTENTIONALLY BLANK

Passage 10 (Questions 52-55)

Understanding the shapes of covalently bonded molecules and ions represents a critical factor in understanding more complex biomolecules. The coupling of Valance Shell Electron Pair Repulsion (VSEPR) theory and Valance Bond (VB) theory has proven to be an extremely useful way to predict molecular shapes and the bonding of small molecules and ions. These theories have formed the basis for computer molecular modeling programs used to understand the complex structures of biopolymers, such as structural proteins and enzymes. In addition to predicting idealized geometries, VSEPR theory can account for subtle distortions of bond angles. For example, the ideal geometric shape of water is based on a tetrahedral geometry, in which two of the tetrahedral vertices are occupied by lone-pairs of electrons. Since the O-H bonding pairs of electrons are shared between two nuclei, the corresponding electron particle wave is elongated, with resulting particle wave amplitude that does not occupy as much space around the oxygen atom as the lone pairs. Since these negatively charged lone-pairs exert an electrostatic repulsive force, the H-O-H angle is reduced from the idealized tetrahedral angle of 109.5° to 104.5°.

In addition to predicting the shapes of molecules and ions of second period elements, VSEPR can also be useful in predicting the idealized shapes and qualitatively predict distortions seen in third period molecules and ions that can expand their octets to form sp^3d and sp^3d^2 hybrid structures, with trigonal bipyramidal (D3h) and octahedral (Oh) geometries, respectively. For example, sulfur hexafluoride adopts an Oh structure, with F-S-F angles of 90° and 180°, but sulfur tetrafluoride adopts a distorted see-saw shaped (C2v) structure (Figure 1), where the idealized F-S-F angles of 180° and 120° are compressed slightly, to 173.1° and 101.6°, respectively, due to the space occupied by the lone-pair of electrons on the sulfur atom.

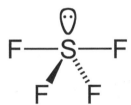

Figure 1 The idealized TBP structure of sulfur tetrafluoride.

52. Which of the following would most likely have a bond angle that is distorted from the idealized geometry?
    A. NH_4^+
    B. H_3O^+
    C. CF_4
    D. BF_3

53. Which of the following does NOT correctly describe the molecular shape?
    A. Sulfur dioxide is bent.
    B. Nitrite ion is bent.
    C. Ammonia is tetrahedral.
    D. Methane is tetrahedral.

54. Which of the following theoretically adopts a distorted see-saw type structure?
    I. PF_4^-
    II. ClF_4^+
    III. XeF_4

    A. I only
    B. III only
    C. I and II only
    D. I, II and III

55. Which of the following is best described as having a fractional bond order?
    A. Carbon dioxide
    B. Carbonate
    C. Elemental nitrogen
    D. Diamond

These questions are NOT based on a passage. (Questions 56-59)

56. Which of the following regions of the infrared spectrum would be most useful in distinguishing an ester from an organic acid?
    A. 3000 to 3700 cm^{-1}
    B. 2800 to 3000 cm^{-1}
    C. 1700 to 1800 cm^{-1}
    D. 1200 to 1400 cm^{-1}

57. What is the oxidation state of the chromium atoms in $Cr_2O_7^{2-}$?
    A. Cr^{2+}
    B. Cr^{3+}
    C. Cr^{6+}
    D. Cr^{12+}

58. Nitrogen dioxide is a brown gas and establishes equilibrium with the colorless gas dinitrogen tetroxide, as described in the following reaction.

$$2 NO_2 (g) \leftrightarrows N_2O_4 (g) + 57 kJ$$

Which of the following changes would most likely cause a sealed glass tube containing these gases to become colorless?
    A. Increase the temperature and decrease the pressure of the system.
    B. Decrease the temperature and increase the pressure of the system.
    C. Increase both the temperature and the pressure of the system.
    D. Decrease both the temperature and the pressure of the system.

59. Which of the following is the most likely O-N-O bond angle in nitrogen dioxide?
    A. 90°
    B. 120°
    C. 134°
    D. 180°

TIMED
SECTION 4
Answers and Explanations

Timed Section 4 Answer Key

Passage 1
1. D
2. A
3. B
4. D
5. C

Passage 2
6. A
7. C
8. A
9. B
10. A

Passage 3
11. B
12. A
13. A
14. B
15. C

Discrete Set 1
16. C
17. A
18. C
19. A

Passage 4
20. D
21. B
22. A
23. A

Passage 5
24. C
25. A
26. D
27. A
28. C

Discrete Set 2
29. B
30. B
31. A

Passage 6
32. D
33. C
34. C
35. A

Passage 7
36. C
37. A
38. D
39. D

Passage 8
40. A
41. A
42. B
43. D

Discrete Set 3
44. A
45. B
46. A
47. B

Passage 9
48. D
49. A
50. A
51. B

Passage 10
52. B
53. C
54. C
55. B

Discrete Set 4
56. A
57. C
58. B
59. C

Passage 1 Explanation

There are over 90 different **radioisotopes** commonly used in medical diagnosis. Radioisotopes can be inhaled, swallowed, or injected. **Imaging techniques** using radioisotopes are similar to traditional **X-ray** photographs in that they require technicians to record varying intensities of radiation. However, rather than emitting this radiation from a source on one side of the person being examined, and detecting radiation intensities on the other side, the radiation comes from inside the person's body, emitted by the material they've taken into their body.

Key terms: radioisotopes, Imaging techniques , X-ray

Contrast: X-ray photography versus radioisotope imaging

Cause-and-effect: imaging is done by identifying location of radioisotopes via their emissions

Of the three main categories of **radiation: alpha, beta, and gamma**, only radioisotopes that emit the last two are used in medical applications. Alpha decay (the emission of a helium nucleus) would be too destructive to internal tissues. Gamma decay (the emission of a high-energy photon) is okay if the dose is hot too high. Unlike the other two types of decay, gamma decay involves a drop in energy levels but no transformation of the isotope itself.

Key terms: radiation, alpha, beta, and gamma

Contrast: alpha and beta produce particles, gamma produces photon; beta and gamma used in medical applications

Cause-and-effect: nucleus emits something, transforms

In beta decay, a neutron emits an **electron (beta particle)** and transforms into a proton, preserving both total charge and mass (a much smaller neutrino is also emitted). The following equation shows a parent isotope (X) decaying to a daughter isotope (Y) and emitting a beta particle (β⁻). Since the number of protons changes, the **chemical identity of the daughter is different from the parent**. The atomic mass for the parent and daughter is approximately equal, however, since the mass of the emitted particles is very small, and the number of nucleons remains constant.

$$\,^{A}_{Z}X \;\rightarrow\; \,^{A'}_{Z'}Y \;+\; \beta^{-}$$

Key terms: electron (beta particle)

Cause-and-effect: beta decay, proton number changes, mass number same

One commonly used beta-decaying radioisotope is **iodine-131**. Like an inefficient incandescent lightbulb, only **10 percent** of the energy emitted by this material is in beta form, the other **90 percent** being in useless (for imaging purposes) gamma radiation, which can cause tissue damage. The radioactive iodine is still deemed safe to use in small doses, however, and since it is very inexpensive compared to other radioisotopes, is used frequently in certain diagnoses, thyroid conditions being one prominent example.

Key terms: iodine-131

Cause-and-effect: only 10% of energy released by I-131 is beta

Iodine-131 has a **half-life of about eight days**. Other commonly used radioisotopes might have half-lives of only a few hours, so compared to these, iodine tracers are much more low-powered, but also more long-lasting. Faster-decaying isotopes tend to be favored for nuclear medical treatment, as they will release all their energy quickly enough to be easily directed towards one target.

Key terms: half-life

Cause-and-effect: fast-decay means longer half-life but lower rate of energy release

1. What is the product of the beta-decay of iodine-131?
   A. Iodine-131 at a lower energy level
   B. Iodine-127
   C. Tellerium-130
   D. **Xenon-131**

Choice **D** is correct. Beta decay of iodine involves a neutron transforming into a proton. Since the total number of nucleons is the same, the atomic mass is still 131, however, the increase in the number of protons means the atomic number is different, and therefore the product cannot be iodine anymore. Xenon-131 is the result of changing one of iodine-131's neutrons to a proton.

2. Uranium-238 will, over time, emit radiation, producing daughter isotopes of thorium-234 (itself radioactive). This is an example of which of the following?
   A. **Alpha decay**
   B. Beta decay
   C. Gamma decay
   D. A chemical reaction

Choice **A** is correct. According to the passage, alpha decay involves the emission of a helium nucleus. Since helium has an atomic mass of four and an atomic number of two, an alpha particle is two protons and two neutrons. These two isotopes clearly have a difference in mass of 4 (238 compared to 234), and only alpha decay can account for that.

Remember a neutron is a proton with an electron attached. In beta decay a neutron sends its electron packing, literally ejecting it from the nucleus at high speed. The result? That neutron turns into a proton! Beta decay increases an atom's electron count by 1 (notice the 1- in the symbol). During beta radiation an atom's proton count grows by one. Gamma rays are electromagnetic radiation similar to light. Gamma decay does not change the mass or charge of the atom from which it originates. Gamma is often emitted along with alpha or beta particle ejection. Forget D, as there is no chemical reaction whereby a single reactant can transform into a single product.

3. A sample of 50 grams of iodine-131 is injected into a patient. Assuming that none of it is excreted from the body in that time, approximately how much of the sample will remain after 24 days?
   A. 2 g
   B. **6 g**
   C. 17 g
   D. 25 g

Choice **B** is correct. The half-life is given in the passage as eight days. That means for every eight days, the original mass can be multiplied by $\frac{1}{2}$. After 24 days, the sample will be 50 x (1/2) x (1/2) x (1/2) = 6.25 g.

4. Approximately 8 out of every 9 times, the beta decay of iodine-131 is followed almost immediately by a gamma emission with energy equal to 364 keV. 1 out of 9 times this photon emission does not occur. If a sample of iodine-131 emits a total of 730 MeV over the course of an eight-day period, what was the original size of the sample?
   A. 4 atoms of iodine-131
   B. 2005 atoms of iodine-131
   C. 4011 atoms of iodine-131
   D. **4512 atoms of iodine-131**

Choice **D** is correct. This is a difficult calculation question, because it involves a trick combination of concepts, a lot of mathematical steps and not very nice numbers. The first thing to recognize is that the energy release of 364 keV signals that decay has occurred. So you need to figure out how many emissions of this amount of energy have occurred to figure out how many decays. 730/364 is very close to 2, but because of the difference in units (MeV versus keV), it's really 730000/364, so that's 2000 emissions. That's very close to answer choice B, but we're not done yet, because the question asks for the size of the sample, not the number of decaying atoms. Note that the question said this happened in an eight-day period, which is the half-life for this isotope. Therefore, these 2000 decays should represent half of the original sample (since half are expected to decay in this period and half are expected to not decay). That gives us 4000, which is a good match for C. But wait, one last twist. Only 8/9 decays result in this energy emission. So for every eight gamma emissions, there's a decay with no emission. Therefore, the true number of decayed atoms, and therefore the true number of atoms in the original sample, are 9/8 of these values, or 1/8 (.125) bigger. That gives us 4500, which gives us our correct answer.

5. Which of the following would be the most appropriate use of iodine-131 as a tracer?
   A. Imaging a system through which fluids must take several weeks to traverse, and which include cells that are highly sensitive to mutation by radiation
   B. Imaging a system which tends to flush out its fluids in a matter of minutes
   C. **Imaging a system through which fluids will spend several weeks passing through, and which is relatively impervious to gamma radiation**
   D. Imaging a system which is resilient against beta radiation and will pass its fluids in a couple of days

Choice **C** is correct. The key questions about the use of iodine-131 or any other radioisotope as a tracer are i) how quickly does it decay, ii) how much energy does it produce? Often these two things are related, as a substance with a very brief half-life produces a lot of energy in a short period of time. In the case of iodine-131, however, you know it produces a lot of extra gamma radiation in addition to the beta particles used for finding its location (and thus imaging the systems in question). So it shouldn't be used in an area that is highly sensitive to radiation, but it's superior for use in an area through which a tracer will be slow-moving, as it will last several weeks. It's inferior in an area where it will be flushed out in a short period of time, as its slow decay process will not provide much information for imaging in that time.

Passage 2 Explanation

Organic acids and alcohols can undergo **esterification by way of an equilibrium involving dehydration**, Reaction 1. In general the equilibrium constants for these reactions are **slightly greater than 1** and the equilibrium concentration of species are significantly affected by experimental conditions as predicted by Le Châtelier's principle. The reaction can be either acid or base catalyzed, increasing the rate at which the reaction reaches equilibrium. Interestingly enough, most esters are perceived as having pleasant odors, and are often used as fragrances, with subtle changes in the alkyl groups having significant effects on the smells you perceive. For example, n-butyl acetate has a smell similar to apples, whereas isoamyl acetate has a smell similar to ripe bananas. On the other hand, methyl butyrate produces a smell like strawberries. These pleasant smells are seemingly in sharp contrast to the smells of the corresponding organic acids, many of which are considered putrid. For example **butyric acid, which can be produced by the anaerobic fermentation of milk**, has a particularly unpleasant smell and taste, often associated with rancid butter, vomit, body odor and feces. Humans are able to detect butyric acid at **levels as low as 10 ppm**, whereas dogs are able to detect butyric acid at three orders of magnitude lower concentrations in air. It is interesting to speculate that the sense of smell in mammals may well have systematically developed in order to avoid ingestion of potentially harmful bacteria and other pathogens that may be present in potentially spoiled foods.

Key terms: esterification, dehydration, Le Châtelier's principle, catalyzed, putrid, and anaerobic fermentation

Cause-and-Effect: Combining an organic acid and an alcohol establishes an equilibrium in which the products are an ester and water and this equilibrium can be shifted based on the concepts of Le Châtelier's principle, i.e. increasing the concentration of the reactants or removal of water shifts the reaction to produce more of the ester.

Cause-and-Effect: The sense of smell depends upon the ability of a molecule to interact with a nerve receptor and the shape and types of intermolecular bonding that is possible between the receptor and molecule that produces the smell has a significant effect on our perception of smell.

Cause-and-Effect: A certain number of molecules are required to generate an action potential associated with a particular smell.

Reaction 1 $RCO_2H + R'OH \rightleftarrows RCO_2R' + H_2O$

Reaction 1 In an esterification, the alkoxide of the alcohol replaces the hydroxyl group of the organic acid, with corresponding loss of a water molecule. This equilibrium reaction is completely reversible and esters can by hydrolyzed to the corresponding acid and alcohol. This reaction can be catalyzed either by acid or by base. An acid catalyst acts by protonating the carbonyl oxygen of the organic acid, making the carbonyl carbon more susceptible to nucleophilic attack by the alcohol. A strongly basic catalyst deprotonates the alcohol, to form the alkoxide, which is then better able to attack the carbonyl carbon, than the alcohol.

By employing special **Lewis acid** catalysts and solvent combinations, it is also possible to synthesize **organic amides** by a similar dehydration reaction between an organic acid and an amine. The equilibrium constants are much less favorable for formation of products and **acidic conditions** tend to protonate the amine, making it a much less effective **nucleophile**.

Key terms: Lewis acid, organic amides, and nucleophile

Cause-and-Effect: The synthesis of organic amides by reaction of an organic acid with an alkyl amine is analogous to esterification, but the equilibrium constant does not favor the formation of the products due to differences in the C-O versus C-N bond energies.

Cause-and-Effect: Unlike esterification, synthesis of amides by dehydration of organic acids and amines is not favorable, because the amine is a much better base than an alcohol and the ammonium ion will not act as a nucleophile and attack the carbonyl carbon of the organic acid.

6. In the reaction between methanol and acetic acid, which of the following would NOT increase the amount of methyl acetate that is formed at equilibrium?
    A. <u>Adding 1 M H_2SO_4 aqueous solution to the reaction mixture</u>
    B. Adding fuming sulfuric acid to the reaction mixture
    C. Using glacial acetic acid as the solvent, rather than water
    D. Using methanol as the solvent, rather than water

Choice **A** is correct.

B: Fuming sulfuric acid is > 98% H_2SO_4. As a result, fuming sulfuric acid is extremely hygroscopic and is an excellent way to promote dehydration reactions, thereby shifting the esterification equilibrium towards products.

C, D: Increasing the concentration of either of the reactants, acetic acid or methanol, will shift the reaction towards products.

Since a 1 M aqueous solution of sulfuric acid has a very high concentration of water, the esterification equilibrium will be shifted towards the reactants. In this case the acid will catalyze the rate at which it reaches equilibrium, but not increase the amount of ester that is formed once it reaches equilibrium. Choice A is the correct answer.

7. Which of the following is the concentration of butyric acid in air that can be detected by a dog?
    A. 10 ppm
    B. 1 ppm
    C. <u>**10 ppb**</u>
    D. 1 ppb

Choice **C** is correct. As stated in the passage, "Humans are able to detect butyric acid at levels as low as 10 ppm, whereas dogs are able to detect butyric acid at three orders of magnitude lower concentrations in air." The unit for concentration is parts per million and three orders of magnitude is a factor of 10^3, so dogs can smell butyric acid at a concentration of 0.010 ppm, which is the same as 10 ppb (parts per billion).

8. Esters react with amines, to form amides. What are the products of the reaction between methyl formate and dimethyl amine?
   A. **Dimethyl formamide and methanol**
   B. Dimethyl formamide and water
   C. Methyl acetamide and methanol
   D. Methyl acetamide and water

The structure of methyl formate is shown below.

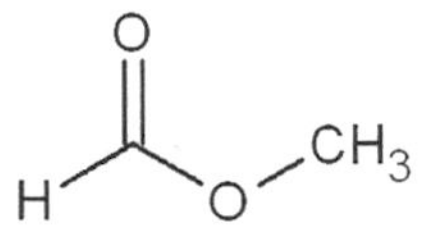

The methoxide group will be replaced by a dimethylamide group to give dimethyl formate and methanol. The best answer is choice **A**.

B, C, D: It would take moving a methyl group from the amine to the organic acid in order to make methyl acetamide, which is extremely unlikely. Choice C and D can be eliminated. There is no hydroxyl group on the formate to eliminate water, Choice B is out.

9. Which of the following best describes the equilibrium involved in forming an ester from an organic acid and an alcohol?
   A. $K_{eq} > 1$ and $\Delta G > 0$
   B. **$K_{eq} > 1$ and $\Delta G < 0$**
   C. $K_{eq} < 1$ and $\Delta G > 0$
   D. $K_{eq} < 1$ and $\Delta G < 0$

Choice **B** is correct. The passage states that the esterification equilibrium constant is "slightly greater than 1", therefore K must be greater than 1. Choice C and D can be eliminated. The relationship between the equilibrium constant and the Gibb's free energy is

$$\Delta G° = -RT \ln K$$

and if the equilibrium constant is >1, then the Gibb's free energy will be negative and the reaction is spontaneous. Choice B is the correct answer.

10. What is the most likely purpose of the acid catalyst in the mechanism for esterification?

    A. **<u>The hydrogen ion protonates the carbonyl oxygen, making the carbonyl carbon more susceptible to nucleophilic attack by the alcohol.</u>**

    B. The hydrogen ion protonates the oxygen of the -OH group of the organic acid, making it a better leaving group for substitution.

    C. The hydrogen ion protonates the alcohol, making it a better nucleophile, to attach the carbonyl carbon.

    D. The hydrogen ion protonates the alcohol, making it a better leaving group for substitution.

Choice **A** is correct. In the second paragraph concerning the comparison between the formation of organic amides by dehydration synthesis to esterification, the passage suggests that protonation of the nucleophile makes it more difficult to attack the carbonyl carbon.

B, C, D: Likewise, protonation of the alcohol would make it an even poorer nucleophile than an alcohol. Choice C can be eliminated. The alcohol is not the leaving group and choice D can be eliminated.

While protonation of the hydroxyl group of the organic acid would make it a better leaving group, this step most likely occurs after the nucleophile attacks the carbonyl carbon. It is generally accepted that the first step in the acid catalyzed substitution of carbonyl compounds, involves an initial protonation of the carbonyl oxygen atom, which produces a resonance structure in which the carbonyl carbon atom has a positive charge, making it more susceptible to attack by an alcohol lone-pair, which is a relatively poor nucleophile. Choice A is the correct answer.

Passage 3 Explanation

A student was asked to **identify an unknown** colorless liquid and was told that the liquid was a component of gasoline. The student initially determined by wafting that the unknown had a familiar odor and a small sample of the liquid readily dissolved in water. When a test tube containing the liquid was placed in a **brine ice/water bath** at approximately -8°C, the unknown remained liquid. After discussing these results with his professor, the student was asked to determine the heating curve of the unknown using a modified melt-temp apparatus that could be cooled to 77 K. To **calibrate** the equipment the student first conducted an experiment using **deionized** (DI) water as a control to ensure that the amount of heat being supplied to the sample was accurate. The student placed 100. g of DI water in a newly purchased thick walled glass tube and inserted a **thermal couple** into the apparatus, followed by adding liquid nitrogen to a reservoir, cooling the sample below its freezing point. The student was able to watch the sample through a small magnifying window as the sample was being cooled. To the student's surprise, the water **did not begin to freeze** until it reached a temperature of - 41°C, at which point the sample slowly solidified. The student initially thought that there was a significant problem with the equipment, but continued on with the calibration experiment.

Cause-and-Effect: Adding heat to a solid will cause the temperature of the material to increase, until the sample reaches its melting point, at which the added heat will break bonds, i.e. intermolecular forces, and cause the sample to become liquid. After the sample has completely become liquid, any additional heat will cause the temperature of the liquid to increase, until it reaches its boiling point. At this stage, adding heat will again break bonds, causing the liquid to become vapor. After all of the liquid has been vaporized, additional heat will cause the temperature of the gas to increase.

Once the sample became completely solid, the remaining liquid nitrogen was drained from the apparatus, and the sample was slowly heated using the **electrical resistor system**. A plot of heat added versus temperature was obtained, as shown in Figure 1a. Then 100. g of unknown was placed in a separate thick walled glass tube and the experiment was repeated, producing the heating curve shown in Figure 1b. After discussing his observations with his professor, the student was told that his observation concerning the differences between the **freezing point** and **melting point** of **DI water was normal**. The professor then asked the student to do one additional experiment using tap water. When the student did the experiment with tap water, he observed that the sample both froze and melted at 0°C, as he would have expected. The professor asked the student to do some literature research in order to explain his observations concerning the differences between the freezing points of DI water and tap water.

Key terms: Brine ice/water bath, calibrate, deionized, thermal couple, electrical resistor, freezing point and melting point

Cause-and-Effect: It is possible to cool pure water below it normal freezing point, because the water molecules need to become oriented in a regular repeating pattern of hydrogen bonding interactions in order to crystalize. This orientation is typically facilitated by dissolved ions, or particles such as dust, scratches in the surface of a container or even proteins from bacteria for more effective snow making at ski resorts.

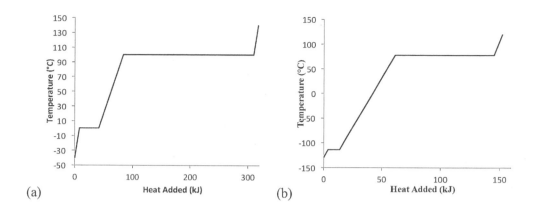

Figure 1 The heating curve for (a) DI water and (b) the unknown sample.

Figure 1 The heating curve of water initially has a region in which the solid is heated. The plateau at 0°C is the phase change in which the ice is melting and all of the heat is causing the phase change, rather than changing the temperature of the material. After all of the ice has melted, the temperature of the liquid water again rises, until it reaches 100°, at which point the temperature again plateaus, as the liquid boils. After all of the liquid has become vapor, the temperature will again increase with the addition of heat. The heating curve for the unknown is similar, but has different slopes for the regions where the temperature changes, because the specific heats of the solid, liquid and gas have different values than for water. The temperature where the plateaus occur are different for the unknown than water, because the melting and boiling points for the unknown are different than water. And finally the horizontal plateaus for the unknown require different amounts of heat than for water, because the unknown has different heats of fusion and vaporization than water.

Finally the student was asked to determine the melting point, **boiling points, heats of fusion** (ΔH_f), **specific heats** (C_p) of the liquid and **heats of vaporization** (ΔH_v) for both his control sample and the unknown. The accepted values for water are given in Table 1.

Key terms: boiling points, heats of fusion, specific heats, and heats of vaporization

Contrast: How well the values of the melting point, boiling point, ΔH_f, C_p, and ΔH_v, for the control sample provides an estimate of the accuracy of the results for the unknown.

Table 1 Literature values of constants related to the heating curve for water

Constant (unit)	Value
ΔH_f (J/g)	334
C_p (J/g°C)	4.18
ΔH_v (J/g)	2260

Table 1 The accepted values of the heat of fusion, heat capacity of the liquid and heat of vaporization for water. The random error associated with these values is ± 1 in the least significant digit.

11. How much heat would be required to change the temperature of 100 g of water from 25°C to 75°C?
    A. 11 kJ
    B. **21 kJ**
    C. 31 kJ
    D. 42 kJ

Choice **B** is correct. You can use the specific heat of liquid water to calculate the heat using dimensional analysis. It is important to remember that the heat involved comes from a temperature change, ΔT, which is 75-25 = 50°C. From the passage, the mass of the water sample was 100 g.

$$4.18 \, J/g°C \times 100 \, g \times 50°C = 21000 \, J = 21 \, kJ$$

A, C, D: You could also look at Figure 1a and estimate the heat (x-axis) required to go from 25°C to 75°C, which is half of the heat required to go from 0°C to 100°C, or about 50 kJ to 90 kJ, which is a change of about 40 kJ (choice D, which is incorrect), so half of this value would be 20 kJ. Choice B is the correct answer.

If you don't use the temperature change, but just use 25°C in the calculation you would get 11 kJ, which is choice A. Likewise, using 75°C in the calculation would give choice C. Both choices A and C are incorrect.

12. If the student measured the amount of heat required to vaporize the control water sample to be 230.0 kJ, what is the percent error in his measurement?
    A. **2%**
    B. 10%
    C. 31%
    D. 98%

Choice **A** is correct. You can use the 230 kJ, or 230,000 J, to calculate the experimental heat of vaporization to be 230,000 J/100 g = 2,300 J/g. Percent error can be calculated by taking the difference between an experimental value and an accepted value, to give the absolute error of 40 J/g. Dividing this by the accepted value, gives a relative error of 40/2260 ~ 40/2000 ~ 0.02. Multiplying this value by 100, gives the percent error of 2%. Choice A is the correct answer.

13. Based on the boiling point data and information in the passage, which of the following components of gasoline is most likely to be the unknown?
    A. **Ethanol, BP is 78°C**
    B. n-octane, BP is 125°C
    C. 2,2,4-trimethylpentane, BP is 99°C
    D. Methyl tert-butyl ether, BP is 55°C

Choice **A** is correct. Looking at Figure 1b, the boiling point is the temperature that corresponds to the second plateau, which is below 100°C. This matches choice A.

Looking at Figure 1b, the boiling point is the temperature that corresponds to the second plateau, which is below 100°C, so choice B can be eliminated. The boiling point is closer to 100°C than 50°C, so choice D can be eliminated. The boiling point is significantly below 100°C and choice C can be eliminated. You can estimate the boiling point to be about 80°C and Choice A is the correct answer.

14. In the heating curve for water, which of the following best describes the sample when the average kinetic energy is NOT changing?
    A. When the solid ice is going from -20°C to 0°C
    B. **When the ice is melting**
    C. When the liquid is going from 25°C to 50°C
    D. The average kinetic energy changes whenever heat is added.

Choice **B** is correct. Temperature is a measure of the average kinetic energy of a system. The two portions of a heating curve in which the average kinetic energy is not changing, are at the melting point and the boiling point. Choice B is the correct answer.

15. As suggested by the professor, the student did some literature research concerning the melting point of DI water and found that it is possible to supercool pure water below its normal freezing point because the water molecules are in a metastable state and can not easily orient to form the crystalline solid state structure of ice. Which of the following changes in the experimental design would prevent this phenomenon from occurring?
    I. Using tap water
    II. Using an old, scratched thick walled glass tube
    III. Using distilled water

    A. I only
    B. II only
    C. **I and II only**
    D. I, II, and III

Choice **C** is correct. As indicated in the passage, when the student used tap water, that contains dissolved minerals and possible microscopic suspended particles that can act as a seed for the crystallization of the water, "normal" freezing and melting at 0°C occurs. Choice B can be eliminated. Using a scratched or dirty glass tube will provide a surface on which the DI water can begin to crystallize. Choice A can be eliminated. Distilled water is purified water being essentially the same as deionized water, which can be super-cooled, because mineral impurities and particles have been removed. Choice C is the correct answer.

These questions are NOT based on a passage.

16. The amount of ethanol in an alcoholic beverage is measure by its "proof". Liquors that are 100 proof are 50% ethanol by volume. When grain alcohol is distilled, it forms an azeotrope that is 5% water. What is the proof value of this distillate?
    A. 10 proof
    B. 95 proof
    C. **190 proof**
    D. 200 proof

Choice **C** is correct. If grain alcohol is 5% water, then it is presumably 95% ethanol. As indicated in the stem of the question, doubling the percentage of ethanol, gives the proof. Doubling 95% gives 190 proof. Choice C is the correct answer.

An alcohol solution that is 10 proof is 5% ethanol, 95 proof is 47.5% ethanol and 200 proof is 100% ethanol. Choices A, B, and D can be eliminated.

17. Which of the following components of gasoline would produce a broad absorption between 3000 and 3700 cm^{-1} in the infrared spectrum?
    A. **Ethanol**
    B. n-octane
    C. 2,2,4-trimethylpentane
    D. Methyl t-butyl ether

Choice **A** is correct. In the infrared spectrum, the 3000 to 3700 cm^{-1} region is where hydrogen bonded O-H stretches are typically observed. Ethanol is the only compound of the answer options that has a hydroxyl group. Choice A is the correct answer.

Only an OH group would cause the peak described by the question. B, an alkane, has no OH groups. C is also an alkane. D, an ether, has the structure R-O-R, which would also not have the necessary OH group.

18. Which of the following would best describe what would happen to the melting point and boiling point of tap water if sodium chloride were dissolved in the solution?
    A. Both the boiling point and the melting point would increase.
    B. Both the boiling point and the melting point would decrease.
    C. **The boiling point would increase and the melting point would decrease.**
    D. The boiling point would decrease and the melting point would increase.

Choice **C** is correct. When a non-volatile solute is dissolved in a solvent, colligative properties cause the melting point to be depressed and the boiling point to be elevated, increasing the range of the liquid phase. Choice C is the correct answer. The boiling point is elevated because the solute solvent intermolecular interactions, reduces the vapor pressure of the liquid.

19. Which of the following compounds are considered radicals?
    I. Nitrogen monoxide
    II. Nitrogen dioxide
    III. Dinitrogen tetroxide
    IV. Ozone

    A. I and II only
    B. III and IV only
    C. I and III only
    D. II and IV only

Choice **A** is correct. Radicals are unstable compounds with unpaired electrons and requires there to be an odd number of valence electrons. Nitrogen monoxide has a total of $5 + 6 = 11$ valence electrons and has a Lewis dot structure with an unpaired electron. Choices B and D can be eliminated.

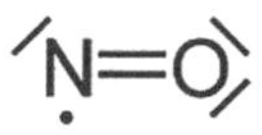

$$\overset{\cdot}{N} = \overset{\cdots}{O}$$

Nitrogen dioxide has $5 + 2(6) = 17$ valence electrons and has a Lewis dot structure with an unpaired electron.

$$\ddot{O} = \overset{\cdot}{N} - \ddot{O}$$

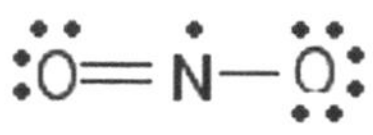

Choice C can be eliminated and choice A is the correct answer.

Dinitrogen tetroxide has $2(5) + 4(6) = 34$ valence electrons, with a Lewis dot structure with no unpaired electrons. Ozone, O_3, has $3(6) = 18$ valence electrons, with a Lewis dot structure with no unpaired electrons.

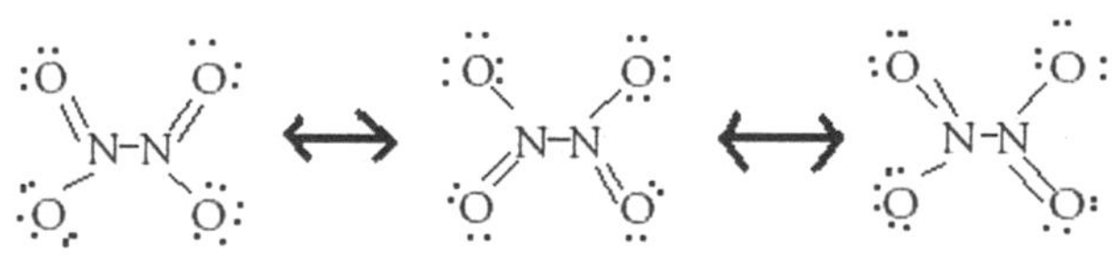

Choices B, C and D can be eliminated because they contain III and IV.

Passage 4 Explanation

Hydrocodone (4,5-a-epoxy-3-methoxy-17-methylmorphinan-6-one) is a commonly prescribed opioid chemically derived from codeine.

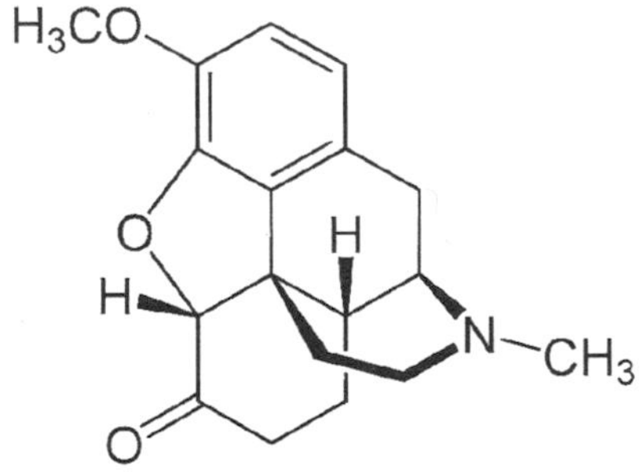

Figure 1 Hydrocodone

It's often administered in **combination with ibuprofen** (isobutyl propanoic phenolic acid, ((RS)-2-(4-(2-methylpropyl)phenyl)propanoic acid), or acetaminophen (N-(4-hydroxyphenyl)ethanamide).

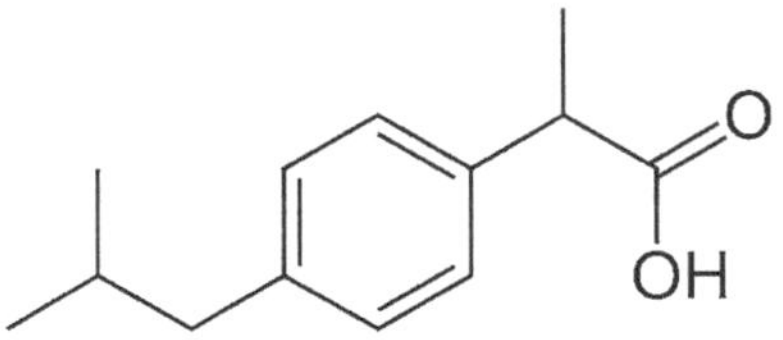

Figure 2 Ibuprofen

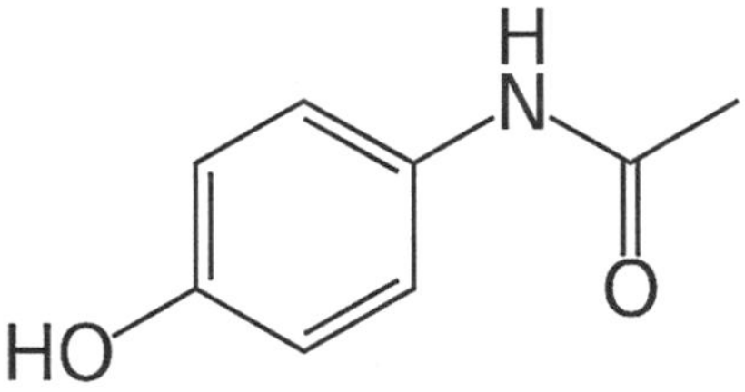

Figure 3 Acetaminophen

Hydrocodone reduces sensation of pain through a receptor-mediated **neurochemical cascade triggered** by binding of certain **metabolites** to opioid receptors in the central nervous system. The breakdown of hydrocodone to primary and secondary metabolites is a **hepatic enzyme-mediated biotransformation**, the principal pathway of which is approximately modelled by the following reaction:

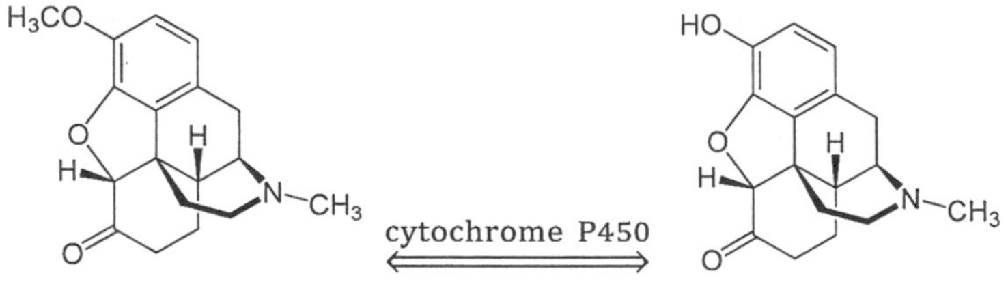

Equation 1   Enzyme-mediated conversion of hydrocodone to hydromorphone

Cause and effect: The word "metabolites" gives us a hint that we're dealing with the ability of the body to chemically alter organic substances upon ingestion. You can also pick up some key clues from the phrase "hepatic enzyme-mediated biotransformation". From the word hepatic, you can conclude that the reaction being described takes place in the liver. From the phrase enzyme-mediated, you can immediately assume that the reaction is catalyzed by enzymes, and that the reaction would be nearly impossible to spontaneously induce without some sort of catalyst. The phrase is also a good hint that you may need to recall basic concepts about enzymatic reactions: for example, the principles of catalysis, some basic vocabulary (e.g., substrate), the different types of inhibition, the basics of Michaelis-Menten kinetics, etc.

Anecdotal evidence suggests that taking hydrocodone with grapefruit juice increases the sensation of any narcotic effects—this is theorized to occur due to **competitive cytochrome P450 inhibition** upon consumption of organic compounds in the juice.

Cause and effect: The phrase "competitive inhibition" rears its ugly head here; you can immediately begin thinking about the kinetic differences between competitive and non-competitive inhibitors, and their different mechanisms of action. For example, competitive inhibitors directly compete with the enzyme's targeted substrate at the active site; to get around the inhibitive effect, you can simply increase the concentration of the target substrate. Non-competitive inhibitors, on the other hand, permanently affect the ability of the enzyme to catalyze the reaction; you can usually presume that the site of reaction is not the active site of the enzyme.

20. Ibuprofen is usually synthesized from its immediate precursor via a mechanism known as palladium-catalyzed carbonylation, a process that adds carbon monoxide to the original organic substrate. It was developed as an alternative to a longer, six-step mechanism that, after a series of synthetic steps, produces ibuprofen from a nitrile. Which of the reactions below represents an approximate illustration of the nitrile precursor to ibuprofen?

A.

C.

B.

D.

Choice **D** is correct. Choice D contains a C triple bonded to an N functional group, making it the correct answer. Nitriles are defined as any organic compound with a carbon-nitrogen triple bond. There is no nitrogen in choice A, therefore it cannot be the correct answer. Similarly, choice B cannot be the correct answer, since it contains no nitrogen. Likewise, the nitrogen in choice C engages in a single π bond with one carbon and a σ bond with a neighbouring oxygen, failing to meet the definition of a nitrile

21. Two students intend to test the hypothesis that a linear increase in compound X, commonly found in grapefruit juice, leads to an exaggeration in observed impairment of test subjects dosed with hydrocodone. Which of the following graphical depictions of cytochrome p450 activity, if generated by the students' data, would appropriately support their hypothesis?

A.

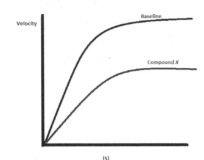

B.

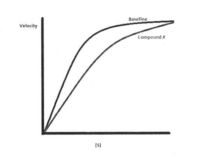

C.

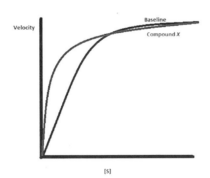

D.

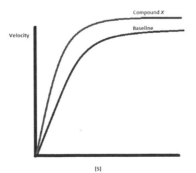

Choice **B** is correct. B correctly depicts an unaffected maximum enzymatic velocity, with delayed achievement of that velocity compared to baseline levels (given equal concentrations of substrate). This precisely meets the definition of competitive inhibition. Choice B must be the correct answer.

Choice A depicts non-competitive inhibition, where the V_{max} is adversely affected by the presence of the inhibitor. The passage specifically states that the theorized inhibition of cytochrome p450 activity is competitive. Therefore, choice A cannot be the correct answer. Choice C depicts an improvement in enzyme performance given equal amounts of substrate, when presented with a competitive inhibitor, and an unaffected maximum velocity. There is no plausible mechanism to explain this phenomenon given the information in the passage; choice C cannot be the correct answer. Choice D depicts an improvement in enzyme performance given equal amounts of substrate, when presented with a competitive inhibitor, and an improved V_{max}. Like choice C, there's no plausible mechanism to explain this phenomenon given the information in the passage; choice D can also not be the correct answer.

22. How many aromatic rings does hydrocodone have?
    A. **1**
    B. 2
    C. 3
    D. 4

Choice **A** is correct. Only the benzyl ring in hydrocodone meets the criteria for aromaticity: a delocalized conjugated π system, coplanar structure, constituent atoms forming a ring, and a number of delocalised π electrons that is even, but not a multiple of 4 (following the 4n+2 rule).

23. The enzymes belonging to the cytochrome p450 (CYP) family are collectively responsible for up to 75% of known xenobiotic (substances that are foreign to living systems or present in much higher concentrations than normal) metabolic reactions in the human body. Certain substances, such as St. John's Wort, are known inhibitors of CYP activity. Which of the following metabolic pathways would be LEAST affected by the consumption of a large amount of CYP inhibitors? Assume that cytochrome p450 enzymes are exclusively involved in xenobiotic metabolism.
    A. **Steroidogenesis by the adrenal glands from fatty acids found in fish oil**
    B. Benzo(α)pyrene toxification upon consumption of burnt meat
    C. Degradation of orally-ingested vitamin D in the case of an infant's unintentional overdose.
    D. Metabolism of polycyclic aromatic hydrocarbons ingested via inhalation

Choice **A** is correct. Steroidogenesis by the adrenal glands from fatty acids found in fish oil involves naturally occurring biological compounds. It does not involve xenobiotics, which are compounds that are either entirely foreign to biological systems, or compounds that are found in unusual concentrations in biological systems. This metabolic pathway would therefore be least affected by CYP inhibitors. Choice A must be the correct answer.

Benzo(α)pyrenes are polycyclic aromatic hydrocarbons (PAHs) commonly produced as a byproduct of incomplete combustion. Its metabolites are highly carcinogenic, and it definitely qualifies as a xenobiotic. Choice B cannot be the correct answer. Degradation orally-ingested vitamin D is a common metabolic pathway. In normal concentrations, vitamin D (or cholecalciferol) would not be a xenobiotic. However, in the case of an accidental overdose, it would be found in concentrations many times higher than the normal range, leading to its official characterization as a xenobiotic. Choice C cannot be the correct answer. Following the same reasoning as choice B, the entire family of PAHs are considered highly dangerous xenobiotics, and therefore a prime target for CYP activity (following the assumptions in the question). Choice D can therefore not be the correct answer.

Passage 5 Explanation

Reactive oxygen species (ROS) and free radicals are oxidative byproducts of metabolism. Oxidative stress results when the production of free radicals exceeds the anti-oxidative capacity of the body. Direct free radical measurement is often inaccurate because of their brief half-lives, but may be measured indirectly by assessing their impact on lipids, proteins and DNA. Lipid peroxidation is a free radical mediated process resulting in the oxidation of **polyunsaturated fatty acids (PUFAs)** to one of several possible secondary products, as shown in Figure 1. The relative amounts of each secondary product produced depend upon conditions in the body.

Key terms: reactive oxygen species (ROS), free radical, oxidative stress, polyunsaturated fatty acids (PUFAs)

Cause-and-Effect: ROSs and free radicals are byproducts of aerobic respiration; oxidative stress occurs when free radical levels exceed the body's anti-oxidant capacity; free radicals have short half-lives and their concentrations are difficult to measure as a result; free radical levels may be indirectly assessed; lipid peroxidation of PUFAs is a free radical mediated process producing secondary products in different amounts depending upon reaction conditions

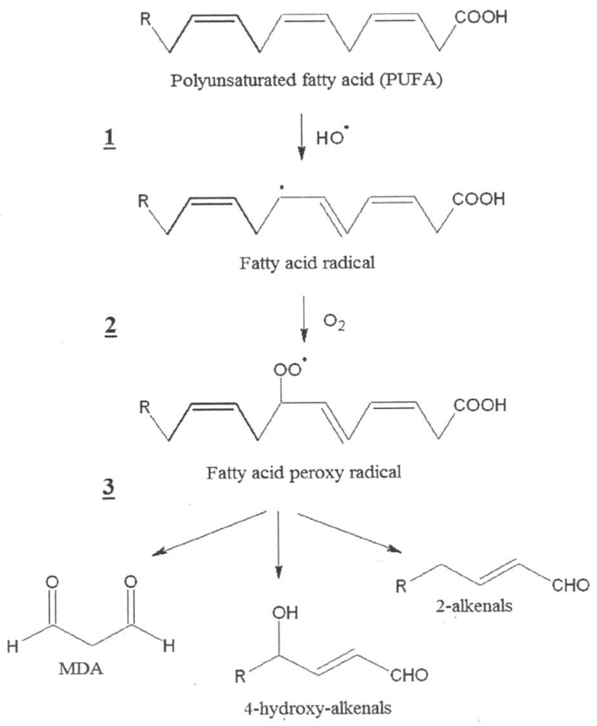

Figure 1 The oxidation of a PUFA to a fatty acid radical, then a fatty acid peroxy radical and finally three different secondary products is shown.

The presence of one such secondary product, **malondialdehyde (MDA)**, is an indicator of oxidative damage to cells. A **colorimetric detection method** for MDA employing the Schiff reagent has long been known. In the presence of aldehydes, **Schiff reagents** undergo a color change. An alternative colorimetric method for assessing oxidative stress was used to measure urinary MDA concentrations in samples collected from healthy individuals. **Thiobarbituric acid (TBA)** was added to serially diluted urine samples, yielding the **chromophoric** product shown in Figure 2.

Key terms: malondialdehyde (MDA), colorimetric detection method, Schiff reagent, thiobarbituric acid (TBA), chromophoric

Cause-and-Effect: MDA is an indicator of oxidative damage to cells; Schiff reagents are used to detect MDA colorimetrically; Schiff reagents determine the presence of aldehydes; TBA can also be used in a colorimetric assay to determine MDA concentration; urinary MDA samples from healthy individuals were screened for a chromophoric product colorimetrically in order to determine MDA concentration

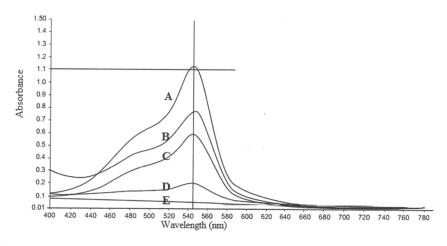

Figure 2 shows the reaction between TBA and MDA to yield a colored product with maximum absorbance at a wavelength of 545 nm.

The **absorbance** of each solution was then measured **spectrophotometrically**. The absorbance curves obtained from the TBA assay for **dilutions A-E** are shown in Figure 3.

Key terms: absorbance, spectrophotometrically, dilutions A-E
Cause-and-Effect: spectrophotometric absorbance for the five dilutions, dilutions A-E, are shown.

Figure 3 TBARS assay absorption curves at five MDA concentrations is shown. Maximum absorbance at 545nm was shown for each dilution other than dilution E (which showed a small absorbance at all wavelengths measured). Maximum absorption declined from dilution A through E.

Absorbance at 545 nm is plotted as a function of sample MDA concentration in Figure 4.

Cause-and-Effect: Absorbance at 545 nm was plotted as a function of sample MDA concentration

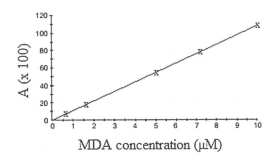

Figure 4 Absorbance at 545 nm increases linearly with MDA concentration

24. The concentration of MDA present in Dilution B is most nearly:
    A. 3 μM
    B. 5 μM
    C. **7 μM**
    D. 10 μM

Choice **C** is correct. Figure 4 indicates that assay absorbance at 545 nm increases linearly with concentration. This suggests that Dilution B, which is shown in Figure 3 to have the second greatest absorbance at 545 nm, should be the second most concentrated sample tested. Figure 3 shows the concentration of the second most concentrated sample, where the absorbance x 100 is nearly 80 (consistent with dilution B's absorbance at 545 nm of .8 in Figure 2), is approximately 7 μM (choice C).

25. Which of the following PUFAs is most susceptible to lipid peroxidation by the pathway shown in Figure 1?
    A. **all-cis-6,9,12,15,18,21-tetracosahexaenoic acid**
    B. all-cis-8,11,14,17-eicosatetraenoic acid
    C. all-cis-9,12,15,18,21-tetracosapentaenoic acid
    D. all-cis-11,14,17-eicosatrienoic acid

Choice **A** is correct. The polyunsaturated, all-cis, omega-3 fatty acids listed in choices A-D differ only in the number of double-bonds they possess. Choice A, the PUFA containing the greatest number of degrees of unsaturation (6) is most likely to be oxidized. Choice B contains 4 double bonds. Choice C contains 5 double bonds. Choice D contains 3 double bonds.

26. All of the following are true of the reaction shown in step 1 of Figure 1 EXCEPT that:
    A. a hydrogen atom is abstracted from a PUFA reactant.
    B. a single electron is transferred to the hydroxyl radical.
    C. water is formed.
    D. **the hydroxyl radical acts as a nucleophile.**

Choice **D** is correct. In the reaction between a PUFA and a hydroxyl radical shown in Step 1 of Figure 1, a proton and a single electron (collectively a hydrogen atom) are transferred from the C-H bond in an α-position relative to an alkene carbon to the hydroxyl radical, producing water, and following a molecular rearrangement, the fatty acid radical shown.

Choices A, B and C are consistent with this information. However, the hydroxyl radical behaved as an electrophile, rather than as a nucleophile. Radical are highly reactive electrophilic species that tend to receive electron density in the form of a single electron transfer (choice D).

27. An aqueous solution containing which of the following molecules will NOT undergo a color change upon addition of a Schiff reagent?

I.

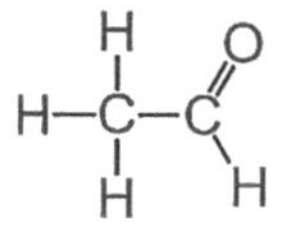

II.

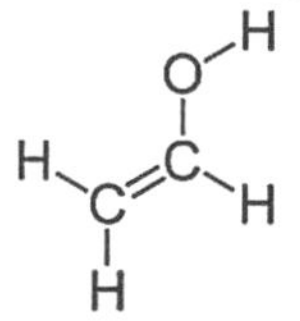

III.

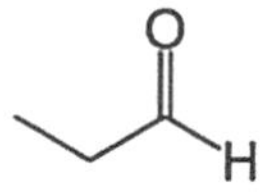

IV.

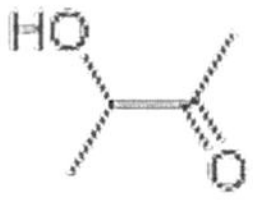

    A. **IV only**
    B. II and IV only
    C. I and III only
    D. III and IV only

Choice **A** is correct. The passage states that a positive Schiff test results in a color change in the presence of aldehydes. As shown, roman numerals I and III are aldehydes and will give return a positive Schiff test. Roman numeral III, a β-hydroxy ketone will not. Roman numeral II will tautomerize in an aqueous environment from its enol form as a vinyl alcohol to its keto form as an aldehyde, resulting in a positive Schiff test. This is consistent with choice A, which indicates that only roman numeral IV will not react with a Schiff reagent.

28. Which statement reflects the most reasonable objection to using TBA assay absorbance at 545 nm as a measure of total cellular oxidative stress?
    A. Determining free radical concentration in the body is a more direct measure of oxidative stress.
    B. Measurements only at 545 nm do not take into TBA assay product absorbance at other wavelengths.
    C. **MDA is produced cellularly as an end product of lipid peroxidation in variable quantities.**
    D. Measured MDA may also be due to oxidation of urinary lipids by the hydrolytic conditions of the reaction.

Choice **C** is correct. The passage states that the relative amounts of each secondary product produced during lipid peroxidation depend upon conditions in the body. While a test for MDA is indicative of the presence of cellular oxidative stress, it would not capture the full range of secondary oxidation products that may result from lipid peroxidation and oxidative stress, and would not necessarily be the best tool for finding a total measure of cellular oxidative stress (choice C).

While direct determination of free radical concentrations in the body is a more direct measure of oxidative stress, the passage provides information that such measures are often inaccurate, and that indirect methods of assessing oxidative stress may be used alternatively (choice A). Measurement of TBA assay product at only its maximal absorbance wavelength would still be a reasonable method of assessing total oxidative stress if that TBA assay product consistently reflected the level of cellular oxidative stress (choice B). Few if any lipids should be present in the filtrate of healthy individuals, making the overestimation of MDA due to their subsequent reaction under the assay condition unlikely.

These questions are NOT based on a passage.

29. Which of the following is an example of β^+ decay?
    A. Sodium-23 decays into magnesium-23.
    B. **Carbon-11 decays into boron-11.**
    C. Carbon-14 decays into carbon-12.
    D. Excited hydrogen decays into ground state hydrogen.

Choice **B** is correct. Like beta-minus decay, beta-plus decay changes the number of protons, which means the chemical identity of the daughter isotope must be different than the parent. That eliminates answer choices C and D. Now, if this kind of decay involves a proton transforming into a neutron, then the atomic number must decrease rather than increase. A involves an increase in the atomic number. B involves a decrease, so B is correct.

A, C, D: The chemical identity of the daughter isotope must be different than the parent. That eliminates answer choices C and D. Now, if this kind of decay involves a proton transforming into a neutron, then the atomic number must decrease rather than increase. A involves an increase in the atomic number.

30. Sound is which type of wave?
    A. Sound is a transverse wave.
    B. **Sound is a longitudinal wave.**
    C. Sound is an electromagnetic wave.
    D. Sound is a wave pulse.

Choice **B** is correct. Sound is a mechanical pressure wave in which individual gas molecules, on average, oscillate in the same direction as the direction that the wave is propagating. This is the definition of a longitudinal wave. Choice B is the correct answer.

Transverse waves oscillate perpendicular to the direction of wave propagation and electromagnetic radiation is an example of a transverse wave. In addition EM is not a mechanical wave, but a simultaneous oscillation of electric and magnetic fields. Choice A and C can be eliminated. A wave pulse is a single input of energy and does not represent simple harmonic motion and therefore is not a wave. Choice D can be eliminated.

31. Which of the following lists of compounds and/or elements contains a substance that is NOT the product of a combustion reaction?
    A. **CO_2 (g), O_2 (g) and H_2O (g)**
    B. CO (g), CO_2 (g) and H_2O (g)
    C. C (s), CO_2 (g) and H_2O (g)
    D. C (s), CO (g) and CO_2 (g)

Choice **A** is correct. This question is associated with the concepts of complete and incomplete combustion reactions, which involve the reaction of an organic fuel with elemental oxygen to form various compounds, including H_2O, CO_2, CO and elemental carbon (soot). The O_2 in choice A is a reactant, not a product of a combustion reaction.

Passage 6 Explanation

Carbon dioxide plays a pivotal role in many chemical, physical, geological, environmental and biological systems. In order to fully understand this central role, it is important to study the **thermodynamic driving forces** (Table 1) behind some of the most important physical and chemical reactions involving CO_2.

Key terms: thermodynamic driving forces

Cause-and-Effect: Thermodynamic driving forces are Gibbs free energy changes (ΔG) associated with going from the reactants to products of a chemical reaction. The two contributing factors to the overall free energy are enthalpy (heat of reaction) and entropy (amount of disorder) changes. If the ΔG for a reaction is negative the reaction will spontaneously convert reactants into products.

Carbon dioxide is the ultimate carbon-containing product of **aerobic respiration**. For most life, an important source of chemical energy is produced by plant **photosynthesis**. Overall, photosynthesis involves combining carbon dioxide, water and sunlight to produce a **carbohydrate**, such as glucose, along with elemental oxygen as a byproduct, Reaction 1. The reverse of this reaction is essentially a combustion reaction, which also happens to be the overall chemical reaction involved in aerobic respiration. **Combustion** reactions release stored chemical energy and can be considered redox reactions that proceed primarily by way of radical mechanisms. The carbon atoms of the reactants are oxidized to carbon's highest oxidation number by the electron acceptor, elemental oxygen. **Incomplete combustion** can lead to the formation of a variety of carbon containing byproducts, with carbon atoms in intermediate oxidation states, such as soot and carbon monoxide. Of course there is a significant difference between the process of combustion and the multistep processes of glycolysis and the Krebs cycle, that are used to produce useful amounts of energy in forms that can be used by living organisms.

Key terms: aerobic respiration, photosynthesis, carbohydrate, combustion, incomplete combustion

Cause-and-Effect: Incomplete combustion is due to an insufficient amount of oxygen and result in incomplete removal of electrons from carbon atoms.

Contrast: Photosynthesis and combustion are the opposite chemical processes in which energy is stored and released, respectively.

Contrast: Combustion releases stored chemical energy in an uncontrolled fashion while aerobic respiration is essentially the same process, but releases the stored energy in a controlled fashion that can be used by living organisms.

In addition, the physical and chemical interactions of carbon dioxide and its associated ions in aqueous solution play a significant role in regulating a variety of biological processes. Carbon dioxide is a **nonpolar molecule** that is sparingly soluble in water at atmospheric pressure and room temperature (Reaction 2). Increasing the pressure and decreasing the temperature dramatically improves the solubility of most gases in water and carbon dioxide is no exception. When dissolved in aqueous solution, carbon dioxide molecules undergo **hydrolysis** to produce carbonic acid (Reaction 3), a weak **diprotic acid** that undergoes successive ionizations (Reaction 4 and 5) to produce bicarbonate and carbonate ions. Many metal cations, including calcium, react with carbonate to form **precipitates** (Reaction 6). Calcium and magnesium carbonate have **solubility product constants** of 5×10^{-9} and 5×10^{-6}, respectively. As most geologists know, these reactions can be reversed. For example, **reaction of limestone** with muriatic acid (concentrated aqueous HCl) causes vigorous bubbling and provides evidence for the origin of this class of sedimentary rock.

Key terms: nonpolar molecule, hydrolysis, diprotic acid, precipitate, solubility product constants

Cause-and-Effect: The nonpolar carbon dioxide molecule is relatively insoluble because its main intermolecular force (London dispersion) is dissimilar to that of waters (H-bonding).

Cause-and-Effect: Precipitates form when metal cations combine with carbonate ions at concentrations that produce reaction quotients that are greater than the value of the corresponding Ksp. Since the solubility product constants for many metal carbonates are very small, precipitates readily form.

Reaction 1
$$6\ CO_2\ (g) + 6\ H_2O\ (g) + photons \rightarrow C_6H_{12}O_6\ (s) + 6\ O_2\ (g)$$

This balanced chemical reaction represents the overall process involved in production of glucose by photosynthesis. Since photons are a form of energy, the process as written is adding energy to the system to form high energy bonds and is endothermic. The reverse of this reaction is the combustion of glucose, which typically releases stored chemical energy primarily in the form of heat and would be exothermic.

Reaction 2 $\quad CO_2\ (g) + H_2O\ (l) \leftrightarrows CO_2\ (aq)$

Reaction 3 $\quad CO_2\ (aq) + H_2O\ (l) \leftrightarrows H_2CO_3\ (aq)$ $\qquad\qquad$ K = 1.7 x 10^{-3} at 25°C

Reaction 4 $\quad H_2CO_3\ (aq) \leftrightarrows HCO_3^-\ (aq) + H^+\ (aq)$ $\qquad\qquad$ K_{a1} = 2.5 x 10^{-4} at 25°C

Reaction 5 $\quad HCO_3^-\ (aq) \leftrightarrows CO_3^{2-}\ (aq) + H^+\ (aq)$ $\qquad\qquad$ K_{a2} = 4.69 x 10^{-11} at 25°C

Reaction 6 $\quad Ca^{2+}\ (aq) + CO_3^{2-}\ (aq) \leftrightarrows CaCO_3\ (s)$

Reactions 2-6. These reactions describe some of the common chemical reactions related to the interactions of carbon dioxide in aqueous solution: Equation 2 represents the phase equilibrium between carbon dioxide gas and carbon dioxide dissolved in water; Equation 3 represents the hydrolysis reaction of aqueous carbon dioxide to form carbonic acid and its equilibrium constant; Equations 4 and 5 represent the stepwise ionization of carbonic acid and the associated acid dissociation constants; Equation 6 represents a precipitation reaction, in which insoluble calcium carbonate is formed from calcium ions and carbonate ions. The reverse of Equation 6 is the solubility reaction for calcium carbonate, which from the passage, has a solubility product constant (K_{sp}) of 5 x 10^{-9}, therefore the K_{eq} for Equation 6 is the reciprocal of the K_{sp}, or 2 x 10^8.

Table 1 Thermodynamic parameters for selected compounds and ions at 25°C.

Compound	Enthalpy of formation, $\Delta H°_f$ (kJ/mol)	Entropy of formation, $S°_f$ (J/mol K)
C (s, graphite)	0	5.74
CO (g)	-110.5	197.7
CO_2 (g)	-393.5	213.8
H_2O (l)	-285.8	69.9
H_2O (g)	-241.8	188.8
H_2CO_3 (aq)	-699.7	187.4
HCO_3^- (aq)	-692.0	91.2
CO_3^{2-} (aq)	-677.1	-56.9
Ca^{2+} (aq)	-542.8	-53.1
H^+ (aq)	0	0
$CaCO_3$ (s) (calcite)	-1206.9	92.9
$C_6H_{12}O_6$ (s)	-1268	-212
O_2 (g)	0	205.1

Table 1: This table contains enthalpies and entropies of formation at room temperature for a number of compounds and ions described in the passage. These thermodynamic values are determined from chemical reactions in which one mole of the compound or ion is made from the most stable form of the elements found in that compound or ion. These values can then be used to calculate the enthalpies and entropies of various other reactions by summing the values for the products and subtracting the sum of the values for the reactants. These values can then be used to calculate the Gibbs free energy change for reactions of interest, by using $\Delta G = \Delta H - T\Delta S$, where the temperature is in degrees Kelvin.

32. Based on the information in the passage, what is the most likely combination of signs for the enthalpy and entropy changes that occur when carbon dioxide gas dissolves in aqueous solution?
    A. ΔH is positive and ΔS is positive.
    B. ΔH is negative and ΔS is positive.
    C. ΔH is positive and ΔS is negative.
    D. ΔH is negative and ΔS is negative.

Choice **D** is correct. This question centers on Reaction 2 and the information presented in paragraph 3, "Increasing the pressure and decreasing the temperature dramatically improves the solubility." This suggests that the enthalpy of the reaction is negative, or heat is a product of this reaction. Based on Le Châtelier's principle, lowering the temperature causes an exothermic reaction to convert reactants into products and a release of heat to counteract the stress imposed on the system. The entropy change of the system must be negative, which contributes to a nonspontaneous free energy change at high temperatures where the $-T\Delta S$ term is positive and greater than the negative enthalpy in the Gibbs free energy equation. At lower temperatures the solubility improves because the $-T\Delta S$ term makes a smaller positive contribution. The negative entropy change for this reaction is best understood in terms of the relative disorder of the gas phase as compared with the relatively ordered liquid aqueous solution.

33. Based on information from Table 1 and the passage, what is the value of the equilibrium constant for the following reaction?

$$CO_2 \text{ (aq)} + H_2O \text{ (l)} + Ca_2^+ \text{ (aq)} \leftrightharpoons CaCO_3 \text{ (s)} + 2 \text{ H}^+ \text{ (aq)}$$

    A. $K = 2 \times 10^5$
    B. $K = 2 \times 10^8$
    C. <u>$K = 4 \times 10^{-9}$</u>
    D. $K = 1 \times 10^{-25}$

Choice **C** is correct. This question requires the summing together of reactions 3 through 6. When adding chemical reactions, the associated equilibrium constants can be multiplied together to give the equilibrium constant for the overall reaction. The equilibrium constant for Reaction 6 is the inverse of the K_{sp} for calcium carbonate given near the end of the last paragraph. Hence the answer is

$$K = (1.7 \times 10^{-3})(2.5 \times 10^{-4})(4.69 \times 10^{-11})(1/5 \times 10^9) \sim (2 \times 10^{-3})(2.5 \times 10^{-4})(5 \times 10^{-11})(1/5 \times 10^9) \sim 5 \times 10^{-9}$$

Hence choice C is the closest answer.

34. What is the approximate Gibbs free energy change for the overall aerobic conversion of solid glucose to carbon dioxide and liquid water at body temperature (37°C)?
    A. +3000 kJ/mol
    B. +700 kJ/mol
    C. <u>**-3000 kJ/mol**</u>
    D. -200000 kJ/mol

Choice **C** is correct. Since the aerobic conversion of glucose to carbon dioxide and water is essentially the same as the combustion of glucose (paragraph 1), and since the combustion reaction is clearly a spontaneous chemical reaction, the ΔG must be negative. Hence you can eliminate the positive answer choices of A and B. While you might anticipate that the combustion of glucose would have a large negative free energy change, answer choice D is an exceedingly large change for a chemical process. Hence choice C is the only reasonable answer.

It is possible to go through the process of calculating the ΔH and ΔS for this reaction from the data presented in Table 1 and then use this in the Gibbs free energy equation ($\Delta G = \Delta H - T\Delta S$), but this will be a very time consuming process. Be sure to use the right values from Table 1 corresponding to the correct phases of matter for the formulas in the reaction. You must multiply by the stoichiometric coefficients in the balanced reaction.

$$C_6H_{12}O_6 \text{ (s)} + 6 \text{ O}_2 \text{ (g)} \rightarrow 6 \text{ CO}_2 \text{ (g)} + 6 \text{ H}_2O \text{ (l)} + \text{photons}$$

Enthalpy in kilojoules per mole (KJ/mol)
$\Delta H_f = [\Sigma \, \Delta H_f \text{ products}] - [\Sigma \, \Delta H_f \text{ reactants}]$
$\Delta H_f = [6(-393.5) + 6(-285.8)] - [(-1268) + 6(0)]$
$\Delta H_f \sim [6(-400) + 6(-300)] - [-1300]$
$\Delta H_f \sim [-4200] + 1300$
$\Delta H_f \sim -2900$ KJ/mol

Entropy in joules per mole kelvin (J/mol K)

$\Delta S_f = [\Sigma \, \Delta S_f \text{ products}] - [\Sigma \, \Delta S_f \text{ reactants}]$

$\Delta S_f = [6(213.79) + 6(69.9)] - [(-212) + 6(205.1)]$

$\Delta S_f \sim [6(200) + 6(100)] - [(-200) + 6(200)]$

$\Delta S_f \sim [1200 + 600] - [-200 + 1200]$

$\Delta S_f \sim [1800] - [1000]$

$\Delta S_f \sim +800 \, \text{J/mol K}$

For calculating ΔG, convert the entropy units into kJ/mol K to agree with the units of the enthalpy, +0.8 kJ/ mol K, which can be approximated as 1 kJ/ mol K. The temperature in Kelvin is $273 + 37 = 310 \, \text{K} \sim 300 \, \text{K}$

$\Delta G = \Delta H - T\Delta S$

$\Delta G \sim [-2900] - [300(1)]$

$\Delta G \sim [-2900] - [300]$

$\Delta G \sim -3000 \, \text{kJ/mol}$

35. Based on the data in Table 1, what is the heat of vaporization of water?
    A. **+44 kJ/mole**
    B. +2260 kJ/mole
    C. -241.8 kJ/mole
    D. -285.8 kJ/mole

Choice **A** is correct. The phase change reaction for vaporization is

$$H_2O \,(l) \quad \leftrightarrows \quad H_2O \,(g)$$

Using the data for the heats of formation of water in the liquid and gas phases, the $\Delta H = [-241.8] - [-285.8] \sim [-240] - [-290]$ which is about +50 kJ/mole. Choice A is the closest answer.

This is an endothermic process. In other words, heat must be added to the liquid water to cause the breaking of the hydrogen bonding interactions in the liquid phase, and the formation of the gas phase molecules. As a result the negative values in choices C and D are not reasonable. The heat of vaporization of water is also given as +2260 kJ per kilogram of water in many reference materials. Note that the units for choice B are kJ/mol, not kJ/kg. Hence choice B is incorrect.

Passage 7 Explanation

The physician Luigi Galvani conducted experiments with static electricity and the **triboelectric effect**. While removing the skin of the frog, accidentally touched a scalpel, that had previously been electrically charged, to the dead frog, resulting in a startling observation. The frog spontaneously moved as if it had come back to life. Galvani was able to reproduce this process numerous times, resulting in his investigations into "**animal electricity**." Frog tissue not only responded to electrical stimulation, but was also a conductor of charge. A number of experiments showed that the electrical conduction was not unique to animal tissue. For instance, Galvani obtained a **similar result** by simply **soaking a paper** towel in a brine solution, which he called an electrolyte. This lead to the discovery that different metals when in contact with brine soaked paper towels would **produce similar effects**, sparking a debate with Galvani concerning the nature of his "cells" that **produced electricity**. Scientists eventually were able to **rank** various **metals** to create the first electrochemical series (Table 1), and associated electromotive forces, based on the idea that various **electrodes** have a **potential to cause charges to move** in a conducting material. Subsequently, a mathematical relationship (**Equation 1**) was developed to **predict the potentials** for electrochemical cells.

Key terms: triboelectric effect, static electricity, electrical conduction, electrolyte, electrochemical series, electromotive force, electrodes, potential, and reaction quotient

Cause-and-Effect: Metals and various other compounds have different abilities to be oxidized or reduced, resulting in the potential for the flow of electrical charge in electrolytes.

Cause-and-Effect: Electrochemical half-cells can be used to measure the potential for a particular compound to undergo oxidation or reduction, resulting is a ranking of cell potentials or an electrochemical series.

$$E = E° - (RT/nF) \ln Q$$

Equation 1 The Nernst equation describes the relationship observed between the cell potential under nonstandard conditions to the potential under standard conditions, where $R = 8.314$ J K^{-1} mol^{-1}, T is the temperature in degrees Kelvin, n is the moles of electrons in the balanced reaction and F is Faraday's constant, 9.65×10^4 C mol^{-1}. Note that at 25°C, $[RT/nF] \ln Q = 0.059/n \log Q$

Equation 1: The Nernst equation is used to predict the overall cell potential of a REDOX process that involves both an oxidation and a reduction half-reaction, in which the cell potential under standard conditions (E°) can be determined by using information from Table 1, in which a reduction half-reaction is combined with an oxidation half-reaction. To obtain the oxidation potential, the reduction half reaction must be reversed and the sign of the potential from Table 1 must be changed. Summing the oxidation and reduction potentials gives the overall cell potential. Do not multiply the half-cell potentials by any stoichiometric coefficient required to balance the overall reaction. The reaction quotient is similar to the equilibrium expression, but is used under non-equilibrium conditions. In the reaction quotient, the concentration of the products are divided by the concentration of the reactants (or partial pressures, for gases), raised to the stoichiometric power of that species based on the balanced redox reaction.

Table 1 Selected standard reduction potentials at 25°C.

Reduction Half-Reaction	E° (V)
$F_2 (g) + 2 e^- \rightarrow 2 F^- (aq)$	+ 2.87
$MnO_4^- (aq) + 8 H^+ (aq) + 5 e^- \rightarrow Mn^{2+} (aq) + 4 H_2O (l)$	+ 1.51
$Cr_2O_7^{2-} (aq) + 14 H^+ (aq) + 6 e^- \rightarrow 2 Cr^{3+} (aq) + 7 H_2O (l)$	+ 1.33
$O_2 (g) + 4 H^+ (aq) + 4 e^- \rightarrow 2 H_2O (l)$	+ 1.23
$Ag^+ (aq) + e^- \rightarrow Ag (s)$	+ 0.80
$O_2 (g) + 2 H_2O (l) + 4 e^- \rightarrow 4 OH^- (aq)$	+0.40
$Cu^{2+} (aq) + 2 e^- \rightarrow Cu (s)$	+0.34
$2 H^+ (aq) + 2 e^- \rightarrow H_2 (g)$	0.00
$Ni^{2+} (aq) + 2 e^- \rightarrow Ni (s)$	- 0.28
$Cd^{2+} (aq) + 2 e^- \rightarrow Cd (s)$	-0.40
$Zn^{2+} (aq) + 2 e^- \rightarrow Zn (s)$	- 0.76
$2 H_2O (l) + 2 e^- \rightarrow H_2 (g) + 2 OH^- (aq)$	- 0.83
$Li^+ (aq) + e^- \rightarrow Li (s)$	-3.05

Table 1: This table provides selected reduction half-reactions, with the associated reduction potentials under standard conditions at 25°C. To obtain an oxidation half-reaction, reverse the side of the reactants and products and change the sign of the voltage. Note that the potential for the reduction of hydrogen ions to elemental hydrogen is zero. This is because the hydrogen half-reaction is used as the reference potential for measuring the potential of All other half-reactions.

36. For an electrochemical cell based on the following redox reaction at 25°C, what is the cell potential when the concentration of Cu^{2+} (aq) is 10^8 times greater than the concentration of Zn^{2+} (aq)?

$$Cu^{2+} (aq) + Zn (s) \rightarrow Zn^{2+} (aq) + Cu (s)$$

 A. -0.18 V
 B. 1.10 V
 C. 1.34 V
 D. 1.57 V

Choice **C** is correct. You can use Equation 1 to answer this question. Note that the constants in Equation 1 are given in the caption, but also that calculation for the combination of the constants is also given and the natural logarithm is converted to the log base 10 form, giving a new form of the equation as

$$E = E° - (0.059/n) \log Q$$

The value of the E° is the sum of the reduction potential of Cu^{2+} and the oxidation potential of Zn, E° = 0.34 + 0.76 = 1.10 V. From the question, the value of the reaction quotient, Q = 10^{-8} and n = 2. Substituting this information into the equation and approximating 0.059 as 6.0×10^{-2} gives

$$E = (1.10) - (6.0 \times 10^{-2})/2 \log (10^{-8})$$
$$E = 1.10 - (3.0 \times 10^{-2})(-8)$$
$$E = 1.10 + (2.4 \times 10^{-1})$$
$$E = 1.34 \text{ V}$$

37. Which of the following species is the best oxidizing agent?
    A. **$\underline{MnO_4^- (aq)}$**
    B. $Cr_2O_7^{2-}$ (aq)
    C. Zn (s)
    D. Li (s)

Choice **A** is correct. An oxidizing agent is a reactant that gets reduced. Both permanganate and dichromate are reactants of a reduction half-reaction, and therefore are potential oxidizing agents. You next need to turn our attention to the voltages and since the more positive the voltage, the more spontaneous the reaction ($\Delta G = -nFE$), permanganate is the best oxidizing agent and choice A is the correct answer.

Since both zinc and lithium metal are both the products of the reduction half reactions in Table 1, they would most likely to be reducing agents, and choices C and D can be eliminated.

38. Which of the following combinations of unit symbols is NOT equivalent to a Volt?
    A. $A \cdot \Omega$
    B. $W A^{-1}$
    C. $J C^{-1}$
    D. **$\underline{Kg\ m\ s^{-2}}$**

Choice **D** is correct. Choice D is mass times acceleration, which is simply force, which is not the same as the electromotive force (EMF), also known as voltage. The definition of voltage is the potential energy per unit charge, so there must be some unit associated with the charge in the answer, which is missing in in choice D, which is the correct NOT answer.

According to Ohm's law, $V = IR$, where I is the current in amperes (and R is resistance in ohms (Ω), therefore choice A can be eliminated. Electrical power in watts (W) is $P = VI$, so $V = P/I$, and choice B can be eliminated. Since a watt is power, or the joules (J) of energy per second, $W = J/s$, and an ampere is the coulombs of charge per second, substituting these units into the units of choice B, gives $W A^{-1} = J s^{-1} C^{-1} s = J C^{-1}$, which is choice C, which can be eliminated. Note the units for the constants in the Nernst equation from the passage also give this set of units.

39. Which of the following statements is true concerning a galvanic cell with a positive potential?

   I. The redox reaction is nonspontaneous because the Gibbs free energy is positive.
   II. Electrons flow through the circuit from the anode to the cathode.
   III. The anode is negatively charged.

   A. I only
   B. II only
   C. I and II only
   D. **II and III only**

Choice **D** is correct. The relationship between cell potential and the Gibbs free energy change (ΔG) is, $\Delta G = -nFE$, where n is the number of electrons involved in the redox reaction, F is Faraday's constant and E is the voltage. Since the question states that the voltage is positive, then ΔG must be negative, which is a spontaneous reaction, eliminating I, and choices A and C. Electrons always flow from the anode to the cathode in any electrochemical cell. The way to remember this is that the RED CAT is a FAT CAT, which stands for, "reduction occurs at the cathode and electrons flow to the cathode." To remember which electrode is positive and which is negative, the mnemonic is the word "gain" = "Galvanic Anode Is Negative".

Passage 8 Explanation

Each person's **voice has a unique** quality, known as **timbre**, and is produced by a system designed to produce **vibrations** and filters based on a series **of resonance chambers**. As air is forced out of the lungs, the vocal cords that are stretched over the opening in the larynx vibrate to create pressure waves. Muscles associated with the vocal cords can adjust the tension of these membranes, affecting the **fundamental frequencies** of vibration. The **sound waves** are filtered, by changing the size and shape of the resonating cavities, which are the lungs, the larynx, the pharynx, the mouth and the sinuses. The frequencies of various **harmonics**, or **overtones**, having significant **amplitudes** also contribute to the timbre of the voice. A person can control the air pressure vibrating the vocal cords using the mussels of the **diaphragm**, abdomen and rib cage, thus affecting the loudness of the sound. The average person has a **lung capacity** of about 1200 cm^3, with a **trachea** representing a tube having an average diameter of about 2 cm and a length of approximately 10 cm. A typical adult male will have a fundamental frequency from 85 to 180 Hz, and a typical adult female from 165 to 255 Hz. The amplitude of the **overtones** can be affected by manipulating the diameter of resonating chambers, i.e. the mouth, at the **nodes** and **antinodes**.

Key terms: Timbre, vibrations, resonance chambers, lungs, vocal cords, larynx, mussels, tension, membranes, fundamental frequencies, sound waves, harmonics, overtones, amplitudes, diaphragm, abdomen, rib cage, lung capacity, trachea, nodes, and antinodes.

Cause-and-Effect: The unique qualities of the human voice result from a complex mixture of the various vibrations that are produced by passing air over the vocal cords, whose tension can be adjusted, and the resonance enhancements that result from the various associated cavities, such as the lungs, trachea, larynx, mouth and sinuses.

A surprisingly good model system for studying the fundamental resonance of the human voice is a bottle whistle. When air is blown over the opening of a bottle, air is forced into the cavity, creating a pressure slightly above **atmospheric pressure**. The system will respond like a **spring**, with air being pushed back out of the bottle, causing the pressure to decrease below atmospheric pressure. Air from outside then rushes back into the bottle and the process is repeated. Thus, the air will **oscillate** into and out of the container at **some natural frequency**. If air is gently blown over the opening, the sound that is produced is primarily due to the fundamental frequency of the resonating cavity. However, blowing air more forcefully can result in the production of one or more overtones as the principle source of the sound. The **pitch of the fundamental frequency** can be changed by adding water to the bottle. The fundamental frequency of a bottle with an irregular shape depends upon a number of variables, including the speed (v) of sound (in air v = 334 m/s), the area (of the opening, the volume (V) of the principle cavity of the bottle, and the length of the neck (l) of the tube. The relationship between frequency (f) and these variables is given in Equation 1. Figure 1 shows the pressure versus time plots for an empty bottle whistle and the same bottle with a small amount of water added using a **microphone** to record the sound.

Key terms: Atmospheric pressure, spring, oscillate, natural frequency, pitch, and microphone.

Cause-and-Effect: The fundamental resonance for the largest cavity associated with the production of sound, the lungs and trachea, can be approximated using a Helmholtz resonance system, in which a vibration is created by blowing air across the opening of a bottle, such that the pressure of air in the cavity oscillates at a particular frequency associated with the size and shape of the cavity.

Equation 1

$$f = \frac{v}{2\pi}\sqrt{\frac{A}{Vl}}$$

Equation 1 This equation describes the fundamental, or lowest frequency produced by what is known as a Helmholtz resonator. The variables are the speed of sound (v) in meters per second, the area (A) of the opening of the tube in square meters, the volume (V) of the cavity of the bottle in cubic meters, and the length (l) of the neck of the bottle in meters. If the units are accounted for properly, the resulting unit is reciprocal seconds (s^{-1}) or hertz (Hz), which is the unit of frequency.

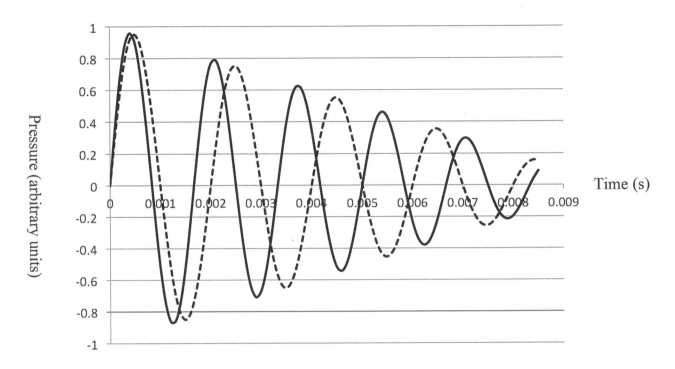

Figure 1 Pressure versus time plots for two different pitches of sound (F_1 = solid line and F_2 = dashed line) produced by a bottle whistle.

Figure 1 The pressure versus time waves for two different pitches produced by a bottle whistle are shown. The highest pitched tone is F_1, since it has the highest frequency, and was produced by adding water to the bottle to reduce the volume of cavity. Since the volume is in the denominator of Equation 1, there is an inverse square-root relationship between frequency and volume. The loudness of the sounds is decreasing because the amplitude (height) of the pressure waves are decreasing with time due to dampening of the vibrations.

40. What is the frequency of the lowest pitched tone produced by the bottle whistle in Figure 1.
    A. **500 Hz**
    B. 600 Hz
    C. 1000 Hz
    D. 1200 Hz

Choice **A** is correct. The lowest pitched sound will have the lowest frequency. Since the period and frequency are inversely related, the wave that takes the longest time to complete a cycle will have the lowest pitch. F_2 has a period of approximately 0.002 s, whereas F_1 has a period of < 0.002 s. The frequency can be calculated by taking the inverse of the period.

$$f = 1/(0.002 \text{ s}) = 500 \text{ s}^{-1} = 500 \text{ Hz}$$

41. Using the information in the passage about the relationship between a bottle whistle and the resonating cavities of the human body, what is the predicted frequency of the fundamental produced by the average person?
    A. **90 Hz**
    B. 500 Hz
    C. 833 Hz
    D. 1500 Hz

It is not necessary to do a calculation. As stated in the passage "A typical adult male will have a fundamental frequency from 85 to 180 Hz, and a typical adult female from 165 to 255 Hz." It is also suggested that the bottle whistle is a good approximation of the fundamental frequency of the human voice, therefore choice A is the only answer in the range quoted.

B, C, D: These answers are a result of miscalculation or failure to recognize the range given in the passage.

42. Based on the information in Figure 1, what is happening to the pitch and loudness of the sounds over time?
    A. The pitches are getting higher and the loudness is staying the same.
    B. **The pitches are staying the same and the loudness is decreasing.**
    C. The pitches are decreasing and the loudness is increasing.
    D. Both the pitches and the loudness are remaining the same.

Choice **B** is correct. The pitch of the whistle is determined by the frequencies of the two sounds. The frequency of the sounds are not changing over time, eliminating choices A and C. The amplitudes of the pressure waves are decreasing and it is the amplitude that determines the loudness of the sound. The sounds are getting softer, quickly over time. Choice B is the correct answer.

The frequency of the sounds are not changing over time, eliminating choices A and C. The amplitudes of the pressure waves are decreasing and it is the amplitude that determines the loudness of the sound. The sounds are getting softer.

43. Which of the following describe the number of nodes and antinodes for a closed tube resonator?
    I. For the fundamental, there is a single node at and a single antinode.
    II. For the third harmonic, there are two nodes and two antinodes.
    III. For the fifth harmonic, there are three nodes and three antinodes.

    A. I only
    B. II and III only
    C. I and III only
    D. **I, II, and III**

Choice D is correct. A node is a position in a standing wave that produces destructive interference, resulting in zero amplitude, and an antinode is a position in a standing wave where there is a maximum constructive interference. For a closed tube, the pressure wave of the fundamental resonance starts at the opening and goes into the tube, is reflected off the closed end and returns to the open end. The tube length represents one quarter of the wavelength, $L = \frac{1}{4}\lambda$, with one node and one antinode each.

Overtones occur by increasing the frequency such that multiples of half a wave length result in standing waves. The first overtone of a closed tube resonator is called the third harmonic, and $L = \frac{3}{4}\lambda$. The name of the harmonic is related to the numerator of the fraction, which is the multiple of $\frac{1}{4}\lambda$. Again the pressure wave starts at the open end, and is reflected off the closed end at a node, as shown below. Now there are two nodes and two antinodes.

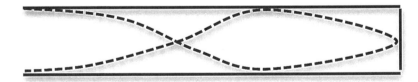

The second overtone is also called the fifth harmonic and $L = 5/4\lambda$. As shown below, there are now three nodes and three antinodes.

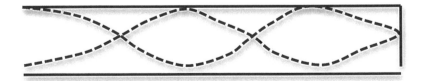

These questions are NOT based on a passage.

44. Which of the following are considered carbohydrates?
    I. Glucose
    II. Formaldehyde
    III. Acetic acid

    A. **I only**
    B. I and II only
    C. I and III only
    D. I, II and III

Choice **A** is correct. The definition of a carbohydrate is a large (greater than 2 carbon atoms) biologically derived molecule that contains carbon, hydrogen and oxygen, usually with an empirical formula of CH_2O. While glucose (a monosaccharide), formaldehyde ($H_2C=O$) and acetic acid (CH_3CO_2H), all have empirical formulas of CH_2O, the latter two are not large molecules with more than two carbon atoms. Hence of the answer options, only glucose is considered a carbohydrate.

While glucose (a monosaccharide), formaldehyde ($H_2C=O$) and acetic acid (CH_3CO_2H), all have empirical formulas of CH_2O, the latter two are not large molecules with more than two carbon atoms. Hence of the answer options, only glucose is considered a carbohydrate.

45. In cases of panic attacks and hyperventilation, the victim is sometimes asked to breath into a paper bag to slow the person's respiration rate. What does breathing into a paper bag do to the concentration of carbon dioxide and the pH of the blood?
    A. The concentration of carbon dioxide increases and pH both increase.
    B. **The concentration of carbon dioxide increases and pH decreases.**
    C. The concentration of carbon dioxide decreases and pH increases.
    D. The concentration of carbon dioxide and pH both decrease.

Choice **B** is correct. By breathing into a bag, the victim will inhale air that has a higher percentage of carbon dioxide and a lower percentage of oxygen than normal air. This will increase the concentration of carbon dioxide in the blood, which will increase the concentration of carbonic acid, increasing the hydrogen ion concentration and lowering the pH of the blood. Choice B is the correct answer.

46. Which of the following best describes the complementary reactions of photosynthesis and combustion?
    A. **Photosynthesis is endothermic and combustion is exothermic.**
    B. Photosynthesis is exothermic and combustion is endothermic.
    C. Both photosynthesis and combustion are endothermic processes.
    D. Both photosynthesis and combustion are exothermic processes.

Choice **A** is correct. Photons, a form of energy, are a reactant in photosynthesis, which makes photosynthesis an endothermic process. Combustion reactions produce energy (heat and light), and are therefore exothermic.

B, C, D: In Photosynthesis energy is a reactant, which makes photosynthesis an endothermic process. Combustion reactions produce (heat and light) as products, making them exothermic.

47. Which of the following best describes the bond angle in ozone?
    A. 90°
    B. 117°
    C. 135°
    D. 180°

Choice **B** is correct. Drawing the Lewis dot structure of ozone, O3, gives (including formal charges)

where there are three electron domains (one lone pair and two bonding domains) on the central oxygen atom, resulting in a bent structure with an O-O-O angle slightly less than 120°. Choice B is the correct answer.

Passage 9 Explanation

Air pollution is a major contributor to public health issues for people living in urban regions. The major sources of **air pollution** are related to energy production and transportation. Recently there has been a significant change in how you produce energy in the United States, with the discovery and use of **new natural** gas reserves, which are replacing coal for electricity production. Burning coal, which can often contain relatively high amounts of sulfur, results in the formation of sulfur dioxide, which can contribute to particulate matter, as well as contributing to problems associated with acid rain. On the other hand, the use of **internal combustion engines for transportation also contributes to the formation of air pollution from the release of volatile organic compounds, as well as the production of nitrogen oxides**, both of which contribute to the production of photochemical **smog** which can produce dangerous concentrations of **ozone**.

Key terms: air pollution, natural gas, nitrogen oxides, smog and ozone

Cause-and-Effect: Incomplete combustion of hydrocarbon based fuels, like gasoline, can result in the formation of reactive volatile organic compounds that when exposed to sunlight, undergo further reaction with gases present in the atmosphere to produce radical compounds, which can promote the conversion of O_2 into ozone, O_3, which is an extremely reactive form of elemental oxygen.

Nitrogen oxides, both nitrogen monoxide and nitrogen dioxide, are formed when air is used as the source of oxygen in high temperature combustion reactions, such as in the internal combustion engine. The reaction between elemental nitrogen and elemental oxygen, Reaction 1, is **thermodynamically favorable, but kinetically hindered**.

Key terms: thermodynamically favorable, and kinetically hindered

Cause-and-Effect: When hydrocarbon based fuels, such as gasoline undergo combustion with air as the source of oxygen, the high temperatures and the presence of elemental nitrogen cause the formation of nitrogen monoxide and nitrogen dioxide.

Reaction 1 $N_2 (g) + O_2 (g) \rightarrow 2\ NO (g)$

Reaction 1 The reaction between elemental nitrogen and elemental oxygen, which are the major component gases in the earth's atmosphere is kinetically slow, due to a very large activation energy. At high temperatures, such as in certain combustion reactions involving air, the collisions can have enough energy to get over the activation energy and form the more thermodynamically stable products.

Nitrogen monoxide reacts further with elemental oxygen to form nitrogen dioxide. This reaction is thought to occur in a two step mechanism, in which two nitrogen monoxide molecules combine in a relatively **fast pre-equilibrium**, forming an intermediate species, dinitrogen dioxide, which then reacts in a slow step with an equivalent of elemental oxygen to form two nitrogen dioxide molecules, Reaction 2 and 3.

Key terms: pre-equilibrium

Cause-and-Effect: Nitrogen monoxide quickly reacts with itself to form an intermediate, N_2O_2, due to the relatively low activation energy for this equilibrium reaction and since this is an equilibrium, the free energy of the reactants and products are fairly similar.

Cause-and-Effect: The activation energy for Reaction 3 is higher than the activation energy for Reaction 2, but the products are more stable, making Reaction 3 slower than Reaction 2, but thermodynamically more favorable.

Reaction 2 $\qquad\qquad$ $2\ NO\ (g) \leftrightarrows N_2O_2\ (g)$ $\qquad\qquad$ fast

Reaction 3 $\qquad\qquad$ $N_2O_2\ (g) + O_2\ (g) \rightarrow\ 2\ NO_2\ (g)$ $\qquad\qquad$ slow

Reactions 2 and 3   These reactions represent the proposed mechanism for the overall reaction

$$2\ NO\ (g) + O_2\ (g)\ \rightarrow 2\ NO_2\ (g)$$

Nitrogen dioxide is a brown colored gas and establishes equilibrium with the colorless gas dinitrogen tetroxide, Reaction 4. The color of nitrogen dioxide is a ubiquitous characteristic of seasonal smog episodes in cities such as Los Angeles California.

Cause-and-Effect: The production of NO_2 as a component of smog, results in the brown haze that is often observed in the summer time in many large urban areas, such as Los Angeles, California.

Reaction 4 $\qquad\qquad$ $2\ NO_2\ (g) \leftrightarrows N_2O_4\ (g) + 57\ kJ$

Reaction 4 Nitrogen dioxide establishes an equilibrium with dinitrogen tetroxide, which is exothermic. The bond that is formed results from sharing a pair of electrons between the nitrogen atoms, which were the unpaired electrons in the reactant NO_2 molecules. The brown color of NO_2 is due to low energy electronic transitions involving the partially filled sp^2 hybridized orbital. This color disappears in the diamagnetic N_2O_4 because all of the bonding orbitals are now completely filled with electrons.

48. Which of the following best describes the thermodynamic changes associated with the equilibrium between nitrogen dioxide and dinitrogen tetroxide?
    A. The enthalpy change is positive and the entropy change is negative.
    B. The enthalpy change is negative and the entropy change is positive.
    C. Both the enthalpy and entropy changes are positive.
    D. <u>**Both the enthalpy and entropy changes are negative.**</u>

Choice **D** is correct. As seen in Reaction 4, heat is a product and hence the reaction is exothermic, with a negative enthalpy.

Choices A and C can be eliminated. Since there are fewer gas molecules as products than reactants, the system becomes more ordered, entropy decreases and the entropy change would be negative. Choice B can be eliminated and choice D is the correct answer.

49. Which of the following best describes the season during which air pollution in Los Angeles most likely has a brown color?

A. Air pollution in Los Angeles has a brown color in the summer due to the increased amounts of nitrogen dioxide that is formed at high temperatures, because the reaction is exothermic.

B. Air pollution in Los Angeles has a brown color in the summer due to the increased amounts of dinitrogen tetroxide that is formed at high temperatures, because the reaction is endothermic.

C. Air pollution in Los Angeles has a brown color in the winter due to the increased amounts of nitrogen dioxide that is formed at low temperatures, because the reaction is exothermic.

D. Air pollution in Los Angeles has a brown color in the winter due to the increased amounts of dinitrogen tetroxide that is formed at low temperatures, because the reaction is endothermic.

Choice **A** is correct. Based on Le Châtelier's principle, since heat is a product of Reaction 4, increasing the temperature would shift the reaction towards the reactants, increasing the amount of the brown NO_2 gas.

Choices B and D can be eliminated. The temperatures in Los Angeles are on average higher in the summer than in the winter. Choice C can be eliminated because dinitrogen tetroxide, N_2O_4, is not the molecule in question..

50. Which of the following energy diagrams best describes Reaction 1?

A.

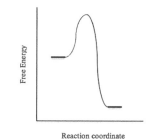

C.

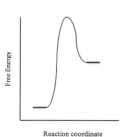

B.

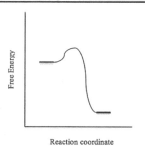

D.

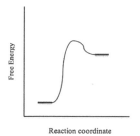

Choice **A** is correct. As stated in the second paragraph of the passage, "The reaction between elemental nitrogen and elemental oxygen, Reaction 1, is thermodynamically favorable, but kinetically hindered."

Choices C and D are not thermodynamically favorable, because the free energy change is positive. Reactions with high activation energies would cause a reaction to be "kinetically hindered". The activation energy in choice A is higher than the activation energy in choice B, making choice A the correct answer.

51. If sulfur dioxide is the major oxide of sulfur initially formed when coal is burned, which of the following acids will be formed when sulfur dioxide reacts with water?
    A. Sulfonic acid
    B. **Sulfurous acid**
    C. Sulfuric acid
    D. Hydrosulfuric acid

Choice **B** is correct. The reaction between sulfur dioxide and water, produces H_2SO_3, which is sulfurous acid, because the anion is sulfite. Choice B is the correct answer.

Sulfuric acid is H_2SO_4, which has the sulfate anion. Sulfuric acid is the product of the reaction between water and sulfur trioxide. Choice C can be eliminated. Hydrosulfuric acid, is H_2S in aqueous solution, with the anion being sulfide, S^{2-}. Choice C can be eliminated. Sulfonic acid is a class of organic acids with the general formula of RSO_3H. Choice A can be eliminated.

Passage 10 Explanation

Understanding the shapes of **covalently bonded** molecules and ions represents a critical factor in understanding more complex biomolecules. The coupling of Valance Shell Electron Pair Repulsion (VSEPR) theory and **Valance Bond** (VB) theory has proven to be an extremely useful way to predict molecular shapes and the bonding of small molecules and ions. These theories have formed the basis for computer molecular modeling programs used to understand the complex structures of biopolymers, such as structural proteins and enzymes. In addition to predicting **idealized geometries**, VSEPR theory can account for subtle distortions of bond angles. For example, the ideal geometric shape of water is based on a tetrahedral geometry, in which two of the **tetrahedral** vertices are occupied by lone-pairs of electrons. Since the O-H **bonding pairs** of electrons are shared between two nuclei, **the corresponding electron cloud is elongated and does not occupy as much space** around the oxygen atom as the lone pairs. Since these negatively charged lone-pairs exert an electrostatic repulsive force, the H-O-H angle is reduced from the idealized tetrahedral angle of 109.5° to 104.5°.

Key terms: Covalently bonded, Valance Shell Electron Pair Repulsion, Valence Bond, idealized geometries, tetrahedral, and vertices.

Cause-and-Effect: The presence of a lone pair of electrons on the central atom of a molecule or ion results in a distortion from the idealized geometry based on VSEPR theory.

In addition to predicting the shapes of molecules and ions of **second period** elements, VSEPR can also be useful in predicting the idealized shapes and qualitatively predict subtle distortions seen in third period molecules and ions that can expand their octets to form sp^3d and sp^3d^2 hybrid structures, with **trigonal bipyramidal** (D_{3h}) and **octahedral** (O_h) geometries, respectively. For example, sulfur hexafluoride adopts an O_h structure, with F-S-F angles of 90° and 180°, but **sulfur tetrafluoride adopts a distorted see-saw shaped structure** (Figure 1), where the idealized F-S-F angles of 180° and 120° are compressed slightly, to 173.1° and 101.6°, respectively, due to the space occupied by the lone-pair of electrons on the sulfur atom.

Key terms: Period, trigonal bipyramid, and octahedral

Contrast: The structure of SF6 adopts the idealized octahedral structure because there are no lone pairs of electrons on the central atom, whereas the structure of SF$_4$ is a distorted structure because the lone pairs of electrons on the central atoms occupies more space than the bonding pairs of electrons.

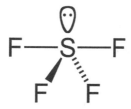

Figure 1 The idealized TBP structure of sulfur tetrafluoride.

Figure 1 The lone pair of electrons on the sulfur atom occupies an equatorial, or trigonal, position having fewer 90° electrostatic repulsive forces than if it were to occupy an axial position of the TBP.

52. Which of the following would most likely have a bond angle that is distorted from the idealized geometry?
    A. NH_4^+
    B. **$H_2O^\pm$**
    C. CF_4
    D. BF_3

Choice **B** is correct. This question is basically asking, "which of the answers options has a lone pair on the central atom." The best answer is choice B. The hydronium ion, H_3O^+, has $6 + 3(1) - 1 = 8$ valence electrons. The three O-H bonds accounts for six of these valence electrons and the remaining pair of electrons complete the octet for the oxygen atom.

The hydronium ion, H_3O^+, has $6 + 3(1) - 1 = 8$ valence electrons. The three O-H bonds accounts for six of these valence electrons and the remaining pair of electrons complete the octet for the oxygen atom. The ammonium ion, NH_4^+, has a total of $5 + 4(1) - 1 = 8$ valence electrons. There are four N-H bonds and therefore there are not any lone pairs on the nitrogen atom. Choice A can be eliminated. Carbon tetrafluoride has a total of $4 + 4(7) = 32$ valence electrons. The C-F bonds accounts for eight of these electrons and there are three lone pairs on each fluorine atom, which accounts for all of the valence electrons. There are no lone pairs on the carbon atom and choice C can be eliminated. Boron trifluoride has a total of $3 + 3(7) = 24$ valence electrons. The B-F bonds account for six of these electrons and there are three lone pairs of electrons on each of the fluorine atoms, which account for all of the remaining valence electrons. The boron atom has not yet completed its octet and a B=F bond can be formed from a fluorine lone pair to complete the octet. There are three resonance structures. There are no lone pairs of electrons on the boron atom and choice D can be eliminated.

53. Which of the following does NOT correctly describe the molecular shape?
    A. Sulfur dioxide is bent.
    B. Nitrite ion is bent.
    C. **Ammonia is tetrahedral.**
    D. Methane is tetrahedral.

Choice **C** is correct. Ammonia has a formula of NH_3 with a total of $5 + 3(1) = 8$ valence electrons. The N-H bonds accounts for six of these electrons and the remaining two electrons represent a lone pair on the nitrogen atom to complete the octet. As a result ammonia has a pyramidal structure. Choice C is the correct answer. Ammonium ion, NH_4^+, is tetrahedral.

Sulfur dioxide, SO_2, has $6 + 2(6) = 18$ valence electrons. The S-O bonds account for four of these electrons and the oxygen atoms each have six additional electrons, representing the lone pairs, giving $18 - 4 - 2(6) = 2$ remaining electrons, which are given to the sulfur atom. However, the sulfur atom only has three pairs of electrons at this point, requiring the formation of a S=O bond to complete the sulfur's octet. The lone pair on the sulfur atom causes the structure to be bent, with an O-S-O angle of slightly less than 120°. Choice A can be eliminated. Nitrite has the same number of valence electrons as sulfur dioxide and also adopts a bent structure and choice B can be eliminated. Methane, CH_4, has $4 + 4(1) = 8$ valence electrons and adopts a tetrahedral structure. Choice D can be eliminated.

54. Which of the following molecules adopts a distorted see-saw type structure?

    I. PF_4^-

    II. ClF_4^+

    III. XeF_4

    A. I only

    B. III only

    C. **I and II only**

    D. I, II and III

Choice **C** is correct. The anion PF_4^- and the cation ClF_4^+ are isoelectronic with SF_4, which as stated in the passage, adopts a distorted see-saw type structure. Therefore answer options I and II also adopt distorted see-saw type structures and Choices A and B can be eliminated. There are two additional electrons in XeF_4, and as a result there are two lone pairs of electrons on the xenon, rather than just one, as in SF_4. Therefore, XeF_4 adopts a square-planar structure, not a see-saw structure, which eliminates choices B and D. Choice C is the correct answer.

55. Which of the following is best described as having a fractional bond order?

    A. Carbon dioxide

    B. **Carbonate**

    C. Elemental nitrogen

    D. Diamond

Choice **B** is correct. A fractional bond order would result from having resonance structures that have different bond orders. This is best determined by drawing the Lewis dot structures. The Lewis dot structure of carbonate has one C=O and two C–O bonds. Therefore, as shown below, there are three resonance structures and the carbon/oxygen bond is best described as having a bond order of 1.33. Choice B is the correct answer.

In carbon dioxide both carbon/oxygen bonds can be described as being double bonds, and choice A can be eliminated. Elemental nitrogen, N_2, has a triple bond, and Choice C can be eliminated.

Diamond is elemental carbon, in which each carbon atom is singly bonded to four other carbon atoms, forming a three-dimensional array of tetrahedral bonded carbon atoms and choice D can be eliminated.

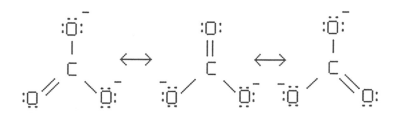

These questions are NOT based on a passage.

56. Which of the following regions of the infrared spectrum would be most useful in distinguishing an ester from and organic acid?
    A. **3000 to 3700 cm^{-1}**
    B. 2800 to 3000 cm^{-1}
    C. 1700 to 1800 cm^{-1}
    D. 1200 to 1400 cm^{-1}

Choice **A** is correct. The best way to differentiate between an ester and an acid is the presence of the hydroxyl group on the acid. The O-H stretching region, 3000 to 3700 cm^{-1}, would suffice.

The C-H stretching region, the C=O stretching region, 1700 to 1800 cm^{-1} and the C-O stretching region, 1200 to 1400 cm^{-1}. The organic acid and ester should both have C-H, C=O and C-O stretching vibrations and choices B, C and D can be eliminated. The O-H stretch will be observed in the organic acid, but not in the ester, therefore choice A is the correct answer.

57. What is the oxidation state of the chromium atoms in $Cr_2O_7^{2-}$?
    A. Cr^{2+}
    B. Cr^{3+}
    C. **Cr^{6+}**
    D. Cr^{12+}

Choice **C** is correct. The total charge of the polyatomic ion (2-) must equal the sum of the oxidation number of the atoms in in the formula. Oxide is given an oxidation number of 2- and you can call the value of the oxidation number of chromium x, giving the formula, which rearranges and gives

$$2- = 2x + 7(2-)$$
$$2- = 2x - 14$$
$$12 = 2x$$
$$6 = x$$

58. Nitrogen dioxide is a brown gas and establishes equilibrium with the colorless gas dinitrogen tetroxide, as described in the following reaction.

$$2\ NO_2\ (g) \leftrightharpoons N_2O_4\ (g) + 57\ kJ$$

Which of the following changes would most likely cause a sealed glass tube containing these gases to become colorless?

   A. Increase the temperature and decrease the pressure of the system.
   B. <u>**Decrease the temperature and increase the pressure of the system.**</u>
   C. Increase both the temperature and the pressure of the system.
   D. Decrease both the temperature and the pressure of the system.

Choice **B** is correct. The reaction is exothermic and heat is a product of this chemical equilibrium. Therefore, based on Le Châtelier's principle, increasing the temperature should increase the rate of the reverse reaction, producing more of the brown NO_2, rather than the colorless N_2O_4. The reaction also has more moles of gas on the reactant side of the reaction than on the product side of the reaction. Therefore, decreasing the pressure would increase the rate of the reverse reaction and produce more of the brown NO_2 gas and less of the colorless N_2O_4 gas.

59. Which of the following is the most likely O-N-O bond angle in nitrogen dioxide?

   A. 90°
   B. 120°
   C. <u>**134°**</u>
   D. 180°

Choice **C** is correct. The Lewis dot structure of NO_2 has a total of 17 valence electrons. There are three electron domains around the central nitrogen atom, which causes NO_2 to have a bent structure, rather than a linear structure. Nitrite ion, NO_2^-, also has a bent structure with an O-N-O angle close to 120°, caused by the repulsive effects of the additional lone pair of electrons on the nitrogen. However, NO_2 only has a single unpaired electron and as a result, the repulsive effects of the single electron causes the O-N-O angle to be less acute. Choice C is the correct answer.

APPENDIX A

Timed Section Scoring Scale

Table 1 Raw Score to Scaled Score Conversion for Science Sections

These scores are rough estimates based on the scaled-to-percentile conversions released by the AAMC in 2015. The raw-to-scaled conversion is based on past released AAMC exams.

Raw Score (Number of Questions Correct)	Scaled Score	Percentile*
58-59	132	100
56-57	131	99
54-55	130	97
51-53	129	93
47-50	128	87
43-46	127	79
39-42	126	67
36-38	125	55
33-35	124	45
30-32	123	32
27-29	122	21
23-26	121	12
18 - 22	120	7
16 - 17	119	3
0 - 15	118	1

* Percentile rank is given in this table as an example of how percentile correlates with scaled score, taken from recent actual MCAT exams. This is for illustration purposes only and does not represent performance of test-takers from the material in this exam.

APPENDIX B

Equation List

Electricity and Magnetism

$F = kQ_1Q_2 / r^2$

$F = qVB\sin\theta$

$F = iLB\sin\theta$

$V = IR$

$P = IV$

$R = \rho L / A$

$V_{rms} = V_{max} / \sqrt{2}$

$I_{rms} = I_{max} / \sqrt{2}$

Resistors in series:

$R_{tot} = R_1 + R_2 \ldots$

Resistors in parallel:

$1/R_{tot} = 1/R_1 + 1/R_2 \ldots$

Capacitors in series:

$1/C_{tot} = 1/C_1 + 1/C_2 \ldots$

Capacitors in parallel:

$C_{tot} = C_1 + C_2 \ldots$

$C = Q/V$

$Energy = (1/2)QV$

$F = qE$

$V = Ed$

$Energy = qEd$

$E = kQ/r^2$

$Energy = kQq/r$

$V = kQ/r$

$\Delta G = -nFE$

$E_{cell} = E_{cath} - E_{an}$

Waves

$v = f\lambda$

$T = 1/f$

Light

$n_1\sin\theta_1 = n_2\sin\theta_2$

$\sin\theta_c = n_2/n_1$

$E = hf$

$m = -d_i / d_o$

$P = 1/f$

$f = (1/2)r$

$n = c/v$

$1/f = 1/d_i + 1/d_o$

Sound

$d\beta = 10 \log (I/I_o)$

$L = n\lambda/2 \ (n=1, 2\ldots)$

$L = n\lambda/4 \ (n=1,3\ldots)$

$f_{beat} = |f_1 - f_2|$

$f = f_e[v\pm v_d]/[v\pm v_s]$

Fluids

$\rho = m/V$

$P = F/A$

$P = P_{atm} + \rho gd$

$F_b = \rho gV$

$Q = Av$

$P + \rho gy + (1/2) \rho v^2 = $ constant

Gases

$PV = nRT$

Boyle: $PV = k$

Guy-Lussac: $P/T=k$

Charles: $V/T=k$

Avogadro: $n/V=k$

$R_1/R_2=\sqrt{(m_2/m_1)}$

$P_A = X_A \times P_{tot}$

Solutions

$pH=pK_a+\log (A^-/HA)$

$M = mol / L$

$m = mol / kg$

$N = M \times \# \text{ of } H^+$

$pH = - \log [H^+]$

$M_iV_i = M_fV_f$

$\Pi = MRT$

$\Delta T_f = ik_fm$

$\Delta T_b = ik_bm$

$X_A = mol_A / mol_{tot}$

Thermo

$\Delta U = Q - W$

$\Delta U = (3/2)nRT$

$W = P\Delta V$

$Q = mc\Delta T$

$Q = mH_L$

$\Delta G = \Delta H - T\Delta S$

$\Delta H_{rxn} = \Delta H_{prod} - \Delta H_{react}$

Kinematics

$v_f = v_o + at$

$d = v_ot + (1/2)at^2$

$v_f^2 = v_o^2 + 2ad$

$a_c = v^2 / r$

$F_c = mv^2 / r$

$v_x = v_o\cos\theta$

$v_y = v_o\sin\theta$

Mechanics

$F = ma$

$F_{a \text{ on } b} = -F_{b \text{ on } a}$

$F_{fric} = \mu F_N$

$F_g = GM_1m_2 / r^2$

$F_g = mg$

$F = kx$

$\tau = rF\sin\theta$

$P = W/t$

$W = Fd\cos\theta$

$E_K = (1/2)mv^2$

$U = mgh$

$U = - GM_1m_2 / r$

Inclined Plane

$F_{incline} = mg\sin\theta$

$F_N = mg\cos\theta$

$F_{fric} = \mu mg\cos\theta$

APPENDIX C

Self-Study Outline

Part I: Physics

1. Translational Motion CL:_____

   _____
   _____
   _____
   _____

   A. Units CL:_____

   _____
   _____
   _____
   _____

   B. Vectors CL:_____

   _____
   _____
   _____
   _____

   C. Vector addition CL:_____

   _____
   _____
   _____
   _____

   D. Speed, velocity CL:_____

   _____
   _____
   _____
   _____

   E. Acceleration CL:_____

   _____
   _____
   _____
   _____

2. Force CL:_____

   _____
   _____
   _____
   _____

A. Newton's 1st Law CL:_____

_____
_____
_____
_____

B. Newton's 2nd Law CL:_____

_____
_____
_____
_____

C. Newton's 3rd Law CL:_____

_____
_____
_____
_____

D. Friction, static and kinetic CL:_____

_____
_____
_____
_____

3. Equilibrium CL:_____

_____
_____
_____
_____

A. Free body diagrams CL:_____

_____
_____
_____
_____

B. Torques, levers CL:_____

_____
_____
_____
_____

4. Work CL:_____

_____
_____
_____
_____

    A. Work Energy theorem CL:_____

_____
_____
_____
_____

    B. Mechanical work CL:_____

_____
_____
_____
_____

    C. Conservative forces CL:_____

_____
_____
_____
_____

5.   Energy CL:_____

_____
_____
_____
_____

    A. Kinetic CL:_____

_____
_____
_____
_____

    B. Potential CL:_____

_____
_____
_____
_____

6.   Thermodynamics CL:_____

_____
_____
_____
_____

    A. Energy Types CL:_____

_____
_____
_____
_____

7.   Periodic Motion CL:_____

_____
_____
_____

    A. Springs CL:_____

_____
_____
_____
_____

    B. Pendulums CL:_____

_____
_____
_____
_____

    C. Transverse and longitudinal waves CL:_____

_____
_____
_____
_____

8.   Fluids CL:_____

_____
_____
_____
_____

    A. Density, specific gravity CL:_____

_____
_____
_____

    B. Buoyancy CL:_____

_____
_____
_____

       1.   Archimedes' Principle CL:_____

_____
_____
_____
_____

C. Hydrostatic pressure CL:_____

1. Pascal's Law CL:_____

2. Hydrostatic pressure CL:_____

D. Viscosity: Poiseuille Flow CL:_____

E. Continuity equation CL:_____

F. Turbulent flow at high velocities CL:_____

G. Surface tension CL:_____

H. Bernoulli's equation CL:_____

APPENDIX D

Self-Study Glossary

Physical Foundations of Biology

Absolute pressure
Is measured relative to the pressure that would occur at absolute vacuum. It is calculated as the force per unit area exerted on an imaginary or real plane surface in a fluid or a gas. $P = F/A$ (pascals)

Acceleration
Is the rate at which the velocity of an object changes over time. An object's acceleration is a result of the net force acting on the object, as described by Newton's Second Law, $F_{net} = ma$

Adiabatic
An adiabatic process is one that occurs without transfer of heat or matter between a system and its surroundings.

Current
In alternating current (AC), the flow of electric charge periodically reverses direction. In direct current (DC, also dc), the flow of electric charge is only in one direction.

Alpha particle
An alpha particle is a fast moving packet containing two protons and two neutrons (a helium nucleus).

Amplitude
In a wave amplitude is the distance from the rest position to the crest position which is half the vertical distance from a trough to a crest.

Antinode
An anti-node is a point where the amplitude of the standing wave is maximum.

Archimedes' principle
Indicates that the upward buoyant force that is exerted on an object immersed in a fluid, is equal to the weight of the fluid that the body displaces.

Atomic mass
Is the mass of an atomic particle, primarily made up by the protons and neutrons in the atom.

Atomic mass unit	An atomic mass unit (amu) is defined as precisely 1/12 the mass of an atom of carbon-12. It is ~ 1.6×10^{-27} kg
Atomic number	The number of protons found in the nucleus of an atom of that element, equal to the charge number of the nucleus. It is represented by the symbol Z.
Beats	Beats are the periodic and repeating fluctuations heard in the intensity of a sound when two sound waves of very similar frequencies interfere with one another.
Beta particle	Beta particles are high-energy, high-speed electrons or positrons emitted by certain types of radioactive nuclei.
Binding energy	Binding energy is the energy required to break apart a system into separate parts. A bound system typically has a lower potential energy than the sum of its parts — this is what keeps the system (e.g. a nucleus) together.
Buoyant force	When an object is submerged in a fluid (completely or partially), there exists an upward force on the object that is equal to the weight of the fluid that is displaced by the object.
Capacitance	Capacitance is the ability of a circuit component to store electrical charge. C = Charge/Volts (C is measured in Farads).
Capacitor	A capacitor is a passive two-terminal electrical component (usually 2 parallel plates) used to store energy electrostatically in an electric field.
Center of gravity	Is the average location of the weight of an object.
Center of mass	The point where the mass of the object is concentrated. When an object is supported at its center of mass there is no net torque acting on the body and it will remain in static equilibrium.
Centripetal force	In the case of an object moving in a circular path, the net force is called the centripetal force, a center seeking force which means that the force is always directed toward the center of the circle.

Conductor	In a conductor, electric current can flow freely. Metals such as copper are great conductors.
Conservative force	A force with the property that the work done in moving a particle between two points is independent of the taken path (e.g. gravity, electrostatics).
Convection	Convection is heat transfer by mass motion of a fluid such as air or water when the heated fluid is caused to move away from the source of heat.
Critical angle	The angle of incidence above which the total internal reflection occurs ($n_2 < n_1$).
Decibel	Decibels provide a relative measure of sound intensity. $dB = 10 \log (I_{sound}/I_o))$
Density	The ratio of a substances mass to its volume (e.g. g/mL, kg/L).
Dielectric	A dielectric material is an electrical insulator that can be polarized by an applied electric field.
Diffraction	The apparent bending of waves around small obstacles and the spreading out of waves past small openings.
Diopter	A unit of measurement of the optical power of a lens or curved mirror, which is equal to the reciprocal of the focal length measured in meters. For example, a 5-diopter lens brings parallel rays of light to focus at 1/5 meter.
Molecular dipole moment	A dipole moment due to non-uniform distributions of positive and negative charges on the various atoms. For example polar compounds like hydrogen chloride, where electron density is shared unequally between atoms.
Dispersion	The change of index of refraction with wavelength. Generally the index decreases as wavelength increases, blue light traveling more slowly in the material than red light. Dispersion is the phenomenon which gives you the separation of colors in a prism.

Displacement
The shortest distance from the initial to the final position of an object. Thus, it is the length of an imaginary straight path, from the path actually travelled by the object.

Doppler effect
Is the change in frequency of a wave (or other periodic event) for an observer moving relative to its source.

Electric dipole
This is a measure of the separation of positive and negative electrical charges in a system of electric charges.

Electric field
The electric force per unit charge emitted by a charged object or particle. The direction of the field is taken to be the direction of the force it would exert on a positive test charge. The electric field is radially outward from a positive charge and radially in toward a negative point charge.

Electric potential
Electric potential (or just potential) at a point in an electric field is defined as the work done in moving a unit positive charge from infinity to that point.

Electromagnetic wave
A changing magnetic field will induce a changing electric field and vice-versa—the two are linked. These changing fields form electromagnetic waves. Electromagnetic waves differ from mechanical waves in that they do not require a medium to propagate. This means that electromagnetic waves can travel not only through air and solid materials, but also through the vacuum of space.

Electromagnetic spectrum
The entire range of light that exists. From radio waves to visible light (ROY G BIV) to gamma rays. Light is a wave of alternating electric and magnetic fields.

Electromotive force
Also called emf (measured in volts, aka Joules/Coulomb), is the voltage developed by any source of electrical energy such as a battery.

Entropy
A thermodynamic quantity representing the unavailable thermal energy for conversion into mechanical work, aka the degree of disorder or randomness in the system.

Field line
These pattern of lines, sometimes referred to as electric field lines, point in the direction that a positive test charge would accelerate if placed upon the line. As such, the lines are directed away from positively charged source charges and toward negatively charged source charges.

Fission   Nuclear fission is either a nuclear reaction or a radioactive decay process in which the nucleus of an atom splits into smaller parts.

Fluorescence   The property of an atoms ability to absorb light of short wavelength and emit light of longer wavelength.

Focal length   A measure of how strongly the system converges or diverges light. For an optical system in air, it is the distance over which initially unfocused rays are brought to a focus.

Focal point   As refraction acts to focus all parallel rays to a point, this point is called the focal point. The distance from the lens to that point is the principal focal length of the lens. For a concave lens where the rays are diverged, the principal focal length is the distance at which the back-projected rays would come together and it is given a negative sign.

Frequency   Frequency is the number of occurrences (cycles, oscillations, waves) of a repeating event per unit time. Units are Hertz (1/sec).

Friction   The force resisting the relative motion of solid surfaces, fluid layers, and material elements sliding against each other.

Fusion   A nuclear reaction in which two or more atomic nuclei collide at a very high speed and join to form a new type of atomic nucleus.

Gamma radiation   Gamma radioactivity is composed of electromagnetic rays. It is distinguished from x-rays only by the fact that it comes from the nucleus. Gamma particles have no mass.

Gauge pressure   The pressure difference between a system and the surrounding atmosphere.

Gravity   The force that attracts a body toward the center of the earth, or toward any other physical body having mass. $F = mg$, where $g = 9.8$ m/s^2.

Ground state   A ground-state atom is an atom in which the total energy of the electrons can not be lowered by transferring one or more electrons to different orbitals. That is, in a ground-state atom, all electrons are in the lowest possible energy levels.

Half-life
The time for half the radioactive nuclei in any sample to undergo radioactive decay. After two half-lives, there will be one fourth the original sample, after three half-lives 1/8 the original sample, and so forth.

Heat
The transfer of energy other than by work or transfer of matter. Heat flows spontaneously from a hotter object to a colder one if they are in thermodynamic contact with one another.

Impulse
Is a measure of change in momentum. The unit of impulse is the same as the unit of momentum, kg m/s

Index of refraction
Is expressed as the speed of light in vacuum divided by the speed of light in the medium. Given by n, where $n = c/v$.

Inertia
The resistance of any object with mass to any change in its state of motion, aka the tendency of objects to keep moving in a straight line at constant velocity (Newton's 1st Law).

Insulator
An electrical insulator is a material whose internal electric charges do not flow freely, and therefore make it very hard to conduct an electric current.

Intensity
Sound intensity is defined as the sound power per unit area. (W/m^2)

Interference
A phenomenon in which two waves superpose to form a resultant wave of greater or lower amplitude.

Isobaric
A thermodynamic process in which the pressure stays constant.

Isothermal
A process resulting in a change of a system, in which the temperature remains constant.

Isotope
A variant of a particular chemical element which differ in neutron number, although all isotopes of a given element have the same number of protons. For example, Carbon-13 has 6 protons and 7 neutrons.

Kinetic energy
An expression that quantifies the amount of work the object could do as a result of its motion. $KE = 1/2 \, mv^2$, measured in Joules (N*m).

Longitudinal wave   Waves in which the displacement of the medium is in the same direction as, or the opposite direction to, the direction of travel of the wave.

Magnetic field   Magnetic fields are produced by electric currents, which can be currents in wires, or currents associated with electrons in atomic orbits. The magnetic field B is defined in terms of force on moving charge (F = qvBsin(theta)).

Mass defect   The difference between the mass of a nucleus and the sum of the masses of the nucleons of which it is composed.

Momentum   The product of mass times velocity. It is a vector quantity. The momentum of a system is the vector sum of the momenta of the objects which make up the system.

Node   A node is a point along a standing wave where the wave has minimum amplitude.

Normal force   The component, perpendicular to the surface of contact between 2 objects, of the contact force exerted on an object. For example the surface of a floor preventing a chair from penetrating the surface of the floor.

Nucleon   A name for the particles that make up the atomic nucleus. There are two kinds of nucleon: the neutron and the proton.

Pascal's principle   The idea that pressure is transmitted undiminished in an enclosed static fluid.

Period   Also known as the reciprocal of frequency, period T is the time needed for one complete cycle of vibration to pass a given point.

Polarized light   Light waves in which the vibrations all occur in a single plane. The process of transforming unpolarized light into polarized light is known as polarization.

Positron   Also known as an antielectron, is the antiparticle or the antimatter counterpart of the electron. It has the same mass and charge as an electron, but it is positively charged.

Potential difference   See electric potential (aka voltage).

Potential energy   The energy which results from position or configuration. An object may have the capacity for doing work as a result of its position in a gravitational field (gravitational potential energy), an electric field (electric potential energy), or a magnetic field (magnetic potential energy). It may have elastic potential energy as a result of a stretched spring or other elastic deformation.

Power   The movement of energy over time, measured in Watts (J/s).

Pressure   See absolute pressure.

Radiation   A process in which electromagnetic waves (EMR) travel through a vacuum or through matter-containing media, carrying energy.

Resonance   The reinforcement or prolongation of sound by reflection from a surface or by the synchronous vibration of a neighboring object.

Reflection   The change in direction of a wavefront at an interface between two different media so that the wavefront returns into the medium from which it originated at the same angle.

Refraction   The bending of a wave when it enters a medium where its speed is different.

Resistance   The ability of an electrical circuit component to resist current. Electrical resistance of a circuit component (R) or device is defined as the ratio of the voltage applied to the electric current which flows through it. R = V/I, measured in Ohms.

Resistivity   The factor in resistance which takes into account the nature of the material the resistor is made of. It is temperature dependent, and it can be used at a given temperature to calculate the resistance of a wire of specified geometry.

RMS current & voltage   Circuit currents and voltages in AC circuits are stated as root-mean-square rather than by the maximum values. That is, you take the square of the current and average it, then take the square root.

Rotation
Is a circular movement of an object around a center (or point) of rotation, can provide and object with rotational kinetic energy.

Rotational equilibrium
When the sum of all torques on an object is equal to zero.

Scalar
A physical quantity that can be described by a single real number, unlike vectors, which are described by several numbers which characterize magnitude and direction.

Simple harmonic motion
A type of periodic motion where the restoring force is directly proportional to the displacement. It can serve as a mathematical model of a variety of motions, such as the oscillation of a spring or pendulum.

Specific gravity
The ratio of the density of a substance to the density (mass of the same unit volume) of a reference substance, typically water.

Specific heat
The amount of heat per unit mass required to raise the temperature by one degree Celsius (c for water is 1 cal/g°C).

Speed
Is the magnitude of an object's velocity (the rate of change of its position). It is a scalar quantity.

Standing wave
Characteristic patterns of vibration associated with resonance in extended objects like strings and air columns. Standing wave modes arise from the combination of reflection and interference such that the reflected waves interfere constructively with the incident waves.

Superposition principle
States that, for all linear systems, the net response at a given place and time caused by two or more stimuli is the sum of the responses which would have been caused by each stimulus individually. Applies to circuits, electric fields, magnetic fields, and mechanical systems.

Thermal expansion
The tendency of matter to change in volume in response to a change in temperature, through heat transfer.

Torque
An influence which tends to change the rotational motion of an object.

Translation

Is movement that changes the position of an object, as opposed to rotation, which does not.

Translational equilibrium

An object is in translational equilibrium if it is not accelerating. Translational equilibrium implies that the sum of all external forces applied to the object is zero.

Transverse wave

For transverse waves the displacement of the medium is perpendicular to the direction of propagation of the wave.

Vector

Any quantity with both a magnitude and a direction. For example, velocity is a vector because it describes both how fast something is moving and in what direction it is moving.

Velocity

A vector that describes both how fast an object is moving and in what direction it is moving.

Viscosity

The quantity that describes a fluid's resistance to flow. Fluids resist the relative motion of immersed objects through them as well as to the motion of layers with differing velocities within them.

Wavelength

The distance between successive crests of a wave, especially points in a sound wave or electromagnetic wave.

Work

When a force acts upon an object to cause a displacement of the object. There are three key ingredients to work - force, displacement, and cause. In order for a force to qualify as having done work on an object, there must be a displacement and the force must cause the displacement.

Chemical Foundations of Biology

1st law of Thermodynamics

States that the total energy of an isolated system is constant; energy can be transformed from one form to another, but cannot be created or destroyed. $U = Q - W$.

2nd law of Thermodynamics

States that the state of entropy of the entire universe, as a closed isolated system, will always increase over time. The second law also states that the changes in the entropy in the universe can never be negative.

Absolute configuration

In stereochemistry is the spatial arrangement of the atoms of a chiral molecular entity and its stereochemical description e.g. R or S. Absolute configurations for a chiral molecule are often obtained by X-ray crystallography.

Achiral

A molecule is achiral if it is superimposable on its mirror image. Most achiral molecules do have a plane of symmetry or a center of symmetry.

Activation energy

The minimum energy which reacting species must possess in order to be able to form an 'activated complex', or 'transition state', before proceeding to the products.

Addition reaction

Reactions in which an unsaturated system is saturated or partly saturated by the addition of a molecule across the multiple bond.

Alkali metals

Are group (column) I in the periodic table consisting of the chemical elements lithium (Li), sodium (Na), etc…

Alkaline earth metals

Are group (column) II in the periodic table consisting of the chemical elements beryllium (Be), magnesium (Mg), etc…

Allyl group

A substituent with the structural formula $H_2C=CH-CH_2R$, where R is the rest of the molecule.

Allylic rearrangement

the migration of a double bond in a 3-carbon system from carbon atoms one and two to carbon atoms two and three.

Alpha-anomer

The specific term used to describe carbohydrate stereoisomers differing only in configuration at the hemi-acetal carbon atom. The anomer in which the hydroxy group or the alkoxy group on the anomeric carbon is pointing down is the alpha anomer.

Amine

Amines are organic compounds and functional groups that contain a basic nitrogen atom with a lone pair.

Amino acid

Amino acids are biologically important organic compounds composed of amine ($-NH_2$) and carboxylic acid ($-COOH$) functional groups, along with a side-chain.

Angle strain   Is the increase in potential energy of a molecule due to bond angles deviating from the ideal values.

Angular momentum number   Determines the shape of an orbital, and therefore the angular distribution. Given by l. Each value of l indicates a specific s, p, d, f subshell on a given energy level.

Anomer   The specific term used to describe carbohydrate stereoisomers differing only in configuration at the hemi-acetal carbon atom.

Aprotic solvent   A solvent that will dissolve many salts, but lack an acidic hydrogen (e.g. ketones).

Aromatic   An organic compound containing a planar unsaturated ring of atoms that is stabilized by an interaction of the bonds forming the ring. It is also cyclic, planar, conjugated, and obeys Huckel's rule (e.g. benzene).

Arrhenius acid   Classifies a substance as an acid if it produces hydrogen ions H^+ or hydronium ions in water.

Arrhenius base   Classifies a substance as a base if it produces hydroxide ions OH^- in water.

Avogadro's constant   The number of constituent particles (usually atoms or molecules) per mole of a given substance. The number is 6.02×10^{23} atoms/mol.

Azimuthal quantum number   See angular momentum number.

Beta-anomer   The anomer in which the hydroxy group or the alkoxy group on the anomeric carbon is pointing up is the beta anomer.

Bimolecular reaction   A chemical reaction in which two species (e.g. molecules, ions) react to form new chemical species. The majority of reactions are bimolecular or proceed through a series of bimolecular steps.

Boiling   The rapid vaporization of a liquid, which occurs when a liquid is heated to its boiling point, the temperature at which the vapor pressure of the liquid is equal to the pressure exerted on the liquid by the surrounding environmental pressure.

Bond energy
The measure of bond strength in a chemical bond. It is the heat required to break one mole of molecules into their individual atoms.

Brønsted-Lowry acid
Classifies a substance as an acid if it donates protons.

Brønsted-Lowry base
Classifies a substance as a base if it accepts protons.

Buffer solution
A solution of definite pH made up in such a way that the pH alters only gradually with the addition of an acid or a base.

Carbocation
A molecule in which a carbon atom bears three bonds and a positive charge. Carbocations are generally unstable because they do not satisfy the octet rule.

Carbohydrate
A biological molecule consisting of carbon (C), hydrogen (H), and oxygen (O) atoms, usually with a hydrogen:oxygen atom ratio of 2:1 (as in water); in other words, with the empirical formula $C_m(H_2O)_n$.

Carbonyl
A functional group composed of a carbon atom double-bonded to an oxygen atom: C=O.

Carboxylic acid
A functional group that contains a carboxyl group (C(O)OH). The general formula of a carboxylic acid is R-C(O)OH.

Catalyst
A substance that increases the rate of a chemical reaction without itself undergoing any permanent chemical change.

Catalytic hydrogenation
The addition of hydrogen atoms to all available unsaturated atoms in an organic molecule, typically aided by a metal catalyst such as platinum.

Chemical equilibrium
The state in which both reactants and products are present in concentrations which will not change with time. This state results when the forward reaction proceeds at the same rate as the reverse reaction.

Chiral center
Tetrahedral atoms (usually carbons) that have four different substituents. Each chiral center in a molecule will be either R or S. As noted above, molecules with a single chiral center are chiral. Molecules with more than one chiral center are usually chiral.

Chromatography

A series of related techniques for the separation of a mixture of compounds by their distribution between two phases. In gas-liquid chromatography the distribution is between a gaseous and a liquid phase. In column chromatography the distribution is between a liquid and a solid phase.

Cis/trans isomers

A form of stereoisomerism describing the orientation of functional groups within a molecule. In general, such isomers contain double bonds, which cannot rotate, but they can also arise from ring structures, wherein the rotation of bonds is greatly restricted.

Colligative properties

Any property of a solution that depends upon the ratio of the number of solute particles to the number of solvent molecules in a solution, and not on the type of chemical species present.

Combination reaction

A combination (synthesis) reaction is a reaction in which two reactants combine to form one product.

Combustion reaction

A reaction that most commonly occurs when a hydrocarbon reacts with oxygen to produce carbon dioxide and water. In the more general sense, combustion involves a reaction between any combustible material and an oxidizer to form an oxidized product. Combustion is an exothermic reaction.

Compound

A pure chemical substance consisting of two or more different chemical elements that can be separated into simpler substances by chemical reactions.

Concentration cell

A limited type of a galvanic (energy producing) cell that has two equivalent half-cells of the same material differing only in concentrations. One can calculate the potential developed by such a cell using the Nernst Equation.

Configurational isomers

Configurational isomers are stereoisomers that cannot be converted into one another by rotation around a single bond (e.g. cis/trans, enantiomers, diastereomers).

Conformational isomer

Isomers can be readily interconverted exclusively by rotations about single (i.e. sigma) bonds. (e.g. chair and boat cyclohexane)

Conjugate acid

The conjugate acid of a base is formed when the base accepts a proton. In the equation, H_2O is the conjugate acid to OH^-, because OH^- accepts a hydrogen ion to form water, the conjugate base.

Conjugate base

The conjugate base of an acid is formed when the acid donates a proton. In the equation, OH^- is the conjugate base to the acid H_2O, because H_2O donates a hydrogen ion to form OH^-, the conjugate base.

Conjugation

A system of connected p-orbitals with delocalized electrons in compounds with alternating single and multiple bonds, which can lower the overall energy of the molecule and increase stability.

Constitutional isomers

Two or more compounds that have the same molecular formula and different connectivity.

Coordinate bond

A coordinate bond is a covalent bond (a shared pair of electrons) in which both electrons come from the same atom.

Covalent bond

A chemical bond that involves the sharing of electron pairs between atoms. These electrons can be shared equally (pure covalent) or unequally (polar covalent) between the atoms.

Critical temperature

The temperature at and above which vapor of the substance cannot be liquefied, no matter how much pressure is applied. Every substance has a critical temperature.

Dalton's law

States that in a mixture of non-reacting gases, the total pressure exerted is equal to the sum of the partial pressures of the individual gases.

Decomposition reaction

A chemical reaction in which a single compound breaks down into two or more elements or new compounds.

Delocalization

Electron systems in which bonding electrons are not localized between two atoms as for a single bond but are spread (delocalized) over the whole group (e.g. pi-bond electrons, in particular the delocalised pi-electrons associated with aromatic molecules).

Deposition

A phase transition in which gas transforms into solid.

Diastereomers
Stereoisomers that are not mirror images of one another and are non-superimposable on one another. Stereoisomers with two or more stereocenters can be diastereomers. They can differ at one or more, but less than all of their chiral centers.

Diffusion
The process by which molecules intermingle as a result of their kinetic energy of random motion (e.g. smoke from a fire rising into the air).

Diol (glycol)
A chemical compound containing two hydroxyl groups (—OH groups).

Disproportionation
A specific type of redox reaction in which a species is simultaneously reduced and oxidized to form two different products.

Double-displacement reaction
A reaction such as NaCl(aq) + AgBr(aq) => AgCl(s) + NaBr(aq) in which the cations and anions exchange partners. Can also be called a metathesis reaction.

Dissociation reaction
A chemical reaction where a compound breaks apart into two or more parts.

E1 reaction
Unimolecular Elimination (E1) is a reaction in which the removal of an HX substituent results in the formation of a double bond. This reaction is 2 steps and proceeds through a carbocation intermediate.

E2 reaction
Bimolecular Elimination (E2) is a reaction in which the removal of an HX substituent results in the formation of a double bond. This reaction occurs in 1 concerted step and is favored by less substituted alkanes.

Effective nuclear charge
The net positive charge experienced by an electron in a multi-electron atom. This can be quantified as the inward pull outermost electrons feel from the nucleus.

Effusion
The process in which a gas escapes from one chamber to another, under pressure, through a small hole. For example blowing smoke out of one's mouth when smoking.

Electrolyte
A substance that ionizes when dissolved in suitable ionizing solvents such as water. This includes most soluble salts, acids, and bases (and Brawndo has 'em).

Electrolytic cell
An electrochemical cell in which the energy from an applied voltage is used to drive an otherwise nonspontaneous redox reaction.

Electron affinity
The release or gain of energy (in kJ/mole) of a neutral atom (in the gaseous phase) when an electron is added to the atom to form a negative ion (aka, the neutral atom's likelihood of gaining an electron).

Electronegativity
A measure of the tendency of an atom to attract a bonding pair of electrons. Fluorine (the most electronegative element) is assigned an EN value of 4.0.

Electronic configuration
Is the distribution of electrons of an atom or molecule (or other physical structure) in atomic or molecular orbitals.

Electrophile
An electron poor species that accepts a pair of electrons to form a new covalent bond.

Element
A pure chemical substance consisting of a single type of atom distinguished by its atomic number, which is the number of protons in its atomic nucleus.

Elementary reaction
A reaction in which one or more of the chemical species react directly to form products in a single reaction step and with a single transition state.

Empirical formula
The simplest formula for a compound. For example, glucose has an empirical formula of CH_2O.

Enantiomers
A pair of stereoisomers which are mirror images of one another (i.e. isomers differing in the configuration at ALL their chiral atoms).

Endothermic reaction
A process in which the system absorbs energy from the surroundings in the form of heat.

Energy diagram
A graph of the energy of a reaction against the progress of the reaction.

Enthalpy
Accounts for energy transferred to the environment at constant pressure through expansion or heating.

Enzyme
A (typically) protein molecule that serves as a catalyst for biological reactions.

Epimerization   Stereoisomers that differ in their configuration at only one chiral carbon atom. For example glucose and galactose are epimers.

Equilibrium constant (K_{eq})   The ratio of products to reactants for a given reaction at a given temperature at equilibrium. According to the law of mass action, for any reversible chemical reaction: $aA + bB = cC + dD$, the equilibrium constant K_{eq} is defined as: $K_{eq} = ([C]^c[D]^d)/([A]^a[B]^b)$

Equivalence point of titration   The point at which chemically equivalent quantities of acid and base have been mixed. It can be found by means of an indicator

Exothermic reaction   A chemical or physical reaction that releases heat. It gives out energy to its surroundings.

Fischer projection   A convention for drawing carbon chains so that the relative 3-dimensional stereochemistry of the carbon atoms is relatively easily portrayed on a 2-dimensional drawing. The horizontal substituents face out of the page while vertical substituents face into the page.

Free radical   Molecules or ions with unpaired electrons which are usually extremely reactive.

Galvanic cell   An electrochemical cell in which energy is released in the form of voltage from a spontaneous redox reaction.

Geminal   Refers to the relationship between two atoms or functional groups that are attached to the same atom.

Gibbs free energy G   The change in the Gibbs free energy of the system that occurs during a reaction is equal to the change in the enthalpy of the system minus the change in the product of the temperature times the entropy of the system. It is a measure of the favorability (spontaneity) of a reaction. This measurement can be measured under any set of conditions. It is a state function because it is defined in terms of thermodynamic properties that are state functions.

Graham's law States that the rate of effusion or of diffusion of a gas is inversely proportional to the square root of its molecular weight. Thus, if the molecular weight of one gas is four times that of another, it would diffuse through a porous plug or escape through a small pinhole in a vessel at half the rate of the other (heavier gases diffuse more slowly).

Half equivalence point The point at which half of the chemically equivalent quantities of acid and base have been mixed. At this point half the original molecules in solution have been converted to its conjugate.

Halogens Are group (column) VII in the periodic table consisting of the chemical elements fluorine (F), bromine (Br), etc…

Heat capacity The amount of heat required to raise the temperature of an object of fixed mass of a substance one degree.

Henderson-Hasselbalch equation $pH = pK_a + \log([A^-] / [HA])$

Heterolytic reaction A reaction in which a covalent bond is broken with unequal sharing of the electrons from the bond.

HOMO The highest occupied molecular orbital of a molecule, ion or atom.

Homolytic reaction A reaction in which a covalent bond is broken with equal sharing of the electrons from the bond.

Hybridization The process where atomic orbitals of similar energies are combined to form a set of equivalent hybrid orbitals. These hybrid orbitals do not exist in the atoms but only in the formation of molecular orbitals by combining atomic orbitals from different atoms.

Hydrogenolysis The chemical reactions wherein C-C, C-N, C-O, or C-S single bonds are cleaved (lysed) by hydrogen.

Hydrolysis The addition of the elements of water to a substance, often with the splitting of the substance into two parts.

Ideal gas law $PV = nRT$. The equation of state of a hypothetical ideal gas.

Inductive effect   The electronic effect due to the polarization of σ bonds within a molecule or ion. This is typically due to an electronegativity difference between the atoms at either end of the bond.

Infrared spectroscopy   The analysis of infrared light interacting with a molecule. This can be analyzed in three ways by measuring absorption, emission and reflection. The main use of this technique is in identifying unknown functional groups.

Inhibitor   A substance that slows down or prevents a particular chemical reaction or other process, or that reduces the activity of a particular reactant, catalyst, or enzyme.

Isobaric   A thermodynamic process in which the pressure stays constant.

Isomers   Two or more molecules with the same chemical formula but different chemical structures (i.e. isomers contain the same ingredients but have different arrangements of their atoms in space).

Isovolumetric   A thermodynamic process during which the volume of the closed system undergoing such a process remains constant.

Kinetic theory of gases   The theory that describes a gas as a large number of small particles which are all in constant, random motion. The moving particles constantly collide with each other and with the walls of the container.

Kinetically controlled product   The product formed as the result of the fastest reaction in a set of competing reaction pathways. (lowest E_a)

Kinetics   The study of the rate of reactions and the species that contribute to reaction rates.

K_w   The equilibrium constant for the auto-ionization of water. $K_w = 1 \times 10^{-14}$

Leaving group   A molecular fragment (usually a weak base) that departs with a pair of electrons in heterolytic bond cleavage.

Lewis acid

A species that accepts an electron pair (e.g. an electrophile).

Lewis base

A species that donates an electron pair (e.g. a nucleophile) and will have lone-pair electrons.

London dispersion forces

The attractive forces that cause even nonpolar substances to condense to liquids and to freeze into solids when the temperature is lowered sufficiently.

LUMO

The lowest unoccupied molecular orbital in a molecule or ion.

Magnetic spin number

The quantum number that describes the energy, shape and orientation of molecular orbitals.

Markovnikov's rule

The halide component of HX bonds preferentially at the more highly substituted carbon, whereas the hydrogen prefers the carbon which already contains more hydrogens.

Mass spectrometry

An analytical technique that identifies the amount and type of chemicals present in a sample by measuring the mass-to-charge ratio of atoms.

Melting

The endothermic physical process that results in the phase transition of a substance from a solid to a liquid.

Meso compound

A molecule with multiple stereocenters that is superimposable on its mirror image, usually due to an internal plane of symmetry within the molecule.

Molality (m)

The amount (in mol) of solute, divided by the mass (in kg) of the solvent, regardless of the identity of the solute.

Molarity (M)

The amount (in mol) of a solute constituent divided by the volume of the mixture (typically in liters).

Mole Fraction(X)

The ratio of the number of moles of molecule A to the total number of moles in the mixture.

Molecular formulas The actual numbers of atoms of each element that occur in the smallest freely existing unit or molecule of the compound (e.g. the molecular formula for glucose is $C_6H_{12}O_6$).

Molecule An electrically neutral group of two or more atoms held together by chemical bonds.

Newman projection A projection obtained by viewing along a carbon-carbon single or double bond.

Noble gases The elements in Group (family) Zero (the far right of the periodic table). These atoms (neon (Ne), argon (Ar), etc.) have a stable octet and are largely non-reactive.

Non-ideal conditions Deviations from ideal gas behavior that tend to occur at very low temperatures and very high pressures.

Nuclear magnetic resonance A method for identifying the chemical nature of nuclei (usually H or ^{13}C) in an unknown molecule.

Nucleophile An electron-rich species that donates an electron pair to an electrophile to form a chemical bond in relation to a reaction. All molecules or ions with a free pair of electrons or at least one pi bond can act as nucleophiles.

Nucleophilic substitution The process by which a nucleophile attacks, and displaces a leaving group from an electrophile, resulting in substitution.

Optical activity The rotating of the plane of linearly polarized light about the direction of motion as the light travels through certain chiral molecules.

Osmotic pressure The minimum pressure which needs to be applied to a solution to prevent the inward flow of water across a semipermeable membrane. This pressure is directly related to the molarity of a solution.

Oxidation The process by which an atom loses electrons.

Partial pressure of a gas
In a mixture of gases, each gas has a partial pressure which is the hypothetical pressure of that gas if it alone occupied the volume of the mixture at the same temperature.

pH
A measure of the acidity or basicity of an aqueous solution. Solutions with a pH less than 7 are said to be acidic and solutions with a pH greater than 7 are basic. Is calculated as $pH = -\log[H^+]$.

Phase changes
Any transitions between solid, liquid, and gaseous phases that usually involve large amounts of energy transfer.

Photoelectric effect
The observation that when light is shone onto a piece of metal, a small current flows through the metal. The light is giving its energy to electrons in the atoms of the metal and allowing them to move around, producing the current.

Pi bond
Covalent chemical bonds where two lobes of one involved atomic orbital overlap two lobes of the other involved atomic orbital.

Planck's quantum theory
The theory that the energy of light is proportional to its frequency, demonstrating that light exists in discrete quanta of energy.

pOH
A measure of the acidity or basicity of an aqueous solution. Solutions with a pOH less than 7 are said to be basic and solutions with a pOH greater than 7 are acidic. Is calculated as $pOH = -\log[OH^-]$.

Polarimeter
A device used to measure the amount of rotation of plane polarized light by a compound, generally prepared in a solution.

Principal quantum number
(n) describes the radial size of the orbital and the energy level of the atoms outermost electrons.

Protecting group
A group that is used to protect a functional group from unwanted reactions. After application the protecting group can be removed to reveal the original functional group.

Protic solvent
A solvent that has a hydrogen atom bound to an oxygen (as in a hydroxyl group) or a nitrogen (as in an amine group).

Q > K

The system has overshot equilibrium, and will spontaneously proceed left to re-establish equilibrium (Le Châteliers principle).

Q < K

The system has not yet reached equilibrium, and will spontaneously proceed right to establish equilibrium (Le Châteliers principle).

Racemic mixture

A 50/50 mixture of two enantiomers, rending the mixture achiral.

Reaction quotient Q

Measures the relative amounts of products and reactants present during a reaction at a particular point in time. Is calculated the same way as K_{eq}.

R,S designation

A formal non-ambiguous, nomenclature system for the assignment of absolute configuration of structure to chiral atoms, using the Cahn, Ingold and Prelog priority rules.

Reduction

A chemical processes in which the proportion of more electronegative substituents is decreased, or the charge is made more negative, or the oxidation number is lowered.

Relative configuration

The position of atoms or groups in space in relation to something else in the molecule (compare to absolute configuration, which is independent of atoms or groups elsewhere in the molecule).

Resolution

The separation of a racemate into its two enantiomers by means of some chiral agent.

Resonance

The representation of a compound by two or more canonical structures in which the valence electrons are rearranged to give structures of similar probability. The actual structure is considered to be a hybrid or the resonance forms.

Reversible process

A reaction or process in which the forward reaction can reach an equilibrium with the reverse reaction.

Ring strain

Is a type of instability that exists when bonds in a molecule form angles that are abnormal. This can result from torsional, steric, angle, or non-bonded strain.

Saturated

An organic molecule that contains the greatest possible number of hydrogen atoms, and so having no carbon–carbon double or triple bonds.

Saturated solution A dissolution reaction that has reached its equilibrium is said to be saturated.

Sigma bond The strongest type of covalent chemical bond. They are formed by head-on overlapping between atomic orbitals. These are the type found in the first bonds formed between carbons and their neighbors.

Single displacement reaction See substitution reaction.

S_N1 reaction A two step, unimolecular nucleophilic substitution reaction that involves a carbocation intermediate.

S_N2 reaction A one step, bimolecular nucleophilic substitution reaction that involves simultaneous attack on the electrophile and loss of a leaving group.

Specific Rotation [α] The observed rotation of an optically active compound, measured using a polarimeter and which depends on the experimental conditions used. It is not a characteristic property of the compound.

Spectrometer An instrument used to measure properties of light over a specific portion of the electromagnetic spectrum, typically used in spectroscopic analysis to identify materials.

Spectrophotometer An instrument which measures the amount of light of a specified wavelength which passes through a medium. According to Beer's law, the amount of light absorbed by a medium is proportional to the concentration of the absorbing material or solute present.

Standard conditions 25°C, 1M concentrations of reactants.

Stereochemistry The study of the spatial arrangements of atoms in molecules and complexes.

Stereoisomers Another name for configurational isomer.

Stereospecific reactions Reactions in which bonds are broken and/or made at a particular carbon atom and which lead to a single stereoisomer. If the configuration is altered in the process the reaction is said to involve inversion of configuration; if the configuration remains the same the transformation occurs with retention of configuration. Commonly seen in drug-target interactions.

Steric strain	The increase in potential energy of a molecule due to repulsion between electrons in atoms that are not directly bonded to each other (e.g. two staggered conformations of 3,4-dichlorobutane).
STP	$0°$ C/273 K and 1 atm
Strong acids	Molecules that near-100% ionize in solution. Hydrochloric acid (HCl), hydroiodic acid (HI), hydrobromic acid (HBr), perchloric acid ($HClO_4$), nitric acid (HNO_3) and sulfuric acid (H_2SO_4).
Strong bases	Molecules that near-100% ionize in solution to release base groups. Most involve group I or group II metals paired with hydroxide ions. (e.g. NaOH, KOH, RbOH, etc.)
Structural isomers	See constitutional isomers.
Sublimation	The transition of a substance directly from the solid to the gas phase without passing through an intermediate liquid phase.
Substitution reactions	A chemical reaction during which one functional group in a chemical compound is replaced by another functional group.
Tautomerism	The inter-conversion of constitutional isomers of organic compounds via a chemical reaction. This reaction commonly results in the formal migration of a hydrogen atom or proton, accompanied by a switch of a single bond and adjacent double bond.
Temperature Kelvin	$T_K = T_c + 273$
Torsional strain	The repulsion caused by the electrons in between different groups when they pass by each other during rotation around single bonds.
Tosylation	A process which introduces the toluene-4-sulphonyl group into a molecule (Generally by reaction of an alcohol with tosyl chloride) to give the tosylate ester.

Transition state   The state containing the highest energy (thus the least stability) along the reaction coordinate. It has more free energy in comparison to the substrate or product.

Triglyceride   An ester derived from glycerol and three fatty acids. It is used primarily by the human body as a storage form of fat.

Unsaturated   A hydrocarbon chain (usually a fat or fatty acid) in which there is at least one double bond within the hydrocarbon chain.

Vapor pressure of solution   The pressure exerted by a vapor in thermodynamic equilibrium with its condensed phases (solid or liquid) at a given temperature in a closed system.

Vicinal   Used to describe any two functional groups bonded to two adjacent carbon atoms. For example the molecule 2,3-dichlorobutane carries two vicinal chlorine atoms and 1,3-dichlorobutane does not.

Vinyl group   Is the functional group $-CH=CH_2$ (an ethylene molecule ($H_2C=CH_2$) minus one hydrogen atom).

Volume of 1 mol of ideal gas   Is 22.4 liters at STP ($0\,°C$ and 1 atm)

Work   In a chemical system is given by Work $= P\Delta V$. Thus for work to be done, a volume change must occur.

Zaitsev's rule   Predicts that in an elimination reaction, the most stable alkene (usually the most substituted one) will be the favored product. This rule has several exceptions.

Zeroth law of Thermodynamics   The law that if two systems are in thermodynamic equilibrium with a third system, the two original systems are in thermal equilibrium with each other.

Remove this page from the book and use the grid below to record your answers. Then check your work and carefully review each question. Don't ignore the ones you got right! Review every single question!

TIMED SECTION 1 - ANSWER SHEET

Key		20		40	
1		21		41	
2		22		42	
3		23		43	
4		24		44	
5		25		45	
6		26		46	
7		27		47	
8		28		48	
9		29		49	
10		30		50	
11		31		51	
12		32		52	
13		33		53	
14		34		54	
15		35		55	
16		36		56	
17		37		57	
18		38		58	
19		39		59	

Remove this page from the book and use the grid below to record your answers. Then check your work and carefully review each question. Don't ignore the ones you got right! Review every single question!

TIMED SECTION 2 - ANSWER SHEET

Key		20		40	
1		21		41	
2		22		42	
3		23		43	
4		24		44	
5		25		45	
6		26		46	
7		27		47	
8		28		48	
9		29		49	
10		30		50	
11		31		51	
12		32		52	
13		33		53	
14		34		54	
15		35		55	
16		36		56	
17		37		57	
18		38		58	
19		39		59	

Remove this page from the book and use the grid below to record your answers. Then check your work and carefully review each question. Don't ignore the ones you got right! Review every single question!

TIMED SECTION 3 - ANSWER SHEET

Key		20		40	
1		21		41	
2		22		42	
3		23		43	
4		24		44	
5		25		45	
6		26		46	
7		27		47	
8		28		48	
9		29		49	
10		30		50	
11		31		51	
12		32		52	
13		33		53	
14		34		54	
15		35		55	
16		36		56	
17		37		57	
18		38		58	
19		39		59	

Remove this page from the book and use the grid below to record your answers. Then check your work and carefully review each question. Don't ignore the ones you got right! Review every single question!

TIMED SECTION 4 - ANSWER SHEET

Key		20		40	
1		21		41	
2		22		42	
3		23		43	
4		24		44	
5		25		45	
6		26		46	
7		27		47	
8		28		48	
9		29		49	
10		30		50	
11		31		51	
12		32		52	
13		33		53	
14		34		54	
15		35		55	
16		36		56	
17		37		57	
18		38		58	
19		39		59	